A History of Women in Ireland, 1500–1800

WOMEN AND MEN IN HISTORY

This series, published for students, scholars and interested general readers, will tackle themes in gender history from the early medieval period through to the present day. Gender issues are now an integral part of all history courses and yet many traditional texts do not reflect this change. Much exciting work is now being done to redress the gender imbalances of the past, and we hope that these books will make their own substantial contribution to that process. We hope that these will both synthesise and shape future developments in gender studies.

The General Editors of the series are *Patricia Skinner* (University of Southampton) for the medieval period; *Pamela Sharpe* (University of Bristol) for the early modern period; and *Penny Summerfield* (University of Lancaster) for the modern period. *Margaret Walsh* (University of Nottingham) was the Founding Editor of the series.

Published books:

Imperial Women in Byzantium, 1025–1204: Power, Patronage and Ideology *Barbara Hill*

Masculinity in Medieval Europe *D. M. Hadley (ed.)*

Gender and Society in Renaissance Italy *Judith C. Brown and Robert C. Davis (eds)*

Widowhood in Medieval and Early Modern Europe *Sandra Cavallo and Lyndan Warner (eds)*

Gender, Church and State in Early Modern Germany: Essays by Merry E. Wiesner
Merry E. Wiesner

Manhood in Early Modern England: Honour, Sex and Marriage *Elizabeth W. Foyster*

English Masculinities, 1600–1800 *Tim Hitchcock and Michele Cohen (eds)*

Disorderly Women in Eighteenth-Century London: Prostitution in the Metropolis, 1730–1830
Tony Henderson

Gender, Power and the Unitarians in England, 1760–1860 *Ruth Watts*

Practical Visionaries: Women, Education and Social Progress, 1790–1930
Mary Hilton and Pam Hirsch (eds)

Women and Work in Russia, 1880–1930: A Study in Continuity through Change
Jane McDermid and Anna Hillyar

More than Munitions: Women, Work and the Engineering Industries, 1900–1950
Clare Wightman

Women in British Public Life, 1914–1950: Gender, Power and Social Policy *Helen Jones*

The Family Story: Blood, Contract and Intimacy, 1830–1960
Leonore Davidoff, Megan Doolittle, Janet Fink and Katherine Holden

Women and the Second World War in France, 1939–1948: Choices and Constraints
Hanna Diamond

Men and the Emergence of Polite Society, Britain 1660–1800 *Philip Carter*

Everyday Violence in Britain, 1850–1950: Gender and Class *Shani D'Cruze (ed.)*

Women and Ageing in British Society Since 1500 *Lynn Botelho and Pat Thane (eds)*

Medieval Memories: Men, Women and the Past, 700–1300 *Elisabeth van Houts (ed.)*

Family Matters: A History of Ideas about Family since 1945 *Michael Peplar*

Domestic Service and Gender, 1660–1750 *Tim Meldrum*

Blood, Bodies and Families in Early Modern England *Patricia Crawford*

A History of Women in Ireland, 1500–1800 *Mary O'Dowd*

Manliness and Masculinity in Nineteenth-Century Britain *John Tosh*

A History of Women in Ireland, 1500–1800

Mary O'Dowd

Harlow, England • London • New York • Boston • San Francisco • Toronto
Sydney • Tokyo • Singapore • Hong Kong • Seoul • Taipei • New Delhi
Cape Town • Madrid • Mexico City • Amsterdam • Munich • Paris • Milan

PEARSON EDUCATION LIMITED

Edinburgh Gate
Harlow CM20 2JE
United Kingdom
Tel: +44 (0)1279 623623
Fax: +44 (0)1279 431059
Website: www.pearsoned.co.uk

First edition published in Great Britain in 2005

ISBN 0 582 40429 0

British Library Cataloguing-in-Publication Data
A CIP catalogue record for this book can be obtained from the British Library

Library of Congress Cataloging-in-Publication Data
O'Dowd, Mary.
A history of women in Ireland, 1500–1800 / Mary O'Dowd.—1st ed.
p. cm. — (Women and men in history)
Includes bibliographical references and index.
ISBN 0-582-40429-0 (pbk.)
1. Women—Ireland—History. 2. Women—Ireland—Economic conditions.
3. Women in politics—Ireland—History. 4. Women and religion—Ireland—History.
I. Title. II. Series.

HQ1600.3.O536 2004
305.4'09415—dc22

2004040144

10 9 8 7 6 5 4 3 2 1
08 07 06 05 04

Set in 9/13.5pt Stone Serif by 35
Printed in Malaysia

The Publishers' policy is to use paper manufactured from sustainable forests.

Contents

PART FOUR Ideas

Acknowledgements

I have received help and support from many people in the preparation of this book. First, I must thank the staff in the many archival institutions and libraries that I visited while researching the volume. I would like especially to express my appreciation of the staff in the library at Queen's University, Belfast: Florence Gray, Mary Kelly, Michael Smallman and Deirdre Wildy, who were unfailingly helpful and often went out of their way to locate material that I requested. My thanks are also due to the staff in four other institutions that I used on a regular basis: the National Archives of Ireland, the National Library of Ireland, the Public Record Office of Northern Ireland and the library and Manuscript Room in Trinity College Dublin. For permission to consult manuscript sources in their possession, I am grateful to these and to the other archival institutions listed in the bibliography.

Secondly, I would like to express my thanks to Margaret MacCurtain who read the text and commented on it with characteristic insight and perceptiveness. The final manuscript is undoubtedly the better for Margaret's observations. I am also indebted to Pamela Sharpe who was the reader for the publishers. Without Pamela's support it is likely that the staff at Pearson Education would have given up the long wait for the appearance of the volume! While writing the book, I benefited enormously from conversations and discussions with my co-editors on the Field Day Anthology of Irish Writing project: Angela Bourke, Máirín Ní Dhonnchadha, Siobhán Kilfeather, Maria Luddy, Gerardine Meaney and Clair Wills as well as Margaret MacCurtain.

Many others provided help and assistance in various forms. They include Toby Barnard, Eileen Black, Caroline Bowden, Ciarán Brady, Richard Butterwick, Nicholas Canny, Aidan Clarke, Anne Crookshank, David Dickson, Mairéad Dunlevy, Alan Ford, Neal Garnham, Ian Green, Ultan Gillen, Angus Haldane, David Hayton, Gráinne Henry, Andrew Holmes, Peter Jupp, James Kelly, Liam Kennedy, Phil Kilroy, Colm Lennon, John Logan,

Marian Lyons, Eoin Magennis, James McGuire, Kerby Miller, James Murray, Katherine O'Donnell, Anne O'Dowd, Jane Ohlmeyer, Kevin O'Neill, Ciarán O Scea, Harold O'Sullivan, Rosemary Raughter, Nini Rodgers, Glenn Thompson, Mary Helen Thuente, Bernadette Whelan and Sabine Wichert.

I acknowledge also my thanks to Queen's University Belfast and the Arts and Humanities Research Board for funding sabbatical leave to enable me to work on the book. In the final stages of the production of the volume, the staff at Pearson Education, particularly Heather Ancient, Barbara Massam, Melanie Carter and Heather McCallum, deserve my gratitude for their endurance and their patience at my failure at nearly every stage to meet their deadlines!

I have dedicated the book to the memory of my maternal grandmother, Anne Brennan. She died before I was born but, like many of her grandchildren, I have always been intrigued by her life. Widowed at a relatively young age, she opened a shop to earn a livelihood for herself and her children. She proved to be a successful business woman and left an impressive legacy to her daughters as well as to her sons. I thought of her often as I explored the economic endeavours of widows in eighteenth-century Dublin with whom she probably had much in common.

Mary O'Dowd
July 2004

Introduction

Natalie Zemon Davis described women's history as being essentially about asking the question 'and what about the women?' of all historical research, even where 'at first glance it may seem hard to find evidence'.[1] Davis's definition encapsulates my central purpose in deciding to write this book. I wanted to explore the role and status of women in early modern Ireland even if the sources for such a study seemed sparse and unyielding. What sorts of questions could be asked and, at least partially, answered of the surviving material concerning women's lives in Irish society over the three-hundred-year time span? Was it possible to identify significant changes in women's lives during the period and could the factors propelling those changes be charted? Were there notable differences in the experiences of women from different economic, religious and ethnic backgrounds? And, as Davis's comment urges us to ask, what was the signficance of the gaps or silences in the surviving documentation concerning women? Did it reflect the absence of women from historical events or have contemporary recorders and later historians overlooked their presence? In other words, how does the history of women relate to the way in which the history of early modern Ireland has been interpreted or written about?

From the perspective of the expanding literature in the field of women's and gender history, my aim may seem relatively modest, closer perhaps to the concerns of women historians in the early 1980s than to the theoretical debate on gender history that prevailed in the 1990s. From the perspective of Irish women's history, however, the aspirations of the volume might be perceived as overambitious, if not foolhardy. Research on women in early modern Ireland has been so sporadic that any attempt at a synthesis might seem premature.

The historiography on women in Ireland from 1500 to 1800 is, in fact, relatively recent, dating back no further than the early twentieth century. And until the 1970s the focus was overwhelmingly biographical. Particular categories of women were selected for study: aristocratic women who left behind a rich collection of private correspondence;[2] religious women, responsible for founding religious communities;[3] women writers[4] and rebellious women.[5] Occasionally other women featured in historical commentaries as victims, for example, of the depressed economy of the late eighteenth century but the tardy development of family and social history in Irish historical studies has meant that such appearances were rare. The interest was mainly in 'notable' or 'notorious' women rather than 'ordinary' women.[6]

A more academic study of women in early modern Ireland was initiated by Margaret MacCurtain who was the first scholar to incorporate the history of women into more general interpretations of the period. In particular, MacCurtain drew attention to the impact of the Reformation and Counter-Reformation on women.[7] MacCurtain's writings and teaching have also stimulated other scholars to undertake research on women in early modern Ireland, especially into women and religious institutions and groups. Consequently, the roles and activities of women in the early modern churches has been one of the most fruitful areas of study in the past twenty-five years.[8]

Many other aspects of women's lives in the period remain, however, unexplored. It was in an attempt to fill some of the gaps in the record that Margaret MacCurtain and I co-edited a collection of essays on the topic in 1991.[9] For the volume, we asked the contributors, most of whom had not written about women before, to write an article on the history of women in their particular specialist area. The result was a wide-ranging collection of essays that clearly demonstrated the intellectual value of examining the role and status of women in early modern Ireland. In addition, the range of sources utilised by the contributors belied any suggestion that historians in Ireland lacked the primary documentation requisite for a history of women during the period. While centuries of war and conflict have led to the loss of most of the local and court records of early modern Ireland, the essays in *Women in Early Modern Ireland* proved the potential of the surviving source base. It was, thus, while working on *Women in Early Modern Ireland* that I became interested in the possibility of attempting a wider survey that would outline the main changes in women's role and contribution to society from 1500–1800 and that could serve as a baseline for other researchers to confirm or challenge with more specialised surveys.

Research for the volume coincided with major advances in Irish women's history. In the past ten years, the number of scholarly books and articles in the field has progressively accumulated. A major impetus for research on women's history in Ireland was supplied by the work of the Women's History Project which identified an impressive array of unpublished sources relating to women in public libraries and archival institutions. At the same time, the production of the fourth and fifth volumes of the *Field Day Anthology of Irish Writing* provided a unique opportunity to edit a varied selection of texts relating to women in Ireland from the earliest times to the end of the second millenium.[10] Although much of this scholarship has focused on the period after 1800, there has also been a steady accretion of information about source material relating to women in the medieval and early modern periods. The secondary analysis still, however, lags behind the listing and editing of primary sources.[11]

The task of the historian of women in Ireland is compounded by the underdevelopment of Irish social history. This dearth is slowly being rectified by the contributions of a number of scholars, some of whom are also utilising gender as one of their tools of analysis.[12] There are, however, still extraordinary gaps in our knowledge, particularly in relation to the history of the family, marriage and private life. In other countries, women's history has been in a position to build on studies of the family and social structure. In Ireland, studies of the history of women have preceded rather than followed the social investigation of the past.

Given the paucity of the secondary literature, it was inevitable that much of the research for this study was based on analyses of primary sources and contemporary printed material. Many of the sources that I have looked at will be familiar to historians of the period. I have made no dramatic new discoveries of long-lost correspondence or diaries lying unrecognised in archives. Instead, I have searched well-known archives (and some perhaps less well known) for what they reveal about women and gender.[13] The process proved rewarding at a number of levels. First, the range of sources for research on women in early modern Ireland is more extensive than I had initially expected, especially for the period before 1660. In many instances, previous researchers (including myself) had ignored or not recognised the gender dimension of the sources. In other cases, the information relating to women had been dismissed as unimportant or dealing with domestic or family matters and, consequently, often left uncatalogued by archivists. Secondly, an archival focus on women has enabled me to identify the significance of women's engagement with some of the most important developments in early modern Ireland. When Patricia Crawford and Sara

Mendelson wrote their history of women in early modern England, they, like Natalie Zemon Davis, wrote of reading sources 'against the grain, of asking where women are absent as well as present in the documents'.[14] I had a similar experience but additionally I found that researching the history of women also meant taking time to identify the presence of women in the sources. Men may dominate the foreground but women are frequently to be found in the background. Women's history is also, of course, about recognising the gendered implications of much-used source material. An obvious example of this is the correspondence of writers such as Mary Delany, the Lennox sisters and Martha McTier that has been widely used in the writing of eighteenth-century Irish history but, apart from the occasional reference to its 'gossipy' nature, it has not normally been assessed from the perspective of the history of women in the period.[15]

The limited pool of secondary literature on women in early modern Ireland and my dependence on primary research has inevitably meant that the coverage of topics has been uneven and highly selective. I have explored some themes and subjects in considerable depth while others are treated more superficially or given only passing consideration. I am very aware, for example, of the absence of attention to the private lives of women and their personal relations with their husbands, children and families, a topic that could well form the central theme of an alternative book on women in early modern Ireland. I have focused instead on major areas of change. From 1500 to 1800, colonialism, Protestantism, capitalism and industrialisation transformed Irish society while Enlightenment ideas opened up new ways of thinking about the state and men's and women's relationship with it. One of my aims was to track the ways in which these developments impacted on women and to contribute a gendered perspective to the analysis of these well-researched topics.

It seemed appropriate, therefore, to begin with an examination of women's political power and influence. Studies of political structure and developments have dominated interpretations of the history of early modern Ireland but women have featured only spasmodically in this analysis. The first section of the book, accordingly, explores the significance of women's political influence and authority and traces the extent to which it changed in the period. Part 2 focuses on another major theme of early modern Ireland: the modernisation of the economy. Chapter 3 examines the impact on women of the transition from Gaelic to English law in relation to property and inheritance while Chapter 4 investigates the opening up of new economic opportunities for women in the eighteenth century. Other changes are considered in the third section of the book which looks at the contribution of women to the religious developments of early modern Ireland. Particular attention is given to women's engagement with some of the key locations of change: Protestant dissent, the revivial of Catholic female religious communities and philanthropic work. Another significant indicator of transition in women's lives is analysed in Chapter 7: their access to education and literacy. A final section assesses the extent to which empirical alterations in women's lives were mirrored by new perceptions and views of women's role in society. The book, thus, makes no claim to be a complete history of women in Ireland, 1500 to 1800. Instead it suggests that a study of women during the period provides not just an interesting footnote to the existing historiography but may also offer a fresh perspective from which to view the history of early modern Irish society as a whole.

Notes

1 Juliet Gardiner (Ed), *What is History Today?* (Atlantic Highlands, New Jersey, 1988), pp. 85–6.

2 See, for example, Brian Fitzgerald, *Emily Duchess of Leinster, 1731–1814. A Study of Her Life and Times* (London, 1949); *Lady Louisa Conolly, 1743–1821* (London, 1950); Brian Fitzgerald (Ed), *Correspondence of Emily Duchess of Leinster, 1731–1814* (3 vols., Dublin, 1949–57).

3 See, for example, Roland Burke Savage, *A Valiant Dublin Woman. The Story of George's Hill (1766–1940)* (Dublin, 1940); T. J. Walsh, *Nano Nagle and the Presentation Sisters* (Dublin, 1959).

4 See, for example, Emily Lawless, *Maria Edgeworth* (London, 1904); Marilyn Butler, *Maria Edgeworth. A Literary Biography* (London, 1972).

5 See, for example, Helena Concannon, *Women of 'Ninety-Eight* (Dublin, 1920); *Daughters of Banba* (Dublin, 1930).

6 For a review of writings on Irish women's history see Maria Luddy, Margaret MacCurtain and Mary O'Dowd, 'An Agenda for Women's History in Ireland, 1500–1900' in *Irish Historical Studies*, **28** (1992), pp. 1–37. See also Mary O'Dowd, 'From Morgan to MacCurtain, Irish Women Historians from the 1790s to the 1990s' in Maryann Gialanella Valiulis and Mary O'Dowd (Eds), *Women and Irish History* (Dublin, 1997), pp. 38–58.

7 For a bibliography of MacCurtain's writings see Monica Cullinan, 'Bibliography of Writings of Margaret MacCurtain' in ibid., pp. 278–83.

8 See, in particular, the work of Phil Kilroy and Rosemary Raughter listed in the bibliography to this volume.

9 Margaret MacCurtain and Mary O'Dowd (Eds) *Women in Early Modern Ireland* (Edinburgh, 1991).

10 For the work of the Women's History Project see Maria Luddy *et al.* (Eds), *A Directory of Sources for Women's History in Ireland* (CD-Rom produced by the Irish Manuscripts Commission, Dublin, 1999). Available online: www.nationalarchives.ie/wh. The Women's History Project also sponsored an edition of McTier's correspondence. See Jean Agnew (Ed), *The Drennan-McTier Letters, 1776–1819* (3 vols., Dublin, 1998–9). For the Field Day project see Angela Bourke *et al.* (Eds), *Field Day Anthology of Irish Writing, Vols. IV–V* (Cork, 2002).

11 Special note should be made of the series of conferences on women in medieval and early modern Europe organised by Professor Christine Meek in Trinity College, Dublin. See Christine Meek and Katharine Simms (Eds), *'The Fragility of Her Sex'. Medieval Irish Women in their European Context* (Dublin, 1996); Christine Meek (Ed), *Women in Renaissance and Early Modern Europe* (Dublin, 2000); Christine Meek and Catherine Lawless (Eds), *Studies on Medieval and Early Modern Women. Pawns or Players?* (Dublin, 2003).

12 See, in particular, the publications of Toby Barnard, Seán Connolly, Neal Garnham, Raymond Gillespie, James Kelly, Colm Lennon and Kevin O'Neill cited in the bibliography and the collection of essays edited by Dáire Keogh and Nicholas Furlong (Eds), *The Women of 1798* (Dublin, 1998). See also Art Cosgrove (Ed), *Marriage in Ireland* (Dublin, 1985). Toby Barnard, *Making the Grand Figure. Lives and Possessions in Ireland, 1641–1770* (New Haven, 2004) appeared too late for consideration in the volume but includes material on men's and women's lives in the seventeenth and eighteenth centuries.

13 For a full list of the primary sources examined see the bibliography.

14 Sara Mendelson and Patricia Crawford, *Women in Early Modern England* (Oxford, 1978), p. 9.

15 Lady Llanover (Ed), *The Autobiography and Correspondence of Mary Granville, Mrs Delany With Interesting Reminiscences of King George the Third and Queen Charlotte* (3 vols., 1st series, London, 1862). For the Lennox sisters' and Martha McTier's correspondence see notes 2, 10 above.

PART I

Politics

CHAPTER 1

Marriage, Lordship and Politics, c. 1500–1692

Politics and marriage networks in sixteenth-century Ireland

In 1574 Edward Fitzgerald, Lieutenant of the Gentlemen Pensioners, was sent on a royal mission to Ireland. He was instructed by Queen Elizabeth to negotiate with the earl of Desmond and to send reports of his progress to his sister or his wife 'so that one of them might deliver the same to her'. Fitzgerald preferred, however, to write to the queen's secretary, Lord Burghley, because 'in my opinion it is too weighty a matter for women to deal with the queen in'.[1] Fitzgerald's comments reveal the gender dilemma of Tudor politics. Despite the courtier's misgivings about women's ability to be trusted with affairs of state, the reality was that the kingdoms of England and Ireland were ruled by two female monarchs for almost fifty years between 1553 and 1602. In order to accommodate the apparent contradiction between the queen as ruler and the queen as a woman, Queen Elizabeth cultivated the notion of herself as androgynous, acknowledging her sex as a woman but not identifying her gender with that of other women. She ruled as a king even though she had 'the body of a weak and feeble woman'.[2] Hence, Fitzgerald could entrust her with 'weighty' matters that he could not impart to his sister or wife.

Nor was the queen the only politically influential woman in Fitzgerald's life. He was in fact surrounded by female relatives who wielded political power and influence. Fitzgerald's mother was Lady Elizabeth Grey, daughter of the marquis of Dorchester, who married Gerald Fitzgerald, 9th earl of Kildare, and solicited support for her husband from her cousin, Henry VIII.[3] Elizabeth was also reported to have learnt to 'read, write and perfectly speake' Irish, a politically useful skill for meeting with and providing hospitality for her husband's Irish supporters.[4] Following Gerald's death and the rebellion of Elizabeth's stepson Thomas in 1534, Elizabeth returned to England where she lived in the home of her brother, Leonard, who served as lord deputy in Ireland, 1536–40. Two of Elizabeth's children, Edward and his sister Elizabeth, secured positions at the royal court. As we have seen, Edward held the post of Lieutenant of the Gentlemen Pensioners while Elizabeth was a maid of honour to Queen Mary. Later, as the countess of Lincoln, she was among the small group of influential women who surrounded Queen Elizabeth and, hence, in the queen's view, if not in Fitzgerald's, was fit to be trusted with affairs of state. Edward's wife was Agnes Leghe, a wealthy heiress and confidante of Queen Elizabeth. Their daughter was also a lady-in-waiting for Queen Elizabeth.[5] Another influential female connection was Edward's sister-in-law, Mabel Browne, a gentlewoman in Queen Mary's privy chamber, who married Edward's half-brother Gerald and who lobbied successfully at court for the political restoration of her husband as the 11th earl of Kildare, a task in which she was assisted by her sister-in-law, the countess of Lincoln.[6] Historians of the Tudor court have acknowledged the political power and influence of ladies-in-waiting in the female courts of Mary and Elizabeth.[7] Hence, the women in Edward's family were among the most politically prestigious in Tudor England. In Ireland, also, Edward's paternal aunts Eleanor and Margaret, daughters of Gerald, 8th earl of Kildare, yielded considerable political power.[8]

The tension between Fitzgerald's view of women's role in public life and the reality as demonstrated by the women in his family was not uncommon in early modern Europe. The theoretical distinction between the private and public worlds of elite men and women rarely reflected the reality. In Ireland, as in England, private acts of marriage, childbirth and the rearing of children were imbued with political significance.

From an Irish point of view, Edward Fitzgerald's mission to Ireland underlined a fundamental characteristic of women's political influence in the sixteenth century. Family connections were of central importance. Fitzgerald was dispatched back to his native country not just because he was an 'influential courtier in his own right'[9] but also quite simply because he was a Fitzgerald. When he was asked to negotiate with the earl of Desmond, Edward Fitzgerald was in fact being asked to talk to his cousin Gerald.[10] Edward was a member of what was left of the great dynastic conglomerate created by his grandfather and father, the 8th and 9th earls of Kildare. Marriage had formed an important part in the development of the Geraldine network as it had in the formation of the rival power bloc of early sixteenth-century Ireland, that of the Butler earls of Ormond.[11]

Consequently, the political potential of noblewomen as prospective marriage partners was crucial for the balance of power in early sixteenth-century Ireland.

The classic demonstration of the use of marriage as a political adjunct was the network established by Edward Fitzgerald's grandfather Gerald, 8th earl of Kildare (c. 1456–1513). Gerald had six daughters, each of whom was married to either an ally of her father's or a lord whose support he wished to acquire. Thus Margaret was married 'for policy' to the earl of Ormond in an unsuccessful attempt to bring the two powerful families together.[12] Eleanor Fitzgerald married Donal MacCarthy Reagh, a prominent Gaelic lord in the southern part of Ireland; her sister Eustacia married Ulick Burke, the lord of Clanricarde, whose territory lay in the west, while Alice Fitzgerald was married to Conn Bacagh O'Neill in the north.[13] Two other daughters married lords from the midlands while the seven sons of the 8th earl of Kildare, by his second wife, were married into prominent Pale families. Thus, through the marital network of his family the earl of Kildare attempted to break down the political fragmentation of early Tudor Ireland and establish a virtual political unity on the island.[14]

Gerald Fitzgerald also extended his links into the Tudor court by his marriage in 1496 to Elizabeth St John, a cousin of Henry VIII. The royal connections established through Elizabeth facilitated the marriage of Gerald's son, Gerald Óg, first to Elizabeth Zouche, in a match arranged by Henry VII and his mother Lady Margaret Beaufort, and secondly, to Edward Fitzgerald's mother Elizabeth Grey, another royal cousin.[15] As James Ware later commented, this marriage 'did afterwards very much advance and promote Kildare affairs acquiring thereby great friends at Court'.[16] Expedient marriage alliances, thus, gave the Fitzgeralds not only control in Ireland but also access to the very centre of the English polity.

Tudor centralisation of government in the course of the sixteenth century gradually eroded the importance of dynastic politics. By the time that Edward Fitzgerald arrived in Ireland in 1574, it was a pale imitation of what it had been forty years earlier and Edward was unable to exploit his family connections to persuade his cousin Gerald to follow his advice. Edward's half-brother, Gerald, had been restored as 11th earl of Kildare in 1554 but he never commanded the same authority and control in Ireland as his predecessors. Thomas Butler, the 10th earl of Ormond (1531–1614) and head of the traditional rival faction group to the Geraldines, had more political influence than the earl of Kildare but Ormond's political strength derived more from his family connections with the queen and members of her court than through his ability to command an extensive factional network in Ireland.[17] By the 1570s, the island of Ireland was no longer held together politically by the marriage networks of the Geraldines or the Butlers.

Marriage alliances remained, however, an important, if no longer a dominating, aspect of political life, particularly at provincial and local level. Within Gaelic Ireland marriage was an important basis for securing political support until the end of the sixteenth century. The O'Neills of Ulster made extensive use of marriage to consolidate their control in Ulster. Shane O'Neill married four times and, as one biographer noted, he changed his marriage partners to suit his political circumstances.[18] His first wife was probably a member of the Maguire family, and she was followed by a woman from the MacDonnell clan. The latter was abandoned when O'Neill made peace with Calvagh O'Donnell, lord of Tyrconnell, in 1560 and married his daughter Mary. The following year Mary was recorded in the annals as having died of shock when her husband imprisoned her father and began a liaison with her stepmother, Calvagh's wife Catherine Mac Lean, the Scottish widow of the 4th earl of Argyle.[19] Catherine may not initially have been a willing partner in the liaison with Shane. One report alleged that Shane tied her to a small boy by day and released her only in the evening when he was present. Subsequently, however, Catherine married Shane with her family's approval and she remained with him until he was killed in 1567.[20]

Despite Shane O'Neill's marriage to Catherine, rumours continued to circulate that he intended to take back his first wife or to marry Lady Agnes Campbell, the daughter of the 4th earl of Argyle and Mac Lean's stepdaughter. The argument that led to Shane O'Neill's murder in 1567 was purported to have arisen during a drunken discussion as to whether or not he planned to marry Agnes Campbell.[21] During his negotiations with the crown in 1561–2 O'Neill also expressed a desire for an English-born wife, a request that encapsulated O'Neill's perception of marriage as essentially a political arrangement.[22]

Hugh O'Neill, 2nd earl of Tyrone (d. 1616), also utilised marriage to build an impressive network of allies. In a complex labyrinth of marriages he established links with all the principal families in Ulster: the O'Donnells, Maguires and MacMahons as well as with families in east Ulster where his direct political influence was weak. O'Neill, himself, married at least four times but his most famous marriage partner was his third wife, Mabel Bagenal. Often portrayed as an audacious snub to her brother, Sir Henry Bagenal, the Marshal of Ireland, or as a romantic joining of 'native' and 'settler', the marriage in fact made sound political sense and fitted into a pattern of O'Neill marriages with east Ulster and Pale families. The Bagenals had established themselves in Newry and had connections with many prominent Pale families as well as members of the Dublin administration.[23] The elopement of Mabel took place from the house of her brother-in-law Sir Patrick Barnewall in County Louth, who was a leading member of the Pale community and married to Mabel's sister Margaret.[24] Thus O'Neill's third marriage linked him into the Old English network of families. It is also worth noting that Sir Henry Bagenal, the brother of Mabel and Margaret, was O'Neill's rival for the position of chief crown representative in Ulster. O'Neill's marriage to Mabel can, therefore, also be interpreted as an attempt to neutralise the threat of the Bagenals to O'Neill's political ambitions.

In the late 1590s, Hugh O'Neill emerged as the leader of the confederacy at war with the Elizabethan forces in Ireland. The expansion of O'Neill's political ambitions is reflected in his marriage plans for his daughter Margaret. In 1596 he negotiated an agreement with Edmond Butler, Viscount Mountgarret, that included the marriage of Margaret to Edmond's son Richard. The Mountgarret alliance not only strengthened O'Neill's links with the Pale community but forged an alliance with a senior branch of the Butler family. The 10th earl of Ormond's only son had died in 1590. Richard was the next male heir. There was, therefore, a distinct possibility that Richard could have become the next earl of Ormond, a move that would have considerably enhanced his father-in-law's political connections.[25]

Marriage in the war-based society of Gaelic Ireland did not normally, as in English society, involve the transfer of property. The political benefits of the union were of more significance than the augmentation of wealth that it may have brought. The acquisition of additional military support was, however, an essential ingredient in the marriages concluded between Ulster lords and Scottish noble families in the late sixteenth century. Scottish brides brought dowries of mercenary soldiers to their Irish husbands as well as alliances with families that had their own reasons for engaging in war against the Tudor monarchy. The English army in sixteenth-century Ireland, until the mid-1580s, rarely exceeded 2000 men. The large number of mercenary soldiers brought as dowries by Scottish women to Ulster lords was, therefore, a significant military factor in the wars of late sixteenth-century Ireland. In his marriage agreement with Catherine Mac Lean's family in 1560, Calvagh O'Donnell received 500 soldiers from the earl of Argyle as well as a gun for ramming castles.[26] Lady Agnes Campbell brought 1000 soldiers with her when she married Turlough Luineach O'Neill on Rathlin Island in August 1569. The marriage was a double one as Agnes's daughter, Finola, married Hugh O'Donnell at the same time and she too provided her husband with access to Scottish military resources.[27]

If marriage in Gaelic society was utilised to extend the military and political resources of the lord, among the Old English families in the Pale marriage was essentially a means of limiting and defining membership of the old colonial elite. Within the Pale, marriage partners were traditionally chosen from a small pool of families, a process which helped to strengthen the identity of the community and protect it from dilution through intermarriage with Gaelic Irish men and women. Throughout the sixteenth century, English-born administrators in Ireland continually expressed their frustration at the 'cousinage' of Old English families. At the height of the rebellion in Munster in 1599, for example, the government was warned that there would be little point in trying to raise an army in the province to attack the rebels because 'they are so linked together by affinity and consanguinity, as they will not for any reward whatsoever do any service one upon another'.[28] In the towns, dominated by Old English merchant families, membership of the burgher community was also defined by family affiliation.

The composition of the Old English community was never, however, as homogenous as its critics claimed. Marriages with Gaelic families did take place as the story of the O'Neills indicates. In the late sixteenth and early seventeenth centuries, politically ambitious members of the New English colonial elite also allied themselves with Old English families. The English captain Sir Henry Bagenal arranged marriages for almost all of his children with local Pale families, a strategy that strengthened the Bagenal regional control in the hinterland of Newry.[29] Another immigrant to Ireland in the sixteenth century was Adam Loftus, Archbishop of Dublin and Irish lord chancellor who was connected by marriage to the Bagenal-Old English network. Loftus, through the marriages of his ten children, built up an alternative network of New and Old English families.[30] In the early 1590s, it was reported that there was not

> *any one house or family, that is of any high degree, name, fame, credit, reputation, or most substantial in riches and forces of followers for the most part of the English Pale, but that one way or another, . . . the Archbishop has allied and strengthened himself, in some kind of degree either of consanguinity or affinity, to purchase himself into a multitude of lines and friendship. . . .*[31]

Marriage was also a means of gaining access to municipal political office, particularly for Englishmen not born into burgher families. The municipal records of Dublin, for example, regularly record the names of men who were enrolled as freemen on the basis of their marriage to the daughters of aldermen. A townswoman's ability to convey the freedom of the city to her husband enhanced her attraction as a marriage partner, particularly for English newcomers in the city anxious to make their 'way into the inner circles of economic and political power fairly rapidly'.[32]

While marriage alliances between the New English settlers and members of the Old English community were socially acceptable to the Tudor administration, those between English men and women from Gaelic society were not. From the earliest colonisation of Ireland in the twelfth century, English commentators denounced intermarriage between Irish and English. Medieval statutes forbidding intermarriage were renewed in the 1530s and not repealed until the reign of James I. Colonial projects re-enforced this legislative programme with forfeiture penalties for any landholder who violated it.[33] Tudor officials were wary not just of the negative impact that Gaelic women could exert on the children of such unions but also of the possible political influence that the women might exert on their husbands:

> . . . . *what mischeiffs have happened by the unfortunate matches of ore Contrimen? by ioyninge such are neere the state wth the Irishe? the minglinge of themselves wth the daughters of ore naturall borne enemies. . . . This womans kinsman must be favoured; that womans Cozin must be protected; the thirdes brother must be pardoned; and the poore Englishe in the meane while must goe to wracke . . . They are professed patronesses . . . for all ofenders: intollerable is the husbandes life, yf their desires be not satisfied . . .*[34]

Inevitably, sexual contact between English soldiers and local women did occur but it was more common in the lower ranks of the army than at officer level. The vast majority of Elizabethan army captains married Englishwomen, often the daughters or wives of other military men. There were close family ties between many of the army captains, resident in small garrisons throughout Ireland. They thus created their own network of alliances within the New English community.[35]

Changing patterns of marriage in the seventeenth century

The political disintegration of Gaelic Ireland, the increased centralisation of government and the consequent extension of English law had changed the political significance and utility of marriage by the early seventeenth century. First, as the Protestant Reformation began to make an impact on

Irish society, religion became a more important criterion for selection of marriage partners than ethnic origin. The sixteenth-century distinction between Catholics of Gaelic and Old English origins was increasingly blurred as intermarriage between the two groups took place more frequently in the later period. Such marriages helped consolidate the political unity of Catholic Ireland and, increasingly, Old English evolved into a term used to define a political group rather than an exclusive ethnic community. Among the leadership of the 1641 rebellion, for example, intricate marriage connections can be traced between Old English and Gaelic families.[36]

It is also possible to identify a strengthening of matrimonial connections between New English and Irish families, particularly those that had conformed to the Church of Ireland. The Elizabethan adventurer Richard Boyle, created earl of Cork in 1622, utilised the marriages of his children to gain entry to a wide social and political circle in Ireland and England. Cork established marital alliances with families from the Old English elite in Munster and the Fitzgerald family in Leinster. As one historian has noted, Cork was 'determined to embrace the whole of the ancient Kildare domain in his dynastic empire' and for this reason he matched his daughter Sarah with Baron Digby, the son of Lady Offaly, who claimed to be the heir general to the Kildare estate; and his daughter Joan to Henry, 12th earl of Kildare.[37] While it is unlikely that Cork had ambitions to be 'the earl of Kildare newly born again'[38] or to set himself up as an old-style Anglo-Irish lord, marrying into what was left of the Geraldine network undoubtedly enhanced the standing of the extended Boyle family in Ireland.

In England, the earl was keen to elevate the status of his family through developing links at the English court. He married four of his sons and a daughter to members of Queen Henrietta Maria's household.[39] Boyle's links with English peerage families reflect another new development in the early decades of the seventeenth century: the increasing number of Irish-born peers who acquired English wives, landed estates and peerage titles. In addition, the sale of Irish peerage titles strengthened the links between Irish and English aristocratic families. Victor Treadwell has suggested that the long-term aim of Edward Villiers, the earl of Buckingham, who masterminded the sale of Irish titles for James I, was the creation of a truly British aristocracy consisting of families that had estates and family interests in both England and Ireland (as well as in some cases in Scotland). Intermarriage was an essential ingredient in Villiers' plan for a new elite.[40]

By the seventeenth century, therefore, a change had taken place in the political value of marriage. In the early sixteenth century it was an essential element in the political world. The choice of marriage partners for the earl of Kildare's daughters could have political resonances for the whole island. The semi-feudal world of lordships and dynastic alliances had disappeared by the early decades of the seventeenth century. Marriage by that time was only one of a number of ways through which families developed connections and influence. Control of government patronage, holding office and having direct personal access to the monarch were also essential. For individual families, accumulation of wealth and annexation of a landed estate were often as important in marriage settlements as the extension of the political connections of the family. The change is most evident in the respective responses of Gerald, 8th earl of Kildare, and Richard, 1st earl of Cork, to the ill-treatment of their daughters. In 1507, when Eustacia Fitzgerald was 'not so used as the earl could be pleased with' by her husband, the lord of Clanricarde, her father seized the opportunity to launch an impressive display of strength against MacWilliam Burke and his western allies in the famous battle of Knockdoe.[41] By contrast in the 1630s, when the earl of Cork became dissatisfied with the manner in which his son-in-law, Gerald's descendant, Henry treated his daughter Joan, he simply took her back to the family home in Lismore.[42] The consequences were important for the Boyle family but they had no wider political significance.

Political influence and power

Women in Anglo-Norman families

If marriage had an important, albeit changing, function in Irish public life in the sixteenth and seventeenth centuries, to what extent did it also confer power on the women involved and was women's public role adjusted as the political significance of marriage underwent alteration? Were women passive partners in the complex networks of marriage alliances that their male relatives engineered or did they have a more active role?

In order to answer these questions it is first necessary to define the meaning of political power. No woman held political office in early modern Ireland. In Gaelic society, women were prohibited from holding the position of lord and the Anglicised Dublin administration was also exclusively male in composition. At local level, women could not be selected as town burghers, sheriffs or justices of the peace. Nor did they have a vote in parliamentary elections. Women did not, therefore, have access to power which was 'formally recognised and legitimated' by the laws of society. Yet, as Merry Wiesner has pointed out, political power can also be defined as an ability to shape and influence political events.[43] In pre-democratic societies considerable political power resided in elite families who monopolised political leadership and government office. Within aristocratic families, women could influence and, at times, directly shape political events, as is evidenced by the women in the Tudor and Stuart courts. In Ireland, also, elite women exercised power and influence.

The women in the Geraldine political networks were clearly in positions of power and authority in their respective husbands' lordships. On her marriage to Donal MacCarthy Reagh, Eleanor Fitzgerald was given half of her husband's lordship and a 'veto over his appointment of "officers and officials" and over his choice of galloglass'.[44] Eleanor's sister Margaret appears to have had a similarly advantageous arrangement with her husband, Piers Butler, earl of Ossory. In the surviving deeds of the Ormond estate, many are assigned jointly to Piers and Margaret and the latter was involved with Piers in developing the estate, expanding and rebuilding manor houses, and establishing a school. Margaret also developed a personal estate on her jointure lands which descended to her younger son Richard, the future 1st Viscount Mountgarret, thus creating a cadet branch of the family.[45] Margaret was described by the family chronicler as 'a lady . . . so politic, that nothing was thought substantially debated without her advice'.[46] Aristocratic women were perceived as representatives of their family and, in the men's absence, widows and, occasionally, married women might exercise leadership roles. When Piers Butler died his wife Margaret took over the ruling of the earldom during the minority of her son. Margaret's daughter Katherine took on a similar responsibility in her husband's territory in south-east Ireland.[47]

The behaviour of several of the women in the Fitzgerald family suggests that they had a deep sense of loyalty to the Geraldine family and were as committed as their male relatives to the extension and strengthening of its interests. They acted as their father's agents in their localities and never lost their identity as Geraldines. Margaret Fitzgerald, wife of the earl of Ossory, for example, signed herself Margaret Fitzgerald of the Geraldines.[48] Gerald Óg, 9th earl of Kildare, entrusted his daughter Alice with crucial political instructions. In 1528 and again in 1534, when Gerald was detained in London, he sent Alice to encourage dissent in the Pale in order to persuade the king that Ireland was ungovernable in his absence.[49] The activities of Alice in 1534 were particularly significant as they led to the rebellion of her brother Thomas, an event which ultimately destroyed the Kildare hegemony. According to the Statute of Attainder of Thomas, Gerald 'willed and commanded his daughter Alice Fitzgerald, wife to the baron of Slane, to repair into this the king's land of Ireland, and in his name to will all his brethern, O'Neill, O'Connor, and all other his friends, servants and allies, to levy, erect stir and rear war against our said sovereign . . .'.[50]

A similar rallying role was performed by Alice's aunt Eleanor in the aftermath of the rebellion. In 1535, Thomas Fitzgerald, the 10th earl of Kildare, and his five uncles were executed in London but the government failed to locate the next male heir, Edward Fitzgerald's half-brother Gerald, who had been taken into hiding by his sister Mary, and later by his aunt, Eleanor.[51] The latter, in the tradition of her family, accepted an offer of marriage from Manus O'Donnell to secure protection for the boy. She brought him with her marriage trousseaux to O'Donnell's lordship in Donegal where she formed a support group for the boy's protection.[52] One government official wrote rather hysterically of Eleanor's success in 1539:

By the pestiferous working of this O'Donnell's wife, the earl of Kildare's sister, they whose ancestors were ever at discension, be made one, and their powers concurring have practised to allure to them, many captains of Irishmen, which never before was towards any of them . . . so that there never was seen in Ireland so great a host of Irishmen and Scots . . .[53]

When Eleanor suspected that her new husband intended to surrender the boy to the government she smuggled him aboard a ship bound for the continent and thus preserved his life and the future of the Kildare earldom.[54] In a dramatic illustration of the use of marriage as a political tool Eleanor, then, informed her new husband that she had only married such a 'clownish curmudgen' to protect her nephew and now that he was safe she felt no further obligation to the marriage and so 'trussing up bag and baggage, she forsook O'Donnell and returned to her country'.[55]

Joan Butler, the wife of the James, 9th earl of Ormond, was also very aware of the political importance of her choice of marriage partner. Following the death of James in 1546, Joan, like Eleanor Fitzgerald, was recognised as co-governor of his estate. She also vigorously defended her son's inheritance, travelling to London to petition the government to secure it. She also indicated her intention to marry her cousin, Gerald Fitzgerald, the 15th earl of Desmond. The Dublin government, fearful of the consequences of the joining of the two largest Anglo-Irish dynasties (and the implications of the marriage for Joan's son by her first husband, Thomas, the future 10th earl of Ormond), opposed Joan's choice of marriage partner. Consequently, Joan was hastily brought to England where she was married to Sir Francis Bryan, a prominent courtier and close friend of Henry VIII. Bryan died within a year of the marriage and Joan, as an older and twice widowed woman, was in a stronger position to exercise a choice over her next husband. She defied the Dublin authorities and married Gerald.[56] Joan's ability to influence the political careers of either her new husband or her son, Thomas, was hampered by the rivalry and tension between the two men. Joan did manage to maintain a peace, however tenuous, between them.[57] It was only after her death in 1565 that military conflict broke out between Desmond and Ormond, a dispute that ultimately destabilised the political order in Munster.

Gerald's second wife, Eleanor Butler, countess of Desmond, was also active in the political affairs of her husband. When her husband was arrested and taken to London, Eleanor endeavoured to preserve the peace in his territories in his absence. Subsequently, Eleanor joined Gerald under house arrest in London where their son was born in 1571. When the couple returned to Ireland in 1573, Eleanor remained closely involved in her family's public affairs. Initially detained in Dublin, Gerald and Eleanor defied the Irish administration's instructions and departed for Munster. They made a dramatic entry into the southern Geraldine territories, symbolically changing their English style dress for Irish garb. Over the next ten years, Eleanor regularly wrote to the queen and her advisers pleading and petitioning for an understanding of her husband's position. She also at times acted as Desmond's spokesperson and intermediary with crown officials in Ireland. When Desmond was proclaimed a rebel in 1579, Eleanor faced a dilemma common to other wives of Irish rebels. If she remained loyal to her husband, she risked the future inheritance of her young son but if she declared her loyalty to the crown, she alienated herself and her son from her husband. Eleanor appears in her correspondence to have chosen the latter option and asked for permission to go to London to speak with the queen in person. The Dublin government, recognising her influence on her husband, refused her permission to leave Ireland. She was still in the country when Gerald died in rebellion in 1583 and his estate was forfeited to the crown. Eleanor was given an annuity to compensate for the loss of her jointure. Eleanor, thus, failed in her political aim to retain her son's inheritance.

The story of Eleanor's marriage to Gerald illustrates the obligation imposed on aristocratic women to take political action. Eleanor felt compelled to defend her husband's and, later, her son's interests. Similarly, after 1596 when she married Donogh O'Connor Sligo, Eleanor acted on behalf of her new husband and for the rest of her life she continued to defend his interests through letters and petitions to the Irish and London administrations.[58] Other women also engaged with the political process to defend their family interests.

Women in Gaelic families

The Butler and Fitzgerald women operated in the hybrid world of Hiberno-Norman and Gaelic lordships and were accustomed to utilising a mixture of English and Irish law. The more literate culture of this society makes aristocratic women more visible in the surviving records than women in the Gaelic worlds of western and northern Ireland. The silence of the historical record may also, however, reflect a historical truth that women in Gaelic society had less space for political action than their counterparts in Anglo-Norman society. Gaelic society gave women little formal political authority. There were no Irish chieftainesses and Irish law prohibited women from inheriting family land or, as noted already, holding the position of lord. The volatile nature of lordly alliances meant that marriages were often of a short duration and wives often had little time to develop a strong political presence in the lordship of their husbands. There is no evidence to suggest that Hugh O'Neill allotted his daughters or wives an active political role. O'Neill did, however, exploit the political potential of marriage, sometimes in a brutal and crude fashion. For example, he claimed that he would remove his daughter from her marriage to Sir Ross MacMahon, if MacMahon did not pay the dowry that had been promised when the marriage was arranged.[59] Similarly, Hugh Roe O'Donnell threatened, on several occasions, to 'cast off' his wife Rose, another daughter of O'Neill's, when the alliance with her father no longer suited his political purposes. Following their eventual divorce, Rose was married to Donal Ballach O'Cahan, described in a contemporary report as her father's 'chief vassal' and who also subsequently abandoned her and sent her back to her father.[60]

Mabel Bagenal, Hugh O'Neill's third wife, could have been a useful intermediary between her Gaelic husband and the English administration but O'Neill never allocated her this role. O'Neill's last wife, Catherine Magennis, also appears to have taken no part in her husband's political affairs and was of little use to the Dublin government when its representation asked her to report on O'Neill's treacherous activities.[61] In September 1607, when O'Neill led the famous flight of Ulster lords and their families to the continent, Catherine had to be persuaded by her husband, at the point of a sword, to follow him. This also suggests that she was not consulted about O'Neill's public affairs.[62]

It is also worth noting that in the many agreements that Gaelic lords made with crown representatives in the sixteenth century, only a small number made provision for wives or widows. Most of the agreements also specified that the inheritance of the lord's estate should descend through male heirs only. Gaelic lords appeared determined to embed the male monopoly on land inheritance that prevailed in Gaelic society into the new order.[63]

The military structure of Gaelic society made it difficult for women to exert political influence. The most famous sixteenth-century woman from a Gaelic background was Gráinne O'Malley who, in her own words, ruled 'by sea and land' for over forty years in the western district of north Mayo.[64] The authority of O'Malley was legitimated in the Gaelic polity through military force, an important point to note because a woman's ability to exercise direct political authority usually depended on her access to resources to make that power effective. Coming from a ship-owning family, Gráinne maintained control of what may have been her dowry of ships when she married. Scottish wives of Gaelic lords such as Agnes Campbell and her daughter, Finola, also enforced their authority through their personal command of large numbers of Scottish mercenary soldiers. The *Annals of the Four Masters*, for example, reported that Finola, or Inghen Dubh, as she was known in the Irish sources, had 'many troops from Scotland, and some of the Irish at her disposal and under her control, and in her own hire and pay constantly'.[65]

Most women from Gaelic Ireland, however, did not have direct control of financial or military resources. In certain lordships, the wife of a chieftain was granted the right to collect rent from a portion of land but there is little evidence that this augmented her political authority.[66] The fact that Hugh O'Neill and his son-in-law, Sir Ross MacMahon, were still disputing the marriage goods promised with O'Neill's daughter almost fifteen years after the marriage had taken place suggests that she (and, most likely, her sisters) did not have access to or control of their dowries.[67] When O'Neill's third wife, Catherine Magennis, complained of her husband's abusive, drunken behaviour, she claimed that if she had sufficient cash to purchase 100 cows, she would leave him, a request that reflected Catherine's lack of access to personal wealth.[68] It should also be remembered that dowries in Gaelic society normally consisted of cattle, other animal stock and household goods. Hence, they gave women limited control of economic resources that might have enhanced their political or military status in the lordship.[69] Nor did the unenclosed pastoral form of agriculture in Gaelic society require women to take on estate management responsibilities that might have given them a quasi-political role.

Gaelic women did not, therefore, have the same obligation to take political action as their counterparts in the Anglo-Norman earldoms of Desmond, Kildare and Ormond. This is not to suggest that women in Gaelic society had no political influence. The annals, for example, regularly praised the good advice and counsel offered by wives of Gaelic lords. It was said of Con O'Neill, 1st earl of Tyrone (d. 1559), that he did nothing without the advice of his wife Mary MacDonnell.[70] Joan Maguire who was the mother of Hugh O'Neill was described in her annalistic obit in 1600 as the 'head and counsel of advice to the gentlemen and chiefs' of Ulster, a role which the annalist did not perceive as contrary to the other attributes that he assigned to Joan: 'demure, womanly, devout, charitable, meek, benignant'.[71] The annalist's fusing of Joan Maguire's 'womanly' virtues of meekness and piety with her role as counsellor for the men of Ulster indicates that, as in Anglo-Norman society, there was no clear distinction between the private and public worlds of aristocratic women. It was Joan Maguire's role as mother of Hugh O'Neill and her membership of a politically important family that bestowed on her the status of a counsellor.

The social structure of Gaelic society also facilitated aristocratic women's political influence in other ways. Childbirth and the rearing of children were imbued with political consequence in Gaelic society. According to custom, the attribution of the paternity of a child lay in the power of the woman and all of the sons attributed to a man were entitled to a share of his inheritance. The most famous example of a woman claiming a politically controversial paternity for her son was that of Alison Kelly who asserted that her son, Mathew, was the result of a night spent with Con O'Neill. Con liked the boy and not only accepted him as his son but also nominated him as heir to his newly acquired title, the earldom of Tyrone, much to the anger of Con's legitimate sons, particularly Shane who never accepted Mathew as his father's heir.[72] Alison's decision to identify Con O'Neill as the father of her child undoubtedly shaped political events not just within Tyrone but also in the wider world of Irish politics, as the dispute between the O'Neills and the Tudor administration dominated the history of sixteenth-century Ireland.

Following the birth and identity of the father, the rearing of children could also have political consequences. Fosterage was used in Gaelic society to cement social and political alliances. According to the English commentator, Fynes Moryson, 'wives of lords and gentlemen' eagerly sought to nurse foster children in order to 'have the protection and love of the parents'.[73] The bond between foster parents and the foster child was strong and was often said to be stronger than that between the child and his or her natural parents.[74] The woman's role as foster mother was obviously an important part of the development of trust between the child and his surrogate parents. Dame Janet Eustace who was foster mother to Thomas Fitzgerald, 10th earl of Kildare, was alleged to have had a strong influence over him, particularly at the time of his rebellion in 1534. She was described as being 'most of secrets with him; and by all probable conjecture, she was the chief counsellor and stirrer of this inordinate rebellion'.[75] Hugh O'Neill's ability to negotiate with English officials was similarly due to his fostering with the Old English family of the Hovendens in the 1560s.[76]

Another domestic task that formed an integral part of the political process in Gaelic Ireland was the provision of hospitality. Feasting and festivities strengthened bonds of loyalty between a lord and his supporters and were also a means through which the lord asserted his authority in an area. Included in the tribute that a lord might expect from his subordinate territories was the lodging of the chiefly retinue on a regular basis.[77] This was a custom also adopted by some of the Anglo-Irish lords and a report of 1537 gives some indication of what was involved:

. . . the earls of Desmond, Kildare and Ossory, their wives, children, and servants, do use, after the custom and usage of wild Irishmen, to come with a great multitude of people to monasteries and gentlemen's houses, and there to continue two days and two nights, taking meat and drink at their pleasure, and their horses and keepers to be shifted or divided on the poor farmers, next to that place adjoining, paying nothing therefore . . .[78]

The chieftain's wife was responsible for providing the hospitality for the visitors. As Richard Stanihurst noted the 'prime place at the table is bestowed upon the woman of the household'.[79] In one of the few accounts which we have of the internal life of the tower house (the typical residence of a Gaelic lord), the author, Luke Gernon, an Englishman, described the warm reception that he received from the lord's wife and her 'female kindred'.[80] Bardic poetry was traditionally sung at such occasions and among the tasks undertaken by the wife of the lord was that of patron and bestower of gifts to the poets. Given the political nature of Irish bardic poetry (it was essentially written to praise the valour and leadership of the lord), the woman's choice of poets determined the political propaganda written for her husband and thus had significant political implications.[81]

The complex family networks that were a consequence of the short-term marriages of Gaelic lords could also embroil women in the faction feuding that was endemic within ruling families. Gaelic lords frequently had children by a number of different wives.[82] A lord's declared heir could often be his eldest son by his first wife and might be opposed by his second or third wife who might favour their own offspring as successors to their fathers. Similarly the wife's loyalty to her new husband's family might be questioned if her new husband engaged in military actions which harmed the interests of her former husband and any children she may have had by him. In the 1550s, Barnabe Fitzpatrick, from the midlands lordship of Ossory, complained bitterly about the activities of his stepmother Elizabeth O'Connor. Elizabeth was Brian Fitzpatrick's third wife. She was the daughter of Brian O'Connor and the ex-wife of Patrick O'More. As local lords in the midlands, Elizabeth's father and first husband had led the resistance against the Tudor army in the region.[83] Barnabe claimed that during the subsequent rebellion of the brothers of the earl of Ormond in 1569,

the governor and ruler of my father, I mean his wife, was confederate and assured to the rebels, and the rebels to her, in such sort as she kept six of the best and strongest castles in the country all the war time, that I nor none that took my part could receive any succour or defence by them for so the ward was commanded that if I came, or any of mine, they should shoot us . . .[84]

Shane O'Neill also fell out with his stepmother, Lady Mary MacDonnell, who passed on to the Dublin government intelligence information about her stepson's activities.[85] Later in the century, Rose O'Toole's hostility towards the eldest son of her husband Feagh O'Byrne created a complex web of intrigue that eventually led to the son's execution in Dublin Castle.[86]

The social structure and customs of Gaelic society, therefore, created the potential for political influence by women in chiefly families and occasionally led to women like Elizabeth O'Connor and Rose O'Toole becoming more directly involved in political or military activity. Lack of resources and the fluidity of the political structure meant, however, that the political influence of aristocratic Gaelic women was often temporary and they did not have the same long-term authority as women in Anglo-Norman society.

It is important to remember, however, that Gaelic society was not a static society in the sixteenth century. Political survival depended on the adoption of new practices and customs. In the absence of an Irish court, access to the royal court became more important as the century progressed. A written petition followed, ideally, by a personal visit to the Tudor Court, became one of the most common means through which elite men and women living in Ireland secured political favours. Politically aware Gaelic lords employed clerks to compose letters and petitions for presentation to the crown and its officials in Ireland and in England. In this increasingly literate political world, the more astute political leaders also recognised the advantages which the right sort of wife could bring.

In 1561 Shane O'Neill, chief of the O'Neills, asked Queen Elizabeth to find him a wife. He wanted, he wrote to the queen, a gentlewoman from a noble family who had had a 'good civil . . . upbringing'. O'Neill suggested to the queen that his new wife would be the means by which he might 'from time to time certify my grief and the country's unto Your Majesty' and through which his country would 'become civil and brought to good reformation'.[87] O'Neill wanted an English noblewoman for the task of advancing the 'civil education' of himself and his people; and he identified Lady Frances Radcliffe, the sister of Lord Lieutenant Thomas Radcliffe, earl of Sussex, as his preferred choice.

O'Neill may have have met Lady Frances when he went to London in 1562 to meet the queen and negotiate directly with her and members of her administration. The negotiations failed and Shane O'Neill never got his English wife.[88] O'Neill's overtures to Sussex's sister may also have been a cynical political exercise designed to annoy the lord lieutenant but his request, nonetheless, identifies the criteria for the ideal wife within the new political world of Tudor Ireland. A wife who could speak English and was literate was a valuable asset to a Gaelic lord. Her facility in the English language could assist mediation between her husband and the English authorities; and an ability to write, or at least read English, meant a wife could compose petitions to the queen and her advisers on her husband's behalf. Shane O'Neill's father Con had such a wife in Mary MacDonnell who met with the Dublin government and petitioned senior administrators for assistance to her husband.[89] And throughout Ireland in the sixteenth century, one can find examples of women acting as mediators between their Gaelic families and the representatives of the crown. In the early 1540s, when Ulick Burke began his discussions with the crown for the agreement that eventually led to him receiving the title of earl of Clanricarde, he abandoned his second wife and married Marie Lynch, the widow of a Galway merchant, who was 'of a civil education and English order of education and manners'. Marie was credited with influencing her new husband to the extent that 'he was brought into such civility and conversation with the King's Council and his subjects, that he was induced to repair into England, to visit the King's Majesty, and to acknowledge his allegiance whereon he was created Earl'.[90]

Educated, literate women developed, therefore, new forms of political influence and, to a limited extent, power in the sixteenth century, as they acted as spokespersons and representatives of their male relatives. As noted already, Eleanor Butler, countess of Desmond, continuously petitioned the Dublin and London administration on behalf of her husband.[91] In 1533, Mairgréag, daughter of the Irish chieftain Ó Conchobhair Failghe, travelled to London and successfully lobbied at the court for the return of her father who was being held as a hostage by the crown. The annals noted that Mairgréag's 'knowledge of the English language' was the primary reason that she was sent.[92] Gráinne O'Malley may have operated within the Gaelic world of the west of Ireland, but she too identified the advantages to be gained from a personal visit to the queen and the composition of a series of petitions in the English language to the queen and her advisers. In 1593, and again in 1595, O'Malley travelled to London and petitioned the queen. She acted as a spokesperson for the men in her family and petitioned for her son's and brother's release from prison and for land titles for her sons. O'Malley also asked that her rights as a widow under English law be respected by the Dublin administration. O'Malley's petitions were successful and she returned to Ireland with royal instructions to have her requests implemented.[93]

The Scottish women who came to Ireland are best remembered for the military assistance that they brought their Irish husbands. It is worth noting, however, that contemporaries also remarked on the women's education and connections that they had with the Scottish court. In 1569, it was noted that Agnes Campbell and her daughter, Finola, were 'trained up in the Scots court and speak both French and English'.[94] Shane O'Neill may not have got his English wife but one of the attractions of his last wife, Catherine Mac Lean, may have been her education. She was described as 'very sober, wise and no less subtle, being not unlearned in the Latin tongue, speaketh good French, and as is said some little Italian'.[95] Given her family background and connections to the Scottish court, it is likely that Mac Lean also spoke English and may indeed have acted as an informal adviser to her Irish husband. Her presence by O'Neill's side when he made his fatal visit to the MacDonnell camp in 1567 is worth considering in this context. The purpose of the visit was political not social so Catherine's presence seems, at first, unusual. If, however, she was there to advise her husband and, possibly, act as an intermediary then her attendance makes more sense.

Catherine's stepdaughter Agnes Campbell also impressed English officials whom she encountered with her political knowledge and negotiating skills. The earl of Essex described her as a 'wise and civil woman' who told Essex that her husband had given her full 'commission to treat' with him.[96] In addition, Campbell was credited with persuading Turlough Luineach to conclude his peace treaty with the crown.[97] Campbell also made an impression on Sir Henry Sidney, who described her as a 'grave, wise and well-spoken lady, both in Scots-English and French, and very well-mannered'.[98] In her conversations with Sidney, Campbell made interesting comparisons between her husband's status as a Gaelic lord in Tudor Ireland and her own family's position in Scotland. The earls of Argyle, she pointed out to the lord deputy, 'challenged as much *jura regalia,* and other sovereignties, as [they] could, and yet contented themselves to submit their causes to the laws of the realm and themselves to the king's pleasure'. William Piers, the English seneschal of Clandeboye in north-east Ulster, who also discussed politics with Campbell was less sanguine about Campbell's ambitions as a Scottish woman based in Ireland, claiming that she was 'wholly bent to make a new Scotland in the north parts of Ireland and . . . she told me plainly that if God should call the Queen that England and Ireland should be both the king of Scotland's own'.[99] The reports of all three Englishmen, however, support the perception of Campbell as a politically well-educated and articulate woman who had a clear understanding of the political situation in Ireland, England and Scotland. And the negotiating skills of Agnes Campbell undoubtedly facilitated her volatile husband's retention of power in Tyrone until his death in 1595.

While the centralisation of power undermined the power of dynastic families, the new colonial context of the sixteenth century provided educated women from Old English and New English families with a potentially more expansive political role. It was, however, a development that was only possible at the time of transition between the Gaelic world of the sixteenth century and the more Anglicised world of the seventeenth century. By the latter period, there was no longer the same necessity for Irish men to look to educated wives to mediate between them and the new state. Women are, therefore, less visibly involved in Irish political life in the seventeenth century as regional and dynastic networks diminished in importance. Personal connections at court in London or, in the latter part of the seventeenth century, in Dublin Castle, consequently assume a new significance.

Dublin Castle and court politics

In the new centralised order of Tudor and Stuart Ireland, the woman with the most political influence should have been the wife of the viceroy, based at Dublin Castle. For much of the sixteenth and seventeenth centuries, however, the spouses of the chief governors are shadowy figures who rarely appear in the official correspondence of their husbands. Not all lord deputies' wives came to Ireland and the absence of a court in Dublin reduced the potential influence such women could have.[100] The wife of the chief governor occasionally offered patronage in the securing of official appointments but this was not a common occurrence and was usually confined to minor posts in the Dublin government. From time to time also a governor's wife might be accused of undue influence over her husband. Anne, wife of Sir William Fitzwilliam, Lord Deputy 1571–5 and 1588–93, aroused the wrath of a number of her husband's colleagues in government. The earl of Essex claimed that it was on Anne's advice that the lord deputy decided to withdraw his support for Essex's campaign in Ulster in 1575. Essex bitterly described how Fitzwilliam resolved to end the enterprise 'without any advice but his lady's who I am credibly informed kept the queen's letters three days and coated every line of it, and in the end gave her final judgement that I and all my soldiers should be cashed'.[101]

Anne Fitzwilliam, who was the sister of Sir Henry Sidney, also solicited the London administration on behalf of her husband, earning a reputation with Lord Burghley as a 'vehement suitor'.[102] Although her husband was refused permission to return to England during the time that he was lord deputy, Anne and her sons were free to travel to London to appeal in person at the Tudor Court.[103] Other wives of senior administrators undertook a similar role. Most men who served in senior administrative posts in Ireland were concerned to retain households as well as political and financial interests in England. If the Irish posting was intended (as most were) to be of short-term duration, then the wife and children often stayed in England to preserve the family interest there. William Fitzwilliam complained relentlessly to the London administration about the cost of maintaining two households but it was not until he was confirmed in the post of lord deputy (he had previously held the temporary position of lord justice) in 1571 that his wife joined him in Dublin Castle.[104] Sir Henry Sidney's wife, Mary, held an official position in Elizabeth's court as her lady-in-waiting when her husband was lord deputy and, consequently, she spent only short periods of time in Ireland but, like Anne Fitzwilliam, she also lobbied on behalf of her husband while at court.[105]

The predominantly military nature of political rule in sixteenth-century Ireland made Ireland an unattractive place for the families of senior administrators, many of whom wrote of the hardship that they endured during their Irish service. The earl of Surrey, for example, brought his wife and family to Ireland in 1520 but he quickly sent them home again when the Irish plague threatened their lives.[106] Nor was Dublin Castle a very appealing residence for wives of lord deputies. It was small and uncomfortable. In the 1560s, Sidney endeavoured to refurbish it to make it more accommodating for his family but neither his wife nor his children spent much time there. Lists of household staff in Dublin Castle in the sixteenth century suggest that it remained an overwhelmingly male military community.[107]

In the more peaceful times of the 1630s, Lord Deputy Sir Thomas Wentworth expressed interest in developing an Irish court in Dublin Castle. He intended to refurbish the Castle buildings and make them an appropriate setting for vice-regal ceremonies. Furthermore, Wentworth encouraged the expansion of the social life in and around Dublin Castle. He was, for example, a strong supporter of the development of theatre in Dublin.[108] In addition, Wentworth planned an impressively large country residence at Jigginstown, County Kildare, where he envisaged entertaining crown administrators and supporters.[109] Events, however, overtook Strafford's plans and the house he built at Jigginstown was never used for his court. Nor did the viceroy have time before his execution in 1642 to shape the sort of social life which he thought his position as vice-regent merited.

It was during the Restoration of the 1660s that the first significant development of Irish court life began. Charles II appointed the duke of Ormond as his first Irish vice-regent and he and his wife Elizabeth Butler entertained political supporters in the Castle and also at their own castles at Kilkenny, Dunmore and elsewhere.[110] In 1662, the writer Katherine Philips visited Dublin and her correspondence reveals the development of a socio-political circle around the duke and duchess of Ormond.[111] Subsequent lord deputies in the 1670s and 1680s endeavoured to maintain the social entertainment initiated in the 1660s. Financial restrictions, however, prevented the further expansion of the Castle buildings and English-born vice-regents did not have the same access to private houses as the Ormonds. Elizabeth Algernon, the wife of the earl of Essex, Lord Lieutenant 1672–7, was noted as the first of the English 'vicereines' to entertain as a social hostess.[112] The male ethos of Dublin Castle survived, however, in the segregation of men and women at social events. In November 1686 when the earl of Clarendon celebrated the king's birthday with an official dinner in the castle, the men dined at his table while the 'ladies . . . were with my wife, and at other tables in the house'.[113]

In 1703, when Lady Mary Somerset, the wife of the 2nd earl of Ormond, arrived in Dublin, she was given an official state welcome, an event that marked the first recorded, formal recognition of the public role of the wife of the lord lieutenant.[114] Within a short time, however, the duchess was complaining about the gendered ethos of Dublin Castle. The household was still predominantly male with only a lady-in-waiting to keep the vicereine company.[115] Consequently, Lady Mary spent most of her time as wife of the Irish lord lieutenant living in their home in London. The political usefulness of the vicereine had, therefore, a much higher profile in the Restoration period than it had fifty or a hundred years earlier but it was not until the eighteenth century that the official position of vicereine was fully developed.

In the absence of a lively or influential Irish court, the London court remained politically important in Irish affairs. The accentuation of the bonds between Irish and English peerage families facilitated a more active role for Irish women in the Stuart Court. The earl of Cork, for example, encouraged his daughter Lettice to lobby the queen and other members of court on his behalf.[116] In his conflict with the Irish Lord Chancellor, Sir Adam Loftus, the Lord Deputy Sir Thomas Wentworth complained vociferously about Loftus's daughter who he claimed 'busieth herself up and down the court' in defence of her father.[117] The collapse of the English court in the turmoil of the 1640s led to a hiatus in the ability of elite women to influence royal policy. Irish women were, however, prominent in the Restoration Court of Charles II. The latter included the first earl of Cork's daughter Katherine, widow of Sir Arthur Jones, Lord Ranelagh, and Elizabeth Butler, the duchess of Ormond.[118]

Rebellion and war

The history of Ireland, 1500–1692, was punctuated by war. There was no decade in the sixteenth century when there was not a military disturbance in some part of the country; and in the seventeenth century the rebellion of 1641 and the Williamite wars, 1689–91, affected all parts of the island. Although there are occasional stories of 'she-soldiers', women did not normally engage in military conflict.[119] Gráinne O'Malley's leadership of her people 'by sea and land' and the command of Inghen Dubh, mother of Hugh Roe O'Donnell, of Scottish soldiers stand out in the historical record because they were so unusual, even to contemporaries.

This is not to imply, however, that women were not present at military engagements. Throughout the early modern period there were large numbers of women living in army camps although their presence was so often assumed that it is only occasionally recorded. The composition of Gaelic military groupings is least well documented but in the few visual representations that we have of sixteenth-century Irish soldiers, women are depicted alongside the men.[120] Scottish troops who travelled to Ireland in the late sixteenth century were also accompanied by women and children.[121] There were regular complaints about the horseboys and 'harlots' who travelled with English soldiers in Ireland. Some of the women were employed as laundresses and kitchen helps but most were either wives, long-term partners of the men or camp prostitutes. Local commanders tolerated the presence of women in the camp but the burden of providing food and lodging in districts where the army was garrisoned was the cause of considerable local bitterness and exacerbated the poor relations between the military and the indigenous community. In 1593, for example, the newly appointed English sheriff Henry Willis entered County Fermanagh with over 100 men, many of whom were also accompanied by women and children. The unruly behaviour of the entourage contributed to Hugh Maguire's decision to initiate military action against crown forces, an event that marked the beginning of the Nine Years War.[122]

In the seventeenth century, army regulations restricted the presence of women and children in regiments but the rules proved difficult to enforce. During the Williamite wars, 1689–91, a local militia was raised. For the first time, men were obliged to serve in regiments far removed from their homes. Rather than abandoning their families, many took their wives and children with them.[123] At times, contemporaries noted that the necessity to provide for the men's families hindered military manoeuvres.[124] On the Jacobite side, officers reported that the soldiers threatened to desert unless their wives and children stayed with them.[125]

Most women who accompanied the army did so out of economic necessity. A smaller number became involved through family circumstances. Wives of English commanders assumed military duties during the temporary absence of their husbands. Katherine Butler, for example, was listed as in charge of a small castle garrison in the 1590s when her husband died, while other wives of English captains negotiated with local Irish lords usually in order to protect their homes from attack.[126] As we have seen, in the sixteenth century a small number of elite women became embroiled in military conflict in order to defend family property and political interests. In the wars of the 1640s, women heads of household found themselves under siege from rebel forces. Some quickly accepted offers of safe convoy for themselves and members of their household but others decided to defend their homes and resist the besiegers. Lady Elizabeth Dowdall appears to have relished the opportunity to command a group of men to defend her castle of Kilfenny in County Limerick. She subsequently wrote an account of her military achievements in which she described how at the beginning of the rebellion she hired a soldier to train eighty men and then sent them out to attack the Irish troops. Her narrative suggests that she was proud of her achievements which she asserted had protected the area from being overrun by Irish forces.[127]

The unsuspecting trust given to women from aristocratic and gentry families by military leaders could be exploited for military purposes. Women were employed to smuggle arms, collect intelligence, pass on messages and act as decoys. In all the military conflicts of early modern Ireland, women risked their lives engaged in such covert activities. None wrote of their reasons for doing so but family loyalty and a desire to protect a child's inheritance were undoubtedly compelling factors. The strength of religious and political beliefs among elite women should, however, not be dismissed as insignificant. As noted already, Agnes Campbell spoke of her dislike of English control in Ireland while Eleanor Butler, countess of Desmond, joined her husband in symbolically changing into Gaelic-style dress when they escaped from house arrest in Dublin in 1573. In the seventeenth century, religious zeal and political commitment to King William or King James motivated women as well as men to engage in clandestine activities.

At a lower social level, economic factors mixed with religious and political beliefs in a complex combination which is difficult to disentangle. Irish rebellions in the sixteenth century were primarily rebellions of the aristocracy and rarely enjoyed or demanded widespread popular support. The rebellion of 1641 was different in the sense that it was the first Irish rebellion that involved spontaneous risings from below, a phenomenon that widened the potential for women to become involved. The risings often began when a crowd assembled and then attacked and looted the homes of local Protestant settlers. Women were recorded as mob leaders as well as participating in the violent activities of such crowds. As the war proceeded, however, the confederate army became more organised and the importance of this type of popular support lessened and, hence, women's active role in the conflict declined.

Popular resistance was relatively unimportant in the war of 1689–91 which was primarily a military conflict between two armies.[128] Both sides were, however, dependent on the support of the local community for provisions and lodgings. The Williamite soldier John Stevens described the passive resistance of men and women who refused hospitality to the army. Local people hid provisions from soldiers and only yielded them up when forced to do so.[129] As in most wars, this type of auxiliary female support service on which all armies depended was provided partly out of loyalty and partly out of fear of intimidation.

Conclusion

The involvement of women in political life in Tudor and Stuart Ireland was manifest in a variety of ways. Far from remaining secluded in the private world of the home, elite women were compelled to participate in political affairs. As Barbara Harris has noted of aristocratic women in early Tudor England, the structures of political life depended on the involvement of aristocratic men and women. In the English-speaking parts of Ireland, those structures were less well developed than in England but there are nonetheless obvious parallels between women in Anglo-Ireland and the aristocratic women of early Tudor England.[130] The distinction between the private and public worlds of women in Gaelic society was as indecipherable as it was among Anglo-Irish women. The social customs of fosterage and hospitality were imbued with political significance. Nonetheless, the political role of women in Gaelic society seems to have been more limited than it was in the English-speaking parts of Ireland. The more militaristic society, the volatility of the political system and the largely pastoral economy meant that there was less need for women to be involved in the political process other than as marriage partners and producers of children. The political role of women in Gaelic society was further diminished with the increased literacy of the political system.

As dynastic politics faded, the political attention of women should have shifted to the Irish capital but the slow emergence of court society in Dublin hindered the development of women's political influence in the seventeenth century. War gave women other ways of engaging with public life and provided glimpses of women who in more peaceful times left no record of their political views. It was not, however, until the eighteenth century that a political system evolved that allotted a more specific role to women.

Notes

1 Mary O'Dowd (Ed), *Calendar of State Papers: Ireland, 1571–1575* (London, 2000), no. 840.

2 Cited in Merry E. Wiesner, *Women and Gender in Early Modern Europe* (Cambridge, 1993), p. 242.

3 See the Marquis of Kildare, *The Earls of Kildare and Their Ancestors: from 1057 to 1773* (Dublin, 1858), pp. 84, 91–3, 99–100, 113–14; Barbara J. Harris, 'Women and Politics in Early Tudor England' in *The Historical Journal*, **33**(2) (1990), p. 272.

4 *The Complete Peerage*; See also Harris, 'Women and Politics in Early Tudor England', p. 272; Barbara J. Harris, 'The View From My Lady's Chamber: New Perspectives on the Early Tudor Monarchy' in *Huntington Library Quarterly*, **60**(3) (1999), p. 234.

5 Kildare, *The Earls of Kildare and Their Ancestors*, pp. 237–8.

6 Vincent P. Carey, *Surviving the Tudors. The 'Wizard' Earl of Kildare and English Rule in Ireland, 1537–1586* (Dublin, 2002), pp. 58, 139; *Calendar of State Papers: Ireland, 1574–85*, p. 284. See also p. 159 below.

7 P. Wright, 'A Change in Direction: The Ramifications of a Female Household, 1558–1603' in D. Starkey (Ed), *The English Court from the Wars of the Roses to the Civil War* (London, 1987), pp. 147–72; Barbara J. Harris, *English Aristocratic Women, 1450–1550* (Oxford, 2002), pp. 210–40.

8 See below.

9 Ciarán Brady, *The Chief Governors. The Rise and Fall of Reform in Tudor Ireland, 1536–1588* (Cambridge, 1994), p. 196.

10 For Edward Fitzgerald's negotiations with the earl of Desmond see O'Dowd (Ed), *Calendar of State Papers: Ireland, 1571–1575*.

11 David Edwards, *The Ormond Lordship in County Kilkenny, 1515–1642, The Rise and Fall of Butler Feudal Power* (Dublin, 2003).

12 Donough Bryan, *Gerald Fitzgerald. The Great Earl of Fitzgerald (1456–1513)* (Dublin, 1933), p. 97.

13 Kildare's sister, Eleanor was married to Conn Mór O'Neill.

14 For a detailed account of the marriages of the Fitzgerald family see Kildare, *The Earls of Kildare and Their Ancestors*, especially pp. 58, 71–9, 84.

15 Harris, 'The View From My Lady's Chamber: New Perspectives on the Early Tudor Monarchy', p. 241; Kildare, *The Earls of Kildare and Their Ancestors*, pp. 58, 60–1.

16 James Ware, *The Antiquities and History of Ireland* (English version, Dublin, 1705), p. 68.

17 Brady, *The Chief Governors in Tudor Ireland, 1536–1588*, pp. 169–208; Edwards, *The Ormond Lordship in County Kilkenny*, p. 102.

18 Thomas Lyons, 'Sean O'Neill – A Biography' (unpublished, MA thesis, University College, Cork, 1948), pp. 202–8.

19 *Annals of the Four Masters*, 1561.

20 Entry for Calvagh O'Donnell in *New Dictionary of National Biography*.

21 Lyons, op. cit., pp. 249–50.

22 See below, pp. 25–6.

23 Paul Walsh, *The Will and Family of Hugh O'Neill, Earl of Tyrone* (Dublin, 1930). See also Hiram Morgan, *Tyrone's Rebellion. The Outbreak of the Nine Years War in Tudor Ireland* (Woodbridge, Suffolk, 1993), pp. 95–7.

24 *Calendar of State Papers: Ireland, 1588–1592*, pp. 433–6; Donald Jackson, *Intermarriage in Ireland, 1550–1650* (Montreal and Minneapolis, 1970), pp. 29–33.

25 David Edwards, 'The Mac Giollapadraigs (Fitzpatricks) of Upper Ossory, 1532–1641' in Padraig G. Lane and William Nolan (Eds), *Laois, History and Society. Interdisciplinary Essays on the History of an Irish County* (Dublin, 1999), pp. 351–3.

26 John MacKechnie, 'Treaty Between Argyle and O'Donnell' in John MacDonald (Ed), *Scottish Gaelic Studies*, **vii** (1953), pp. 94–9.

27 G. A. Hayes-McCoy, *Scots Mercenary Forces in Ireland (1569–1603)* (Dublin and London, 1937), pp. 98–107.

28 *Calendar of State Papers: Ireland, 1599–1600*, p. 366.

29 Jackson, *Intermarriage in Ireland 1550–1650*, pp. 29–37.

30 Ibid., pp. 20–8.

31 Document dated c. 1592. See *Calendar of State Papers: Ireland, 1588–1592*, pp. 534–6.

32 Colm Lennon, *The Lords of Dublin in the Age of Reformation* (Dublin, 1989), pp. 78–9. See also pp. 72–4.

33 Mary O'Dowd, 'Women and Colonisation: the Irish Experience, 1550–1650' in Terry Brotherstone and Oonagh Walsh (Eds), *Gendering Scottish History: an International Approach* (Glasgow, 1999), pp. 156–71. See also pp. 250–2 below.

34 Willy Maley (Ed), 'The Supplication of the Blood of the English Most Lamentably Murdered in Ireland Cryeng Out of the Yearth for Revenge (1598)' in *Analecta Hibernica*, **36** (1995), pp. 31–2.

35 Nicholas Canny, *Making Ireland British 1580–1650* (Oxford, 2001), pp. 66–103; Ciarán Brady, 'The Captains' Games: Army and Society in Elizabethan Ireland' in Thomas Bartlett and Keith Jeffery (Eds), *A Military History of Ireland* (Cambridge, 1996), pp. 136–59; Brady, *The Chief Governors*, p. 274.

36 Aidan Clarke, 'The Genesis of the Ulster Rising of 1641' in Peter Roebuck (Ed), *Plantation to Partition* (Belfast, 1981), pp. 29–45.

37 Victor Treadwell, *Buckingham and Ireland 1616–1628. A Study in Anglo-Irish Politics* (Dublin, 1998), pp. 120–1. See also P. J. Little, 'The Geraldine Ambitions of the First Earl of Cork' in *Irish Historical Studies*, **xxxiii** (2002), pp. 151–68.

38 A charge levied against Edward Fitzgerald's uncle, Sir Leonard Grey when he was lord deputy of Ireland, 1536–40 (*State Papers, Henry VIII*, vol. III, part 3, p. 32).

39 Caroline Hibbard, 'The Role of a Queen Consort: the Household and Court of Henrietta Maria, 1625–1642' in R. Asch and A. Birke (Eds), *Princes, Patronage and the Nobility: the Court at the Beginning of the Modern Age, c. 1450–1650* (London, 1991), p. 411. See also P. J. S. Little, 'Family and Faction, the Irish Nobility and the English Court, 1632–42' (unpublished M.Litt, University of Dublin, 1992).

40 Treadwell, *Buckingham and Ireland 1616–1628*, pp. 103–47. Professor Jane Ohlmeyer is currently undertaking a major study of seventeenth-century aristocratic families in Ireland.

41 Bryan, *Gerald Fitzgerald*, pp. 236–7. For an account of the battle of Knockdoe see Colm Lennon, *Sixteenth-Century Ireland: the Incomplete Conquest* (Dublin, 1994), pp. 65–7.

42 A. B. Grosart (Ed), *Lismore Papers* (10 vols., London, 1886–8), 1st series, vol. 4, pp. 42–4, vol. v, pp. 45–6.

43 Wiesner, *Women and Gender in Early Modern Europe*, p. 240.

44 Kenneth Nicholls, 'Irishwomen and Property in the Sixteenth Century' in Margaret MacCurtain and Mary O'Dowd (Eds), *Women in Early Modern Ireland* (Edinburgh, 1991), p. 20.

45 See Edmund Curtis (Ed), *Calendar of Ormond Deeds. Volume IV, 1509–1547* (Dublin, 1937), pp. 1, 19, 21, 36, 53, 59, 62, 64, 78, 87–8, 99, 109, 114, 116, 142, 144, 145, 146, 180, 188; Edwards, *The Ormond Lordship in County Kilkenny, 1515–1642*, pp. 69, 93, 148–9.

46 Angela Bourke *et al.* (Eds), *Field Day Anthology of Irish Writing, Vols. IV–V* (Cork, 2002), **V**, p. 14.

47 Ibid., pp. 14–16.

48 Curtis, *Calendar of Ormond Deeds. Volume IV, 1509–1547*, pp. 11–13.

49 Kildare, *The Earls of Kildare and Their Ancestors*, pp. 107–8; 28 ch. Henry VIII, ch. 1.

50 Ibid.; *State Papers, Henry VIII*, vol. II, part 3, pp. 146–7.

51 Edward Fitzgerald was an infant at the time of the rebellion and brought to England by his mother. See above.

52 For the wider political background see Brady, *The Chief Governors*, pp. 1–44.

53 Kildare, *The Earls of Kildare and Their Ancestors*, p. 189. See also *State Papers, Henry VIII*, vol. III, part 3, p. 44.

54 Ibid., pp. 190–1. See also Bourke *et al.* (Eds), *Field Day Anthology of Irish Writing, Vol. V*, pp. 13–14.

55 Ibid., p. 14.

56 Edwards, *The Ormond Lordship in County Kilkenny*, pp. 94–5, 97, 178; PRO, SP61/2, no. 50. For correspondence of Joan as a widow see PRO, SP61/1/1, no. 4.

57 See, for example, PRO, SP63/8, no. 56.

58 For a biography of Eleanor, Countess of Desmond see Anne Chambers, *Eleanor Countess of Desmond, c. 1545–1638* (Dublin, 1986). See also Bourke *et al.* (Eds), *Field Day Anthology of Irish Writing, Vol. V*, pp. 16–19.

59 Walsh, *The Will and Family of Hugh O'Neill, Earl of Tyrone*, p. 33.

60 Ibid., pp. 37–8.

61 John McCavitt, *The Flight of the Earls* (Dublin, 2002), pp. 60–2.

62 Ibid., p. 95.

63 Based on an examination of agreements made in the sixteenth century. See also comments of Gráinne O'Malley cited on p. 99.

64 Anne Chambers, *Granuaile. The Life and Times of Grace O'Malley c. 1530–1603* (Dublin, new edition, 1998), p. 195.

65 Bourke *et al.* (Eds), *Field Day Anthology of Irish Writing, Vol. V*, p. 20.

66 Katharine Simms, 'The Legal Position of Irishwomen in the Later Middle Ages' in *The Irish Jurist*, **x**, n.s. (1975), pp. 108–9; Kenneth Nicholls, 'Irishwomen and Property in the Sixteenth Century' in MacCurtain and O'Dowd (Eds), *Women in Early Modern Ireland*, pp. 19–20.

67 See Walsh, *The Will and Family of Hugh O'Neill, Earl of Tyrone.*

68 *Calendar of State Papers: Ireland, 1603–1606*, pp. 408–10.

69 See below, pp. 76–7.

70 *State Papers During the Reign of Henry the Eighth* (11 vols., London, 1830–52), p. 131; PRO, SP62, vol. 4, no. 85.

71 *Annals of the Four Masters*, 1600.

72 Ciarán Brady, *Shane O'Neill* (Dublin, 1996).

73 C. L. Falkiner, *Illustrations of Irish History and Topography, Mainly of the Seventeenth Century* (London, 1904), p. 318; Kenneth Nicholls, *Gaelic and Gaelicised Ireland in the Middle Ages* (Dublin, 1972), p. 79. See also Fiona Fitzsimons, 'Fosterage and Gossiprid in Late Medieval Ireland: Some New Evidence' in Patrick J. Duffy, David Edwards and Elizabeth FitzPatrick (Eds), *Gaelic Ireland. Land, Lordship and Settlement c. 1550–c. 1650* (Dublin, 2001), pp. 138–49.

74 See, for example, Lennon, *Sixteenth-Century Ireland*, pp. 61–2, 75–6; Morgan, *Tyrone's Rebellion*, pp. 95–6.

75 *State Papers, Henry VIII*, vol. II, part 3, p. 228.

76 Morgan, *Tyrone's Rebellion*, pp. 92–3, 214–15.

77 Katharine Simms, 'Guesting and Feasting in Gaelic Ireland' in *Journal of the Royal Society of Antiquaries of Ireland*, **108** (1978), pp. 67–100.

78 Kildare, *The Earls of Kildare and Their Ancestors*, p. 117.

79 Colm Lennon, *Richard Stanihurst. The Dubliner 1547–1618* (Dublin, 1981), p. 150.

80 Falkiner, *Illustrations of Irish History and Topography*, pp. 357–62.

81 Bernadette Cunningham, 'Women and Gaelic Literature, 1500–1800' in MacCurtain and O'Dowd (Eds), *Women in Early Modern Ireland*, pp. 147–59.

82 See for example, M. D. O'Sullivan, 'The Wives of Ulick, 1st Earl of Clanricarde' in *Journal of Galway Archaeological and Historical Society*, **xxi** (1945), pp. 174–83.

83 Edwards, 'The Mac Giollapadraigs (Fitzpatricks) of Upper Ossory, 1532–1641', pp. 339–42.

84 J. T. Gilbert (Ed), *Facsimiles of the National Manuscripts of Ireland* (4 vols., Dublin, 1874–84), vol. iv, i, appendix ix, p. 79.

85 Lord Deputy Sir William Fitzwilliam to Sir William Cecil, 11 April 1560 (PRO, SP63/2, no. 11).

86 B. G. McCarthy, 'The Riddle of Rose O'Toole' in Séamus Pender (Ed), *Féilscríbhinn Torna . . . Essays and Studies Presented to Professor Tadhg ua Donnachadha (Torna)* (Cork, 1947), pp. 171–82.

87 Shane O'Neill to Queen Elizabeth, 8 February 1561 (PRO, SP/63/3, no. 4); same to Sir William Cecil, 18 November 1563 (PRO, SP63/9, no. 63). See also Richard Bagwell, *Ireland Under the Tudors* (3 vols., London, 1885–90), vol. 2, pp. 17–18, 40, 52, 63–4; Brady, *Shane O'Neill*, pp. 52–3.

88 Ibid.; Bagwell, *Ireland Under the Tudors*, vol. 2, pp. 17–18.

89 See Bagwell, *Ireland Under the Tudors*, vol. 2, pp. 8, 15; Mary, Countess of Tyrone to the Duke of Northumberland, 13 February 1562 (PRO, SP63/4, no. 10); *Calendar of State Papers: Ireland, 1509–1572*, p. 131; PRO, SP62/4, no. 85.

90 Cited in O'Sullivan, 'The Wives of Ulick, 1st Earl of Clanricarde', pp. 178–9.

91 Mabel Browne exploited her family contacts at court to endorse her petitions on behalf of her husband, Gerald, the restored 11th earl of Kildare (see note 6 above); D. G. White, 'Tudor Plantations in Ireland Before 1571' (2 vols., unpublished Ph.D. thesis, University of Dublin, 1968), vol. i, pp. 389–93. For other examples of wives acting as intermediaries for their husbands see Donal Moore, 'English Action, Irish Reaction: the MacMurrough Kavanaghs, 1530–1630' (unpublished MA thesis, St Patrick's College, Maynooth, 1985), p. 60.

92 Bourke *et al.* (Eds), *Field Day Anthology of Irish Writing, Vol. IV*, p. 339.

93 Chambers, *Granuaile. The Life and Times of Grace O'Malley*, pp. 127–50, 155–7, 195–204.

94 Cited in Hayes-McCoy, *Scots Mercenary Forces in Ireland*, pp. 345–6.

95 Lord Deputy Fitzwilliam to Sir Robert Cecil, 30 May 1561 (PRO, SP63/3, no. 84).

96 *Calendar of State Papers: Ireland, 1571–75*, nos. 1423, 1466.16, 1466.19.

97 Bagwell, *Ireland Under the Tudors*, vol. 3, pp. 304–5.

98 Ciarán Brady (Ed), *A Viceroy's Vindication? Sir Henry Sidney's Memoir of Service in Ireland, 1556–1578* (Dublin, 2002), pp. 75–6; Hayes-McCoy, *Scots*

Mercenary Forces in Ireland, pp. 98–121 is the most detailed account of Agnes Campbell's Irish activities. See also the many references to her in the Irish state papers of the period.

99 William Piers to Sir Francis Walsingham, 18 August 1580 (PRO, SP63/75, no. 58).

100 Ciarán Brady, 'Political Women and Reform in Tudor Ireland' in MacCurtain and O'Dowd (Eds), *Women in Early Modern Ireland*, pp. 69–90.

101 *Calendar of State Papers: Ireland, 1571–75*, no. 1358.

102 Ibid., nos. 124, 135, 163, 287, 304.

103 Ibid., no. 1404.

104 Ibid., nos. 124, 351.

105 Francis Berkeley Young, *Mary Sidney, Countess of Pembroke* (London, 1912), pp. 10–26; Philip Sidney, *The Sidneys of Penshurst* (London, no date given).

106 *State Papers, Henry VIII*, vol. II, part 3, p. 39.

107 See, for example, PRO, SP63/161, no. 66; A Brief Declaration of the Order and Forme of the Government in Sir John Perrot's House During the Time He Was Lord Deputy of Ireland (Bodleian Library, Oxford, MS Add C 39). See also Chapter 3 below.

108 William Smith Clark, *The Early Irish Stage. The Beginnings to 1720* (Westport, Connecticut, 1973), pp. 26–38. See also A. J. Fletcher, *Drama, Performance and Polity in Pre-Cromwellian Ireland* (Cambridge, 2000), pp. 261–7.

109 J. F. Merritt, 'Power and Communication: Thomas Wentworth and Government At A Distance During the Personal Rule, 1629–1633' in J. F. Merritt (Ed), *The Political World of Thomas Wentworth, Earl of Strafford, 1621–1641* (Cambridge, 1996), p. 115; Toby Barnard, 'The Viceregal Court in Later Seventeenth-Century Ireland' in Eveline Cruickshanks (Ed), *The Stuart Courts* (Stroud, Gloucestershire, 2000), pp. 256–8.

110 Ibid., pp. 258–9.

111 Philip Webster Souers, *The Matchless Orinda* (Cambridge, Harvard, 1931); Carol Barash, *English Women's Poetry, 1649–1714. Politics, Community, and Linguistic Authority* (Oxford, 1996), pp. 78–83. Smith Clark, op. cit., pp. 43–67.

112 Charles O'Mahony, *The Viceroys of Ireland. The Story of the Long Line of Noblemen and Their Wives Who Have Ruled Ireland and Irish Society For Over Seven Hundred Years* (London, 1912), p. 100. Smith Clark, op. cit., 72–3.

113 *The State Letters of Henry Earl of Clarendon . . . During the Reign of King James the Second* (2 vols., Oxford and Dublin, 1765), vol. ii, pp. 86–7, 156. See also vol. i, p. 331.

114 F. Elrington Ball, Introduction to *Calender of the Manuscripts of the Marquess of Ormonde, Preserved at Kilkenny Castle* (11 vols., London, 1895–1920), vol. 8.

115 T. C. Barnard, 'Introduction: the Dukes of Ormond' in T. C. Barnard and Jane Fenton (Eds), *The Dukes of Ormond, 1610–1745* (Woodbridge, 2000), p. 33.

116 Little, 'Family and Faction, the Irish Nobility and the English Court, 1632–42'.

117 Cited in ibid., p. 125.

118 There is no satisfactory study of either woman's life but for Katherine Boyle, Lady Ranelagh, see Lynette Hunter, 'Sisters of the Royal Society: the Circle of Katherine Jones, Lady Ranelagh' in Lynette Hunter and Sarah Hutton (Eds), *Women, Science and Medicine, 1500–1700: Mothers and Sisters of the Royal Society* (Stroud, Gloucesteshire, 1997), pp. 178–97. For Elizabeth Butler, Countess of Ormond see Bourke *et al.* (Eds), *Field Day Anthology of Irish Writing, Vol. IV*, pp. 30–4, 66; Barnard, 'Introduction: The Dukes of Ormond' in Barnard and Fenton (Eds), *The Dukes of Ormond*, pp. 31–5.

119 Mary O'Dowd, 'Women and War in Ireland in the 1640s' in MacCurtain and O'Dowd (Eds), *Women in Early Modern Ireland*, pp. 94–5; Bernadette Whelan, 'Women and the "War of the Three Kings" 1689–91' in Ronit Lenin (Ed), *In From the Shadows: The UL Women's Studies Collection*, vol. ii (Limerick, 1996), p. 45.

120 H. F. McClintock, *Handbook of the Traditional Old Irish Dress* (Dundalk, 1958), plate 3; John Derricke, *The Image of Ireland* (London, 1581; reprinted, Belfast, 1985).

121 See, for example, *Calendar of State Papers: Ireland, 1586–88*, pp. 175, 179.

122 PRO, SP63/170, no. 23(7). For another example, see White, 'The Plantations in Ireland Before 1571', vol. i, pp. 94–5.

123 R. H. Murray (Ed), *The Journal of John Stevens* (Oxford, 1912), pp. 199–200. See also Whelan, 'Women and the "War of the Three Kings" 1689–91', p. 44.

124 See, for example, Andrew Hamilton, *A True Relation of the Actions of the Inniskilling-Men From Their First Taking Up Arms in December 1688 for the Defence of the Protestant Religion, and Their Lives and Liberty* (London, 1690), p. 22.

125 Murray (Ed), *The Journal of John Stevens*, p. 99.

126 See *Calendar of State Papers: Ireland*, 1599–1600, p. 437; (SP63/207, no. 70); PRO SP63/176, no. 60, ix; See also *Calendar of State Papers: Ireland, 1599–1600*, pp. 41–2; PRO SP63/186, no. 86, xxi.

127 See Bourke *et al.* (Eds), *Field Day Anthology of Irish Writing, Vol. V*, pp. 22–4. For other examples see O'Dowd, 'Women and War in Ireland in the 1640s' in MacCurtain and O'Dowd (Eds), *Women in Early Modern Ireland*, pp. 91–111. Similar stories were recorded during the Williamite wars. See Whelan, 'Women and the "War of the Three Kings" 1689–91'; J. T. Gilbert, *A Jacobite Narrative of the War in Ireland, 1688–1691* (Dublin, 1892; reprinted, 1971), pp. 91–2; K. Danaher and J. G. Simms (Eds), *The Danish Forces in Ireland,*

1690–1691 (Dublin, 1961), p. 30; Philip H. Bagenal, *Vicissitudes of an Anglo-Irish Family 1530–1800.*
A Story of Romance and Tragedy (London, 1925), pp. 129–31.

128 Maurice Lenihan, *Limerick: Its History and Antiquities* (1866, reprinted, Cork, 1967), pp. 243–5.

129 Murray (Ed), *The Journal of John Stevens*, p. 157. See also pp. 50–1.

130 Harris, *Aristocratic Women in Early Tudor England, 1450–1550.*

CHAPTER 2

Politics, Patriotism and the Public Sphere: Women and Politics, 1692–1800

Parliamentary politics

In July 1782, Elizabeth Hastings, countess of Moira, wrote to her daughter Selina:

All the Cavendishes out and the Ponsonbys of course have fallen here . . . If the Duke of Rutland comes over, we are connected there both by him and her, so that at the Castle we shall be well received.[1]

The countess's comments reflect the impact that the appointment of a new lord lieutenant had on the social life of eighteenth-century Dublin. Familial relationships and friendships were exploited to establish links with the new incumbent and his spouse. As Lady Moira implicitly recognised, identifying such connections was about more than securing an invitation to a ball or dinner at Dublin Castle. The factional basis of eighteenth-century Irish political life meant that family networks could also be political networks. Families that did not have a point of contact with the new incumbents could find that they were excluded not just from social events but also from political circles.

A crucial difference between politics in the sixteenth and seventeenth centuries and politics in the eighteenth century was the change in the status and role of parliament. At best a sporadically summoned and ineffective institution in the earlier centuries, the Irish parliament began to meet regularly from the 1690s and rapidly developed as the central forum for political debate. Initially English party divisions prevailed but after 1714 parliamentary groupings were formed through a complex and shifting labyrinth of marriage and family connections. As one historian has commented, the early eighteenth-century Irish House of Commons was a 'fairly incestuous institution' with over half of the MPs being related to at least one other member.[2] Alan Broderick (Speaker of the House, 1703, 1713, and Lord Chancellor, 1714–25), for example, was connected through his two marriages to nine MPs while William Conolly (Speaker of the House, 1715–29), was related through his marriage to Kathryn Conyngham to an extended family that returned a total of thirteen MPs.[3] The factional-family alliances that dominated eighteenth-century Irish political life were reminiscent of the dynastic networks of the sixteenth century in which, as we have seen, elite women had a political role as influential marriage partners and intermediaries. In the later period, women in political families performed a similar role but by that time the structure of Irish political life had changed and new mechanisms were in place which facilitated a widening of women's political influence and participation in Irish public affairs.

First, as the comments of the countess of Moira note, Dublin Castle developed a socio-political role. The hosting of an intensive social programme in the Castle complex was an important means through which eighteenth-century lord lieutenants managed parliament. The court life of Dublin evolved alongside that of the legislature as the public rooms in the Castle were expanded and lord lieutenants hosted weekly levees, drawing rooms, balls and dinners.[4] Some of these events, as in the seventeenth century, were gendered and were closed to women. The levees at which there was an opportunity to lobby the lord lieutenant personally for positions and favours were male-only affairs as were some of the political dinners hosted by the viceroy.[5] Women, however, regularly attended other events in the Castle such as the weekly balls and some of the private and public dinners arranged by the vice-regal couple.

The expansion of the court life of Dublin Castle enhanced the socio-political role of the lord lieutenant's wife or social partner. Unlike in earlier times, most lord lieutenants' wives spent some time living in Dublin and their arrival was hailed in the press as a noteworthy public event. As the countess of Moira's correspondence reveals, the familial connections of the vicereine were as carefully scrutinised as those of her husband for political advantage. The social achievements of a vice-regency were important criteria for assessing its overall success. The positive image of the Carterets (1724–31) was attributed to the 'full social programme' mounted by the couple. The duchess hosted a weekly ball at Dublin Castle to which a large number of people were invited.[6] Later in the century, in the 1780s, the duke and duchess of Rutland were also very popular hosts and were reported to have 'enmeshed all factions in a continuous round of pleasure'.[7] Other chief governors and their wives were noted, on the other hand, for their lack of hospitality.[8]

Most vicereines took their social tasks seriously and not only hosted events jointly with the viceroy but organised social programmes of their own.[9] While the lord lieutenant presided at the male levee, his wife received female guests formally in the mornings and in the drawing room in the evenings.[10] The vicereine also hosted ladies' nights at the theatre.[11] The higher public profile of the vicereine was acknowledged in the appointment of a gentleman usher to attend her on formal occasions and in the establishment of a recognised protocol to be followed when the lord lieutenant's wife travelled through the streets of Dublin on official visits to charity balls and private dinner parties.[12]

Invitations to Dublin Castle were prized for the political influence and patronage that they might foster. Some invitations were, however, more highly prized than others. Large balls at the Castle, designed to elicit as much support for the executive as possible, were crowded and noisy affairs that made personal contact and conversation difficult.[13] There were over 400 women at the Queen's Birthday Ball in 1781 while more than 150 ladies were frequently presented at Drawing Room evenings. A Catholic woman, Mary Scully, who attended a ball at the Castle in 1802 described it, accurately, as 'a kind of public meeting'.[14] Far more valued were invitations to smaller, more intimate social events such as dinner parties or the cribbage parties hosted by Lord and Lady Carlisle in the 1780s.[15] A list of guests at the dinners hosted by lord lieutenants, 1761–70, indicates that parliamentary representatives regularly dined at the Castle in small groups of twelve to fifteen. Lord Lieutenants Northumberland and Harcourt included women on their guest lists while others appear to have maintained the gender exclusiveness of previous generations.[16] Most women who attended the official dinners at the Castle were in the company of their husbands but a small number appear to have been unattended by a male partner. Amongst the women on the guest list in the 1760s were spouses of prominent politicians including Lady Betty Ponsonby, Lady Shannon, Mrs Clements, Mrs Grattan, Louisa Conolly and Lady Brandon.

Invitations to events such as small dinner or card parties and concerts in Dublin Castle confirmed the women's membership of the political elite and the favoured status of their families and their families' connections in the eyes of the administration. The dinners presumably also gave the guests an opportunity to lobby for particular projects and patronage. Many of the women who dined at the Castle were also engaged in philanthropic work that benefitted from public funding. One of Lord Northumberland's dinner guests in the early 1760s was Lady Arbella Denny who undoubtedly exploited her political connections to lobby for public funding for her charitable foundations. Other women on the Castle's dining list were also involved in charities that were supported by the Irish parliament.[17]

Balls and dinners were of course also held in private houses and eighteenth-century correspondence reveals a busy social programme for members of the Protestant network that dominated Irish political life. In 1782, an Irish correspondent of Lady Louisa Stuart noted 'nothing can be so gay as Dublin is – the castle twice a week, the opera twice a week, with plays, assemblies and supper to fill up the time'.[18] In March of the same year, Lady Carlow described her social programme for a week. On Monday there was a dinner at Mrs Gardiner's, on Tuesday a dinner at the home of Louisa and Thomas Conolly in Castletown House during the day, followed by a ball in the evening at Mr O'Neill's or an assembly at Lady Ely's; on Wednesday there was a ball at Mr Trench's and on Thursday there were two balls and on Friday two concerts.[19] Invitations to such events, like attendance at the Castle, could carry an implict political message. Exclusion from a guest list was interpreted politically. In 1758 Charles O'Hara wrote to his wife Mary that the duchess of Kildare had hosted a ball from which he and the 'old set' were excluded. In response Lady Macartney held an alternative social evening for those shunned by the Leinster House event.[20]

The relatively small size of the Protestant elite determined the limits of its social world and reinforced its incestuous nature. Dublin appears not to have developed the salon society for which Paris and to a lesser extent London were renowned. Moira House, the home of Francis Rawdon, 1st earl of Moira and his third wife, Elizabeth Hastings, was exceptional.[21] The countess took a keen interest in public affairs and wrote knowledgeably about Irish and international politics. After her husband's death, she and her son John, the 2nd earl of Moira, entertained supporters of parliamentary reform at Moira House including Wolfe Tone and Thomas Russell as well as men connected to the Catholic Committee. Lady Moira's daughter Selina, wife of Lord Granard, also participated in the political discussions at Moira House.[22] In 1798, Lady Pamela Fitzgerald, wife of United Irishman Lord Edward Fitzgerald, found refuge in Moira House when her husband was arrested and later executed by the government.[23]

The possession of a large landed estate within a day's riding distance from Dublin could aften be a more important political asset than a town house in Dublin, particularly prior to the purchase of the lord lieutenant's rural residence in Phoenix Park in 1782. The presence of the lord lieutenant and his entourage at a country demesne for a day's hunting provided many opportunities to exert political influence. Emily Fitzgerald, 1st duchess of Leinster, wrote of receiving politicians at Carton House while successive lord lieutenants also made use of the neighbouring estate of Castletown for a day's relaxation. The choice of hunting location or venue for festive celebrations might also reveal political loyalties. In the 1720s, for example, the duke of Grafton spent Christmas at Carton but the Carterets opted to remain in Dublin, signalling their independence of the Kildare network.[24] Carton, Castletown and other large estate houses thus, as Toby Barnard has noted, 'functioned as something more than a private habitation'.[25]

Elite women had, therefore, numerous opportunities to exercise political influence although it is more difficult to identify specific occasions when any of them directly influenced the political process. Private correspondence makes clear, however, that women were actively engaged in communicating political 'news' and exploiting their family status to lobby for patronage and political support. In the 1720s, Kathryn Conolly wrote regularly to prominent politicians in England as well as in Ireland on behalf of her husband and their political allies. She described gathering her 'friends' to support particular bills in the House of Commons and passed on to the London administration information on political life in Dublin that was damaging to her husband's political opponents. Kathryn also lobbied officials in London on appointments to the Irish establishment.[26] In 1778–9, Louisa Conolly, who married Kathryn's nephew Thomas, used her family links to the lord lieutenant, the duke of Buckinghamshire, to petition and secure jobs and appointments for family and friends.[27]

Attendance at social engagements enabled elite women to hear political gossip that might prove useful to their families' political involvement. When she visited London, Lady Emily Fitzgerald regularly sent her husband political news and advice that she gleaned from her brother-in-law, Charles Fox.[28] The countess of Moira and her daughter, Lady Selina Granard, wrote to one another on a daily basis about political events and the public actions of their male relatives. They also corresponded with others, passing on news and information on the most recent political developments in Dublin and elsewhere.[29]

Contemporaries recognised the political role of women. Political satire that mocked the interference of aristocratic women indirectly confirmed the women's public role. Wives and relatives of politicians were frequently petitioned to exert their influence to secure patronage and official positions. Even after the death of her husband, Kathryn Conolly was still considered a woman with political influence.[30] Similarly, following the death of the duchess of Leinster's first husband, her eldest son still believed that his mother had sufficient political influence to 'make interest' against a parliamentary bill.[31] His aunt, Louisa Conolly, complained of the large number of petitions that she received during the duke of Buckinghamshire's lord lieutenantship, while Lady Moira expressed her frustration that rumours that her son might secure public office had led to what she described as 'a renewal of visiting friends'.[32] In the aftermath of the 1798 rebellion, women in influential families were frequently approached to plead clemency for those accused of rebellious activities.[33]

Parliamentary elections could also provide women with the potential for political influence. It appears to have been accepted by the electorate that female relatives of candidates and political patrons were involved in the selection and election of suitable nominees. The countess of Moira and her daughter, Lady Granard, were both actively involved in canvassing for the constituency of Granard. One potential voter described how Lady Selina visited him and noted down in a pocket book his request for a favour in return for securing his vote.[34] This and other comparable requests were usually related to securing positions in the public service. Lady Moira received similar requests when she took over the management of the Granard electoral interests in the 1780s when her daughter and her husband lived abroad. The voters of Granard were, in fact, long accustomed to female political involvement. For much of the eighteenth century, the borough was controlled by two sisters, Alice Macartney and Frances Greville, who had inherited it as co-heirs of their grandfather, James Macartney.[35] Alice Macartney was described by a contemporary as 'the matron-like producer of Members of Parliament'[36] while her sister endorsed Lady Moira's candidate in 1783 and promised that she would 'have her interest in conjunction with that of Lord Longford and Mr Harman'.[37] The mother of Luke Gardiner, Florinda, also canvassed the electorate on her son's behalf in the by-election in Dublin in the 1770s. She too received letters of support from women as well as men. Margaret Dunne, for example, promised Mrs Gardiner that she would use 'any influence that I have . . . or any person that I can influence'.[38]

Nor did the control of the women necessarily cease when the family candidate had been successfully elected. Members of parliament could find themselves under pressure to vote as directed by their female relatives. In

1770, Sir Edward Newenham claimed that he had 'received orders to vote against' certain bills from his female patron whom he described as the 'friend that purchased my seat in parliament for me' while the Jacobite countess of Donegal was noted as having 'two or three boroughs at her disposition which return members of parliament to which she will only allow to be chosen people of her own sentiments'.[39]

Public sphere

The regular meetings of parliament from 1662 advanced the politicisation of Irish society not just at elite level but in the long term at all levels of society. Public and private debate on political issues became a normal part of social discourse. A key factor in the formation of a more politically aware public was the growth in the number of people who could read. Literacy rates increased, particularly among the 'middling sort' of Irish Protestant society, a development that triggered a massive expansion in Irish published material. Newspapers, books and political pamphlets proliferated as the print medium became an essential component of political discourse.

Coinciding with the advances in the literate society was a widening of the public places where issues of public interest were discussed. Printing businesses established coffee houses where newspapers and pamphlets were made available to be read and discussed. Societies, clubs and associations dedicated to particular public causes and social reforms were formed. Many of these developments conform to what the German philosopher Jürgen Habermas called the bourgeois public sphere that emerged 'from the intimacy of private reading, letters, salons, into the public associations and voluntary societies, the periodicals and the press'.[40]

Women's engagement with the new sociability was undoubtedly more circumscribed than men's but it is also clear that the eighteenth century witnessed a significant expansion of the public space accessible to women. The rise in literacy statistics for women, the targeting of a female readership by newspapers and magazines, and women's membership of some of the new societies and associations have all been identified as indicators of women's involvement in the new public sphere.[41]

We have no specific figures for literacy rates among women in eighteenth-century Ireland but from mid-century on there were more and more schools being established in Irish towns for the education of girls.[42] Another indicator of an increase in female literacy is the number of newspapers and magazines that began to include material that was specifically directed at a female readership. As Máire Kennedy has documented, by the mid-eighteenth century Irish monthly magazines frequently included articles and illustrations on fashion and clothing.[43] *Hibernian Magazine* (later *Walker's Hibernian Magazine*) was one such monthly magazine that was very popular in the last quarter of the eighteenth century. It regularly printed material addressed to its women readers. Nor was this material confined to items on fashion or the latest social gossip from London and elsewhere. From the 1770s through to the 1790s, *Hibernian Magazine* included articles on women's role in society and, in particular, on women's education.[44] *Hibernian Magazine* also printed reports on parliamentary debates and as a supporter of the Volunteers carried many of the statements issued by local as well as the national branches of the organisation. It is hard to believe that this political material was not read by at least some of the magazine's female readership.[45] Women correspondents recorded in their letters that they were reading newspapers on a regular basis; and some like Martha McTier and the countess of Moira and her daughter, Selina, were also keeping up with the latest political pamphlets. Even when women could not read, the new public spaces of eighteenth-century Dublin could give them access to the content of newspapers. In 1766, the *Freeman's Journal* reported that 'several Housekeepers of St. Anne's Parish meet at a friendly Club, and have the Freeman's Journal constantly read to them, in order to make observations, and if necessary to make them public for the Good of their Fellow-citizens'.[46]

Another way in which women were involved in the public world of print was through their role as editors and publishers of books and newspapers. Robert Munter's dictionary of Irish eighteenth-century printers demonstrates the family nature of the printing trade and the involvement of women in it. Women inherited printing businesses from male relatives and maintained them as widows. The business was also enmeshed in political controversy throughout the eighteenth century. Women not only printed political books and pamphlets but were often very involved and committed to certain political causes. Elizabeth Dickson, who in partnership with her second husband and son published the *Dublin Intelligence*, managed several coffee houses and printed various pamphlets and polemics largely in the Whig cause. Sarah and John Harding published pamphlets for Swift. When John died, Sarah remained as Swift's printer and printed *The Present Miserable State of Ireland*, and Swift's *Modest Proposal*. She was taken into custody by the Irish House of Commons in 1725 for her association with Swift, but despite her brief confinement Sarah Harding continued to publish politically controversial work. In 1728, she printed a newspaper and a satirical poem (not by Swift) for which she suffered a second short imprisonment.

Another politically aware woman printer was Elizabeth Pue who managed a coffee house and printing business after her husband died in the 1720s. She was responsible for the well-known Dublin newspaper *Pue's Occurrences* and during her time as manager of the newspaper it became a strong supporter of the government. Elizabeth Pue was secretly paid by the administration to include material which attacked printers like John Harding who produced anti-government propaganda.[47] Other women editors of newspapers can be found in towns outside Dublin. Esther Crawley was one of the principal printers in Waterford in the mid-eighteenth century and edited the *Waterford Journal* while Catherine Finn edited *Finn's Leinster Journal* for many years.[48]

Many of the new clubs and societies that appeared in Irish towns in the second half of the eighteenth century had a male only membership but some such as the Friendly Society noted above admitted women. The Constitutional Free Debating Society met in the Music Hall in Dublin from 1771. It held weekly evening debates for which seats were reserved in the orchestra for 'ladies'.[49] Women's wider involvement in charity work also gave them an opportunity to join public organisations and to participate in the public sphere in ways in which they had not done before.[50]

The theatre was a political space in eighteenth-century Dublin and women attended plays in large numbers. Wealthy women hosted theatre evenings for charity and, as noted already, lord lieutenants' wives patronised command performances that were attended only by women.[51] Poorer women were among the crowds in the stalls who cheered and booed according to their political preferences. Contemporary political messages were read into stage performances. In 1754, at the height of the Money Bill dispute, a performance of Voltaire's *Mahomet* in Smock Alley was perceived to have direct relevance to the political crisis unfolding in Dublin. An actor's refusal to repeat a particularly provocative speech led to a riot that destroyed the theatre.[52] Attendance at plays by the lord lieutenant and his wife could also be perceived as a political gesture and their presence was applauded or denounced by political admirers and detractors accordingly.

An important development in the politicisation of Dublin society was the opening of the new parliamentary building in 1731. The new building was designed to encourage public participation. The purpose-built parliamentary complex incorporated not just the debating chambers of the Houses of Lords and Commons but also committee rooms, coffee and dining rooms as well as a large hall or lobby where people assembled during the sitting of parliament, often as members of delegations presenting petitions to be read before the House.[53]

The House of Commons' Chamber included a public gallery that was open to male and female visitors. On the occasion of important debates, the gallery could become very crowded. Jonah Barrington noted that the House of Commons' gallery was designed to seat 700 people and that the front row of the gallery was 'generally occupied by females of the highest rank and fashion.'[54] Barrington and others recorded the presence of women in the House of Commons' gallery at debates on Irish parliamentary independence in the 1770s. Later, during the long sessions on the Act of Union in the spring of 1799, Barrington noted that:

immense numbers of ladies of distinction crowded at any early hour into the galleries, and by their presence and their gestures animated that patriotic spirit, upon the prompt energy of which alone depended the fate of Ireland.[55]

Given the public interest in the debates on independence and the Act of Union it was not perhaps surprising that women relatives of the MPs attended in large numbers. There is evidence, however, that women's presence in the gallery was a regular occurrence not confined to the most significant debates. On her first visit to Dublin in 1731, Mary Delany recorded that she spent the whole day in the parliament. She described how she and her party arrived at 11.00 and heard a dispute about an election. At about 3 o'clock they were brought chickens, ham and tongue and

everything we could desire. At 4 o'clock the speaker adjourned the House 'till five. We then were conveyed, by some gentleman of our acquaintance, into the Usher of the Black Rod's room, where he had a good fire, and meat, tea, and bread and butter . . . When the House was assembled, we re-assumed our seats and staid till 8; loth was I to go away then . . .[56]

Other women are also recorded spending some time in the parliamentary building although some complained that the crowds made it an uncomfortable experience. In 1760 when Mary Delany wrote of another visit, the gallery was so crowded that she and her companion were given seats in the Chamber of the House of Commons.[57] Attendance by women in the Irish parliamentary buildings was in contrast to the situation in the English House of Commons where women were discouraged from attending debates. Jonah Barrington who wrote such vivid descriptions of the women in the Irish House of Commons commented on how different was the scene in its English counterpart. Votes in the English House of Commons were usually taken in private but in Ireland the gallery was normally not cleared during a vote and so everyone could see who voted for whom.[58]

The vehemence of supporters in the gallery could exert an influence on the voting choices of the MPs. During the Money Bill dispute in the 1750s, Chief Secretary Bedford asserted that 'scarce a man in parliament gives his opinion if he thinks it is not the opinion of the gallery, and popularity, as they call it, must take the place of service and reason'.[59] There were also suggestions that the defeat of the first Union Bill in the spring of 1799 was due to pressure from the gallery on the MPs in the Chamber. Barrington's description of the vote also suggests that the men in the Chamber were aware of the views of those in the gallery:

The gratification of the Anti-Unionists was unbounded; and as they walked deliberately in, one by one, to be counted, the eager spectators, ladies as well as gentlemen, leaning over the galleries, ignorant of the result, were panting with expectation. Lady Castlereagh, then one of the finest women of the Court, appeared in the Serjeant's box, palpitating for her husband's fate. . . . A due sense of respect and decorum restrained the galleries within proper bounds; but a loud cry of satisfaction from the female audience could not be prevented; and no sooner was the event made known out of doors, than the crowds that had waited during the entire night. . . . sent forth loud and reiterated shouts of exultation. . . .[60]

On the occasion of another long debate (extending over an afternoon and all night) on the Commercial Proposals in 1785, the women in the gallery sat in two divisions, indicating their support for the men in the Chamber.[61]

Talking politics was clearly part of the social scene in Ireland. Elizabeth Hamilton, the writer, commented following her visit to Dublin in 1782:

The people here [ie. In London] are not such great politicians as in Ireland; there politics engross the greatest part of discourse in every company; and man, woman and child enter as zealously into every debate, as if they had been perfectly acquainted with all the hidden springs of government.[62]

Other women complained of the dominance of politics in the social conversation. Charlotte Fitzgerald, the daughter of the duke and duchess of Leinster, complained in the early 1780s that everyone was talking non-stop about the 'papist bill' although she claimed that she did not really understand what the conversations were about.[63]

More women were, therefore, involved in public life and engaged with political discourse in eighteenth-century Ireland than at any time previously. There were, however, serious limits to that involvement and much of it could be characterised as a passive rather than an active engagement. Women were reading political literature but only a tiny number were writing it and mainly in verse or novel format.[64] Similarly, women could attend, watch and listen to political debates in the Constitutional Club or in the parliament but they did not participate in them. Expressing one's view either in print or in a public forum was not considered an appropriate occupation for a respectable woman. Societies and associations that did admit women as members were concerned above all with charitable work and social reform, tasks deemed suitable for women. The new public world was also only open to wealthy women who had the leisure and the means to acquire an education and read newspapers and books. As Margaret Jacob has noted, 'only literacy, enhanced by access to learned opinion about books and journals that told what was worth reading, offered full citizenship or conferred identity within the anonymous public sphere'.[65]

The denominational affiliation of the women who participated in the public sphere in however limited a fashion should also be acknowledged. In general, Catholic participation in eighteenth-century Irish politics was restricted but it was gradually widened from the 1760s when the penal laws were relaxed or removed completely from the statute book and the Catholic Committee was formed among Catholic peers and wealthy merchants. The historical record is, however, largely silent on Catholic women's involvement in public affairs. The alternative political world of Catholic Ireland was more conservative than its Protestant counterpart and women were not encouraged to take an active public role. The close kinship of Irish Catholic landed and middle-class families may have occasionally allowed a woman to exercise some influence in Catholic Committee circles but it was not until the nineteenth century that middle-class Catholic women emerged as visible political activists.[66]

Outside the incestuous world of the Catholic Committee, however, popular politics assumed a new significance in the course of the eighteenth century as riots, secret societies and other forms of communal protests became a means through which pressure could be exerted on parliament. As in other countries, women were often involved in this type of popular protest. In rural areas membership of agrarian secret societies was gender specific, as names such as the Whiteboys or Rightboys imply, but support for their activities was community based. Surviving Irish poetry indicates that women poets and keeners were given responsibility for expressing the communal voice of protest through the *caoineadh*. This is evident, for example, in the *caoineadh* for Father Nicholas Sheehy by his sister and the most famous *caoineadh* of the eighteenth century, Eibhlín Ó Laoghaire's lament for her husband, Art.[67] The poetry of Mháire Bhuidhe Ní Laoghaire also conveys a sense of the community's outrage.[68] There were also other developments in eighteenth-century Irish political life that widened the possibilities for Irish women to become involved in the public world of politics. In particular, the development of patriot politics enhanced the political participating of Irish women in general.

Popular politics and patriotism

The emergence of patriot politics in eighteenth-century Ireland has been analysed by historians but the extent to which it encouraged women's involvement in the political process has not been appreciated. Up until its transformation in the last quarter of the eighteenth century, Irish patriotism drew its theoretical basis from classical republicanism that defined patriotism 'in terms of a commitment to civic virtue and active citizenship'.[69] Consequently, until the 1770s, Irish patriotism was more about demonstrating a sense of civic awareness than railing against the evils of English colonial government.[70] Patriotism fostered a sense of good citizenship and public spiritness, a concept that was manifest in much of the political discourse of the first half of the century.[71] Pamphleteers debated the best ways to improve the trade and commerce of Ireland, proposing a myriad of schemes and projects designed to eradicate or at least alleviate Irish poverty. Virtue and patriotism were perceived as being intertwined. Virtuous citizens demonstrated their patriotism through support for Irish manufactured goods and produce.

The importance of women in this patriotic endeavour was recognised by the pamphleteers. A favourite theme of the pamphleteers was the extravagance of wealthy women who imported at great expense the latest French and English fashions rather than support local Irish manufacturers. In 1722, Jonathan Swift specifically targeted such women in his pamphlet entitled *A Proposal That All The Ladies and Women of Ireland Should Appear Constantly In Irish Manufactures*. Swift's publication was followed by others encouraging women to purchase Irish cloth and fashions. In 1735 Bishop Berkeley devoted some of his famous queries to the issue. Among his queries were 'whether a woman of fashion ought not to be declared a public enemy?' and 'how far the vanity of our ladies in dressing and of our gentlemen in drinking contribute to the general misery of the people?'[72] Wealthy, vain women were perceived to embody all the characteristics of the unpatriotic citizen: a follower of fashion who squandered money on of imported goods rather than support the poor through the wearing of Irish cloth.

Successive wives of lord lieutenants attempted to set a good moral example by making the wearing of Irish cloth fashionable and issuing invitations to social events in Dublin Castle with instructions that only Irish manufactured cloth was to be worn.[73] Although such campaigns made little impact on the Irish textile industry, they did transform the wearing of Irish cloth into a symbol of virtuous patriotism. By the middle decades of the eighteenth century, elite women viewed the occasional purchase of Irish produced textiles as an appropriate form of public charity. Patriotism thus gradually evolved into both a fashionable and a gender inclusive sentiment. Aristocratic women began to be praised for their support for Irish manufactures rather than being condemned for their extravagant and careless vanity, as had been the case in earlier decades.

The Wear Irish campaign was, however, more than simply a fashionable game for bored society women. It brought women into the public discourse, placed a value on their consumer power and expanded their engagement with the public sphere. The patriotic Irish woman demonstrated her virtue through the clothes that she wore. Civic patriotism was also closely linked to the Protestant evangelicalism supported by many Irish Protestant women in the mid-eighteenth century. Religious belief reinforced the view that acts of charity contributed to the public good. More particularly, the activities of Lady Arbella Denny gained official recognition for women's contribution to the alleviation of Irish poverty that was at the core of much of Irish patriotic endeavour and women's charitable work. Arbella Fitzmaurice, daughter of the 1st earl of Kerry, was the widow of Colonel Arthur Denny, a member of parliament for County Kerry who died in 1742 when Arbella was thirty-five years of age. Childless, Denny did not remarry but devoted the rest of her life to charity work. Following a devastating report to the Irish House of Commons in 1758 on the appalling conditions in the Dublin Foundling Hospital, Denny suggested to the Governors that she and a group of other women be given permission to visit and introduce reforms into the organisation of the hospital. Denny's work in the hospital was publicly recognised through a formal vote of thanks in the Irish House of Commons in 1764 and in July of that year she received the Freedom of the City of Dublin from the Corporation. Denny, a supporter of Methodism, founded the Magdalen Asylum in Dublin in 1766 and, as she had done in the management of the Foundling Hospital, she used the device of a committee of female patronesses in its organisational structure. The Asylum Chapel was opened in 1768 and quickly became one of the most fashionable venues for charity sermons in Dublin. Public sermons in the chapel attracted large congregations drawn from the wealthiest and politically most prominent people in the city.[74]

In 1763, the Irish parliament granted £8000 to the Dublin Society to encourage Irish industries. One of the first sectors to benefit from the Society's financial aid was the flagging Irish silk manufacturing business. In 1764 the Society opened the Hibernian Silk Warehouse in Parliament Street near to the parliament buildings and Dublin Castle. The warehouse offered a 10 per cent premium to all Irish manufactured silk, a gesture that helped in the short term to revive the flagging industry.[75] The opening of the warehouse was reportedly attended by 'the principal ladies of rank and fortune in Dublin, who made considerable purchases on the occasion'.[76] Two years later, possibly at Denny's prompting, the Dublin Society resolved to nominate fifteen patronesses who would advise the warehouse on the latest fashions and promote the purchase of Irish silk. Lady Denny was, not surprisingly, among the first patronesses and the lord lieutenant's wife, Lady Townshend, was given the 'office of presiding patroness'. All of the other women patrons had close connections with the Irish political establishment and most can be documented as having attended dinners in Dublin Castle in the 1760s. They included the duchess of Leinster, Lady Louisa Conolly, Lady Betty Ponsonby, Mrs Clements and Lady Brandon.[77]

The opening of the Silk Warehouse was a typical example of the patriotic endeavour of the Dublin Society. Its appointment of women patrons also, however, exemplifies the way in which the charity work of wealthy women merged with the patriotic discourse of mid-eighteenth century Ireland. The billhead of the Warehouse was suitably adorned with a lady in a full-flowing Irish dress sitting at an Irish harp.[78] Thus public expressions of patriotism went hand in hand with the more traditional charitable work normally undertaken by wealthy women. Charlotte Fitzgerald described for her mother a meeting at which a group of mainly aristocratic men and women resolved to assist the economic distress of cloth manufacturers in Dublin by

buying nothing but Irish manufactures. . . . It was therefore settled that everybody should buy a piece of linen for a gown and to make a pleasant thing of it, the following scheme was proposed. Colonel Burton the promoter of it all gave a breakfast to a large party of gentlemen and ladies; out of whom there was a committee of ladies chosen: Lady E. Clements, Lady De Vesci, Lady Ross, Lady Charlemont, Lady Charlotte Fitzgerald in the chair. They were to determine upon a uniform. . . . The colour green was not liked by anybody as not becoming, but as everybody could not have exactly the same coloured printed linen, it was agreed that green would suit with everybody's linen. It was fixed that we should all go to the Gardens upon such a day in our uniform that the mob might see that the nobility and gentry were inclined to favour the Irish manufactures. . . .[79]

The events described by Charlotte Fitzgerald took place in the spring of 1778 when the Irish economy was beginning the feel the impact of the outbreak of war in North America. The war depressed the Irish economy as American markets were closed to Irish exports, particularly cloth. The prosperity that the country had enjoyed in the middle decades of the century began to evaporate as the Irish textile industry found it increasingly difficult to compete with cheaper imported cloth from Britain and elsewhere. Consequently, there were renewed calls for women in Ireland to support locally manufactured cloth.

More generally in Ireland in the 1770s, there was a growing recognition that there were strong similarities between the demands of the American colonists and Irish patriots. Both wanted greater freedom and particularly economic freedom from Britain. The campaign to lift the restrictions on Irish trade encapsulated in the phrase 'Free Trade' became a very popular cause in Ireland in the late 1770s.[80]

In the spring and summer of 1779, the poor state of the Irish economy and the campaign for Free Trade began to merge. The demands for women to buy Irish cloth as an act of charity to help the Irish economy mutated into a more overtly political gesture. Mirroring the tactics used in America, non-importation associations were formed and a popular campaign was launched urging people, and particularly women, to buy Irish.[81] Women in Ireland were urged to follow the example of women in America, who had boycotted British cloth and donned homespun garments to indicate their support for the revolution.[82]

Women, therefore, who had initially supported the buy Irish campaigns for charitable reasons, found themselves by the early summer of 1779 at the centre of a more political and anti-English campaign. In May 1779, the *Hibernian Journal* addressed an editorial to the 'female patriots of Ireland' in which it explicitly linked the boycott campaign to the political protest against English restrictions on Irish trade:

Let the glorious Cause in which you my fair Countrywomen are embarked, fire your Emulation, and let Fame tell the surrounding nations, that the Daughters of Ireland restored to Happiness and Prosperity their Country long groaning under the Shackles of Restriction, and revived that Commerce, rendered languid by the unmerited Opposition of an envious Kingdom.[83]

In December 1779, the *Freeman's Journal* also addressed an editorial to Irish women that linked women's patriotism, their private virtue and the public good. It exhorted women:

> *Do not imagine, that public spirit ill becomes the graceful reserve, and amiable timidity of the female character, no, public spirit is the accomplishment and perfection of private virtue.*[84]

Women responded to these calls individually and collectively. In Dublin, a group of women formed a non-importation association following a public meeting in April 1779. The members of the association resolved that 'we will not wear any article that is not the product or manufacture of this country, and that we will not permit the addresses of any of the other sex who are not equally zealous in the cause of this country'.[85] In the autumn of that year, the women involved in the Silk Warehouse also formed a non-importation association and a 'Ladies Agreement' was left at the warehouse and signed by 'a great number of respectable names'.[86] The *Freeman's Journal* and other newspapers urged other Irish women to follow the example of the women in Dublin.[87]

The Volunteers were formed in 1778 for the military purpose of defending Ireland against French attack while the regular British troops were engaged in the war in North America. The Volunteer movement quickly, however, emerged as a popular organisation with a political agenda of Free Trade and greater independence for the Irish parliament. The organisation and widespread campaigning of the Volunteers expanded the opportunities for women to engage with public life. Women attended Volunteer reviews in large numbers, either as participants in the crowd or as wives and relatives of the men in the regiments. It was common practice for officers' wives to appear on the reviewing stand, some dressed in the uniform of the regiment and wearing 'white silk belts, with small bayonets or daggers'.[88] The English artist Francis Wheatley painted a number of women in their Volunteer uniform, suggesting that it was a fashionable attire in the years 1779–80.[89] Women in the crowds at Volunteer reviews also used fashion to demonstrate their political allegiance by donning Volunteer-coloured ribbons and rosettes in their hats and hair.[90] Women were also among the crowds who cheered and waved ribbons and handkerchiefs at the Volunteers when they marched through the streets of Dublin to attend the Convention in the Rotunda building in 1783, and they were also admitted to the Convention debates.[91] The Volunteers thus provided women with a new means of demonstrating their patriotism in public.

The heightened public role for women in the Volunteer campaigns was, however, of short duration. In December 1779, the English parliament conceded to Volunteer demands and passed legislation that relaxed restrictions on Irish trade. In the 1780s public debate shifted to the issue of parliamentary reform and, in particular, the extension of the franchise to enable more men to sit in parliament. There was disagreement among those who participated in the debate as to how many and which men should be enfranchised but none of the contributors advocated granting women any formal role in the parliamentary process. The shift of focus to parliamentary reform reduced the political usefulness of incorporating women into political campaigns. The involvement of women in the Volunteer movement sparked a reaction against women participating in public affairs and the women who attended Volunteer reviews and listened to the Convention debates began to be mocked and scorned in Volunteer literature.[92]

In 1784 the debate on the protective duties imposed by Britain led to calls to revive the non-importation associations and the boycott of English imports. Sporadic attempts were also made to encourage women to join together once again in non-importation associations. At a public meeting in Belfast in April 1784, the ladies of the town were urged to follow the virtuous example of the women in America by forming an association and 'proving that our public virtue is not confined to sex'.[93] In May the silk weavers of Dublin formally approached 'several ladies of the first rank and distinction' for their patronage of the silk industry that had been 'nearly annihilated in consequence of the preference shown for India goods'. And, according to the *Freeman's Journal*, resolutions were passed by ladies attending a number of assemblies in Dublin that they would not 'wear any India goods, but more particularly muslins and calicoes'.[94] The duchess of Rutland, the wife of the lord lieutenant, also promoted the wearing of Irish cloth at social events in the Castle.[95] The debate was, however, half-hearted in its appeal to women's patriotism and was, in fact, more notable for a return to the earlier condemnation of wealthy women for not doing enough to support Irish products than praise for the women who supported the campaign. The earlier enthusiasm for campaigning women had disappeared.[96]

By the end of the 1780s, public expressions of patriotism by women were manifested more in their writings than through overt public demonstrations. Among the virtue associated with women writers in the late eighteenth century was an adherence to patriotic sentiments and a number of women authors such as Charlotte Brooke and Mary Birkett embraced patriotism in their writings.[97] Patriotism continued to be admired as a female virtue in the early decades of the nineteenth century, as the writings of Lady Sydney Morgan indicate.[98] By that time, however, the philanthropic associations of patriotism had been overtaken by the more overt politics of republicanism.

Rebellion, republicanism and women

The formation of the Society of the United Irishmen in 1791 introduced radical republicanism into Irish political discourse. The Society supported the Volunteer aim of reforming parliament and reducing the influence of the British political elite on the Irish administration. A small group within the Society advanced more radical views and advocated the establishment of a republic. Neither group, however, gave serious consideration to the extension of the franchise to women. A number of United Irishmen who had visited Paris in their attempts to win French assistance for a rebellion in Ireland expressed their horror at the behaviour of the women who supported the Revolution on the streets of Paris. They clearly held very conservative views on the role of women in society.[99] Only William Drennan, brother of Martha McTier, appears to have thought a female franchise worth at least considering but even he believed that the 'time for female suffrage . . . had not yet arrived'.[100]

Nor, it should be added, did any women associated with the United Irishmen argue for the inclusion of women in the franchise debate. Two of the most well-known female supporters of the movement, Martha McTier and Mary Ann McCracken, enthusiastically encouraged their brothers' involvement but neither chose to be active in public life. Public reaction in Ireland to events in France, particularly the execution of the royal family, combined with what Nancy Curtin has described as the 'paramilitary homosociability' of the United Irishmen, strengthened rather than undermined traditional views of women's domestic role in the 1790s.[101]

Women were involved in the rebellion of the United Irishmen in 1798 but it was in an auxiliary role as providers mainly of domestic services. The army of the United Irishmen in 1798 relied on the safe houses and hospitality maintained by women. The memoirs of Joseph Holt, a commander of the United Irishmen's forces in Wicklow, describe the provision of food and lodging given to his 'boys' by women. Holt demanded domestic servicing from the women for his men and was not so much grateful for its provision as indignant when it was refused. One on occasion, he reprimanded a woman who claimed she had no food to spare for Holt's 'men'. Holt ordered his 'boys' to seize the sheep of the woman, denouncing her as an 'inhuman woman' and a 'disgrace to your sex'. The young men in Holt's regiment, like the male members of agrarian societies, expected to be supported by the whole community.

As was the case in earlier wars, sizeable numbers of women travelled with the rebel troops in the 1790s. Holt describes the presence of wives and other women in his camp. Some were utilised as messengers and occasionally as spies. Holt, in particular, employed a woman whom he called his 'moving magazine' who went to the enemy camp ostensibly to sell a basket of fruit and gingerbread but also carried two large bags under her petticoats in which she stored ball cartridges and ammunition that she obtained, by one means or another, from the government troops. In addition, the 'moving magazine' supplied Holt with 'a very accurate account' of all the military stations she had visited.[102]

Women also followed the government troops. When the militia was formed in 1793, it was decreed that men would not serve in their home counties, a decision which led to the riots of that year when it was realised that conscription into the militia would deprive many households of their principal breadwinner. A series of family acts attempted to solve this problem by providing financial assistance while the man was away but it was not sufficient to maintain most families and large contingents of women and children accompanied the militia on their manoeuvres. There were, for example, considerable numbers of women with Cornwallis in the west and also on Vinegar Hill in 1798.[103] The presence of women and children in the army camps was not only a considerable drain on the army's resources but also hindered, at times, the efficient operation of the soldiers. In 1798, a captain was court-martialled for failing to march when ordered to do so. He explained in his defence that he had to find provisions for soldiers' wives before he could start moving.[104]

Conclusion

Despite the utilisation of women, the republicanism of the United Irishmen never adopted the concept of republican motherhood that emerged in the early years of the republic in America. The American historian Linda Kerber defined republican motherhood as creating the deferential female citizen who was expected to influence the political system if only in a limited way through the education of her sons as good republican citizens.[105] The rhetoric of Irish republicanism did not allot a similar role to women before the nineteenth century.

It is, however, worth nothing that the rhetoric of Irish patriotism – as distinct from republicanism – opened up a new public role for women and clearly articulated the view that women should exercise public as well as private virtue. While there was no support for republican motherhood in late eighteenth-century Ireland, there was considerable enthusiasm for the concept of the patriotic woman. In other ways, too, the last decades of the century involved women in forms of public life which were developed in the early nineteenth century. Attendance at public meetings and debates and participation in protest crowds facilitated the ease with which women joined in the O'Connellite movement from the 1820s through to the 1840s. Indeed, it is difficult to comprehend the success of O'Connell's mass mobilisation of popular support without considering the involvement of women. It was only in the puritanical society of the late Victorian era that women's attendance at public meetings and crowds began to be frowned upon as unacceptable behaviour for ladies.

Notes

1 Public Record Office of Northern Ireland (PRONI), T/J/9/1/25, 3 July 1782.

2 Patrick McNally, *Parties, Patriots and Undertakers: Parliamentary Politics in Early Hanoverian Ireland* (Dublin, 1987), p. 54.

3 Ibid.

4 Joseph Robins, *Champagne and Silver Buckles. The Viceregal Court at Dublin Castle 1700–1922* (Dublin, 2001), pp. 3–82; Edward McParland, *Public Architecture in Ireland, 1680–1760* (New Haven and London, 2001), pp. 91–121.

5 See, for example, Thomas Bartlett (Ed), *Macartney in Ireland 1768–72. A Calendar of the Chief Secretaryship Papers of Sir George Macartney* (Belfast, 1978), pp. 166, 175, 268; National Library of Ireland (NLI) MS 8064; *The Prelude to a Levee; Calculated for the Meridian of the Castle of Dublin* (Dublin, 1757).

6 Robins, *Champagne and Silver Buckles*, pp. 18–19.

7 Ibid., p. 8; Francis Hardy, *Memoirs of the Political and Private Life of James Caulfield, Earl of Charlemont* (London, 1810), pp. 282–3; Jonah Barrington, *The Rise and Fall of the Irish Nation* (London 1833, reprinted Dublin, 1843), pp. 398–9.

8 Toby Barnard has suggested that viceroys often lacked adequate resources to offer lavish hospitality. See T. C. Barnard, '"Grand Metropolis"or "The Anus of the World"? The Cultural Life of Eighteenth-Century Dublin' in Peter Clark and Raymond Gillespie (Eds), *Two Capitals. London and Dublin 1500–1840* (Oxford, 2001), pp. 189–92.

9 Robins, *Champagne and Silver Buckles* documents the social activities of eighteenth-century lord lieutenants and their wives.

10 Vernon-Bardon Papers, vol. 3 (National Archives of Ireland); Extracts from printed Gazette, 1777–8 (NLI, MS 1471). See also Robins, *Champagne and Silver Buckles*, p. 24.

11 Ibid., p. 21.

12 Vernon-Bardon Papers, vol. 3.

13 Robins, *Champagne and Silver Buckles*, pp. 46–7; Mrs Godfrey Clark, *Gleanings From an Old Portfolio* (3 vols., Edinburgh, 1895), vol. i, pp. 165–6, 167–8.

14 Brian MacDermot (Ed), *The Catholic Question in Ireland and England, 1798–1822* (Dublin, 1988), p. 59. See also Vernon-Bardon Papers, vol. 3; Robins, *Champagne and Silver Buckles*, pp. 21–2, 46–7.

15 Vernon-Bardon Papers, vol. 3.

16 NLI, MS 1467–70.

17 NLI, MS 1468.

18 Clark, *Gleanings from an Old Portfolio*, vol. i, pp. 188–9.

19 Ibid., p. 186. See also Toby Barnard, '"Grand Metropolis" or "The Anus of the World"?', p. 190.

20 Letter dated 6 Feb. [1758], O'Hara Papers, NLI, MS 20389.

21 J. T. Gilbert, *A History of the City of Dublin* (3 vols., Dublin, 1854–5), vol. i, p. 395. For literary salons, see pp. 220–1.

22 MacDermot (Ed), *The Catholic Question in Ireland and England, 1798–1822*, pp. 7–56.

23 Gilbert, *A History of the City of Dublin*, vol. i, pp. 395–7, 399.

24 Brian Fitzgerald (Ed), *Correspondence of Emily Duchess of Leinster, 1731–1814* (3 vols., Dublin, 1949–57), vol. i, p. 16; Fragment of Earl of Halifax's Journal in 1761 (NLI, MS 8064, 7 November. See also 23 November); McNally, *Parties, Patriots and Undertakers*, p. 129; Bartlett (Ed), *Macartney in Ireland 1768–72*, 23 December 1772.

25 Toby Barnard, *Irish Protestants. Ascents and Descents, 1641–1770* (Dublin, 2004), pp. 283–4; *A New Anatomy of Ireland. The Irish Protestants, 1649–1770* (New Haven and London, 2003), p. 74.

26 For Kathryn Conolly's correspondence see PRO, SP63/391, fos. 46, 71, 167–8, 392; Trinity College Dublin (TCD), MS 3974–84/29, 30.

27 Anthony Robert Black, 'An Edition of the Cavendish Irish Parliamentary Diary: 1776–1778' (unpublished Ph.D. thesis, University of Notre Dame, 1969), pp. 84–6. See also NLI, MS 13049, Heron Papers. The duke was married to Thomas Conolly's sister.

28 Fitzgerald (Ed), *Correspondence of Emily Duchess of Leinster, 1731–1814*, vol. i.

29 See the transcripts of the Granard papers in PRONI, T/3765; MacDermot (Ed), *The Catholic Question in Ireland and England, 1798–1822*, p. 59. See also Countess of Ilchester and Lord Stavordale (Eds), *The Life and Letters of Lady Sarah Lennox 1745–1826* (2 vols., London, 1901), vol. ii, pp. 74–129.

30 Barnard, *Irish Protestants. Ascents and Descents, 1641–1770* (Dublin, 2004), pp. 272–89.

31 NLI, MS 13022, folder 15.

32 Angela Bourke *et al.* (Eds), *Field Day Anthology of Irish Writing, Vol. V* (Cork, 2002), p. 45; Transcripts of the Granard Papers, PRONI, T/3765.

33 Thomas Bartlett, 'Bearing Witness: Female Evidences in Courts Martial Convened to Suppress the 1798 Rebellion' in Dáire Keogh and Nicholas Furlong (Eds), *Women of 1798* (Dublin, 1998), pp. 84–5; Peter O'Shaughnessy (Ed), *Rebellion in Wicklow. General Joseph Holt's Personal Account of 1798* (Dublin, 1998), pp. 101–2, 108.

34 Bourke *et al.* (Eds), *Field Day Anthology of Irish Writing, Vol. V*, pp. 47–8.

35 Edith Mary Johnston-Liik, *History of the Irish Parliament, 1692–1800; Commons, Constituencies and Statutes* (6 vols., Belfast, 2002), vol. ii, pp. 282–3.

36 Ibid., p. 283.

37 See the transcripts of the Granard Papers, PRONI, T/3765.

38 Letter-book contained bound-in letters to Florinda Gardiner (PRONI, Calendar, Registers of Irish Archives, Miscellaneous Collections). See also the 1783 canvassing letter by Anne, dowager, countess of Massereene on behalf of her son, *Irish Elections, 1750–1832* (PRONI, *Education Facsimiles* (Belfast, 1972)); G. O. Sayles, 'Contemporary Sketches of the Members of the Irish Parliament in 1782' in *Proceedings of the Royal Irish Academy*, **56** (1953–4), section C, p. 262; Anthony Malcomson, 'A Woman Scorned?: Theodosia, Countess of Clanwilliam (1743–1817)' in *Familia*, **15** (1999), pp. 11–18. See also Judith S. Lewis, *Sacred to Female Patriotism, Gender, Class and Politics in Late Georgian Britain* (New York and London, 2003) that includes a number of case studies of women canvassing in Ireland in the late eighteenth and early nineteenth centuries.

39 Cited in McNally, *Parties, Patriots and Undertakers*, p. 77. See Bartlett (Ed), *Macartney in Ireland 1768–72*, 16 March 1770. See also Toby Barnard, *Irish Protestants. Ascents and Descents*, pp. 268–9 for a reference to Anna Hill who lobbied for votes for her preferred candidate for the speakership of the House of Commons.

40 Jane Rendall, 'Women and the Public Sphere' in *Gender and History*, **11** (3) (November 1999), p. 479.

41 Ibid., pp. 475–88; Margaret Jacob, 'The Mental Landscape of the Public Sphere' in *Eighteenth-Century Studies*, **28** (1994), pp. 95–113.

42 See pp. 210–13 below.

43 Máire Kennedy, 'Women and Reading in Eighteenth-Century Ireland' in Bernadette Cunningham and Máire Kennedy (Eds), *The Experience of Reading: Irish Historical Perspectives* (Dublin, 1999), pp. 78–98. See pp. 224–5 below.

44 See pp. 213–15, 258–9 below.

45 From the 1770s reports on the proceedings in the Irish parliament were included in many Irish newspapers. See James Kelly, 'Reporting the Irish Parliament: the *Parliamentary Register*' in *Eighteenth-Century Ireland*, **15** (2000), pp. 158–71; R. B. McDowell, *Ireland in the Age of Imperialism and Revolution 1760–1801* (Oxford, 1979), p. 127.

46 Kennedy, 'Women and Reading in Eighteenth-Century Ireland', pp. 78–98.

47 See Robert Munter, *A Dictionary of the Print Trade in Ireland 1550–1775* (New York, 1988).

48 Kennedy, 'Women and Reading in Eighteenth-Century Ireland', pp. 78–98.

49 Gilbert, *A History of the City of Dublin*, vol i, p. 81. See also Andrew Carpenter (Ed), *Verses in English From Eighteenth-Century Ireland* (Cork, 1998), pp. 278–80.

50 See pp. 192–5 below.

51 Fitzgerald (Ed), *Correspondence of Emily Duchess of Leinster, 1731–1814*, vol. i, p. 13; Gilbert, *A History of the City of Dublin*, vol. ii, pp. 71–2; Stephen Gwynn, *Henry Grattan and his Times* (Dublin, 1939), pp. 191–2; Esther K. Sheldon, *Thomas Sheridan of Smock-Alley* (Princeton, 1967), pp. 92, 109, 113, 199–206.

52 Fintan O'Toole, *A Traitor's Kiss. The Life of Richard Brinsley Sheridan* (London, 1997), pp. 19–20.

53 Edward McParland, 'Building the Parliament House in Dublin' (unpublished paper). I am grateful to Dr McParland for sending me a copy of his paper. McParland, *Public Architecture in Ireland 1680–1760*, pp. 177–205. M. McDonnell-Bodkin, *Grattan's Parliament, Before and After* (London, 1912), p. 69.

54 Jonah Barrington, *Historic Memoirs of Ireland; Comprising Secret Records of the National Convention, the Rebellion and the Union; With the Delineations of the Principal Characters Connected with Those Transactions* (2 vols., Dublin, 1835), vol. i, p. 296. There were alterations made to the gallery of the Irish House of Commons in 1789, as a result of which the space was curtailed and limited to 280 people, all of whom were seated.

55 Ibid., vol. ii, p. 300. See also Gilbert, *A History of the City of Dublin*, vol. iii, pp. 148–50.

56 Bourke *et al.* (Eds), *Field Day Anthology of Irish Writing, Vol. V*, pp. 37–8; see also Lady Llanover (Ed), *The Autobiography and Correspondence of Mary Granville, Mrs Delany With Interesting Reminiscences of King George the Third and Queen Charlotte* (3 vols., 1st series, London, 1862), vol. iii, p. 590.

57 G. H. Bell (Ed), *The Hanwood papers of the Ladies of Llangollen and Caroline Hamilton* (London, 1930), p. 51; Llanover (Ed), *The Autobiography and Correspondence of Mary Granville, Mrs Delany*, vol. iii, p. 590; Robins, *Champagne and Silver Buckles*, pp. 34, 70.

58 See, for example, Barrington, *Historic Memoirs of Ireland*, vol. ii, pp. 311–12. See also P. D. G. Thomas, *The House of Commons in the Eighteenth Century* (Oxford, 1971), pp. 148–9; Janet Todd, *The Sign of Angellica. Women, Writing and Fiction, 1660–1800* (London, 1989), p. 104.

59 McDowell, *Ireland in the Age of Imperialism and Revolution, 1760–1801*, p. 209.

60 Barrington, *Historic Memoirs of Ireland*, vol. ii, pp. 311–12; Francis Plowden, *An Historical Review of the State of Ireland, From the Invasion of That Country under Henry II, to its Union with Great Britain* (2 vols., London, 1803), vol. ii, part 2, p. 920.

61 Gwynn, *Henry Grattan and his Times*, pp. 202–3.

62 *Memoirs of the Late Mrs Elizabeth Hamilton With a Selection From Her Correspondence and Other Unpublished Writings By Miss Benger* (2 vols., London, 1818), vol. i, pp. 88–9.

63 Charlotte Fitzgerald to Emily Fitzgerald (NLI, Leinster Papers, folder 14). See also the correspondence of Charlotte's aunt, Lady Sarah Lennox, which conveys the social interest of women in contemporary politics (Ilchester and Stavordale (Eds), *The Life and Letters of Lady Sarah Lennox 1745–1826*).

64 These include women such as Harriet Battier, Mary Birkett and Mary O'Brien. See Siobhán Kilfeather, 'The Profession of Letters, 1700–1810' in Angela Bourke *et al.* (Eds), *Field Day Anthology of Irish Writing, Vol. IV*, pp. 772–832; Mary O'Dowd, 'The Political Writings and Public Voices of Women, c. 1500–1850' in ibid., Vol. V, pp. 6–68; Kevin O'Neill, 'Mary Shackleton Leadbeater: Peaceful Rebel' in Keogh and Furlong (Eds), *The Women of 1798*, pp. 137–62; Mary Birkett, *A Poem on the African Slave Trade, Addressed To Her Own Sex* (Dublin, 1792).

65 Jacob, 'The Mental Landscape of the Public Shere', p. 100.

66 Thomas Reynolds claimed that his grandmother used her influence to have her son elected to the Catholic Committee in place of her dead husband. See Thomas Reynolds, *The Life of Thomas Reynolds* (London, 1839), p. 64.

67 Bourke *et al.* (Eds), *Field Day Anthology of Irish Writing, Vol. IV*, pp. 1365–84.

68 Ibid., pp. 287–90. See also Donncha Ó Donnchú (Ed), *Fíliocht Mháire Bhuidhe Ní Laoghaire* (Dublin, 1931) and Angela Bourke, 'More in Anger than in Sorrow: Irish Women's Lament in Poetry' in Joan Newlon Radner (Ed),

Feminist Messages. Coding in Women's Folk Culture (Urbana and Chicago, 1993), pp. 160–82.

69 Sean Connolly, *Religion, Law and Power: the Making of Protestant Ireland, 1660–1760* (Oxford, 1992), p. 123.

70 Joep Leerssen, *Mere Irish and Fíor Ghael* (Cork, 1996), pp. 294–376.

71 Patrick Kelly, 'The Politics of Political Economy in Mid-Eighteenth Century Ireland' in Sean Connolly (Ed), *Political Ideas in Eighteenth Century Ireland* (Dublin, 2000), pp. 105–29.

72 George Berkeley, *The Querist Containing Several Queries Proposed to the Consideration of the Public.* Edited by J. M. Hone (Dublin and Cork, 1935). See also *To the Ladies of Dublin, A Poem. To Which is Added, Ierne's Answer to Albion. By a Lady* (Dublin, 1745).

73 One of the first vicereines to encourage the purchasing of Irish cloth was Mary Somerset, 2nd duchess of Ormond, see *Calendar of the Manuscripts of the Marquess of Ormonde, K. P. Preserved at Kilkenny Castle* (London, 1920), new series, vol. 8, pp. xli–xlii; Robins, *Champagne and Silver Buckles*, pp. 54–5.

74 The information on Denny is taken from Beatrice Bayley Butler, 'Lady Arbella Denny, 1707–1792' in *Dublin Historical Record* (1946–7), 9 (1), pp. 1–20. See also Bourke *et al.* (Eds), *Field Day Anthology of Irish Writing, Vol. V*, pp. 737–40; *Debates Relative to the Affairs of Ireland; In the Years 1763 and 1764. Taken By a Military Officer* (2 vols., London, 1766), vol. 2, pp. 731–6.

75 J. J. Webb, *Industrial Dublin Since 1698 and the Silk Industry in Dublin – Two Essays* (Dublin, 1913), pp. 131–47.

76 Gilbert, *A History of the City of Dublin*, vol. ii, p. 27.

77 Ibid., pp. 27–8.

78 Transcripts of Granard Papers in PRONI, T/3765.

79 Charlotte Fitzgerald to Emily Fitzgerald, 3 June 1778 (NLI, Leinster Papers, folder 14).

80 George O'Brien, *The Economic History of Ireland in the Eighteenth Century* (Dublin, 1918), pp. 227–35; Maurice O'Connell, *Irish Politics and Social Conflict in the Age of the American Revolution* (Philadelphia, 1965), pp. 129–67.

81 Thomas MacNevin, *The History of the Volunteers of 1782* (5th edition, Dublin, 1846), pp. 96–101; O'Connell, *Irish Politics and Social Conflict in the Age of the American Revolution*, pp. 129–67.

82 *Freeman's Journal*, 30 October–2 November 1779.

83 *Hibernian Journal*, 21–24 May 1779.

84 *Freeman's Journal*, 18–21 December 1779.

85 Cited in Alice E. Murray, *A History of the Commercial and Financial Relations Between England and Ireland from the Period of the Restoration* (London, 1903), pp. 203–4. See also *Hibernian Journal*, 23–25 April 1779; 21–24 May 1779. *Freeman's Journal*, 30 October–2 November 1779.

86 *Freeman's Journal*, 5–7 October 1779; 30 October–2 November 1779.

87 See also Mary O'Dowd, 'The Women in the Gallery. Women and Politics in 18th Century Ireland' in Sabine Wichert (Ed) *From the United Irishmen to the Act of Union* (Dublin, 2004, pp. 35–47).

88 *Memoirs of the Life and Times of the Right Honourable Henry Grattan* (5 vols., new edition, London, 1849), vol. 2, p. 124; Breandán Mac Suibhne, 'Whiskey, Potatoes and Paddies: Volunteering and the Construction of the Irish Nation in Northwest Ulster, 1778–1782' in Peter Jupp and Eoin Magennis (Eds), *Crowds in Ireland, c. 1720–1920* (London and New York, 2000), p. 72; Barrington, *Historic Memoirs of Ireland*, vol. 2, p. 182, note.

89 Mary Webster, *Francis Wheatley* (London, 1970), frontispiece, pp. 29–41.

90 See, for example, the women in the windows of the buildings overlooking the Volunteer review in College Green on 4 November 1779 in Francis Wheatley's famous painting of the event (National Gallery of Ireland).

91 Barrington, *Historic Memoirs*, vol. 2, pp. 173–5, 178–9.

92 See, in particular, the articles in the *Volunteer Evening Post*, 4–6 December 1783; 24–26 February 1784.

93 Henry Joy, *Historical Collections Relative to the Town of Belfast* (Belfast, 1817), pp. 285–9.

94 *Freeman's Journal*, 29 May–1 June 1784.

95 Ibid. 18–20 May 1784.

96 John Nevill, *Seasonable Remarks on the Linen-Trade of Ireland With Some Observations on the Present State of that Country* (Dublin, 1783), pp. 24–5; Richard Griffith, Junior, *Thoughts on Protecting Duties* (Dublin, 1784), pp. 38–9.

97 Charlotte Brooke, for example, described her translations of Gaelic poetry as 'an acceptable service to my country' (cited in Leerssen, *Mere Irish and Fíor Ghael*, p. 364); Birkett, *A Poem on the African Slave Trade*. See also O'Neill, 'Mary Shackleton Leadbeater: Peaceful Rebel', pp. 137–62.

98 O'Dowd, 'The Political Writings and Public Voices of Women, c. 1500–1850', p. 11.

99 R. B. McDowell, *Irish Public Opinion, 1750–1800* (London, 1944), pp. 151–9. See also C. J. Woods, *Journals and Memoirs of Thomas Russell, 1791–5* (Dublin and Belfast, 1991), p. 153.

100 R. B. McDowell, op. cit., pp. 196–7. See also R. B. McDowell, 'Historical Revisions: the United Irish Plans of Parliamentary Reform, 1793' in *Irish Historical Studies*, **iii** (1942–3), pp. 39–59.

101 See below p. 259; Nancy Curtin, 'Women and Eighteenth-Century Irish Republicanism' in MacCurtain and O'Dowd (Eds), *Women In Early Modern Ireland*, pp. 133–44.

102 O'Shaughnessy (Ed), *Rebellion in Wicklow. General Joseph Holt's Personal Account of 1798*, pp. 37–8, 59, 68, 76, 92. See also Ruan O'Donnell, 'Bridget "Croppy Biddy" Dolan: Wicklow's Anti-Heroine of 1798' in Keogh and Furlong (Eds), *The Women of 1798*, pp. 87–112.

103 Anna Kinsella, 'Nineteenth-Century Perspectives: The Women of 1798 in Folk Memory and Ballads' in ibid., p. 192.

104 Henry McAnally, *The Irish Militia, 1793–1816* (Dublin, 1949), pp. 265–77; Kinsella, 'Nineteenth-Century Perspectives: The Women of 1798 in Folk Memory and Ballads', pp. 187–99; O'Donnell, 'Bridget "Croppy Biddy" Dolan: Wicklow's Anti-Heroine of 1798', pp. 87–112; Kenneth P. Ferguson 'The Army in Ireland. From the Restoration to the Act of Union' (unpublished Ph.D. thesis, Trinity College, Dublin, 1980).

105 Linda Kerber, *Women of the Republic. Intellect and Ideology in Revolutionary America* (Chapel Hill, North Carolina, 1980).

PART II

The Economy

CHAPTER 3

Portions, Property and Home: Women and the Economy, 1500–1696

Single women and marriage portions

Sometime in the late sixteenth or early seventeenth century, Joan St Michael lodged a bill of complaint against her brother James in the Dublin Chancery Court. James was the eldest son and heir of their father, Gerard St Michael. Gerard had provided in his will for his six daughters, the youngest of whom was Joan. He had instructed James to fund marriage portions for the women from rents on the family property in County Kildare. James had honoured his father's instructions for four of his sisters but, according to Joan, neither she who was twenty-five nor her sister who was twenty-eight could get a groat out of him. When Joan was seventeen, her brother took her 'against her will' from the house of her foster father where she was living and brought her back to the family home. James also took some kine, sheep and corn which Joan had kept in her foster father's house.[1]

The St Michaels lived in the English Pale and Joan's bill reveals the financially dependent status of single women in landed families under English law. The life choices facing Joan and her sister seemed bleak. If they did not secure their portion from their brother, they might not marry. If they did not marry, they were dependent on their brother's goodwill to maintain them. Statistical evidence for the age of marriage in sixteenth- and seventeenth-century Ireland is scant but fathers occasionally stipulated in their wills that daughters should not marry before they were fifteen and provided maintenance for them until they were twenty-five.[2] From fifteen to twenty-five appears, therefore, to have been the optimum age for marriage.[3]

Joan's sister at twenty-eight was already past the normal age of marriage, and Joan was also in danger of being considered too old to be a suitable marriage partner.

Apart from their dependence on their brother's goodwill to carry out their father's wishes, the sisters were also dependent on their father to leave them an adequate legacy that could be paid within a reasonable length of time. The misfortune of Joan and her elder sister was that they had four other sisters and that Gerard had stipulated that all the portions were to be paid from rents from the same lands on the family estate. Marriage portions were often paid according to a daughter's place in the family with the eldest receiving the first and, sometimes, the largest portion.[4] The consequence was that in a family with six girls, the youngest daughter could be waiting a considerable length of time before she was entitled to her portion, a circumstance which could in turn make her less attractive as a potential marriage partner. James St Michael, for his part, might argue that it was his misfortune to have six sisters who had to be provided for from his inheritance; and it is possible that when the time came for the portions of the youngest daughters to be paid, it was not financially possible to release the funds to them. On some estates, landlords tried to limit the potential burden that financial provision for daughters and widows could impose on the eldest son's inheritance by directing that one part of the estate be used to provide both dowries and jointures for daughters and widows. This type of arrangement might, of course, mean that a daughter could only claim her inheritance after arrangements for her father's widow had been settled and she might also have to wait for the widow's death before she could claim her full portion.

Under English law a single woman could take legal action in her own name against the heir if he refused to fulfil the wishes of a testator. The surviving records of the Dublin Chancery Court – where such cases were normally heard – suggest that few women availed of this option. Instead, most appear to have waited in the expectation that the heir would eventually pay the marriage portion or, alternatively, if they were fortunate, until they married and initiated a joint suit with a husband against the heir. It is likely, therefore, that Joan and her sister had already been waiting many years for their portion before they sought the assistance of the chancellor.[5]

The St Michael sisters were not totally dependent on their brother's goodwill for maintenance and material wealth. In considering a single woman's economic status, a distinction should be made between her marriage portion and a daughter's entitlement to a share in her father's movable goods. In Ireland under English law, until 1696, all children were entitled to a share in their father's movable goods. A man's goods were divided into three parts on his death: a third was assigned to his children, a third to his wife and a third was at his own disposal and was normally used to pay his debts. If a man had no children, then his wife's share increased to a half. A daughter's right to her child's portion was legally separate from any legacy that her father might leave her as a marriage portion although some fathers specified that the value of the goods should be deducted from the cash value of the portion.[6] For a woman from a non-landowning family, her marriage portion may, in fact, have consisted entirely of her child's share of her father's goods.

The distribution of the movable goods depended on the testator's instructions, if there were any, and on the size and wealth of the estate. In some parts of the medieval Irish colony, the custom was that the eldest son had the first choice or 'principal' of the goods although it was also possible for a testator to specify how he wanted his goods distributed. Thomas Shortall from County Kilkenny, for example, left instructions in his will that his daughters should have their child's portions only from his cattle and corn and no other part of the estate.[7] The kine and sheep that Joan St Michael had kept in her foster father's home may well have been her child's allocation from her father's goods and which she, subsequently, would have brought to her husband on marriage. The women in the family normally inherited their mother's clothes and other household goods such as brass pans (used for brewing and cooking), griddle irons and, occasionally, a flock or feather bed and bed and table linen as well as animal stock.[8]

In addition to the distribution of his goods among his wife and children, a father, like Gerard St Michael, was concerned, when he could, to make provision for the future livelihood of all his children. Under English common law, the eldest son inherited the landed estate but younger sons were usually given the means to live independently of their older brother through the provision of a cash annuity, a portion of land or a lump sum to finance their education or apprenticeship. By contrast, the main concern of a father in relation to his daughters was to ensure that they had the means to attract a suitable marriage partner. Marriage portions for daughters in landowning families who observed English law were nearly always in the form of a cash sum. It was this money that was in dispute between James St Michael and his sisters.

In wealthy families, portions could also be used to provide a separate maintenance for the daughter while she remained single. Testators often left instructions that the portion was to be paid when the girl reached a certain age – usually between fifteen and twenty-five – or when she was married, whichever occurred first. Other wills provided for an annual sum to be paid to a daughter by the main heir to the estate until she married. Edward Dowdall of County Meath arranged for each of his four daughters to be given a clothing maintenance of £4 per annum until they were ten years of age, and then each was to receive £10 per year from ages ten to fourteen.[9] In 1623, Sir John Dowdall of Kilfenny, County Limerick, was more generous to his four younger daughters, leaving them £10 per year until they were fifteen when they were to be given portions of £500. Sir John's eldest daughter Anne, who was also his heiress, was to receive £1000 at the age of fifteen as her portion.[10] In 1620, Sir Christopher Nugent arranged for his daughters an annual maintenance of £20 until they married while in the same decade Richard Boyle's daughter, Mary, had an annual allowance of £100 from her father which he stopped temporarily when she refused to marry the man he had chosen as her husband.[11] Sir John Wilson from County Donegal in 1636 arranged for his only daughter's maintenance to be incrementally increased from the age of twelve to twenty-one.[12]

Prior to marriage, young girls in landed families often spent some time in the home of another gentry family. Richard Boyle, for example, sent most of his children to be educated by foster parents;[13] and, as noted already, Joan St Michael was staying with her foster parents when her brother requested that she return to the family home. James's insistence that Joan reside in the family residence when she was seventeen may have been motivated by a reluctance to continue paying separate maintenance for her to her foster father. Her brother took on the role of *parentum locis* providing her with food and lodging and probably deciding on her future marriage partner.

The provision of maintenance in the form of a cash sum for single women was an English custom. We have less information about the economic provision for single women in Gaelic families. It is unlikely that they were paid maintenance but spending some time in the household of a foster parent was a common experience for girls in landed Gaelic families.[14] Marriage portions in sixteenth-century Gaelic society usually took the form of animal stock and household goods rather than cash. In those parts of the country with a predominantly pastoral economy the dowry was measured in cattle. Thus, for example, Ambrose Madden from Galway provided £100 worth of cows with his daughter Margaret in 1621 and when Thomas McGerrott of County Mayo married Margaret Marriott he received twenty milch cows and sixteen in-calf cows.[15] In areas where the economy was more mixed, a woman's marriage portion included a wider variety of animal stock as well as a small number of essential household goods. Ross McDonoghe

MacGeoghegan from MacGeoghegan's Country in the midlands received six milch cows, twelve kine, five garrans, twenty-four swine, twenty-four sheep, a pan and a griddle iron from his prospective father-in-law.[16] Traditionally, a lord collected his daughter's dowry from his tenants and followers. On the O'Sullivan Beare lands in County Kerry, for example, lands were charged with 'marriage cows' payable on the marriage of a daughter of the chief.[17] In 1537, the gentlemen of County Waterford complained that the ruling family, the Powers, collected a sheep from every husband in the region and a cow from every village when their daughters married.[18] By the early seventeenth century, Gaelic landowners were increasingly adopting the English custom of making wills and assigning portions in cash to their daughters although the custom of dowries in the form of animal stock, particularly cattle, was retained in some families down to the end of the eighteenth century.[19]

The size of the marriage portion varied, depending on the family's circumstances and the father's personal deposition but it is clear that the amount considered as an adequate marriage portion increased significantly in the late sixteenth and early seventeenth centuries. Among landowning families in the 1570s and 1580s, amounts of between £200 and £400 were common. By the 1630s, marriage portions of £300 to £500 were more normal in families at gentry level while the largest landowners were by that time leaving portions of between £1000 and £3000 to their daughters, and occasionally more.[20] The most noticeable increase was in the 1630s and scattered evidence suggests that this was a time when contemporaries recognised that portions were rising sharply. In his will of 1629, Randal MacDonnell, 1st earl of Antrim, raised the portions of his daughters to £2700 because their former portions were too small so that they 'can hardly be matched according to their ranks and descent'.[21]

Assessing the size of marriage portions after 1660 is a difficult process as the negotiations for a pre-marriage settlement, particularly between large landowning families, often involved a complex legal process which can be difficult to unravel from the surviving documentation. Portions cited in wills suggest, however, that increases were less dramatic in the second half of the century with amounts of £500 and less still considered acceptable among landowning families at gentry level. This figure may, however, also reflect the fact that more smaller landowners made wills after 1660 than before. Nevertheless, at aristocratic level, £3000 was still a very acceptable portion in the 1690s and this suggests that the disruptive impact of war and the Commonwealth land settlement prevented a sharp escalation in the size of marriage portions before the beginning of the eighteenth century.

In the towns, among merchant families, marriage portions for daughters were lower than among rural-based landholding families. In the sixteenth century, dowries of between £20 and £40 were common in Cork and Dublin. This figure also rose in the 1630s when amounts of between £100 and £300 were more normal. By the end of the century, there was an increase in these figures with portions of £500 being more frequent among Dublin merchants, although some of the wealthier families were agreeing much larger settlements for their daughters' marriages by that time. The relatively small legacies left to merchants' daughters could be offset by other material assets that they could offer potential husbands. In large towns, the dowry of a merchant's daughter could take forms other than cash. Among Galway merchant families in the late fifteenth and early sixteenth centuries, a dowry included quantities of goods which were traded in the town such as wine, linen cloth and Spanish coins.[22] In Dublin, marriage to the daughter of an alderman entitled her spouse to apply for the freedom of the city and the facility to trade in the town. When sometime after 1642 Elizabeth Cransey married Charles Morgan, her father provided not only a marriage portion (£40) and some household stuff but he also procured for Charles the freedom of Dublin and membership of the Company of Blacksmiths; and gave the couple free board for a year, presumably to give Charles time to set up his own business as a blacksmith.[23]

In a similar arrangement, John White provided his new son-in-law with £100 to stock and begin the 'trade of merchandise'.[24] Daughters in Dublin and elsewhere were also given leases of houses and other town property as marriage portions.[25] In Cork, in the 1580s, tavern keeper Richard Mathew left his eldest daughter his 'best brewing pan' and brand iron and a tavern for three years while his second daughter received his second brewing pan and the tavern for two years. Two of his younger sons also received years' shares in the tavern. Presumably it was intended that the children receive the profit of the tavern for a specified period of time.

Among the new British urban communities in Munster, it was also not uncommon for a father to bequeath a share in the family business to his daughter as a marriage portion. In 1666, William Weber, a mariner and ship owner in Cork, left his second daughter a share in one of his ships, while twenty years later, in 1686, a Cork cordwainer, Baptist Looby, left his daughter a 'brewing furnace and all necessaries belonging to brewing trade' after the death of his wife, so that she could continue the brewing business of her mother. Other townswomen on the plantation lands, like their counterparts in Dublin, received leases or freeholds of houses from their merchant fathers.[26]

The escalation in the cash amounts required for a respectable dowry meant that finding the cash for dowries was an increasing problem within the Irish landed community in the early decades of the seventeenth century. Richard Boyle recorded in his diary that he had lent money to men to pay for their daughters' portions while other landlords borrowed money through the Irish statute staple.[27] Although provision of dowry money was never a popular charitable cause in early modern Ireland, it is probably no coincidence that the earliest references to charitable provision for dowries for poor girls date to the 1620s and 1630s when portions began to increase. In 1633, Sir Henry Lynch left money in his will to establish a fund for dowries for poor girls while, in the 1620s, Richard Wadding's father left money to be used towards the assistance of the marriages of poor orphans and virgins. Occasional legacies to servants directed that the money was to be used for a marriage portion. The importance of securing a sizeable portion is also evidenced by the fact that uncles and other male relatives frequently left small cash legacies or animal stock to nieces, sisters and cousins which could augment the sum of money which they had received from their fathers.[28]

As the St Michael case demonstrates, payment of marriage portions was always a source of potential conflict between an heir and his siblings as well as with his in-laws, a phenomenon that was not alleviated by the increases of the seventeenth century. Even when the money was paid, it was often done so in instalments and it could take years for the full sum to be paid. Testators occasionally acknowledged in their wills that their brother-in-law or son-in-law was still owed part of a marriage portion. In England, it was common practice for a daughter to be given control of part of the property of her father's estate until she secured her portion but this was not the custom in Ireland. The only recourse that a woman or her husband had against a defaulting heir was to go to court. The surviving Dublin chancery records suggest that cases involving non-payment of all or part of a marriage portion constituted a considerable proportion of the family dispute cases heard by the chancellor. In most cases equity demanded that the heir fulfil the intentions of his father or predecessor in relation to the unpaid portion. Nonetheless, a married couple needed also to bear in mind that there was no legal obligation in common law for a father to provide a portion for his daughter's marriage. A father could leave as little or as much as he wished as a marriage portion for his daughter; and many inserted a clause in their will that the payment of a marriage portion was conditional on the daughter marrying with the consent of her mother and her father's heir or the executors or overseers of the will. When Margaret Purcell tried in 1622 to claim her marriage portion of £140 through the Chancery Court, she and her husband, Edmond Butler, were reminded that the portion was in her father's gift and was not his legal obligation. Margaret, it was claimed, had married against her father's wishes 'a man of no estate or quality'. Her father had, therefore, reduced her legacy to goods to the value of £39 which probably represented her child's share of her father's goods as distinct from her marriage portion.[29] Christian Hamilton was also dependent on the goodwill of her father, William, for her marriage portion. In 1686, William Hamilton who had an estate in County Down left his daughter five shillings because she had married without his consent. The birth of a grandchild seems to have softened William's attitude and he subsequently added a codicil leaving Christian £1000 as well as a bequest of £200 to his granddaughter.[30] Other women were not so lucky and were deprived of their marriage portion through their choice of marriage partner.

Sexual intercourse before marriage or even rape could also lead to a woman losing her marriage portion. When Luke Rochford 'ravished' a young woman, it was alleged that she had consented to the sexual intercourse. Although the couple subsequently married, the feoffees of the woman's father refused to give her the portion that her father had provided for her in his will. Citing the law of rape, they argued that as she had consented to the rape, she could not claim a dowry from her father's estate.[31]

As the cash-based economy became more widespread in seventeenth century Ireland, the transition from the Gaelic to an English form of marriage portion was completed within landed families. The change made little effective difference to the daughters' economic dependence. A more significant change occurred in 1696 when the legal entitlement of children to a share in their father's movable estate was abolished. Thereafter, like the marriage portion, the father was free to leave as much or as little to each child as he chose. Although most men continued to bequeath their daughters a portion of household goods, nonetheless, by the end of the seventeenth century the single woman's legal entitlement under English law from her father's estate was more restricted than it had been in 1500. Other changes in the law were more benign and could be said to have benefitted women. This was particularly the case for women identified as heiresses to their father's inheritances.

Heiresses

Heiresses were rare in sixteenth- and early seventeenth-century Ireland. It was unusual for marriage to result in the permanent transfer of land prior to the second half of the seventeenth century. Gaelic law did not permit women to inherit family land. As the men in the O'Farrell family told the lord chancellor in 1588, the land in their lordship 'always beyond man's memory hath been by the general custom and manner of gavelkind, that is to say, the lands descended from the ancestor to be divided between the next heirs males, excluding all daughters and females'.[32] In areas where English law was recognised, it was theoretically possible for a daughter to inherit land if her father had no sons but, in reality, an analysis of inquisitions and wills suggests that heiresses among Old English landowning families were exceptional. In 737 post mortem inquisitions held in County Dublin from 1515 to the end of the reign of Charles 1, only twenty-four identified women as the next heirs.[33]

In the sixteenth and early seventeenth centuries, among Old English families, the most common legal method by which landholders ensured the future security of their landed estates was through a deed of enfeoffment by which the ownership of the lands was passed to a group of feoffees who held it to the use of the landowner. The latter then made a will in which he outlined how he wanted the feoffees to distribute his estate after his death. The will identified the principal heir (usually the eldest son) and provided a jointure for the widow of the testator (which was often the subject of a separate deed) and normally, but not always, made financial and other provision for younger sons and marriage portions for daughters.

The enfeoffment of land to uses had developed in the later Middle Ages, partly as a means of avoiding the payment of feudal fees to the crown but also to facilitate landholders wishing to entail their lands to male heirs only.[34] The practice of entailing land, which was widespread among Irish landowning families before the Statutes of Uses and Wills in 1635, meant that women were often explicitly excluded from inheriting their family estates. In families without sons, nephews, male cousins and grandsons and even illegitimate sons were named as heirs before daughters. In his will in 1608, Peter Bermingham, for example, nominated his illegitimate son among his heirs male before the land could pass to his 'right heirs' and therefore, possibly, to a woman.[35] Even when a man wished to recognise his daughter as his heir, he may have been prevented from doing so through the will of his father or grandfather which had entailed the land to male heirs only. A woman could, therefore, be identified as an heiress to her father in a post mortem enquiry but this did not necessarily mean that she was granted possession of the estate. If the land was entailed, it would pass to the next named heir who was usually a man.[36]

A landholder was freer to dispose of property that he had purchased subsequent to the entail. This land was not encumbered in the same way as the land listed in the entail and so the owner could bequeath it to his daughters or female heirs, if he so wished. When Mark Barnewall made his will in the early 1570s, he distinguished between that part of his estate that was entailed to male heirs and other land that he had bought and left to his female heirs, with remainder to his sister in tail male and remainder to her issue female.[37]

A significant amount of new land was acquired by Old English landowners in the course of the sixteenth century, either in the form of dissolved monastic property or that of attainted rebels. The proportion of land that could be bequeathed to women heiresses was, therefore, increasing. Significantly, however, there was no corresponding rise in the number of heiresses. The conservative attitude of Irish landholders towards property rights meant that they were reluctant to leave estates to daughters even when they were legally in a position to do so. When Martin Blake was urged, before his death in 1605, to leave land that he had by purchase or mortgage to his daughter and heiress Mary, he refused claiming it would beggar his brother who had inherited the family estate as his next male heir.[38] Among the cadet branches of Old English families settled in the west of Ireland on newly acquired crown property in the late sixteenth or early seventeenth centuries, heiresses were also rare. The Old English concern, like that of their Gaelic counterparts, was to preserve the estate intact for future generations of the family. The marriage of a female heiress would have led to the permanent alienation of the property from the family as ownership would have been transferred to her husband. Many testators would have sympathised with John O'Connor of Carrigafoyle, County Kerry, when he made his will in 1638. O'Connor had no sons but 'adopted' his cousin, Connor, as heir, for, and as 'the legitimate masculine line . . . [so] that the [inheritance] may be continued in my name and family'. O'Connor asked his family, including his two daughters, not to challenge Connor's right to the estate.[39] This was a sentiment echoed by John Tuite of County Roscommon when he left instructions that his property was to descend 'successively to whosoever shall be the eldest male descendant for ever'.[40] Potential heiresses might occasionally be compensated (or, possibly, discouraged from asserting their claim to an inheritance) through being provided with an expanded portion if they were side-stepped in favour of a male heir. In his will of 1635, for example, James Fitzgerald of Cloyne nominated his cousin germane, Sir John Fitzgerald, as his heir but instructed Sir John to give his sister, Ellen, £700 or a 'better' portion 'if occasion doth soe require' because she was expected to release her claim and title to the land to Sir John.[41]

In the Irish urban community, there was more willingness to permit female inheritance. In the Dublin post mortem inquisitions of the sixteenth century, merchant families predominate among those who recognised female heiresses.[42] The contrasting practices among urban and rural families reflect the different priorities of the two groups. In landed families the preservation of the estate in the family name was considered essential while in merchant communities the economic imperative of continuing the business was the main concern.

The legal process by which landholders passed their estates on to the next generation changed in the course of the seventeenth century in ways that exposed up more estates to the possibility of female inheritance. First, common law courts and government policy were increasingly opposed to long entails on land. In England in the later Middle Ages, the courts had fought a largely successful battle against them. In sixteenth-century Ireland, it is possible to detect a similar administrative dislike of entails. Post mortem inquisitions, for example, identified female heiresses to their father's property even though the existence of an entail barred them from the inheritance; and a number of high profile legal cases were fought over the issue of female inheritance with the government appearing to favour inheritance by women at the expense of preserving an entail on an estate. The most famous heiress of seventeenth-century Ireland, Elizabeth Butler, succeeded to her father's estate only after a royal order from James I broke the entail on the estate. The male heir, her cousin Walter, was so outraged at what he perceived as unjust interference that he went to jail in protest at the king's actions.[43] Lady Lettice Fitzgerald also fought a long legal battle to have her claim as heir general to her father, the 12th earl of Kildare, recognised. Again, the case went to London where another royal decree gave Lettice a sizeable portion of the estate as well as the title of Baroness Offaly.[44]

Among new British landowners, long entails were not as common as they were within the Old English community. In part, the reason for this was the difference in attitude between the new and old landowning families. Unlike their Anglo-Irish or Gaelic predecessors, the new English and Scottish colonial families were concerned to establish their family as a member of the elite rather than to preserve an existing lineage. If the family was to survive as a landed unit, then it made sense to recognise immediate female heiresses, rather than entail the land to absentee male heirs.[45]

Another major reason why enfeoffment of land to uses was abandoned was the passing of the Irish Statute of Uses in 1635, after which date Irish inheritance law and practice converged more with that followed in England. The Irish Statute of Uses was a copy of the English statute. It converted equitable estates (i.e. estates held to the use of another) into legal interests which were recognised at common law.[46] Consequently, Irish landlords ceased making use of deeds of enfeoffment to determine the future of their estates. Small landholders, tenants, tradesmen and merchants increasingly relied on a last will and testament to instruct their executors on the distribution of their real and personal estate after their deaths. Landowners with larger estates, many of whom had links to English-based landed families, began to utilise legal arrangements for inheritance that had developed in England after the Statute of Uses of 1534. Particularly after 1660, Irish landed families increasingly made use of pre-nuptial settlements and deeds of trust. The marriage, or strict settlement as it developed in the late seventeenth century, had many of the same components as the earlier enfeoffment process: a last will and testament accompanied by deeds and a settlement agreed prior to marriage. Above all, the legal process allowed a landlord to determine the future inheritance of his estate.

For women, the significant difference between the two processes was that the earlier form of marriage agreement did not always include provision for the portions of the children of the marriage and was primarily concerned with the wife's jointure. The strict settlement of the late seventeenth century could more accurately be described as a family settlement, as marriage portions, jointures and the amount to be given to younger children were all determined before a marriage took place.

The emergence of family settlements after 1660 led to the reintroduction of entail but not in such a restrictive format as in the earlier deeds of feoffments and wills. In the later settlements, entail could take several forms. Some families revived the older practice of entailing to male heirs only but most entailed to sons and their heirs male and then to daughters and their heirs male. In other words, a daughter was recognised as an heiress if a man's sons died without male heirs. The entail might list the landholder's daughters successively, according to age or it might follow common law practice and divide the property among all the daughters of a man without sons or heirs male. This type of entail expanded the potential for land passing to female heirs but it had one important advantage for landed families in an increasingly sectarian society. It facilitated the retention of the property within the religious denomination supported by the person who drew up the entail. This was particularly the case in the surviving Catholic propertied families, most of whom, by the second half of the seventeenth century, would have had relatives who had converted to Protestantism. Stipulating that the estate should pass through male heirs only opened up the strong possibility that the property would pass at some stage to Protestant ownership. Confining inheritance to the smaller family unit of the owner's own sons and daughters made it easier to maintain the property in Catholic ownership.[47]

The practice of compensating daughters if they were by-passed in an entail seems also to have become more common in the second half of the seventeenth century, an indication, perhaps, of a greater awareness of the legal rights of heiresses. In his will of 1695, Donogh McCarthy, earl of Clancarthy, entailed his land to his sons and then to his cousin germane and other males members of the extended family with the proviso that if his youngest son died without heirs, then each of his daughters was to receive £3000 from those in remainder, presumably in lieu of a daughter claiming her inheritance as an heir of her father under common law.[48] Other potential heiresses were compensated by their fathers in a similar fashion.

The possibility of a woman inheriting a landed estate widened, therefore, after 1660 as did the potential for a son or grandson to claim a right to landed inheritance through his mother or grandmother. An analysis of Lodge's *Irish Peerage* and the *Complete Peerage* indicates that many of the large landowning families of late seventeenth-century Ireland had their property enhanced through marriage to an heiress or had lands descend through the female line.[49] Many of the heiresses were from English landed families but there was also an increasing number of Irish-born heiresses or co-heiresses to large estates. The recognition of female heiresses was not only significant for the establishment of individual landed families but it was also central to the integration of the new Protestant landlords of the Commonwealth and Restoration periods with older, more established Protestant families. Intermarriage was one of the principal means by which the two groups united. The new importance of female heiresses is underlined by David Dickson's estimate that 'about 60 of the [144] resident Irishmen who were created peers during the eighteenth century, were the sons or husbands of an heiress (some indeed were in the happy position of being both), the creation of a peerage setting a seal on the merger of two landed fortunes'.[50]

The expansion of the potential for women to inherit land did not, however, diminish the patrilineal aims of most landed families. The greater recognition of female heirs developed alongside the growing complexity of marriage settlements that imposed legal restrictions on husbands in relation to the real and movable property that their wives brought to the marriage. Fathers' began to leave instructions in their wills that their inheritance to their daughters was for their 'sole and separate use' or that their sons-in-law were not to 'intermeddle' with it.[51] This property was often encumbered with entails and other agreements specified in marriage settlements so that neither the woman nor her spouse derived a financial benefit from it.[52] Other testators requested that the daughter's husband (who would on marriage secure control of his wife's estate) or her next male heir change his surname to that of the woman.[53]

Single women in poor families

The vast majority of people at the lower levels of society in sixteenth- and early seventeenth-century Ireland did not make wills. It is, therefore, difficult to document the economic experiences of single women in non-landed families. The absence of markets or villages in many parts of rural Ireland in the sixteenth century, particularly in the west and north, meant that opportunities for financially remunerative work for single women were limited. The main form of trade was through barter with travelling merchants or by private sales or exchanges of goods and services between neighbours. The custom of young women working to save for their dowry that was normal in other parts of early modern Europe would not have been common in Gaelic society. As already noted, dowries consisted not of cash but of household goods and animal stock and were more likely to have been gathered from neighbours than accumulated over many years by the young bride. At the lower levels of Irish rural society, the number of cows and other animals appears to have been calculated according to agreed or customary rates or contributed by neighbours and friends, presumably in sufficient quantities to provide the means by which the couple could live as a separate household. One chancery pleading referred to marriage goods being calculated 'after the reckoning of the country'[54] and in a sixteenth-century marriage agreement between Laughline O'Hykie and Ownye Ny Teig in County Clare, Ownye agreed to give Laughline eight in-calf cows and 'all such cattle as she shall be able to get amongst her friends'.[55] Similarly, in his account of County Westmeath in 1682, Henry Piers described how 'the father or next of kin to the bride, sends to his neighbours and friends, . . . and every one gives his cow or heifer, . . . and thus the portion is quickly paid'.[56] For poorer families, the gathering together of a couple of animals and some household goods remained the most popular form of dowry until the nineteenth century.

A small number of poor single women may have found remunerative employment in the local tower house, performing menial tasks such as water carrying. The community in the tower house was, however, predominantly male with a strong military ethos. The principal female residents were the lord's wife, his daughters, foster daughters and possibly one or two female attendants who came from the families of the lord's followers. The woodcuts of John Derrick, depicting scenes from Gaelic lordly society, also suggest an overwhelmingly male society in which even the cooking was done by men.[57]

In the more Anglicised households in the eastern part of the country, English-style male and female domestic servants were employed in the sixteenth century. The surviving wills of Pale landlords include bequests to servants and arrangements for them to be paid outstanding wages.[58] Similarly, on the Butler estate in the early seventeenth century, household accounts indicate that Kilkenny Castle provided employment for a small number of local women who worked as domestic servants in the kitchen and elsewhere in the house.[59] When Lord Deputy Sir Henry Sidney travelled through County Louth in the 1560s, he gave small amounts of cash to maids and other servants who tended to his domestic needs in castles and inns where he and his retinue lodged. At Dundalk, for example, he paid out 3s. 4d. to be distributed as a 'reward' among the maids and servants and at Mellifont, the home of the Moore family, he paid 16s. for the cook, butler, porter, maids in the dairy and the boys of the chamber and kitchen.[60]

A surviving household account book for the Sidney family gives some idea of the structure of a household (albeit an English one) in the Pale in the mid 1550s. Most of the staff listed as receiving wages were men, including those employed in the kitchen. Women were hired on a part-time and casual basis to clean or scour the pewter.[61] Occasional payments were also made to women who worked in the fields at harvest time.[62] Four to six women attended Sidney's wife, Lady Mary and these were the only women recorded as being employed in the household on a full-time basis.[63] At least one of Lady Mary's ladies-in-waiting, Anne Holt, was Welsh and had probably travelled with her to Ireland from the Sidney's home in Penshurst. When Sidney moved to Dublin Castle as lord deputy in the 1560s, he appears also to have presided over a household which had few female employees. The only woman who was listed on the official establishment was the laundress.[64]

In the course of the seventeenth century, the demand for domestic servants grew as the new English and Scottish landlords built houses which required a large staff to maintain them. Some, like Lady Sidney, brought English attendants with them to Ireland, but these were gradually replaced by Irish-born servants. English and Irish literature mocked the Irish servants who took over the tasks of English servants in the new households. As a mid-seventeenth century poet noted cynically:

Donnough the groome steps in, in Richard's place
And Shevane Oge, doth turne out gentle Grace . . .
. . . Owna, Sive . . .
And Moar great beastly Drones; creep into th' Hive
Who so bewitch the Captaine and his wife
That these must be Followers, all their life.[65]

The diary of Richard Boyle contains frequent references to the women employed on his Lismore estate. Boyle also records occasionally paying additional sums of money to a female servant when she married, which suggests that domestic service was beginning to be a more common means by which young single women could accumulate a small cash dowry.[66]

More regular paid employment for single women was available in towns. By comparison with English and European urban centres, Irish towns were, however, small prior to the late seventeenth century. In the older towns, established in the medieval period, trade was controlled by guilds and town corporations from which women were excluded. In Dublin, women apprentices are occasionally recorded in the town records and single women were admitted to the freedom of the city in the fifteenth and early sixteenth centuries, but increasingly in the late sixteenth century women were entered on the town freedom rolls as daughters of aldermen rather than as traders in their own right.[67] The main economic opportunities for young, unmarried women were located outside the formal world of guilds and town corporations on the edge of the market place and in the streets, peddling and dealing in local produce. The corporation repeatedly endeavoured to control the number of women 'going about the city' selling a mixture of agricultural produce and more exotic goods such as oranges, lemons, and 'sneezing tobacco', as well as apples, nuts and salt, presumably purchased in small quantities from the ships docking in the port of Dublin.[68]

Prostitution provided another less formal economic opportunity for single women in urban centres, particularly in the garrison town of Dublin where large numbers of soldiers were based in the aftermath of the wars of the 1590s. Dublin corporation tried to control the problem of prostitution and issued directions in 1616 to its aldermen to report the numbers of single women in their wards who were selling ale. The city authorities suspected that many of the women were also offering sexual services. Similar bans were proclaimed in other towns against single women selling ale, while in Munster the provincial council endeavoured to prevent women working as prostitutes in coastal towns frequented by pirates.[69]

In the early decades of the seventeenth century, the urbanisation of Irish society was accelerated by the arrival of British settlers who formed small urban communities of artisans and craftsmen, particularly in the southern plantation of Munster.[70] The surviving records are not expansive enough to examine the extent to which such centres provided paid employment for women. It is likely that, as in craft workshops in English towns, most of the work done by single women was within their own family home although some may have been hired out on a seasonal basis.

In summary, it can be argued that Anglicisation of Irish life brought new economic opportunities and opened up a new labour market for single women outside the landed classes.

Married women in landed families

When a woman married her tasks and work depended on the social and economic background of her family and that of her husband. At the highest level in the early sixteenth century, most landowning families, Gaelic and Old English, lived in stone tower houses. Although English-style houses began to be built in the late sixteenth century, the tower house remained a common form of dwelling for landowners until the mid-seventeenth century. Even in towns such as Galway, Sligo and Carrickfergus wealthy merchant families lived in tower houses. At its simplest, the tower house was a three or four storied stone building with one room on each floor accessed by a spiral staircase at the side of the building.[71] The living quarters for the lord's family were normally on the top floor. This room usually had a large fireplace with stone seats built into the walls. Some tower houses, particularly in the Pale, had a more complex layout with small chambers off the main living room on the top floor and a privy chamber. Others such as Dunsoghley in County Dublin developed the basic plan into a more sophisticated building with four towers and a small chapel, built by Sir John Plunkett and his wife, Genet Sarsfield, in 1573.[72] In the simplest form of tower house, internal furniture was at a minimum consisting of little more than some low stools and a table. In the Pale, tables and wooden chests were also recorded in inventory lists. Bundles of rushes and straw were used for bedding but more luxurious flock beds appear among the marriage goods of families in the towns and in the larger houses of the Pale.[73]

As noted in Chapter 1, feasting was central to the Gaelic political system and it was the wife's duty to act as an hospitable hostess to her husband's client supporters. Luke Gernon described how he was greeted by a Gaelic lord's wife when he visited a tower house in the first decade of the seventeenth century:

The castles are built very strong, and with narrow stayres, for security. The hall is the uppermost room, let us go up, you shall not come downe agayne till tomorrow . . . The lady of the house meets you with her trayne. . . . Salutations paste, you shall be presented with all the drinkes in the house, first the ordinary beere, then aquavitae, then sacke, then olde ale, the lady tastes it, you must not refuse it. The fyre is prepared in the middle of the hall, where you may sollace yourselfe till supper time, you shall not want sacke and tobacco. By this time the table is spread and plentifully furnished with variety of meates, but ill cooked, and without sauce. . . . They feast together with great iollyty and healths around; towards the middle of supper, the harper begins to tune and singeth Irish rymes of ancient making. If he be a good rymer, he will make one song to the present occasion.[74]

Even in the English household of the Sidneys in the 1550s, Lady Mary Sidney supervised hospitality, issuing instructions for payments to musicians and other entertainers including her husband's 'fool', and to visiting servants who accompanied guests to the house. Lady Mary Sidney, along with her husband, also received gifts from local dignitaries on feast days such as New Year's Day and St George's Day.[75]

The Sidneys made elaborate changes to the house in Kilkane as their household accounts reveal. Architecture was in fact the most visible sign of the changing nature of early modern Irish society. Gradually in the late sixteenth and early seventeenth centuries, the tower house went out of fashion and was replaced by English-style large houses with multiple rooms, each allocated to a specific task such as cooking, sleeping and dining.[76] In the Sidney household in the 1550s, builders and carpenters worked on Lady Mary's chamber and a chapel as well as the brewhouse, buttery, laundry, kitchen, and a garden. The carpenters also built cupboards for the buttery, set up bedsteads and built a brushing board for Lady Sidney's clothes. Furniture in the house included tapestries from England and chairs from Flanders. The range of food purchased for the household also reflected a wider market than that available locally. Walnuts, chestnuts, oil, nutmegs, aniseed, marmalade, cinnamon, sugar and a wide variety of fruit were all on the menu and were imported through local port towns such as Waterford.[77] As Toby Barnard has noted, the new domestic architecture 'made manifest the aims of the protestant settlers'.[78] The acquisition and display of material wealth communicated the status and importance of the family. In his new house in County Cork in the mid-seventeenth century, Lord Orrery:

displayed not only wealth and position but his awareness of continental currents and court standards. . . . When guests came to dine, as they frequently did, they would be seated on chairs upholstered in 'Turkey' work, could admire the gilt leather hangings, the painted images of family and royalty, the green curtains at the three windows, the burnished wall sconces and fire dogs and the three turkey-work carpets removed from the tables only when the food was served.[79]

The employment and supervision of servants in the estate house were tasks normally assigned to the women in the house. On the Boyle estate in Lismore and Youghal in the 1620s and 1630s, Richard Boyle's mother-in-law, Lady Alice Fenton, dealt with much of the day-to-day management, supervising staff and overseeing building and other work on the estate.[80] One of the earliest accounts of a woman settler in seventeenth-century Ireland also describes her involvement in estate management. Lady Elizabeth Montgomery encouraged British tenants to settle on the Montgomery estate in County Down, providing them with a house and some land to sow flax and potatoes. She also, according to a late seventeenth-century descendant, encouraged linen and woollen manufactures.[81] In the 1660s and 1670s Lady Elizabeth Butler closely supervised the employment of staff and their work on the Butler family estates in Kilkenny and Tipperary, even when she lived in London. The agent, George Mathews, sent her regular reports on estate affairs which she recorded in her own account book in London.[82] Elizabeth Petty, the wife of the surveyor, William, spent most of her married life in London but this did not prevent her from supervising affairs on the family estates in Kerry. When she visited Ireland, she busied herself with a wide range of tasks on the estate: interviewing and receiving petitions from tenants, collecting rents, granting abatements to defaulters, drafting new leases and discussing a new forge with some workmen.[83]

The household management role undertaken by women in Ireland was similar to that of women in landed families in England and other parts of Europe. In Ireland, however, women may have been expected to perform these roles more independently of their husbands than their counterparts elsewhere. The small pool of suitable recruits for service in the Irish administration meant that many Irish landlords held official positions that demanded their attendance in Dublin or London. As the Montgomery family chronicler noted, Lady Elizabeth Montgomery's husband Sir Hugh was 'by business much and often kept from home' and during his absence Lady Montgomery ran the estate.

A survey of the Ulster plantation lands in 1622 also records a number of women living on their family's Ulster lands alone. Some were widows who had taken over their husbands' responsibilities as undertakers but in other instances, the surveyor noted that the husband was in England or in Scotland. In Fermanagh, for example, Lady Worrall was resident on the lands of her husband while he was noted as being in England. Sir Robert Hamilton was also in England but his wife, children and 'many servants' were living on his Irish estate. Captain Callum was in England although his wife, children and family were in residence on his lands. In Cavan, William Hamilton's wife and some servants were found on his lands but the survey recorded that Hamilton 'resides not upon it'. Hugh Mitchell and his wife and family were 'usually' resident 'but he is now himself in Scotland'. It is likely that among these settler families two households were being maintained, one in England or Scotland and another in Ireland with the wife being given responsibility for maintaining one of them. Family papers that might enable us to document this in detail do not exist but in one of the few families for which we do have records, a dual household was clearly maintained in Scotland and Ireland. Scottish undertaker Robert McClelland left his daughter, Marion McClelland, in charge of his Ulster estate while he remained in Scotland and Marion kept a written account of her expenditure and estate management in her father's absence. Later, when Marion married Robert Maxwell, she returned to Scotland where she managed her family's lands while her husband 'while not canvassing favours at court, was looking after their estates and children in Ireland'.[84]

The wars of the 1640s followed by the dislocation and land transfers of the 1650s led to an expansion in the number of women widowed or left on their own for long periods of time. Wives of royalist supporters like Elizabeth Butler, countess of Ormond, spent much of the Commonwealth period in Ireland while her husband remained on the continent with the exiled King Charles II. In the aftermath of the war, women from Catholic landed families were often left in Ireland when the men in their family travelled abroad to secure military and other positions in the Spanish army and administration. Initially perceived as a temporary arrangement, many married couples must have remained separated for the rest of their lives. Wives and widows were not only left behind by the menfolk but they were often also obliged to take on the role of head of the surviving kin in Ireland and protector of the family estates. When William Neylan departed for Spain in 1652, he made a will in which he nominated his mother, the famous Máire Rua O'Brien, as manager of his property; and there must have been many other married women given legal custody of the family property.[85] Women heads of household also worked their way through the legal minefield of the Commonwealth and Restoration land settlements as best they could. In the 1650s they appealed against the forfeiture of family estates and their legal entitlements as widows and when these pleas failed, the women heads of households led the small entourages of surviving family, servants and animal stock in the long trek across the country to claim land in the transplantation to Connacht scheme.[86] Women also attended the 1662–3 Court of Claims in large numbers. Over a third of the plaintiffs in the court were women and over half of those were women presenting petitions on their own, usually widows claiming jointures or other entitlements from their husbands' estates. The court officers seem to have been particularly sympathetic to the latter group and normally issued instructions that the widows be restored to the jointure property that had been agreed in family settlements dating back to the 1620s and 1630s.[87]

War and its aftermath, therefore, gave women new obligations as they took on the responsibilities of estate management and head of household. Political circumstances also frequently compelled women to take legal responsibility for property. It is difficult, however, to discern if the new financial responsibilities undertaken by women led to any significant change in attitudes to them but the fact, as we shall see, that more men were willing to nominate their wives as executors may reflect a new respect for their financial and legal skills.[88]

Married women in non-landed families

Outside the tower house and big house in rural areas, the most common form of dwelling in the sixteenth and seventeenth centuries was what was described by English visitors as a 'cabin', made of clay or mud and covered with a turf or thatch roof. These were usually one-roomed dwellings with no chimneys. Furniture was basic, some stools and a low table, with beds made of bundles of wool, straw or rushes. Until the early years of the seventeenth century, rent or chiefly tribute (the two were virtually indistinguishable by the sixteenth century) was paid in kind and normally consisted of a specified numbers of beeves or other animal stock as well as quantities of food such as butter, flour and bread and labour on the lord's land.[89] A woman's marriage goods of animal stock and household utensils identified her economic role in the marriage. She brought the cows that she would milk and from which she would produce butter and other milk products, as well as the utensils that she would use for cooking. Most food was cooked on a griddle iron or in a large pot, both of which were often included among the marriage goods of a bride and were clearly considered essential items in the household. Brewing of ale was also a household chore undertaken by women. Pans and other utensils used in the brewing process were included among marriage goods as well as being considered valuable enough to be bequeathed in wills. Women's work, thus, not only fed the household but also produced produce which contributed to the rent.

Crops such as oats and barley were grown in small quantities with the corn being ground by women, usually by hand, to make oatcakes and bread baked on a griddle iron. John Dunton memorably described the making of a meal in a house in the west of Ireland in the late seventeenth century. Three generations of women in the household (daughter, mother and grandmother) were involved in the food preparation which included grinding of oats by hand, grilling an oat cake over an open fire, churning butter, straining milk through straw and boiling meat in butter.[90] Women also spun linen and woollen yarn, mainly for household use.[91] Other agricultural work undertaken by women included the moulding of turf sods for fuel, the collection of seaweed for fertiliser and, in fishing communities, the gathering of worms for bait.[92] The absence of markets or villages in many parts of rural Ireland, particularly in the west and north, must have meant that many households were virtually self-sufficient with women making a significant contribution to the family economy.[93]

The size and ethnic mix of the tenant population of Ireland expanded in sixteenth- and seventeenth-century Ireland. No accurate estimates of the extent of the settler population are available, so we can only guess at the gender divisions among the newcomers.[94] In the sixteenth century the majority of British people who came to Ireland were single or married men who left their wives and family in England. Administrators and soldiers in the sixteenth century often came alone and only brought over wives and children if they made the decision to settle permanently in Ireland. Initially, therefore, the majority of the New English community in Ireland was male. In the first official plantation scheme in Laois and Offaly, soldiers predominated among the proposed settler population and very few, if any, English women settled on the plantation lands.[95] Of the two large plantation schemes in Munster and Ulster, the southern scheme was the most successful in attracting married couples in the early years of the project. In 1589 the Munster undertakers were obliged to certify the number of English tenants on their lands and some provided a gender breakdown. On Sir Walter Ralegh's estate 144 men were listed, seventy-four of whom were accompanied by wife and 'family'. The agent for Sir Christopher Hatton recorded fifteen English men and eight English women on his lands and on another estate it was reported that thirty-two out of thirty-five

Englishmen were accompanied by their wives and children.[96] Out of a list of twenty-two tenants on the lands of Sir William Herbert in Castleisland, only one was recorded as not being accompanied by a wife and he lived with his sister on the estate. The households on the Herbert lands ranged in size from two to ten persons but the average was four.[97] Other settlers in Munster also recorded households of four or five persons although a small number were much larger. Thus at a rough calculation over half of the men on the Munster plantation were accompanied by their wives and most lived in small households which probably consisted of a man, his wife, children and one or no servants.

In Ulster, the government-sponsored surveys suggest that the initial population of British women on the plantation lands was lower than it was in Munster. A survey of 1611 gives an impression of a small number of undertakers in residence with their wives and 'family'. The fact that the presence of wives and 'family' is recorded in the case of some undertakers suggests that this was a positive point to be noted. In the majority of cases where no reference is made to wives or 'family' it might be assumed that they were not present. Tenants with wives were more thinly scattered. There are references to promises to bring over more tenants with wives and children and to tenants having returned home allegedly for the purpose of bringing back their families. By the time of the survey of 1618–19, although the number of undertakers and tenants in residence with their wives had risen, they still represented only a small proportion of the total.

T. W. Moody recorded that the majority of the settlers who came to Ulster through the London companies' efforts were the workmen employed in building on the city's lands in the new county of Londonderry. Some of these workmen brought their wives and children with them intending to settle permanently but the surviving records give the impression that the vast majority came alone.[98] Elsewhere on the plantation, however, there were undertakers who actively encouraged settlement and may also have succeeded in establishing a more balanced sex ratio in a shorter period of time than is evident in County Londonderry. In the 1622 survey the composition of the 'families' on one English proportion was recorded. The return recorded a total of thirty-nine families consisting of sixty-eight men, sixty-two women and seventy-seven children on the land in the barony of Oneilland in County Armagh. The average household size was five. Eighteen families had an equal number of men and women and in eleven of these the household consisted of a man, a woman and children. Six families had two men, two women and children which may have represented a married couple and grandparents. As in Munster, therefore, households were generally small and the nuclear family formed the core of the family unit and in many cases its entirety. Thirteen families had more men than women while only eight had more women than men. It is impossible to discern how representative these figures are but they do at least suggest that in some parts of the Ulster plantation the sex ratio by 1622 was beginning to be more balanced.[99]

It is important to note, however, that a low sex ratio did not have the same long-term implications for society in Ulster as it did in other colonies located thousands of miles from the 'home' country. In Ulster, the close proximity of the home country, particularly Scotland, meant that a scarcity of women in an Irish colony could be relatively easily eliminated. There is evidence, for example, that Scottish men returned home to seek wives; and Professor Canny found that by 1641 the majority of male British deponents in Munster and in Ulster were married to wives of British origin.[100]

From the Drapers' Company records we can identify the life of one married woman in the new settlement. Jane Russell and her husband Roger ran a 'lodging house' where the mason on the Drapers' Company's lands, George Birkett, was 'dieted'. Jane was described as a camp follower who had travelled with the English army from the Low Countries to Ireland. The Russells provided hospitality for the soldiers based in the local garrison as well as the workmen on the Drapers' Company's lands. The company's records indicate that brewing and selling of beer was the most profitable business in the new town. When George Birkett's wife eventually joined her husband in Ireland, she decided to start selling beer in her house, partly to pay off her husband's debts but also to 'keep him [i.e. her husband] at home'. Mrs Birkett was in competition not only with the Russell establishment but also with the many other 'cabin brewers' in the town where the brewing appears to have been done mainly by Irish women. Irish men and women mixed freely with the settlers in the shebeens making 'rhymes and songs . . . and such like behaviour to the raising of quarrels and breaches of the peace'.[101] It was not the ideal community envisaged by the planners of the plantation project but it nonetheless provided economic opportunities for women as brewers and sellers of beer.

Twenty years later, by the time of the 1641 rebellion, the plantation was more settled with a more balanced sex ratio which also led to a more inward-looking community. The depositions taken after the outbreak of rebellion in October 1641 convey an impression of a close-knit settler society in which intermarriage was common and in which most married couples lived on small farms and engaged mainly in pastoral farming. Despite the fact that a significant number of the deponents were women (often widows whose husbands had been killed in the course of the wars of the 1640s), the depositions are not that enlightening on the economic contribution of women to the new economy. The work of the women is not identified as separate from that of the men and much of what we can extract from the depositions on women's work is by inference rather than by direct evidence.

The details that the women deponents provided of the animals and stock lost convey an impression that they worked on the farm alongside their husbands. Many of the widows had a detailed knowledge of the stock on the farm, including the age and value of the animals. Thus in County Cavan, Jane Oliver recorded the loss of fifteen English and one Irish cow, worth £3 each; six two-year-old English heifers, worth 25s each, six one-year-old heifers worth 10s each, a horse worth £1. 10s. as well as grain and household stuff. Jane Taylor listed among her losses: twenty milch cows and a bull, five two-year-old heifers and a young bull, one fair breeding mare in foal, as well as leases and hides and leather in a tan house. Christian Stanhope noted that she and her husband had lost seven travelling geldings and nags, one stand horse, twenty-four mares, fillies and other horses and colts (all English breed), twenty English cows, ten fair oxen of English breed, six Irish fatted beeves, two bulls, twenty-five heads of young cattle (all English breed), fifty-four English sheep and wool and fourteen swine.[102] The thoroughness with which the women listed their losses suggests that they were involved in the rearing and caring for the animal stock on the farm.

As Nicholas Canny has documented, the British people in Ulster, who came mainly from Scotland, retained the existing pastoral economy and bred cattle, sheep, horses and other animal stock while also growing small amounts of corn for domestic consumption. The settlers in the border counties of Fermanagh, Cavan and Monaghan made a living by supplying beef, milk, butter and cheese for the Dublin market. Carriers laden with butter travelled regularly to Dublin.[103] Dairy utensils are rarely listed among the items lost but it is highly likely that the production of the dairy products was undertaken by the women in the family which is probably why they had such a detailed knowledge of the cows on the farm. A tantalising glimpse of one woman's involvement in the dairy industry survives in an itemised account of butter collected by Katherine Dunkan in the Fermanagh area in 1675. Dunkan collected the butter in the hinterland of Belturbet from where she sent it by boat to Dublin.[104]

In Munster and Leinster, the settlers were more specialised in their craft skills and farming than in Ulster and Connacht. Tillage farming was undertaken and the textile business, particularly in wool, was 'expanded out of all proportions by British manufacturers'.[105] The depositions provide no details as to how woollen cloth was manufactured but as in the south-west counties of England, from where the majority of the new British community in Munster originated, woollen merchants operated a family workshop in which the women and the children carded and spun the wool while the men wove and managed the sale of the wool and cloth.

Poor married women could also avail of the new economic opportunities offered by the expanding urban economy. Single and married women carried produce into towns and cities to sell. In the coastal regions of the south-west, married women traded with pirates for small quantities of sugar and other smuggled goods that they subsequently sold in the local town.[106] War also left many women destitute. Many fled to the towns looking for work and sustenance. In the 1650s, Dublin was reported to be 'swarming' with beggars, many of them women and children with no other means of survival. Not surprisingly, claims that prostitution was on the increase often coincided with the reports of expanding numbers of beggars in Dublin.[107]

Paradoxically, while British emigration into Ireland increased in the seventeenth century, there was also a growing exodus of Catholic men from the country. While women in Catholic landed families stayed in Ireland to preserve as much of the family lands as possible, poor women often had little option but to follow their male relatives to the continent. In the 1650s and again in the 1690s, women and children are reported to have accompanied the 'wild geese' abroad. For the fortunate few, life on the continent was good as the men pursued successful careers in the Spanish army and their wives were accepted into the upper levels of Spanish society. Other women, however, were not so fortunate and many were reduced to begging on the streets of Brussels and other European towns, particularly after a husband's death.[108]

Widows, dower and jointures

Most marriages ended with death although Gaelic customs of divorce and separation continued to be observed into the seventeenth century. On divorce in customary law, a woman was entitled to a return of her marriage goods. On widowhood, she had a similar entitlement. In Gaelic society, as part of the marriage agreement, the groom's family arranged to mortgage land as security for the dowry. In the event of a marriage breakdown, the wife's family was entitled to a return of the dowry. Thus, for example, in 1546 Ulick Ó Bruadair gave a dowry of twenty-one cows, a bull and three horses with his daughter for which the groom provided sureties for repayment and mortgaged lands as well.[109] When the husband died, the land was redeemed and the goods paid to the widow or alternatively the land was given to the widow. As Kenneth Nicholls has noted, the Irish redeemable jointure survived into the early decades of the seventeenth century.[110] In 1633, Dermot McOwen Carthy of County Cork enfeoffed land to the use of his wife, Syly, for her lifetime in return for her marriage goods of twelve in-calf cows, twelve cows of two years, six yearling heifers, eight horses and mares and a nag (total value estimated at £8. 4s.). If Syly survived Dermot, the feoffees were to hold on to property to the use of Syly until the marriage goods were repaid by Dermot's heirs.[111] The Gaelic provision for widows thus differed from the English system in that it did not grant women an automatic right to a third of her husband's property.

As Gráinne O'Malley informed Queen Elizabeth:

Among the Irishry the custom is, that wives shall have but her first dowry without any increase or allowance for the same, time out of mind, it hath been so used, and before any woman do deliver up her marriage to her husband she receives sureties for the restitution of the same in manner and form as she hath delivered it, in regard that husbands through their great expenses, especially chieftains at the time of their deaths, have no goods to leave behind them but are commonly indebted, at other times they are divorced upon proof of precontracts; and the husband now and then without any lawful due proceeding do put his wife from him and so brings in another; so as the wife is to have sureties for her dowry for fear of the worst. . . .[112]

For O'Malley and other Irish women, the English system of a woman's right to dower or a third of her husband's estate for her lifetime was more attractive than the Gaelic custom. New husbands of former widows agreed and in the late sixteenth and early seventeenth centuries an increasing number of men, usually in conjunction with their wives, began to claim the widows' entitlement to English-style dower. In the surviving chancery records, it is possible to document the conflict over dower which occurred in many Irish families in the late sixteenth century as heirs tried to resist the alienation of property for the lifetime of the widow. By the 1630s, the battle had been largely won; and most Irish landlords by that stage followed English legal practices in their provision for their wives.[113]

As noted already, until 1696 a widow was also entitled to a share in her husband's movable goods: a third if there were children and a half if the couple was childless. Outside of the larger landed families, testamentary evidence suggests that the attitude which a man adopted to future provision for his widow depended to a large extent on the age and size of the family. If a couple had young children, the widow was usually left custody of all the personal goods, the dwelling house and, often, of all the real estate until the children were of age. The widow was charged with the maintenance of the children and sometimes she was given instructions for their education. If, however, the children were already of age, then the widow was normally left her jointure of land or a cash annuity, a share of the household goods and, usually, the dwelling house of the couple and, occasionally, an additional cash sum.

The legislation of 1696 abolished a widow's legal entitlement to a share in her husband's goods and, thereafter, the husband was entitled to dispose of his goods as he saw fit. Most husbands continued to bequeath household goods and other possessions to their wives but legally they were no longer obliged to do so. The distribution of the testator's goods was sometimes left to the discretion of the wife, but among wealthier families the instructions were more specific. Jewellery and other valuable items such as silver or gold plate and utensils were normally given to the eldest son or, if he was a minor, the widow had to take out a bond to undertake to preserve them for the heir as she had received them.[114] Other goods might be given into the widow's custody for her lifetime provided she did not remarry.

Another important development in the economic provisions for widows was that by the early seventeenth century jointures had replaced dower as the most popular means of providing for a widow in landed families. There were a number of reasons for this. First, the practice of enfeoffing land to the use of the landowner was a legal impediment to a woman claiming dower. Strictly speaking, a widow could not claim her third from land held to a husband's use. Under common law, 'dower attached only to lands of which her husband stood seized'.[115] A jointure was arranged by enfeoffing the land to the joint use of the husband and wife for life. If the wife survived her husband, she enjoyed the land for her lifetime and on her death it passed to her husband's heir. Apart from legal necessity, arranging a jointure enabled a husband to determine his wife's claim to his estate prior to his death. It could be included in his will or deed of enfeoffment along with portions for younger children. The landlord also hoped that stipulating the bequest to his wife would prevent family disputes over the estate after his death. Unusually, in 1640, Robert Meath FitzDavid, an alderman from Cork, allowed his wife to choose between having a cash jointure of £500, an annuity of £60 or 'other dower or thirds'. Most widows, however, were not given the choice.[116]

A frequent clause in wills was that if the wife did not accept her jointure then she was to be excluded from the benefit of the will and 'shall betake herself to the benefit of her dower at common law'.[117] This might suggest that the jointure usually constituted more than a third of the estate. However, given that a widow could not claim dower to any of her husband's property which was enfeoffed to uses, it might also be interpreted as a veiled threat to a widow that if she did not accept the jointure she would receive nothing other than a share of the personal estate of her husband.

Apart from the 1696 Act and the transition from jointure to dower, the most significant change in the provision for widows was a consequence of the adoption of family settlements by many Irish landed families in the second half of the seventeenth century. In the family settlement, jointure became a mathematical calculation based on the size of the woman's marriage portion. Thus the widow's jointure was limited by the amount which she brought to the marriage. The money for the jointure could be raised in a number of ways. A sum of money might be invested and the widow paid from the interest; or, alternatively, some land on the estate could be set aside to yield the required sum in rents.

The move to a cash calculation of the value of the jointure also led to a transformation in the very nature of the jointure itself. In the sixteenth and early seventeenth centuries, jointures in Ireland were usually in the form of land. Although land jointures can still be found in wills in the late seventeenth century, the movement towards cash annuities was strong and was considered standard practice by the mid-eighteenth century. Eileen Spring has argued that the move from land to cash jointures had profound implications for the economic power and status of the widow.[118] Before the middle decades of the seventeenth century, a widow with a large jointure was in control of an extensive territory for her lifetime. Property conveyed power in ways that a cash annuity could not do. The widow was free to choose what she would do with the land: she could lease it or manage it herself. She might also have responsibility for looking after the tenants on the estate. In 1587, James Aylmer of County Meath instructed his wife to continue to hold the manor court on the estate.[119] If the widow wished to remarry, her jointure could add to her attraction for a prospective husband. The cash annuity deprived the widow of these opportunities and, therefore, diminished her status and influence in the community.

It should, however, also be acknowledged, that widows might not necessarily have wanted the burden of managing an estate. From the woman's point of view, control of property was not always the most convenient way of earning an income from her late husband's estate, particularly if she remarried and moved away from the area. The account books of Richard Boyle indicate that he offered widows an attractive alternative by offering to buy out their jointure or dower. In return for a cash sum, Boyle secured the widow's life interest in the property.[120] In Gaelic families, unaccustomed to providing property for widows, a cash annuity was also an attractive alternative. In 1618, Owna Callaghan, described as of Killarbry in County Donegal, widow of Tadhg O'Hara, leased her jointure in Sligo to her son-in-law, Tadhg O'Hara. The agreement stipulated that if Owna wished to live on the land, she was to give Tadhg six months' notice. A similar arrangement was made on the McCarthy estate in County Cork.[121]

As was the case in relation to single women and heiresses, the economic provision for widows among merchant families differed from that to be found within landed families. Testators were concerned, above all, to maintain the commercial profit of the business. The smoothest way to do this was frequently to leave the business in the overall control of a widow or arrange for a man to manage the business and give part of the profit to the widow for herself and any dependent children. In other words, the responsibility for the continuation of the family business was often bequeathed to the widow by the husband. This did not always mean, however, that the widow was obliged to run the business herself. In 1640, Sir William Caulfield left his wife a lease of a house in Dublin called the London Tavern but he clearly expected her to sub-let it rather than manage it herself.[122] In 1642, James Mathew Fitz James, a merchant of Cork City, left his wine tavern and licence for retailing wine for two years after his death to his servant and nephew, instructing his wife to provide the nephew with meat and drink while he worked in the tavern.[123] Other men left their wives with the means of making a living as a widow. Thomas Rice, a burgher of Dingle, bequeathed his wife the use of his boat during her life, if the boat survived that long.[124] Presumably, again, it was intended that the widow would hire a crew for the boat. If a business was left to a widow, a testator often made it clear that she was simply acting as custodian while the heir was a minor. In 1642, for example, when Griffith Mathew left his widow a malt house he left instructions that she was 'to put in security to preserve my estate from embezzling and wasting or else to stand to her thirds, so the rest to be preserved for my grandson'.[125]

Some widows successfully continued the family business and became wealthy women in their own right. In Drogheda in the 1680s, Margaret Coole had a substantial business importing a large stock of silk and other types of cloth and millinery goods.[126] In Dublin, widows are recorded leasing land, collecting rents and lending money. But if some women opted to continue their husbands' businesses others preferred to sell up or pass the business on to others. The documentation is not sufficiently detailed to estimate the proportion of women who chose to do this but in the late sixteenth and early seventeenth centuries, the chancellor heard a large number of pleas from widows asking for help and assistance. Widows, undoubtedly, came under pressure from their husbands' partners to sell out. Margaret Cusack, a widow of a Dublin merchant in the late sixteenth century, claimed that her husband's partners were putting pressure on her to sell her widow's share of the business. Another merchant's widow from Drogheda, described herself as a 'simple soul' and 'unskilful' in the 'trade of merchant' and claimed that her husband's partner told her that her husband's debts were greater than they actually were and so she 'not knowing the greatness of her husband's estate' made it over to him.[127]

The remarriage of the widow, the coming of age of the heir or his marriage changed the relationship of the widow with her former husband's estate. The widow's custody of the family home was nearly always limited to her widowhood and, consequently, she was expected to leave it if she remarried. The marriage or the entry of the heir into his inheritance could also have implications for the widow's place of residence. Testators normally instructed their heirs to provide the widow with a room in the family house while she remained unmarried. Cork merchant James Mathew Fitz James directed that if his son married then his mother should have during her widowhood a chamber and cellar in the dwelling house besides the 'common use of the hall, kitchen, buttery and backside'. Other testators urged mother and son to live in harmony. William Jones, for example, asked that his wife and son 'live amiably together as mother and son should do'. John Cloud, a yeoman, in 1675 instructed that all his goods 'should continue entire' until his wife and children 'marry or go out into the world'. Nevertheless, the widow's legal rights were reduced when the heir came of age. She was often no longer entitled to live in the home that she and her husband had shared during their married life but was dependent on the goodwill of the heir.[128]

Despite deathbed requests for family harmony, conflicts inevitably arose between widows and sons and particularly between widows and stepsons. The remarriage of a widow could, in particular, lead to family tension and conflict. Statistically, we have no information on the number of widows who remarried but Colm Lennon concluded that remarriage was common among women in Dublin merchant families. Not all surpassed Genet Sarsfield's achievement of six husbands but many had two or three.[129] The new husband had a legal right to all the property of his wife, including her jointure or dower from previous marriages. He might also take custody of his wife's children's portions and legacies left to them by their respective fathers. When the children came of age, legal disputes might arise as the children claimed their inheritance. A widow remarrying was often in a strong position to negotiate her own marriage settlement with her new husband and might try to protect the interests of her existing children. For example, in the early seventeenth century, when Margaret Taaffe married her second husband, Nicholas Gernon, she gave him her jointure land but said that she never intended to harm the inheritance of her sons by her first marriage. Following her marriage to Gernon, he persuaded Margaret to move to his house and took goods from her first husband's house, promising to return them when the children came of age, a promise he did not fulfil and, consequently, Margaret and Nicholas became embroiled in a legal dispute with Margaret's eldest son, Richard Taaffe, who disputed his mother's right to a jointure from his father's lands.[130] Margaret's legal position became more complex when Gernon died and she married for a third time. Gernon's death provoked an additional conflict with his son, George, who questioned the dowry that Margaret should have had from her second husband's estate.[131]

A widow's control over her former husband's estate depended not just on the particular legacies bequeathed to her by her husband but also on whether or not she was nominated as executor or administrator of her husband's will. In seventeenth-century England, it was common for men to appoint their wives as executors to their estates and frequently the wife was the sole executor.[132] In Ireland, however, it was rare for men to nominate their wives as sole executors before the mid-seventeenth century. Prior to that time, when wives were nominated as executors they were usually given the responsibility in conjunction with other male relatives: the testator's sons, uncles or brothers. An executor had considerable legal as well as financial responsibility in overseeing the execution of the will. If the estate was tied up in deeds of enfeoffment or marriage or trust settlements, the potential legal complications for the executor could be considerable. Many women may have preferred not to have to deal with such issues. Equally, the emphasis placed on male heirs by Irish landlords up to the mid-seventeenth century militated against nominating a woman to execute the will. Even when a woman was appointed as sole executor, overseers were nominated to assist her. In England overseers had only an advisory role but in Ireland they were usually expected to take a more active role in the administration of the estate. If the children were minors, the overseers took on the role of guardians and occasionally the testator instructed his overseers to keep a careful eye on his widow's management of the estate's finances.

In the second half of the seventeenth century more testators nominated their wife as sole executor. The change reflected the more general changes in Irish society as Irish legal practice began to follow more closely that of England. The newly established landowning families of the seventeenth century, in particular, bequeathed more legal responsibilities to women. The disruption of family life during the wars of the 1640s also meant that women were forced to take on a management role in relation to the family estates and this may also explain why more testators trusted them with an executor's role. It is intriguing, therefore, to speculate that the disruption of the middle decades of the seventeenth century bestowed on women in landed families a new esteem and status, at least within the extended family unit.

Conclusion

By 1696, the legal framework for women's relationship with property and inheritance in Ireland had been established and was to remain largely unchanged for the rest of the early modern period. As Anthony Malcolmson and, more recently, Deborah Wilson, have documented, the marriage settlement was an essential component of any marriage proposal within Irish landed families in the eighteenth century.[133] Below the level of landlord, the mechanics of marriage arrangements are more difficult to detect before the second half of the eighteenth century.[134] By that time, Irish rural society was more clearly divided into a middling farming or large tenant group and a labouring or cottier class than it had been in the sixteenth or seventeenth centuries. Within farming families, a pattern of arranged marriages and marriage agreements was well established by the 1750s. The negotiations may have lacked the legal sophistication of the settlements within the landlord class but the principles were very similar. Considerations of property and family dominated the discussions for marriage. The bride's family was required to provide a dowry while the groom's family normally offered property as its part of the negotiations. This suggests that the inheritance practices developed among landed families in the seventeenth century had filtered downwards to other social groups by the mid-eighteenth century. The next chapter will explore further the ways in which women's lives changed during these years.

Notes

1 Undated bill (National Archives of Ireland, Chancery Pleadings, Box O/142).

2 The information extracted from wills in this chapter is based on an analysis of almost 500 transcripts and copies of wills. The main collections used are

the wills cited in chancery pleadings transcribed by the Record Commission in National Archives of Ireland, RC 5 and RC 10 and the transcripts of seventeenth-century wills in PRONI T/561, 564, 581, D3045. These were augmented by single transcripts and copies of wills printed in family histories and local journals. For a full list see the bibliography.

3 See also David Dickson, 'No Scythians Here: Women and Marriage in Seventeenth Century Ireland' in Margaret MacCurtain and Mary O'Dowd (Eds), *Women in Early Modern Ireland* (Edinburgh, 1991), pp. 223–35.

4 See, for example, National Archives of Ireland, RC 5/5, pp. 406–10.

5 See Mary O'Dowd, 'Women and the Irish Chancery Court in the Late Sixteenth and Early Seventeenth Centuries' in *Irish Historical Studies*, **xxxi** (November, 1999), pp. 470–87.

6 See, for example, Margaret C. Griffith (Ed), *Calendar of Inquisitions Formerly in the Office of the Chief Remembrancer of the Exchequer Prepared from the Mss of the Irish Record Commission* (Dublin, 1991), p. 169.

7 Will dated 27 March 1628 (National Archives of Ireland, RC 5/1, pp. 125–41).

8 See, for example, undated bill (National Archives of Ireland, Chancery Pleadings, Box G/303); Will of Walter Cottell, 1642 (National Archives of Ireland, RC 5/5, pp. 527–43).

9 National Archives of Ireland, RC 5/8, pp. 385–400.

10 Will dated 6 Nov 1616 (National Archives of Ireland, RC 5/21, pp. 26–36).

11 Will dated 15 December 1620 (National Archives of Ireland, RC 5/8, pp. 24–9; Nicholas Canny, *The Upstart Earl: A Study of the Social and Mental World of Richard Boyle, First Earl of Cork, 1566–1643* (Cambridge, 1982), pp. 107–8; Angela Bourke *et al.* (Eds), *Field Day Anthology of Irish Writing Vol. iv* (Cork, 2002), p. 500.

12 Will dated 13 April 1636 (National Archives of Ireland, RC 5/25).

13 Canny, *The Upstart Earl*, pp. 100–4.

14 On Gaelic customs of fosterage and gossiprid see Kenneth Nicholls, *Gaelic and Gaelicised Ireland in the Middle Ages* (Dublin, 1972), p. 79; Fiona Fitzsimons, 'Fosterage and Gossiprid in Late Medieval Ireland: Some New Evidence' in Patrick J. Duffy, David Edwards and Elizabeth FitzPatrick (Eds), *Gaelic Ireland. Land, Lordship and Settlement c. 1250–c. 1650* (Dublin, 2001), pp. 138–49.

15 National Archives of Ireland, Chancery Pleadings, Box G/327; L/32.

16 Loc. cit., Box J/166.

17 W. F. T. Butler, *Gleanings From Irish History* (London, 1925), p. 41.

18 Herbert J. Hore and James Graves (Eds), *The Social State of The Southern and Eastern Counties of Ireland in the Sixteenth Century, Being the Presentments of the Gentlemen, Commonalty, and Citizens of Carlow, Cork, Kilkenny, Tipperary,*

Waterford, and Wexford, Made in the Reigns of Henry VIII and Elizabeth (Dublin, 1870), p. 186.

19 See, for example, John O'Donovan (Ed), *The Genealogies, Tribes and Customs of Hy Fiachrach* . . . (Dublin, 1844), pp. 399–400, 404–5. In the O'Connell family, dowries were still in the form of cattle and other animals in the eighteenth century (see UCD Archives, O'Connell Papers, P12/5/197).

20 These figures are based on an analysis of wills and cases involving marriage portions in the Chancery Pleadings in the National Archives. Richard Boyle offered marriage portions of £3000 to £4000 with his daughters (see, for example, A. B. Grosart (Ed), *The Lismore Papers* (10 volumes, 2 series, London, 1886–8), 1st series, vol. 2, pp. 14–15, 228.

21 National Archives of Ireland, RC 5/24, pp. 55–8.

22 See, for example, Martin J. Blake (Ed), *Blake Family Records, 1300 to 1700; A Chronological Catalogue With Copious Notes and Genealogies* (2 vols., 1902, 1905), i, pp. 56, 60–1, 86–7.

23 National Archives of Ireland, Chancery Pleadings, Box T/15.

24 National Archives of Ireland, Chancery Pleadings, Box H/120.

25 National Archives of Ireland, Chancery Pleadings, Box K/282; Box K/319; Box G/141.

26 Richard Caulfield (Ed), 'Wills and Inventories, Cork, temp. Elizabeth' in *The Gentleman's Magazine* (May 1861–September 1862); PRONI, T/581, 2.

27 A. B. Grosart (Ed), *The Lismore Papers*, 2nd series, vol. 2, pp. 95–6; Jane Ohlmeyer and Éamonn Ó Ciardha (Eds), *The Irish Statute Staple Books, 1596–1687* (Dublin, 1998), p. 11.

28 O'Donovan (Ed), *The Genealogies, Tribes and Customs of the Hy Fiachrach*; 'Old Waterford Wills' in *Journal of the Waterford and South-East Archaeological Society* (1906), pp. 151–3.

29 When the testator's debts had been cleared, all that remained were goods to the value of £30. (Undated Bill, National Archives of Ireland, Chancery Pleadings, Box BB/172.)

30 PRONI, T/681, pp. 64–9.

31 Undated Answer, National Archives of Ireland, Chancery Pleadings, Box R/22.

32 Cited in K. W. Nicholls, 'Some Documents on Irish Law and Custom in the Sixteenth Century' in *Analecta Hibernica*, **6** (1970), p. 108.

33 See Griffith (Ed), *Calendar of Inquisitions Formerly in the Office of the Chief Remembrancer of the Exchequer.*

34 See J. M. W. Bean, *The Decline of English Feudalism 1215–1540* (Manchester, 1968), pp. 118–79 for the popularity of this type of settlement in fourteenth- and fifteenth-century England.

35 Griffith (Ed), *Calendar of Inquisitions Formerly in the Office of the Chief Remembrancer of the Exchequer*, pp. 354–5.

36 Ibid., p. 338

37 Ibid., pp. 216–17.

38 Ibid., pp. 331–2.

39 National Archives of Ireland, RC 5/20, 367–9.

40 Griffith (Ed), *Calendar of Inquisitions Formerly in the Office of the Chief Remembrancer of the Exchequer*, p. 352. The Old English cleric Geoffrey Keating identified a man having no sons to inherit as one of the evil consequences of adultery (Bourke *et al.* (Eds), *Field Day Anthology of Irish Writing, Vol. IV*, p. 278).

41 National Archives of Ireland, RC 5/19, pp. 99–108.

42 See, for example, Griffith (Ed), *Calendar of Inquisitions Formerly in the Office of the Chief Remembrancer of the Exchequer*, pp. 390, 391–2, 394, 403–4.

43 David Edwards, *The Ormond Lordship in County Kilkenny, 1515–1642, The Rise and Fall of Butler Feudal Power* (Dublin, 2003), pp. 108–25.

44 The royal decrees in both cases were also motivated by a desire to prevent a Catholic heir succeeding. (See Victor Treadwell, *Buckingham and Ireland, 1616–1628: A Study in Anglo-Irish Politics* (Dublin, 1998), pp. 114–30.

45 See, for example, the 1641 will of Sir Philip Perceval in which he remaindered his estate to his father in Somerset (PRONI/T581/1, 152).

46 On the impact of the Statute of Uses in England see Lloyd Bonfield, *Marriage Settlements, 1601–1670. The Adoption of the Strict Settlement* (Cambridge, 1983), pp. 1–45; Eileen Spring, *Law, Land, And Family. Aristocratic Inheritance in England, 1300–1800* (Chapel Hill and London, 1993).

47 See, for example, the history of the Blake and Brown families.

48 Will dated 29 July 1665 (National Archives of Ireland, RC 5/19, p. 7).

49 Among the families where the property descended through a female heir in the seventeenth century were the Berminghams, Chichesters, Fentons, Hamiltons, Hills, Kings, Lamberts, Loftuses and Masterons. Families in which the heir married an English heiress include the Aungiers, Joneses, Kings, Rawdons, Ridgeways and Talbots.

50 Cited in Anthony Malcolmson, *The Pursuit of an Heiress: Atistocratic Marriage in Ireland, 1750–1820* (Belfast, 1982), p. 2.

51 See, for example, PRONI, T/581/3, p. 41; T/581/5, p. 229; T/581/6.

52 Deborah Wilson's recently completed doctoral thesis documents the complexity of family settlements in eighteenth- and early nineteenth-century Ireland (Deborah Wilson, 'Women Marriage and Property in Ireland, 1750–1850' (unpublished Ph.D. thesis, Queen's University, Belfast, 2003)).

53 The earliest example of this practice in the wills examined for this study dates to 1660 when Sir William Brownlow requested that his grandson, Arthur Chamberlain, the son of his daughter Lettice, change his name to Brownlow before he inherit the estate through his mother (Will dated 22 November 1660, National Archives of Ireland, RC 5/25, pp. 179–85). See also Anthony Malcomson, 'A Woman Scorned?: Theodosia, Countess of Clanwilliam (1743–1817)' in *Familia*, **15** (1999), p. 2.

54 National Archives of Ireland, Chancery Pleadings, Box I/78.

55 National Library of Ireland, Inchiquin Papers, Folder 1812.

56 Henry Piers, *A Choreographical Description of the County of West-Meath* (Meath Archaeological and Historical Sociey, 1981), p. 122.

57 See John Derricke, *The Image of Irelande With A Discouerie of Woodkarne* (first printed, London, 1581, reprinted, Belfast, 1985). See also Luke Gernon, 'A Discourse of Ireland, Anno 1620' in C. L. Falkiner, *Illustrations of Irish History and Topography, Mainly of the Seventeenth Century* (London, 1904), pp. 345–62.

58 See, for example, the series of wills cited in chancery inquisitions (National Archives of Ireland, RC/5).

59 Household Account Book, Ormond Manuscripts (NLI, MS 2549).

60 De L'Isle and Dudley Papers, O28/19, no date (Centre for Kentish Studies). I am grateful to Lord De L'Isle for permission to consult these papers.

61 Book of payments of wages under Sir Henry Sidney, c. 1557 (Centre for Kentish Studies, De L'Isle and Dudley Papers, U1475/O22); Daily Account Book, 1558–9 (loc. cit., U1475/O25/1); list of payments made to Lady Sidney (loc. cit., U1475/O21).

62 Declaration of the accompt of Edward Cowley, the bailiff of husbandry at Kilky (loc. cit., U1475/O28/4).

63 Account of Sir Henry Sidney, 1556–1559 (loc. cit., U1475/O18). One of these was a chamber maid and another was the wife of the bailiff of husbandry who may not have been officially employed in the household.

64 A book of accompts of household in Ireland, August 1566–September 1568 (loc. cit., U1475/O31). See also list of payments made (loc. cit., U1475/O48/21). Anne Holt was from Denbigh. She later married Captain William Piers, seneschal of Clandeboye. See *New DNB* entry for William Piers.

65 *The Moderate Cavalier or the Soldier's description of Ireland and of the Country Disease with Receipts for the Same. A Book Fit for All Protestant Houses in Ireland* ([?] Cork, 1675).

66 See, for example, Grosart (Ed), *The Lismore Papers* 1st series, vol. 1, pp. 48–9; vol. 2, pp. 255, 264.

67 The disappearance of women from urban records also occurs in English towns and has been attributed to the expanding population of the late medieval period, following the decline after the Black Death when women were welcomed as traders. See Caroline M. Baron, 'London 1300–1540' in D. M. Palliser (Ed), *The Cambridge Urban History of Britain, vol. i, 600–1540* (Cambridge, 2000), pp. 427–8.

68 J. T. Gilbert and Rosa Mulholland (Eds), *Calendar of Ancient Records of Dublin in the Possession of the Municipal Corporation* (18 vols., Dublin, 1889–1922), vol. iv, pp. 211–12.

69 See Bourke *et al.* (Eds), *Field Day Anthology of Irish Writing, Vol. V*, pp. 496–7; Samuel MacSkimin, *The History and Antiquities of the County of the Town of Carrickfergus From the Earliest Records Till 1839* (new edition, Belfast, 1909), p. 385; J. C. Appleby, 'Women and Piracy in Ireland: From Gráinne O'Malley to Anne Bonney' in MacCurtain and O'Dowd (Eds), *Women in Early Modern Ireland*, pp. 60–1.

70 Nicholas Canny, 'The 1641 Depositions as a Source for the Writing of Social and Economic History: County Cork as a Case Study' in Patrick O'Flanagan and Cornelius Buttimer (Eds), *Cork: History and Society* (Dublin, 1993), pp. 249–308; Nicholas Canny, *Making Ireland British, 1580–1650* (Oxford, 2001), pp. 336–47.

71 H. G. Leask, *Irish Castles and Castellated Houses* (Dublin, 1977), pp. 75–124.

72 Ibid., pp. 120–1.

73 Ibid., pp. 91–2.

74 Falkiner, *Illustrations of Irish History and Topography, Mainly of the Seventeenth Century*, pp. 60–1.

75 Daily Account Book, 1558–9 (Centre for Kentish Studies, De L'Isle and Dudley Papers, U1475/O25/1, 26 March, 2 April).

76 Leask, *Irish Castles and Castellated Houses*, pp. 124–41; Mairéad Dunlevy, 'Changes in Living Standards in the Seventeenth Century' in M. Ryan (Ed), *Irish Archaeology Illustrated* (Dublin, 1991), pp. 207–8.

77 Daily Account Book, 1558–9 (Centre for Kentish Studies, De L'Isle and Dudley Papers, U1475/025/1).

78 Toby Barnard, *Irish Protestants. Ascents and Descents, 1641–1770* (Dublin, 2004), p. 35.

79 Ibid., p. 52.

80 Grosart (Ed), *The Lismore Papers*, 1st series, vol. i, pp. 6, 10, 23, 28, 205.

81 Bourke *et al.* (Eds), *Field Day Anthology of Irish Writing, Vol. V*, pp. 493–4.

82 Ibid., pp. 501–3.

83 Paper presented by Rosemary Raughter at the conference on medieval women's history held in Trinity College, Dublin on 12 April 2003.

84 Canny, *Making Ireland British, 1580–1650*, pp. 224–5, 292.

85 Máire Mac Neill, *Máire Rua. Lady of Leamaneh* (Whitegate, Co. Clare, 1990), pp. 60–1.

86 See, for example, J. P. Prendergast, *The Cromwellian Settlement of Ireland* (3rd edition, Dublin, 1922), pp. 363–85.

87 Gerald Tallon (Ed), *The Court of Claims* (Dublin, 2005).

88 See below, pp. 104–5.

89 See, for example, Mary O'Dowd, *Power, Politics and Land in Early Modern Sligo, 1568–1668* (Belfast, 1991), p. 64; Katharine Simms, *From Kings to Warlords. The Changing Political Structure of Gaelic Ireland into the Later Middle Ages* (Woodbridge, Suffolk, 1987), pp. 129–50.

90 Edward MacLysaght, *Irish Life in the Seventeenth Century* (Cork, 1939; reprinted, New York, 1969), pp. 331–2.

91 For the export trade in Irish cloth in the late Middle Ages see Timothy O'Neill, *Merchants and Mariners in Medieval Ireland* (Dublin, 1987) pp. 58–76.

92 Gerard Boate, *Ireland's Natural History* (London, 1652), pp. 155–60; National Archives of Ireland, Chancery Pleadings, Box J/170.

93 O'Dowd, *Power, Politics and Land*, pp. 63–87.

94 Canny, *Making Ireland British, 1580–1650* is the best study of the British settler community in Ireland.

95 Mary O'Dowd, 'Women and the Colonial Experience in Ireland, c. 1550–1650' in Terry Brotherstone, Deborah Simonton and Oonagh Walsh (Eds), *Gendering Scottish History. An International Approach* (Glasgow, 1999), pp. 156–71.

96 *Calendar of State Papers: Ireland, 1588–92*, pp. 168–72; Public Record Office, London, SP 63/144, nos. 11a, 28, 68, 73; SP 63/145, nos. 40, 42.

97 National Library of Ireland, MS 7861, fos. 177–8.

98 T. W. Moody, *The Londonderry Plantation, 1609–41: The City of London and the Plantation in Ulster* (Belfast, 1939). See also Canny, *Making Ireland British, 1580–1650*, p. 394.

99 National Library of Ireland, MS 8014/9. See also Michael Perceval-Maxwell, *The Scottish Migration to Ulster in the Reign of James I* (London, 1973), p. 126.

100 Canny, 'The 1641 Depositions as a Source for the Writing of Social and Economic History', pp. 249–308.

101 O'Dowd, 'Women and the Colonial Experience in Ireland, c. 1550–1650', p. 162.

102 Trinity College, Dublin, MS 833, fos. 67, 181; MS 836, fo. 75.

103 Canny, *Making Ireland British, 1580–1650*, p. 351.

104 National Archives of Ireland, Undated Chancery Pleadings, Box 6.

105 Canny, *Making Ireland British, 1580–1650*, p. 392.

106 J. C. Appleby, 'Women and Piracy in Ireland: From Gráinne O'Malley to Anne Bonney' in MacCurtain and O'Dowd (Eds), *Women in Early Modern Ireland*, p. 61.

107 Patrick Fitzgerald, 'Poverty and Vagrancy in Ireland, 1500–1770' (unpublished Ph.D. thesis, Queen's University, Belfast, 1995) is the only study of vagrancy in Dublin in the period.

108 Jerrold Casway, 'Irish Women Overseas, 1500–1800' in MacCurtain and O'Dowd (Eds), *Women in Early Modern Ireland*, pp. 112–32; G. Henry, *The Irish Military Community in Spanish Flanders 1586–1621* (Dublin, 1992), pp. 84–90; Micheline Walsh, 'Some Notes Towards a History of the Womenfolk of the Wild Geese' in *The Irish Sword*, **v** (1961), pp. 98–106; 'Some Further Notes Towards a History of the Womenfolk of the Wild Geese' in *The Irish Sword*, **vi** (1962), pp. 133–45.

109 Kenneth Nicholls, 'Irishwomen and Property in the Sixteenth Century' in MacCurtain and O'Dowd (Eds), *Women in Early Modern Ireland*, p. 23.

110 Ibid., p. 23.

111 National Archives of Ireland, RC 5/19, pp. 172–80.

112 Bourke *et al.* (Eds), *Field Day Anthology of Irish Writing, Vol. V*, pp. 21–2.

113 O'Dowd, 'Women and the Irish Chancery Court in the Late Sixteenth and Early Seventeenth Centuries', pp. 470–87.

114 See, for example, the will of Thomas Carey, 8 September 1637 (National Archives of Ireland, RC 5/21, pp. 335–44).

115 Bonfield, *Marriage Settlements, 1601–1670*, p. 1.

116 National Archives of Ireland, RC 5/19, pp. 195–203.

117 See, for example, will of John Rochford, 15 September 1616 (National Archives of Ireland, RC 5/4, pp. 90–100).

118 Spring, *Law, Land, and Family. Aristocratic Inheritance in England, 1300–1800*, p. 9.

119 Griffith (Ed), *Calendar of Inquisitions Formerly in the Office of the Chief Remembrancer of the Exchequer*, p. 277.

120 For Boyle's dealings with widows see, for example, A. B. Grosart (Ed), *The Lismore Papers*, 1st series, vol. 1, pp. 7, 19–20, 24, 25, 39–40, 106, 225.

121 National Archives of Ireland, RC 5/30, pp. 310–21.

122 National Archives of Ireland, RC 5/25, pp. 122–5.

123 Will dated 1642 (National Archives of Ireland, RC 5/19, pp. 203–30). See also p. 78 above.

124 Will dated 20 September 1633 (National Archives of Ireland, RC 5/20).

125 PRONI, T/581.

126 J. T. Dolan 'Drogheda Trade and Customs, 1683', in *Co. Louth Archaeological Journal*, vol. iii (1912–15), pp. 83–103.

127 National Archives of Ireland, CP, Box C, no. 146; Box I, no. 220.

128 Will dated 1642 (National Archives of Ireland, RC 5/19, pp. 203–30); PRONI, T/581.

129 Colm Lennon, *The Lords of Dublin in the Age of Reformation* (Dublin, 1989), p. 84.

130 National Archives of Ireland, CP Box AA/135.

131 Loc. cit., Box BB/234.

132 Amy Louise Erickson, *Women and Property in Early Modern England* (London, 1993), pp. 159–61; 'Property and Widowhood in England, 1660–1840' in Dandra Cavallo and Lynda Warner (Eds), *Widowhood in Medieval and Early Modern Europe* (London, 1999), p. 187.

133 Malcolmson, *The Pursuit of an Heiress: Artistocratic Marriage in Ireland, 1750–1820*; Wilson, 'Women, Marriage and Property in Ireland, 1750–1850'.

134 S. C. Connolly, 'Marriage in Pre-Famine Ireland' in Art Cosgrove (Ed), *Marriage in Ireland* (Dublin, 1985), pp. 78–98.

CHAPTER 4

Women and Economic Opportunities in Eighteenth-Century Ireland

Family businesses

Elizabeth Eken was born in the early decades of the eighteenth century. Her family was in the seed business in Coleraine. Elizabeth married a local businessman, Robert Shipboy, a clothier, who was also based in Coleraine, and in the 1770s the couple managed a shop in the town as a joint enterprise. Robert was in charge of the main business while Elizabeth advertised a mantua or gown-making service. Robert and Elizabeth had two children, Jane and James. When Robert died he bequeathed the business to Elizabeth with instructions that James, behaved himself towards his mother and sister, then she should bequeath the business to him in her will.[1] Elizabeth ran the Coleraine shop on her own for a number of years but in 1793 she sold up and moved to Belfast where she joined with James to establish a millinery and carpet business in High Street.[2] From 1793 until Elizabeth's death two years later, she and James appear to have been partners in the business. They signed receipts for money jointly and individually. They advertised, however, under the name 'Elizabeth and James Shipboy' and it is clear from a surviving letter from James to Elizabeth that Elizabeth was in charge.[3]

When Elizabeth died, she was sufficiently well known to merit a brief obituary notice in the *Belfast Newsletter*. In her will Elizabeth fulfilled her husband's wishes and left the business to James although she instructed him to give half the value of the enterprise to his sister, Jane, as her marriage portion.[4]

The story of the Eken-Shipboy family exemplifies one of the most important economic developments of eighteenth-century Ireland: the growth in the commercial life of Irish towns and the corresponding expansion in economic opportunities for enterprising individuals including women. The transformation in the Irish urban landscape was dramatic. The population of Dublin increased from 4500 in 1685, to 100,000 by 1750 and had reached 180,000 by 1800. And, in other towns the demographic increase was equally startling.[5]

As the business interests of the Eken-Shipboy family document, the development of Irish urban life was fuelled largely by a rapid expansion in the Irish textile industry. The development of linen production in Ulster led to the growth of smaller towns in the 'linen triangle' in the eastern part of the province. In the southern part of the country, woollen exports brought increased prosperity to Cork and other urban centres. In Dublin, by the mid-eighteenth century, over 10,000 men and women were employed in the city's silk and woollen trades.[6]

Urban expansion widened the involvement of women in paid work. The Eken-Shipboy story documents women's engagement with the economy of towns and, in particular, their role within family businesses. As was the case in the sixteenth and seventeenth centuries, women in trading families were expected to contribute to the family enterprise. From an early age daughters helped in the shop or provided assistance in the home so that their mother would be free to work in the business. In 1795, Elizabeth Eken's brother, Joseph, expressed his gratitude that following the death of his wife he had been left with two daughters, 'one my housekeeper, the other my shopkeeper'.[7] In her will, Elizabeth Eken left instructions that her daughter Jane should assist her son James with the business and housekeeping while she remained unmarried.[8]

Elizabeth recognised the contribution that Jane had made to the family business by dividing its value equally between her daughter and her son. An analysis of a selection of Irish merchants' wills suggests that this was common practice by the early eighteenth century. Testators with small family businesses frequently instructed that their estate be divided among all their children and often also their wife, 'share and share alike'. If the enterprise was a large one, daughters could be left a share of its profits, including urban properties and income from rents.[9] If a businessman had no sons, it was common practice to leave the family enterprise to a daughter. The trend, therefore, noted in the last chapter, of merchant families recognising the economic contribution of women to the family business was accelerated in the eighteenth century. A daughter in an urban middle- or upper-class family could, accordingly, have personal access to a considerable amount of cash or wealth in the form of a business and might, indeed, provide a more attractive marriage portion to a potential spouse than a woman in a landed family where the estate was entangled by several generations of marriage settlements.

Working in the family business gave a young girl valuable training in paying bills, collecting debts, identifying and ordering up-to-date and attractive stock and, most importantly, dealing personally with customers. Mercantile families were often closely connected by marriage and so this experience could be of practical use if the girl subsequently married into a business or trade family. Jane Shipboy, like her mother Elizabeth, married a trader, James McAdam from Belfast, and worked in her husband's business after she married.[10]

When a woman married a merchant or tradesman there were a number of ways in which she could contribute to the family enterprise. Apart from maintaining the house and providing food for the household, she might also keep the accounts and run the business in her husband's absence. Jane McAdam's husband James, for example, wrote regularly to her when he travelled to England on business, giving her instructions on what to do with goods and stock which he had shipped back to Belfast.[11] Other women provided a similar back-up service for their husbands.[12]

A wife might also set up a separate, but auxiliary business to that of her husband as Elizabeth Shipboy did in her husband's cloth shop in Coleraine in the 1770s.[13] In a similar fashion, the wife of David Murray ran a cloak-making business in her husband's fur shop in Aungier Street in Dublin in the 1780s, and the Dublin trade directories also suggest that other married couples established separate businesses in the same or adjoining premises.[14] In small towns where shops were less specialised than in Dublin, a wife might look after a particular aspect of the business. In Broughshane in County Antrim in the 1760s, the wife and son of Robert Cabeen sold groceries and hardware while he managed a woollen drapery business.[15] Similarly, in Armagh in the 1770s, Robert Scott operated an apothecary business while his wife sold millinery and grocery goods, probably in the same premises.[16] In small craft workshops involved in the production of wool, such as those described by L. A. Clarkson in Carrick-on-Suir, the work of the women in the family was also a crucial part of the production of the woollen cloth, even if it frequently went unrecorded.[17]

Urban growth also meant the expansion of the services offered in town centres. In earlier times, travellers to Ireland regularly complained of the lack of inns and taverns that were a familiar feature of the English landscape. In the eighteenth century, the range of public facilities in Irish towns became more varied. By 1800, most large towns had at least one hotel and a number of public houses. Other new urban-based instititutions included hospitals and prisons as well as schools. Many of these establishments were run jointly by a husband and wife team or by women, usually widows, on their own.

If daughters were bequeathed an equal share in the family business as sons, so too widows were commonly left in charge of the family business on the death of their husband. As in the sixteenth and seventeenth centuries, some widows welcomed the challenge of managing a business and retained control during their lifetime, bequeathing ownership to their eldest son or other children on death. In this situation the son remained a junior partner in the business while his mother was alive and only assumed complete control on her death. He might also, at that stage, like James Shipboy, be legally compelled to raise the funds to pay his sisters' or other siblings' parental legacies.

Through the computer index to the *Belfast Newsletter* it is possible to follow the trading career of a number of widows who like Elizabeth Shipboy chose to continue trading after their husband's death. Frances Seed was the widow of a Belfast salt merchant, Stephen Seed, who died in 1755. Like Elizabeth Shipboy, Frances continued the family business. She traded on her own for a number of years and then in 1769 went into partnership with William Seed who was probably her son. For three years, Frances and William worked jointly, but from 1773 William began to advertise on his own. He expanded the original salt business into other areas, importing coal, oats and flour and taking shares in ships. William was, however, overambitious. He went bankrupt in 1776 and was forced to sell much of his stock. In 1777, Frances started to trade again in the salt business on her own. This suggests that she had, like Elizabeth Shipboy, retained control of the original family business and was, therefore, in a position to rescue it from William's bankruptcy. When she died in 1778, she left the business to her daughter, Elizabeth, with instructions that her house and furniture were to be sold on Elizabeth's behalf. The intention may have been to keep the business from William's creditors. In the 1780s, William was again trading from the family premises, which implies that he had come to some arrangement with his sister and, consequently, partly due to his mother's business acumen, the family business had survived.[18]

The economic relationship of Elizabeth Shipboy and Frances Seed with their sons was a complex one. They both appear to have retained legal ownership of the business until their death but took on their sons as partners. Catherine Cox found similar arrangements between widows and sons in Dublin. In one case, the husband Jonathan Barclay specified in his will that the business was to trade under the name of 'Ann Barclay and son', emphasising the junior status of the son, a business arrangement that echoes that of Elizabeth and James Shipboy.[19] An analysis of women traders listed in the Dublin trade directories indicates that this type of arrangement between mother and son was not uncommon.

Widows who ran successful businesses over a long period of time achieved recognition and status in urban society. As already noted, the death of Elizabeth Shipboy was noted in the *Belfast Newsletter* as was that of other business widows.[20] Part of the admiration for such women may have been that they had achieved success in what was considered a male world. A woman trading, particularly in a business not normally associated with women, might have to overcome considerable hostility from both customers and employees. Male apprentices could resent taking orders from a woman or could perceive a woman to be easy prey for fraud and deception. Newspaper advertisements and announcements occasionally reveal tension between a woman employer and her staff. In 1756, Ruth Smith, the widow of a smith in Dublin, announced that she had discharged Peter Mullan, who worked with her and kept her books for over four years 'on account of his behaving in a very dishonest manner to her, by working underhand, in her name'.[21] Frances Seed had to defend herself in court against a man fraudulently claiming to be a creditor of her husband and with 'carmen and others' attempting to sell her 'Irish salt claiming it was English salt'.[22] Frances Seed also had problems with her husband's former employees. Andrew Wills 'who lived with Mr Stephen Seed' and was, presumably his apprentice, established a rival salt business on Seed's death. Wills's premises was located close to the cellar of Mrs Seed.[23]

Wills may have been disappointed that Frances Seed had chosen to take on the management of the business herself rather than appointing him as manager. The latter was an option chosen by many widows who did not want to become directly involved in running a business. When Thomas Reynolds's grandfather died in 1788, he left his cloth business and property in Dublin to his wife 'to be disposed of as she should think proper for her own and his children's support, making her sole executrix'.[24] There were eight children to be provided for. Mrs Reynolds who was, according to her grandson, 'totally unacquainted with mercantile affairs' appointed one of her husband's long-term employees, Thomas Warren, to run the business on her behalf in return for a third of the profit. The widow reserved the right to place one of her children as a partner in the business, with the intention that her eldest son would eventually join Warren in managing the family firm. Mrs Reynolds subsequently fell out with Warren who, her grandson later claimed, had brought the business to the brink of bankruptcy.[25]

Newspaper advertisements frequently refer to the fact that a widow had appointed a man, often a former apprentice, to run the business on her behalf. The settlement could be a formal one, agreed before the death of the husband.[26] It was not unusual for a testator to leave instructions that apprentices should be given a share in the business or were to continue to manage it on behalf of his wife. In the 1790s, Benjamin Yeats, a Dublin linen draper arranged for his wife after his death to take into partnership his two apprentices, Edward Butler and Gerald Geoghegan and to trade under the name 'Yeats, Butler and Geoghegan'.[27] Such an arrangement also served the purpose of reassuring customers that the business would continue under male control. In trades where the business depended on a particular skill or craft, continuity of personnel not only reassured customers that the business would proceed as before but it also ensured that the widow was not left to find a replacement for the skilled work undertaken by her husband.

Even when a widow wished to continue the business on her husband's death it was not always economically feasible for her to do so. A businessman's death led to an assessment of his debts and assets and a widow could frequently discover that the former outweighed the latter. More widows were appointed executors and administrators of their late husbands' estates in the eighteenth century than was the case in the earlier period. This bestowed greater economic responsibility on the women but it also meant that the widow, as the executor, was responsible for paying her husband's debts and in such circumstances she might have had little option but to sell the business. There were, therefore, formidable financial, legal and social obstacles facing widows who chose to continue trading after their husbands' death. Statistical analysis suggests that women like Frances Seed and Elizabeth Shipboy were in fact in a minority and that the majority of widows decided not to continue with the business following their husband's demise. Catherine Cox estimated that out of a sample of ninety-three widows in Dublin in the late eighteenth century, only fifteen opted to continue in the trade of their husband. Similarly, Leslie Clarkson and Margaret Crawford concluded that widows were more likely to be poor and without any means of making a living than to be prosperous managers of a family business.[28]

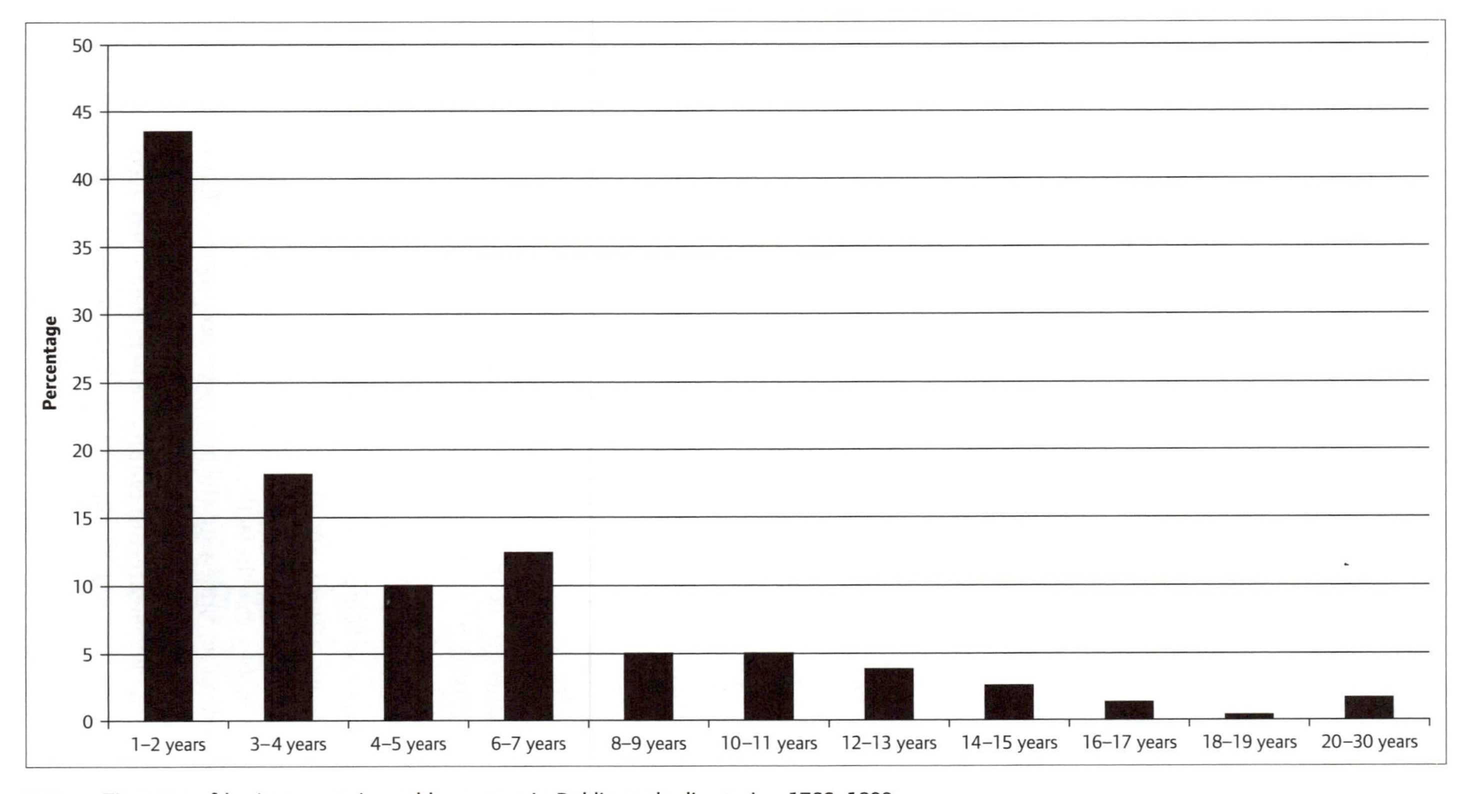

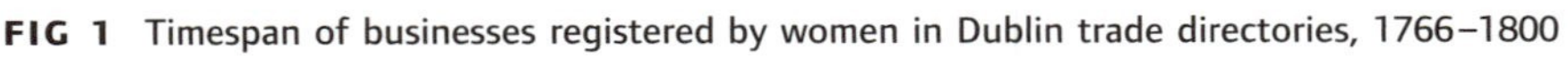
FIG 1 Timespan of businesses registered by women in Dublin trade directories, 1766–1800

An analysis of women traders listed in the trade directories for Dublin from 1766–1800 confirms the view that most women, when possible, chose not to operate within the world of commerce. As Figure 1 demonstrates, over 70% of women were registered in the directories for less than five years while almost 42% appear for one year only. Fewer than 10% of the female business owners can be tracked over a ten-year period.[29] It is likely, therefore, that the majority of widows traded in their own name for a few years while their son was a minor, but, unlike Elizabeth Shipboy and Frances Seed, opted to transfer the business to him when he came of age.

There may also have been a religious denominational element to the extent to which women became involved in the family business or continued with it following their husband's death. Maureen Wall's co-relation of the Catholic convert lists with the trade directories suggests that the proportion of Catholic women trading on their own was below the more general average for women traders.[30] In addition, women in Catholic merchant families feature rarely in studies of the business and family networks established by Catholic merchants in Ireland and overseas. The priority for aspiring Irish merchants was to establish marital connections with business families on the continent rather than in Ireland. Hence, a continental wife was perceived to have more commercial advantages than one based in Ireland.[31] The conservative ethos within the Irish Catholic community may have encouraged women to remain aloof from business affairs and to delegate responsibility for the family business when they were widowed. This seems to have been the intended plan of Thomas Reynolds's grandfather for his widow, an aim which was explicitly supported by popular Catholic writers such as Francis de Sales who encouraged widows to devote their lives to good works and charity rather than engage in business enterprises.[32]

Women traders

Wives, daughters and widows in established commercial families could, therefore, be involved in various ways and with varying degress of intensity in the family business but perhaps the most interesting aspect of the expansion of towns in eighteenth-century Ireland was that it opened up the possibility of women establishing businesses in their own right. In particular, the development of shops and service industries in the larger towns and cities provided single and widowed women with the means of making an independent living. Documentation on shops in early modern Ireland is scarce but trade directories outline the range of businesses registered by women. A study the Dublin trade directories from 1766 to 1800 indicates that the majority of women listed were in the food or cloth business. A 1787 trade directory for Irish towns in the south of Ireland confirms that female trading outside the capital followed a similar pattern.[33] Apart from the cloth and food businesses, women were also listed as tallow chandlers, proprietors of book, printing and paper businesses as well as sellers of some of the new consumer goods of the eighteenth century, particularly those used by women such as china, delph and glass. By the end of the century, they were also recorded as owners of schools for girls in many small towns in Ireland.

Within the food business, the most common form of shop listed with a woman proprietor was a grocery shop, although by the end of the century more specialist skills such as confectionery and tea were also being advertised by women in Dublin.

Detailed information on the extent of the stock of eighteenth-century shops is limited.[34] In large grocery shops in Dublin, the range of goods for sale included teas, coffee, chocolate, spices, spirits, wines, mineral water, pickles, fruit, rice, mustard and liquorice. Most of the goods were imported although some Irish produce was also sold.[35] In smaller towns, the stock was probably less exotic and more home produced. Groceries were sold alongside other sorts of goods. In Armagh in the 1760s John Oakman sold hardware, millinery items as well as wine and food while in Moira, Elizabeth Perry sold garden seeds, millinery items and groceries. The produce sold in the shop may have been produced on the premises. Small shopkeepers in rural towns were often also part-time farmers. In the 1770s, Elizabeth Blair kept a 'little shop' in Newry in which she sold among other things flax seed that probably came from land that Elizabeth owned in the vicinity of her shop and home. Blair's income was, therefore, partly derived from trading and partly from farming, a combination that would have been common in many small Irish towns.[36]

Most women who opened shops selling food probably managed very small enterprises that were never advertised or listed in trade directories. They were included among what one visitor to Ireland called the petty shopkeepers whose stock in trade consisted of 'half a dozen eggs, a platter of salt, a few pipes, a roll of tobacco, a yard of tape, a ball of twine, a paper of pins'.[37] The capital outlay in such a shop was minimal. The business could be opened in the downstairs room of a house and provided its owner with a small income. The death of a father or guardian could have furnished single women with the necessary capital to stock a shop. Others received loans or gifts

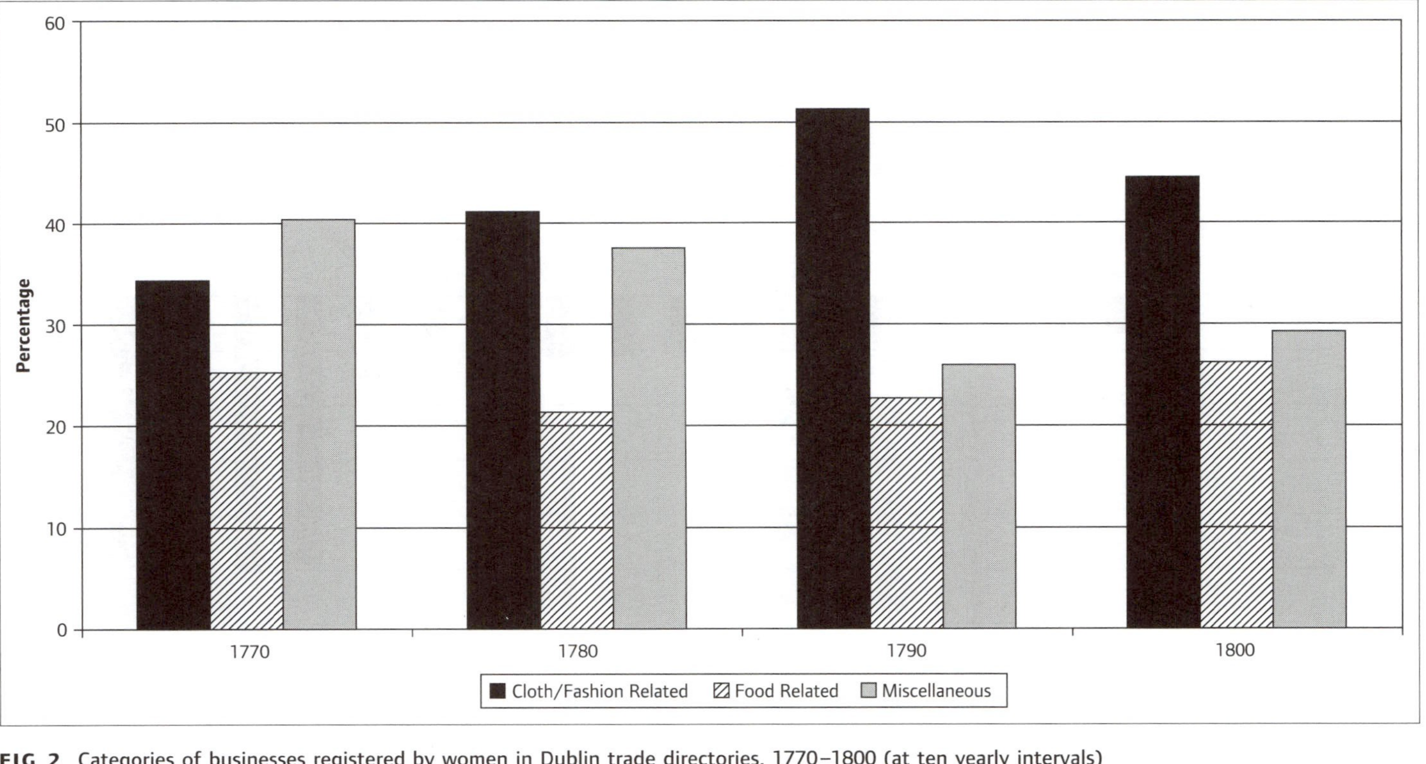

FIG 2 Categories of businesses registered by women in Dublin trade directories, 1770–1800 (at ten yearly intervals)

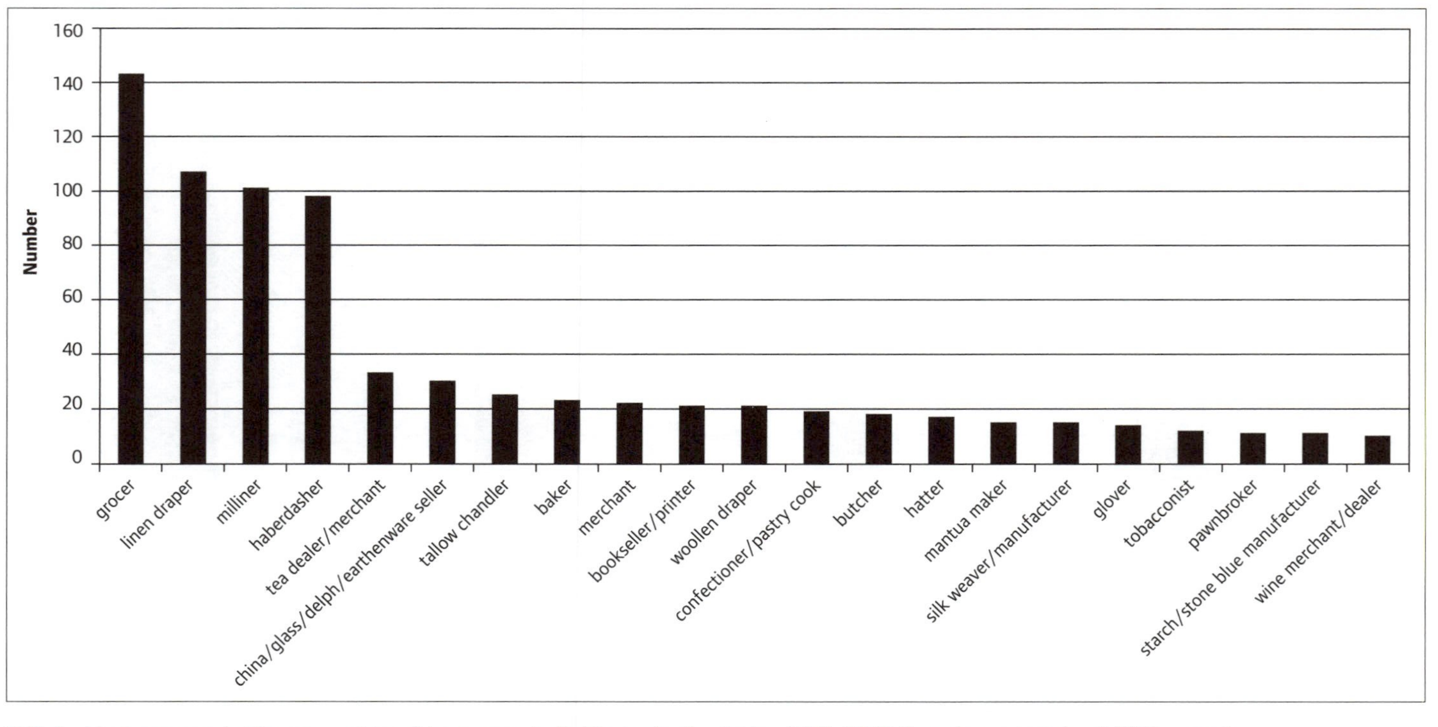

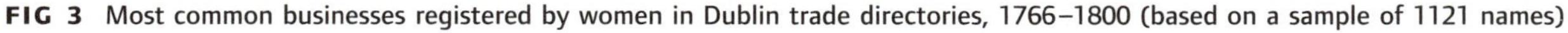

FIG 3 Most common businesses registered by women in Dublin trade directories, 1766–1800 (based on a sample of 1121 names)

from relatives or, in some cases, philanthropic-minded individuals. Jonathan Swift, for example, lent a woman in Dublin £20 to set up a fruit shop.[38]

The stories of Mary Leadbeater, based on the lives of the people who lived in her neighbourhood of Ballitore, County Kildare, included accounts of women (usually impoverished widows) who opened shops with a small stock of goods. Although imbued with Leadbeater's admiration for enterprising poor women who, through their own endeavours, overcame their poverty, Leadbeater's writings on the lives of women in the Ballitore area, nonetheless, provide a rare insight into the means by which a woman could establish a small business. In *Cottage Biography*, Leadbeater related the story of Elizabeth Curran who on her husband's death started a business by baking cakes and selling tripe and 'neats-foot-oil' and herring which she bought at a local fair.[39] Another woman, whose husband had deserted her, lived with her sister and with 'the flour of a barrel of wheat, bought on credit, she baked bread in her sister's oven, from the sale of which she paid for the wheat and continued her traffic'.[40] Dorothy Finn, another widow, used ten guineas acquired from selling an acre and a half of oats to hire

a room in the village, went to Dublin, and laid out the little capital obtained from her crop in such goods as were in constant demand. With these she attended the markets and increased her stock . . . After four months residence in her lodging, she ventured to take a decent house, opened a huckster's shop, and when she could, let lodgings, and accommodated boarders.[41]

Statistically, the textile industry, apart from that of the grocery business, provided urban based women with the most common way of making a living and seems, in particular, to have attracted single women. The types of businesses which women ran within the cloth business changed, however, in the second half of the eighteenth century. Initially, in the 1770s when traders were first listed in the Dublin directories, the majority of women were registered as proprietors of traditional businesses such as linen or woollen drapers, hatters, glovers or as owners of silk works. By the 1790s, however, this emphasis had changed with more women recorded as running millinery or haberdashery establishments and a small number listed as mantua makers. In other words, the new fashion market of the eighteenth century widened the options for women in the industry.

Trade directories distinguish between milliners, mantua makers and haberdashers but in many small premises the distinction was more theoretical than real. Initially, milliners were makers of hats for women but by the mid-eighteenth century hat-making was only a small part of the millinery business. Far more important was the sale of cloth of various kinds and of a wide range of accessories necessary for making fashionable women's clothes as well as additional items such as perfume, combs and hair decorations. Milliners also sold ready-made accessories, namely gloves, caps, veils and stockings and some also sold cloaks and shawls. Two 'old maiden ladies' in Kilkenny in the mid-eighteenth century

kept a kind of inland slop shop – that is to say, they sold every possible article for the dress, toilet etc., of men and women; – millinery, mercery, haberdashery, woollen drapery, hosiery, linen-drapery, ready-made shoes for men and women, hats of every description, furs, rugs, carpets, blankets; in short, they kept a universal magazine.[42]

The shop was stocked through an annual visit to merchants in Dublin.

The only garment not normally sold by a milliner was a gown, a task usually allocated to the mantua maker. By the mid-eighteenth century, mantua makers, like milliners, had widened their original business. The fashion for mantuas began in London in the seventeenth century and spread to other parts of England in the course of the eighteenth century. A mantua was a loose-fitting over-garment worn with stays. They were easily put together, did not require fitting and so could be made cheaply by women dressmakers. As mantuas went out of fashion, mantua makers began to manufacture other garments for women including 'gowns of all sorts, as well as cloaks and petticoats'.[43] The number of mantua makers who had premises of their own in eighteenth-century Dublin was small. Most mantua makers operated from the business of a milliner or a linen draper and were not, therefore, listed in trade directories nor would they have normally advertised their services in their own name. In late eighteenth-century Belfast, for example, mantua makers are recorded as working within other businesses.[44]

Outside Dublin and Belfast, the number of mantua makers listed in trade directories is also small but household accounts indicate that mantua makers were regularly employed making gowns in many parts of Ireland. Nor was their custom confined to the gentry or wealthy members of local communities. Accounts for servants' wages include payments to local mantua makers for making up gowns, petticoats and cloaks.[45] A distinction is clearly made in household accounts between payments to a mantua maker and a local seamstress. The latter made up small items such as shifts, children's clothes and men's shirts but the more complex task of gown making was left to the mantua maker.[46] In the accounts of Louisa Conolly for Castletown House, for example, separate payments were made to mantua makers, milliners in Leixlip as well as women who made up shifts, small items for children and shirts for the men in the family.[47]

Once a gown was made, it could be kept in fashion for a number of years by adding or replacing ribbons, lace and buttons or adding a new petticoat, apron or shawl (usually listed as a handkerchief), all of which were stocked by the milliner. As Beverly Lemire has noted:

To elevate oneself to the ranks of the fashionable might entail no more than the wearing of a petticoat of the prescribed colour, an apron suitably embroidered set at the right length, a printed handkerchief agreeably draped, or the retrimming of a gown or petticoat to meet the current mode.[48]

It was, therefore, important for milliners to advertise not just their goods but also their personal knowledge of the latest fashions. Milliners in Dublin stressed their connections with London while those outside the capital city emphasised their links with Dublin. In 1796, for example, a Miss Shaw and Miss Collins advertised that they were opening a millinery business in Suffolk Street in Dublin and that they had established correspondents in the London millinery business and intended also to visit the city at the 'different seasons' to keep up to date with the latest fashions.[49]

As in the grocery business, there were, undoubtedly, gradations in the size and range of millinery shops established by women. In London and other large cities a millinery business required an initial capital investment of between £25 and £75.[50] To stock a fashionable millinery business in Dublin must have required a similar if not higher amount, as many of the goods would have been imported from England or the continent. Money was sourced in a number of ways through legacies or loans. Alternatively, women trading on their own may have begun with a small stock and then expanded it as the business prospered. In 1771, Jane Otway advertised that she was opening a new shop in Parliament Street in Dublin. While her new premises in one of the most fashionable streets in the capital must have involved a substantial investment, it is worth noting that Otway's original business was at the Dove and Pendant in Castle Street.[51] Jane may have begun her enterprise by renting a room at the public house and when her venture grew she moved to a bigger establishment at a more prestigious address. Other women traded from their own homes or at the place where they were lodging.[52] Many of the items which they sold initially may have been made on the premises. Mary McAulay had a millinery business in Lisburn in the 1780s and noted in her advertisements that 'every article in the millinery line made up on the shortest notice'.[53] When Jane Greer opened a sewing school at the Sign of the Spinning Wheel in Scotch Street in Armagh in 1762, she announced that she would 'furnish the ladies in town and country with millinery work in the newest fashion'.[54] Greer's expectation was, presumably, that the sale of the goods made by the girls and the revenue from the school fees would finance the business. If the enterprise succeeded, a wholesale trade might also develop providing stock for country merchants and travelling pedlars and market sellers. Jane Otway, for example, noted in her advertisement that she traded with merchants in the country as well as the public in general.[55]

For young women with few financial resources, an alternative means of entering the millinery or mantua making business was through apprenticeship. In London, formal apprenticeships were available and a young girl starting in the industry might also be obliged to pay apprentice fees.[56] In the 1750s, in Waterford and Dungarvan young girls were apprenticed to mantua makers for a fee of £5.[57] Less formal apprenticeships were also available for young girls willing to work as shop assistants and this type of apprenticeship was advertised in Irish newspapers. Having served an apprenticeship a woman could venture into her own business and her qualifications could be used as a means of attracting custom. In 1767, Elizabeth Hamilton, for example, who 'has for a considerable time past been qualifying and improving herself in the millinery business with Mrs Mercer in Capel Street in Dublin' opened a millinery shop in Belfast.[58] In smaller towns, mantua makers were probably self-taught. In Mary Leadbeater's *Cottage Biography*, when Elizabeth Curran's shop failed to prosper she turned to sewing for a livelihood, making caps for sale and 'listing shoes or down tippets' and eventually she 'undertook the business of mantua maker'.[59]

Another way of reducing costs and sharing the risks involved in establishing a business was to establish a partnership with another woman. Sister partnerships were common in the millinery business. The most well-known sister trading partnership in eighteenth-century Ireland was that of Mary Ann McCracken and her sister Margaret. The sisters established a muslin manufacturing business in Belfast in the last quarter of the eighteenth century. The correspondence of the McCracken sisters gives some impression of the logistics of running a small textile enterprise in Belfast in the last decades of the eighteenth century. The McCrackens' mother, Ann Joy, was from a well-established Belfast merchant family and had a small cloth business of her own so that the decision of the sisters to go into business was not that unusual from the family point of view.

The production line of the sisters' venture began with the buying of cotton yarn that was then distributed to weavers in and around Belfast. The weavers wove the cloth and returned it to the McCrackens. The sisters encouraged the weavers to be innovative in their work and they were pioneers in the production of patterned and checked muslin. The woven cloth was sold, either through personal orders or through travelling salesmen employed by the McCrackens. The sisters also had agents in Dublin.[60] When their brother Henry was in jail in Dublin, they travelled from Belfast to visit him, armed with a large consignment of muslins, which they hoped to sell.[61] In their absence their mother looked after the business while at the same time continuing to produce and sell cloth herself.[62] The McCrackens appreciated the central role that personal connections played in a successful business in the eighteenth century as orders came through friends and friends of friends. The financial profit which the sisters made from their business is not recorded although on one occasion the £90 which a man was employed to collect on their behalf was quickly used to pay the legal expenses for the defence of Thomas Russell of the United Irishmen and a family friend.[63] Despite a declining market in the early nineteenth century, the business survived until 1815.

What is striking about the McCracken experience is the fact that mother and daughters ran separate but probably very similar businesses. This suggests that businesses established by single women were often small scale and required only a small amount of capital to be established. They could be run from the family home with no special room allocated to their operation and sales depended on the personal connections of the family. If the family had a trading background then knowledgeable advice, finance and business networks were also available in the home. The businesses may also have been a part-time rather than a full-time occupation for many single women who may not necessarily have depended on the business for their livelihood. Mary Ann McCracken claimed that she persuaded her sister to start the business 'so that she might have a little money to use as she pleased'.[64] Poverty or the need to make a living were, therefore, not the only motives which persuaded single women to start a business in the late eighteenth century. To 'make a little money to use as she pleased' may also have been the motive of the women in the O'Connell family who included their own cloth among the goods to be sent abroad for sale by their male relatives.[65]

The McCracken business lasted over twenty years but most businesses established by single women appear to have been of much shorter duration. While the trading career of some Belfast widows can be traced through their advertisements in the *Belfast Newsletter* over many years and usually until their death, it is not possible to do the same for single women. Most of the latter advertised for limited periods of time, often no more than two or three years. This suggests that single women operated on their own for only a small portion of their lives, a trend corroborated by the trade directories which, as Figure 1 indicates, provide evidence that few women, single or otherwise, maintained a business on their own for any length of time. The trade directories also reveal that some married women continued to run separate businesses after they were married but they were in the minority. Occasionally, the change in the Christian name of the proprietor indicates that the management had been passed on to another female relative, possibly a single sister or daughter. Marriage was undoubtedly the most common reason for the dissolution of the business. The expansion in the textile industry in eighteenth-century towns, therefore, increased the opportunities for single women to earn an independent income but for many it represented only a brief period in their lives before they got married.

Poor women

Unlike middle-class women such as the McCracken sisters who worked for leisure money, the urban-based women who were compelled to earn a living by working outside the home could not afford to advertise their services or register their name in trade directories.[66] The women hucksters and pedlars who so annoyed the Dublin corporation in the seventeenth century continued to flourish in the eighteenth century. Some of these women may have had a regular business supplying dairy products and fruit to houses on a daily or weekly basis.[67] Others sold baskets of vegetables and fruit in the street or found work as charwomen or washerwomen. The textile and manufacturing industries provided employment for women, particularly in the Liberties where most of the city's textile production took place. Rural-based women also moved into local towns to work as charwomen, washerwomen, pedlars, hawkers and hucksters.[68]

Prostitution had always been a problem in the garrison town of Dublin but as the city expanded in the middle decades of the eighteenth century, it became a haven for young girls anxious to leave home and find employment in the city. One of the most famous prostitutes in Dublin was Margaret Leeson who in 1797 published a memoir of her life. Leeson had come to Dublin as a young girl, fleeing, she claimed, from a violent home where her brother had beaten her with a horsewhip. While in Dublin she became pregnant and was disowned by her family and lover. She subsequently presided over the most well-known brothel in the city, counting lord lieutenants and other members of the Irish establishment among her customers.[69]

For Leeson, prostitution proved a financially rewarding occupation but most of the women who worked as prostitutes in eighteenth-century

Dublin lived less glamorous lives and received far less reward for their services. They worked from the streets or in small one-roomed brothels in inner city districts such as the Smock Alley neighbourhood, notorious for its night life. These women appear only fleetingly in the historical record, usually to be condemned as corrupters of morals or as the inmates of public institutions concerned with their reform and rescue. The first Irish institution aimed exclusively at reform of female prostitutes was the Magdalen Asylum founded in Dublin in 1766 by Lady Arbella Denny. Denny's aim was pre-eminently practical: to give young prostitutes an alternative means of making a living. The women in the Asylum were trained in needlework and general domestic duties. Denny kept a detailed list of the girls whom she selected for the Asylum, noting their age, the length of time that they spent in the Institution and her opinion of their general demeanour and behaviour. Denny endeavoured to find a home and work for all the women when they left the Asylum, information about which she also entered in the women's notes. The Asylum records thus provide some insight into the background and life of young prostitutes in eighteenth-century Dublin.[70] Between 1767 and 1798, 388 women entered the Asylum. The girls chosen had an average age of nineteen although the youngest was twelve and the eldest thirty-two. Most were recommended by a governor of the institution or a clergyman but by the 1780s, members of the girls' family, often a girl's mother, petitioned Lady Denny directly on their relatives' behalf. A small number of women opted to petition for entry in their own name. The vast majority of the women admitted lived in Dublin prior to admittance and most entered with few or no possessions of their own.

Included among the inmates were ten mantua makers and a woman who had worked as apprentice to a glover for five years, but the majority were unskilled in any occupation apart from being able to do some plain or coarse needlework, adequate for undergarments but not for gown making or embroidery and of little economic value in an increasingly crowded textile market. Others were skilled in 'country business', suggesting that they had been reared on a farm or had worked as domestic servants in farming households. The average stay in the Asylum was two years and 64 per cent of the 388 stayed for the full time. There were significant material rewards for those who abided by the rules of the institution. On entry each applicant was given a new set of clothes that could be taken away if an inmate was evicted for bad behaviour. When a woman was expelled for violating a rule or being deemed unsuitable for the institution's reform programme, Lady Denny was always careful to note that they were sent away in old clothes having not earned the right to new garments. The appeal of a new set of clothes clearly drew some of the women to the Asylum as the records frequently note that the women arrived in borrowed clothes which were returned to their owners when the inmates acquired their new outfit.

The girls were trained in needlework, embroidery and tambour work and general domestic skills. Reading and writing skills were also taught albeit with mixed success, judging by the number of girls who could not sign their name on leaving the institution. When the women left they were initially given a cash bounty of three guineas as well as religious books and needles and tambour handles to set themselves up in the textile business. Discovering that the bounty was taken by girls who subsequently returned to prostitution, Lady Denny changed the rules to pay it in instalments: a guinea on departure from the Asylum and two guineas after two years if the woman had not worked as a prostitute in the meantime.

There appears to have been a high rate of payment of the full bounty which suggests that the majority of women convinced Lady Denny that they had reformed their lives. Most were found work in domestic service, often in the household of one of the patronesses of the Asylum, although some married or returned to their families. Twenty-three of the women emigrated as indentured servants to North America, with the institution paying their passage and giving them money as well as blankets and other comforts for the journey. Positions as domestic servants were arranged for them on arrival in America.

Religious affiliation is not recorded for every woman but of the 129 for whom we have information, forty-nine were Catholic, seventy-six members of the Church of Ireland, one was a Quaker and another was Presbyterian. Two women who were probably Catholic claimed to prefer to be designated as Protestants. Given that preference was given to Protestant applicants, it is highly likely that some of those registered as Protestant were in fact Catholic. The fact that women lied about their religion to gain admission and that the majority stayed for the full time suggests that the material benefits of the Asylum were recognised and appreciated. Elizabeth Kehoe who petitioned in her own name to be admitted into the Asylum said that her Catholic friends had urged to 'take the character of a Magdalen' so that she could gain training in needlework and learn to read, both of which she accomplished. She left the Asylum after two years with new clothes and a tambour handle and needle, signing her name on receipt of them. Mary Roche, another Catholic, aged twenty said that 'distress and a desire to be instructed in needlework were her only motives for coming to the house'.[71] Other women were sent to the institution by mothers anxious that their daughters would learn a skill by which they could lead a more respectable life.

Domestic service

Whether they found work as a prostitute or in the food or textile business, urbanisation opened up new economic opportunities for women from poor backgrounds in the eighteenth century. In rural Ireland the opportunities for remunerative work for women also increased. As elsewhere in western Europe, domestic service provided many young women with access to waged work. As noted in Chapter 3, the expansion in the number of domestic servants employed in Ireland began in the second half of the seventeenth century with the building of large estate houses. The new multi-roomed houses were built on the assumption that there would be staff available to maintain and service them. Most large estate houses employed a staff establishment that included a female housekeeper, housemaid, kitchenmaid and dairymaid. Many households had a lady's maid, nurserymaids for the children, a governess and a laundress as well as additional house- and kitchenmaids. In the mid-eighteenth century, on the Brownlow estate- in County Antrim, a total of twenty-six staff were employed and of those eleven were women.[72]

Recruitment of staff at the higher levels of housekeeper, governess and cook was usually through personal recommendations and preference was given to English or non-Irish women. Emily Fitzgerald, duchess of Leinster, went to some trouble to appoint an English housekeeper for Carton House in the 1760s. French or English governesses were also preferred to women from Irish backgrounds. Three of the six governesses employed on the Brownlow estate in County Armagh between 1772 and 1778 had French surnames while two others may have been English.[73] The large number of governesses employed over such a short period of time testifies to the difficulties of recruiting non-Irish staff to rural estate houses. The search for a satisfactory cook is also evident in the household accounts of many Irish houses. A good male cook, preferably English or French, was the ideal but many Irish households had to settle for a succession of Irish women instead. On the Brownlow estate, a total of ten cooks (seven men and three women) were employed in the twenty-two-year period from 1772 to 1794, some only staying for a few months, before being discharged because they were 'not a good cook'.[74]

Within the hierarchy of the domestic staff of the estate house, local Irish women found most opportunities for employment at the lower levels as maids in the house, kitchen, nursery or dairy. The most sought-after position was lady's maid. In the 1790s, the *Dublin Evening Post* regularly carried advertisements from women looking for employment as a lady's maid.

The advertisements outline the skills that the applicants considered to be the main requirements of the job. Many of the women had worked as mantua makers or milliners and clearly expected that their dressmaking and sewing skills would be useful for the duties of a lady's maid. Most also proclaimed their ability to 'get up small linen' or underwear. All the women claimed that they could dress hair and some also noted that they could also write and keep accounts.[75] The advertisements suggest that a lady's maid was perceived to have a certain status in society. For poor girls who had worked as assistants to milliners and mantua makers, the post of lady's maid could bring social promotion as well as better wages.[76] The position was also attractive to impoverished middle-class women for whom a respectable address and accommodation was of more importance than wages.

Women who took employment in the lower grades of domestic staff as house-, kitchen- or dairymaids came from poor, rural backgrounds. These positions involved more menial work than that of lady's maid or housekeeper and families from the middling ranks in society declined to send their daughters into this type of service considering it shameful to do so. In the mid-eighteenth century, for example, Charles O'Hara distinguished between the very poor families of County Sligo in which the daughters 'generally go to some sort of service when grown up' and better-off families in which the daughters and sons stayed at home until marriage.[77]

Most staff in large estate houses were recruited through word of mouth and personal recommendation rather than through newspaper advertisements. A recommendation might come from servants whose families lived on the estate. Edward Synge, Bishop of Elphin in the west of Ireland, recruited the niece of his housekeeper as a maid for his daughter in Dublin. Certain families may also have provided servants over several generations to the same house. Sisters are, for example, recorded working in the same household while other women were employed in a house because their husbands were employed outside on the estate. A servant who performed satisfactorily could receive a reference on leaving that could be used as a recommendation for her next employer.[78]

It is difficult to generalise about the wages earned through domestic service in a 'big house' because estates differed in the amounts and the method by which staff were paid. In some households the basic wage was supplemented by an allowance for tea or clothes. 'Board money' was also paid on a regular basis on Irish estates. Board money was normally a cash allowance given for food and other expenses when the staff travelled outside the estate, usually to the Dublin or London homes of the family. On some estates, however, board wages were a permanent part of the wage, paid to staff who did not live in the main estate house. Another problem in comparing wages is that owners of large estates were often in a position to pay higher wages than some of the less well-off landlords. The basic wage of servants was also often supplemented by tips from house guests, rewards for special services and legacies left by grateful employers. Women staff might also be given presents of second-hand clothes, particularly gowns which were expensive to purchase.

The method by which estate staff were paid also varied. In large households, wages were paid in two instalments, in summer and winter or early spring each year. In other households, small sums of money were made throughout the year for the purchase of goods by the servant. Part of the wage might also be sent to the servant's family. Thus on the O'Hara estate in County Sligo, Catherine Cole was hired in February 1745 as a nurserymaid for an annual wage of £3 and remained in service until May 1747. During that time money was paid on her behalf to her mother and to her father as well as to a shoemaker. While she was working Catherine received in cash £1. 2s. of her total wages and when she left service she was paid the remainder of her wages which amounted to £2. 5s. $5^1/_2$d.[79]

Staff who remained in service for a long time and who were not paid their full wage every year could build up considerable credit with their employer. Mrs Burn who was employed as a lady's maid on the French estate in Monivea, County Galway, in 1748 was owed £73. 13s. by 1761 from her annual wages of £10 and her employer agreed to pay her interest on the money which he owed her.[80] Mrs Burn was using her employer as a form of banker while her employer was in effect borrowing money from his servant. Elizabeth Cahill who worked all her life in the Reynolds household in Dublin 'accumulated some property during her long service, and had . . . assisted her family, and given marriage portions to three or four relatives'.[81] Cahill and other long-term servants were also in a position to lend money to friends and acquaintances.[82]

Most women, however, did not stay in service long enough to accumulate large sums of money. The majority of women employed on the O'Hara estate stayed for less than a year. Of eleven kitchenmaids employed between 1744 and 1757, only three stayed for more than a year.[83] A similar pattern emerges from other estates. On the Domville estate in County Dublin, in the years 1769–73, for example, many of the maids were employed for less than twelve months.[84] On other estates, lengths of service of a year to two years were common. The highest turnover of staff was among the lower grades of kitchen- and housemaid while the longest-serving staff was usually to be found in the higher grade of housekeeper. While long-term servants could, therefore, accumulate impressive savings, women who stayed in service for short periods of time left with far smaller sums or no cash at all. Typical of the money accumulated by the majority of female servants was the £2. 5s. 5½d. that Catherine Cole received on leaving her position after two and a quarter years' service.

An account book among the Brownlow estate papers notes the reasons why staff left their employment. Of thirty-three female staff, twelve were dismissed for unsatisfactory service. This usually included what was perceived as negligent or dishonest behaviour. Mary Black, Mrs Brownlow's maid, for example, was dismissed in 1779 after less than a year's service because she was 'silly and careless, spoiled or broke more things than double her wages'.[85] Esther Duffin, a housemaid, was discharged in 1783 after four years' service because 'a great deal of China and other articles being missing supposed to be stolen by a woman she had taken into the house'.[86] A housekeeper was dismissed after a year's service because she was 'negligent and extravagant' while a children's maid was discharged after four years because she 'behaved ill and not honestly', another because she was 'drinking and whoring'.[87] As one newspaper advertisement noted, 'sobriety, honesty and cleanliness' were the main qualities looked for in a good servant.[88]

The Brownlow account book suggests, however, that the service of the majority of women servants was satisfactory and that they left at their own choice rather than being dismissed. Sixteen women were noted as leaving 'at her own desire' or because they were ill or about to be married or to give birth. Two older women were retired with a pension and a nurse was discharged because there was 'no further occasion for her'.[89] She was presumably a wet nurse who had been employed to nurse an infant for eighteen months.

Marriage was clearly the main reason why most women left service. Although pregnancy (within marriage or outside it) may have led on some estates to dismissal, at least one of the women on the Brownlow estate, employed as a nurserymaid, continued to work until she was to 'lie in and nurse'.[90] Others continued to work after marriage but the majority of female domestic staff were young, single women who worked full-time for a wage for a short period of their lives. They did not expect, or presumably wish for, long-term employment. It might also be suggested that employers considered that most female domestic staff were short-term employees who could be dismissed when circumstances suited. The seasonal movement of the family to Dublin or London could result in a dismissal of all but a caretaker staff and new employees taken on when the family returned. Keane Oge O'Hara, for example, advised his wife to 'turn off all unnecessary servants and idlers' when she moved from their country house in County Sligo to join him in Dublin in the spring of 1715.[91] On the Domville estate in County Dublin, staff wages were calculated on a quarterly basis suggesting that it was expected that many of the women employed were not perceived as long-term employees. This may also explain the high turnover of household staff on the estate.[92]

For the small number of women who continued in employment on a long-term basis, domestic service provided a career structure in which satisfactory service was rewarded with higher wages and promotion. Peggy Watson was employed on the Brownlow estate in the 1770s as a nursery-maid at an annual wage of 4 guineas. She subsequently became a housemaid and in 1785 was promoted to the position of Mrs Brownlow's maid at a wage of 8 guineas, a position which she held for at least five years.[93] In 1774, Catherine Magee was promoted from her position as lady's maid to that of housekeeper which gave her an annual income of £15.[94]

Long-term employees could also be entrusted with considerable responsibility by their employers which must also have given them a certain status within the household. As housekeeper, for example, Catherine Magee would have been responsible for supervising the recruitment, work and the payment of the other women staff in the household. Other servants were entrusted with the maintenance of the house or the care of children during the absences of the landowner and his wife.[95]

Women who remained in service for a long time, however, constituted a tiny minority of the total number of women employed in domestic service. Overall, the evidence of household account books suggest a continual movement of female staff in and out of employment in the 'big house'. Apart from those who were employed full-time, many other women were employed on a part-time or occasional basis to work as nurses or maids during the illness of a member of a household or to help out with spring cleaning or some particular task. Estate accounts also indicate that local women provided other services such as washing clothes or supplying food produce for the staff and family in the house. Locally-based seamstresses were also employed to make underwear and other small items of clothing.

Domestic service expanded rapidly as a form of employment for women in the course of the eighteenth century. Outside the big estate house, many large and small farming households also began to employ young girls as maids. The Elphin census of 1744 suggests that it was common for farmers and, even cottiers, to employ two servants, one male and one female.[96] As in eighteenth-century England, domestic servants were 'an integral part of all but the poorest households'.[97]

In many parts of Ireland, women and men were hired on an annual basis at hiring fairs and were expected to perform a multitude of tasks both inside and outside the house. The hard work involved in these one-maid households was vividly described by Mary Leadbeater in her fictional dialogue between two young female servants, one of whom complained that there was 'no end to my work'.[98] The maid's tasks included dairy work, making butter and keeping the milk vessels spotlessly clean, baking and preparing meals in the kitchen, washing, sweeping and dusting the floors, stairs and furniture in the house, laundry work and serving food at mealtimes as well as making the beds.[99] Other female servants were expected to help out in the fields in the springtime and during the harvest. Limerick tenant farmer Nicholas Peacock recorded in his diary that the maids in his household worked outside picking barley, reaping and binding and pulling flax and peas as well as performing domestic chores in the house.

Relations between the head of the household and his or her domestic staff were often affectionate and caring but much depended on the financial resources and personality of the employer.[100] Bachelor Nicholas Peacock referred to his servants as his 'family' and gave them presents of cloth and money.[101] On large estates, like that of the Brownlows, long-term servants were provided in old age with a small pension or lodgings on the estate.[102] On the French estate, an old servant woman was kept on as a 'hen woman to attend the barn' and subsequently died in service.[103] Many servants, however, particularly those who worked in small households, must have been reduced to penury when they were no longer in a position to work. Edward Synge advised his daughter against employing an elderly married couple: 'I think it not prudent to engage with a deaf wizen'd old woman and gouty old man.'[104] Servants who remained in domestic service all their lives might, therefore, find themselves in a precarious economic position when, either through sickness or old age, they were no longer of use to their employers. Former servants were frequently to be found among those begging on the streets or seeking charity.[105]

Farm work and servants

The increased employment opportunities for young rural women in domestic service reflected the more general growth in the labouring classes of eighteenth century Ireland. The expansion in intensive forms of tillage farming such as the growing of flax and potatoes led to an increased demand for agricultural labour and farmers began to hire more outside labour to help with agricultural work.

For women, however, much of the paid agricultural work available was seasonal and occasional. In the spring women were hired on a daily basis to prepare the ground for planting. The majority of women worked for only three to four days a week. They picked stones, weeded and sowed potatoes. Later, at harvest time, large numbers of women were employed to make hay. Women were also hired to assist with turf making. On the Flower estate in Durrow, County Dublin, in the 1720s, women were paid 2d. to 3d. a day for such work and similar rates were recorded for other farms throughout the eighteenth century with no noticeable increase in the daily rate.

Arthur Young, however, noted that women were paid 4d. to 8d. a day for agricultural work on flax-growing farms in the 1770s, a wage which may reflect the relatively prosperous economy of flax-growing areas, particularly in the middle decades of the eighteenth century. Young itemised the different tasks performed by men and women in growing and harvesting flax and the economic value of each. The women's work involved clearing and weeding the ground, pulling the flax when it was ripe, rippling it to save the seed and spreading it to dry. Women then beat the flax to extract the fibre and finally spun it into yarn. The well-known prints of William Hinck provide a visual record of the nature of women's labour in the domestic linen industry.[106]

In the households of many tenant farmers and cottiers, particularly in the west and north-west, linen cloth and yarn production was a vital part of the family economy. On some farms, the entire process from the growing of flax seed to the production of the cloth was done in-house with the whole family engaged in the field work in the spring and summer while in the winter the girls (as young as seven) and women spun and the men and boys wove. The cloth was then sold in the local market.[107] On other farms, no weaving took place. Instead, the yarn was taken to be sold in the market.

As Brenda Collins pointed out, the efficient operation of the family economy was dependent on the composition of the household.[108] This could change over time as sons and daughters grew up and left the family home. A family without the 'appropriate age and sex mix' had two options.[109] Yarn could be given out to be spun by women in separate households, or labour in the shape of itinerant weavers or live-in spinners could be hired for specified periods of time. In Limerick, in the 1740s, the bachelor, Nicholas Peacock regularly gave out yarn to be spun by local women.[110] A woman could earn 3d. to 5d. a day for spinning yarn in her own home. Such work was attractive to married women because they could combine spinning with their own household chores or 'little family trifles' as Young described them.[111] Among poor families in the west of Ireland, the money earned by women for spinning could often lift the family above subsistence level as the cash was used to pay the rent.[112] In Westport, Arthur Young noted that: 'In their domestic economy, they reckon that the men feed the family with their labour in the field, and the women pay the rent by spinning.'[113] Payment could also be made in kind. Nicholas Peacock regularly paid his spinners with quantities of produce or cloth, recording on one occasion that a woman to whom he gave a peck of oats was to 'give me work or money' in return.[114]

In all of the households where women spun, a 'family economy' prevailed but the relative contribution of men and women varied. In the first type of household, described by Collins, all members of the household worked on the same product with the men ultimately producing the cloth which could be sold in the market for cash. In the second, it was the women's spinning work which brought the cash, or sometimes the food, into the house. Among poor families in the west of Ireland, the traditional gender roles were reversed. Men provided the food while the work of the women earned the cash income in the household.

In households where spinners were hired, yet another version of the household economy can be detected. Women were hired to spin for a specified period of time, usually six to twelve months. The amount which they were paid varied, depending on the locality and size of the farm and the number of spinners available for hire. On large farms in the 1770s, women spinners were hired for £3 per year and their board and lodgings. Household accounts for smaller farms record lesser payments ranging from £1 to £1.10s. per year.[115]

Hired spinners were expected to do 'some drudgery in the house' as well as spinning a certain amount of yarn per day.[116] Household accounts also suggest that payment could often take the form of seed and other agricultural produce which was delivered to the girl's family. When the girls were paid cash, it was, like the payments to domestic servants in estate houses, in small sums to pay for specific items bought from a local dressmaker, travelling pedlar or at the market or fair. Thus in the account book of the Orr family who had a farm in County Down, payments were recorded to women farm servants for purchases of muslin, buckles, shoes, hats, handkerchiefs and other clothing items as well as when they attended the local fair. Money and flax seed were also given to members of the girls' families.[117] On the Rossiter farm in County Wexford in the 1780s, women spinners were paid in bundles of linen as well as cash.[118] Income earned by women hired for spinning could, therefore, form part of the family economy, even though the girls were living outside the home.

In the south of Ireland, spinning of wool was more common than the spinning of flax yarn. The export of wool and woollen goods was an important part of the Munster economy in the middle decades of the eighteenth century. It is estimated that at its peak in the 1760s about 30,000 rural women were regularly employed in the southern parts of Ireland in spinning wool for the English market.[119] As in the flax producing areas, the family economy could take different forms in households which concentrated on wool and woollen cloth production. In the households of independent weavers, all members of the family were involved in the process with the women assisting with the combing and carding processes as well as spinning the wool.[120] Large woollen manufacturers also gave out wool to be spun by poor women in their own households.[121] Spinning of wool does not, however, appear to have been as financially rewarding as the spinning of linen. Young noted that most women earned 9d. to 12d. a week for spinning wool in the 1770s while the average payment for spinning linen yarn was 3d. to 5d. per day.[122]

Milking of cows and making butter were traditionally tasks associated with women but the commercialisation of the dairy industry in the southern part of Ireland in the eighteenth century gave new status to women's work in the dairy. On farms which specialised in the production of milk and butter, the work of women was central and most of the labour was distributed among family members with women being responsible for the milking of cows and the production of butter.[123] The commercial sale of butter was dominated by Cork butter merchants but on small farms with one or two cows, surplus milk and butter could be sold locally and it is likely that such sales were frequently undertaken by women. In the 1770s, a visitor to Ireland recorded that cabin holders hung out a white rag on a stick to indicate that milk was on sale.[124] The business accounts of the O'Connell family include small quantities of butter received from local women and shipped overseas from Cork.[125]

Dairy work could also provide opportunities for waged work as large farms and most large estate houses in eighteenth-century Ireland employed dairymaids. The work involved a certain amount of specialised skill in which maintaining high standards of hygiene was at a premium. A good dairymaid was 'treated with a degree of respect',[126] and could be rewarded with higher wages than the less skilled housemaid. She could also earn more than other hired female labour in rural Ireland such as the spinners of linen and wool.

Conclusion

The eighteenth century was a time of expanding economic opportunities for women in urban and rural Ireland. Women working outside the family home became a common sight as they found work as domestic servants, shopkeepers and farm workers. Far from condemning the working woman, economic reformers identified paid work for poor women as a means by which the economy of Ireland could prosper. Contemporaries recognised the contribution which working women made to the family economy, particularly in rural areas.

The opening of new ways in which single women could earn a living was the most dramatic change from previous centuries. Few single women, however, worked for long or in large enterprises. Most abandoned their businesses and regular employment on marriage. Once married, women's incomes merged with those of their husbands, although among trading families women sometimes established auxiliary enterprises alongside the business of their husbands. The majority of widows also abandoned their involvement in commerce when they could with only a relatively small proportion continuing to manage their husbands' affairs.

Despite the limited periods of time during which women earned a paid income for their work, the evidence suggests that it could give them a certain amount of financial independence. A number of eighteenth-century writers record the presence of female servants at markets spending their money on fashionable clothes. Mary Leadbeater's moral tales warned of the poor quality of bought goods and urged the servants to save their money and make their own clothes. Her depiction of Nancy, the maid who got into debt with the local shopkeeper, was probably, however, more typical than that of Rose who saved money to buy wool and cloth to make her own garments.[127] Mary Delany lamented that dairymaids had abandoned their traditional dress for 'large hoops and velvet hoods'.[128] In rural communities young domestic servants may, in fact, have been among the small number of people who had regular access to surplus cash, albeit in small quantities. Nicholas Peacock, for example, who managed a middling-sized tenant farm in north Limerick in the 1740s, recorded in his diary that he borrowed cash from his maids on a number of occasions.[129] And, as noted already, a woman who served the Reynolds's family for many years accumulated sufficient cash to pay marriage portions for some of her nieces.

As migrant workers often did, young, unmarried women living away from home expanded their social life and had an opportunity to return home dressed in fine clothes. Spinners participated in spinning competitions or *keatings*.[130] Nicholas Peacock noted in his diary that his servants went to the local patterns and he gave them money to celebrate St Patrick's Day and Christmas. Nuala Cullen has also pointed to the new skills in cooking and housework acquired by servants while the writings of Mary Leadbeater and others unwittingly testify to the excitement of young women with money to spend on fashionable clothes and the to try out newfangled customs such as the drinking of tea.[131]

Economic opportunities for women remained, however, highly volatile and subject to the overall state of the Irish economy. The textile industry was in decline from the 1780s and, consequently, the income to be derived from it also diminished. The establishment of charitable institutions, catering for specific categories of women: widows, orphans and young prostitutes, gives some idea of where the impact of the downward trend in the economy fell hardest. Unemployed and destitute women crowded into inner city Dublin, which experienced 'unprecedented overcrowding' in the 1790s.[132]

The decline in the textile industry coincided with changes in the demographic pattern of Irish society. The reasons for the dramatic rise in the Irish population in the second half of the eighteenth century has been the subject of intense debate among historians for several decades. A number of factors have been identified as crucial including a reduction in the age of marriage and a decline in infant mortality.[133] Marriage at a young age expanded the size of families and improvements in diet and general health meant that a larger number of children had a better chance of survival to adulthood. The changing circumstances of Irish society in the late eighteenth century had catastrophic consequences for many rural families. As income from spinning disappeared or dramatically declined, more and more women from poor families were giving birth to children that they could not afford to feed. Increasingly, the main economic contribution of women to the family economy was earned not through spinning but through begging. The economic advantages that women may have gained in the boom time of the eighteenth century had, therefore, begun to disappear by 1800.[134]

Notes

1 Will of Elizabeth Shipboy, undated, PRONI, D/530/13. See also Kerby Miller *et al.* (Eds), *Irish Immigrants in the Land of Canaan. Letters and Memoirs From Colonial and Revolutionary America, 1675–1815* (New York, 2003), pp. 331–5 for an account of Robert's brother Thomas, who emigrated to North America from where he wrote to Robert and Elizabeth.

2 *Belfast Newsletter*, 19–22 February 1788, 12–16 June 1789, 3–6 August 1790, 3–6 July 1792, 28 December 1792–1 January 1793, 20–23 June 1794, 1–5 June 1795; PRONI D/530/14; 22/6, 7. See also T. H. Mullan, *Coleraine in Georgian Times* (Belfast, 1877), pp. 92–3.

3 PRONI, D/530/22/19.

4 Will of Elizabeth Shipboy, undated, PRONI, D/530/13; obit in *Belfast Newsletter*, 4 June 1795.

5 David Dickson, *New Foundations: Ireland, 1660–1800* (revised edition, Dublin, 2000), p. 109.

6 David Dickson, 'Capital and County: 1600–1800' in Art Cosgrove (Ed), *Dublin Through the Ages* (Dublin, 1988), p. 69.

7 PRONI, D/530/22/10.

8 Will of Elizabeth Shipboy, undated, PRONI, D/530/13.

9 Based on an analysis of wills cited in the transcript books of the Registry of Deeds, Dublin and PRONI, T/581.

10 Will of Elizabeth Shipboy, undated PRONI, D/530/13; correspondence from James McAdam to Jane McAdam (PRONI, D/530/22/20-23); *Belfast Newsletter*, 4 May 1774.

11 Correspondence from James McAdam to Jane McAdam (PRONI, D/530/22/20-23).

12 See, for example, PRONI, D/1140/20.

13 *Belfast Newsletter*, 4 May 1774.

14 *Freeman's Journal*, 10 February 1780.

15 *Belfast Newsletter*, 9 May 1766.

16 Ibid., 12 March 1771.

17 L. A. Clarkson, 'The Carrick-on-Suir Woollen Industry in the Eighteenth Century' in *Irish Economic and Social History*, **xvi** (1989), p. 34.

18 The story of the Seed business can be traced through the index of the *Belfast Newsletter* (www.ucs.louisiana.edu/~jcg3525/Main.html). See also Michaela Collins, 'Women in the Belfast Newsletter 1738 to 1770' (unpublished MA dissertation, Queen's University, Belfast, 1994), pp. 40–4.

19 Catherine Cox, 'Women and Business in Eighteenth-Century Dublin: A Case Study' in Bernadette Whelan (Ed), *Women and Paid Work in Ireland, 1500–1930* (Dublin, 2000), p. 40. See also Imelda Brophy, 'Women in the Workforce' in David Dickson (Ed), *The Gorgeous Mask. Dublin, 1700–1850* (Dublin, 1987), pp. 51–63.

20 See, for example, the obituary of Mrs Elizabeth Clark, *Belfast Newsletter*, 21 February 1764.

21 *The Universal Advertiser*, 6 January 1756.

22 Collins, op. cit. See also *The Universal Advertiser*, 6 January 1756 for another example in Dublin.

23 Collins, op. cit.; *Belfast Newsletter*, 7 June 1757.

24 Thomas Reynolds, *The Life of Thomas Reynolds, Esq.* (2 vols., London, 1839), vol. i, pp. 61–2.

25 Ibid., vol. i, pp. 61–2, 68–9, 78–9, 88–90.

26 *Dublin Evening Post*, 19 January 1796.

27 *Freeman's Journal*, 20 May 1798. See also PRONI, D/1721/1, p. 13.

28 Cox, 'Women and Business in Eighteenth-Century Dublin: A Case Study', p. 41; L. A. Clarkson and E. M. Crawford, 'Life After Death: Widows in Carrick-on-Suir, 1799' in Margaret MacCurtain and Mary O'Dowd (Eds), *Women in Early Modern Ireland*, (Edinburgh, 1991), pp. 236–54.

29 See Figure 1.

30 Maureen Wall, 'The Catholic Merchants, Manufacturers and Traders of Dublin, 1778–1782' in *Reportium Novum*, **2** (2) (1959–60), pp. 298–323.

31 For a study of the Irish merchant community see, for example, L. M. Cullen, *The Irish Brandy Houses of Eighteenth-Century France* (Dublin, 2000). For marital strategies see Amala Bilbao Acedos, *The Irish Community in the Basque Country, c. 1700–1800* (Dublin, 2003), pp. 23, 54–5.

32 See pp. 160–2, 257 below.

33 See Figures 2–3. Richard Lucas, *The Cork Directory for 1787, Including the Adjacent Outports of Youghal, Kinsale, Cove, Passage and the Manufacturing Towns of Inishannon and Bandon* (Cork, 1787). For women in the print business see Robert Munter, *A Dictionary of the Print Trade in Ireland, 1550–1775* (New York, 1988).

34 Toby Barnard, 'The World of Goods and County Offaly in the Early Eighteenth Century' in William Nolan and Timothy P. O'Neill (Eds), *Offaly History and Society. Interdisciplinary Essays on the History of an Irish County* (Dublin, 1998), pp. 371–92; Sarah Foster, 'Going Shopping in 18th Century Dublin' in *Things*, **4** (Summer, 1996), pp. 33–61.

35 See, for example, receipt for goods supplied by James and John Hamilton whose shop was on Upper Ormond Quay in Dublin (PRONI, T/3765/L/3/3/1).

36 *Belfast Newsletter*, 6 June 1769, 22–25 March 1774; PRONI, D/717/1-27.

37 Richard Twiss, *A Tour in Ireland in 1775* (London, 1776), p. 34.

38 A. C. Elias, Junior (Ed), *Memoirs of Laetitia Pilkington* (2 vols., Athens, University of Georgia, 1997), vol. i, p. 313. See also Amy M. Froide, 'Old Maids: the Lifecycle of Single Women in Early Modern England' in Judith M. Bennett and Amy M. Froide (Eds), *Single Women in the European Past 1250–1800* (Philadelphia, 1999), pp. 99–100.

39 Mary Leadbeater, *Cottage Biography. Being a Collection of the Lives of the Irish Peasantry* (London, 1822; new edition, Athy, Co. Kildare, 1987), pp. 43–4.

40 Ibid., p. 87.

41 Ibid.

42 Reynolds, *The Life of Thomas Reynolds, Esq.*, vol. i, pp. 82–3.

43 John Styles, 'Clothing the North: the Supply of Non-élite Clothing in the Eighteenth-Century North of England' in *Textile History*, **25** (2) (1994), p. 152; Mary Prior, 'Women and the Urban Economy: Oxford, 1500–1800' in M. Prior (Ed), *Women in English Society, 1500–1800* (London, 1985), pp. 110–13.

44 Collins, op. cit.

45 See, for example, Account Book of Patrick Rossiter for 1780, Business Records, Wex 15/1 (National Archives of Ireland); Household Accounts in Story Papers (PRONI, T/2854/1).

46 See Mairéad Dunlevy, *Dress in Ireland. A History* (Dublin, 1989), p. 128.

47 Accounts kept by Lady Louisa Conolly, 1778–1788 (Trinity College, Dublin MS 3955). See also Maria Luddy (Ed), *The Diary of Mary Mathew* (Thurles, 1991).

48 Beverly Lemire, 'Developing Counsumerism and the Ready-Made Clothing Trade in Britain, 1750–1800' in *Textile History* **15** (1984), p. 22.

49 *Dublin Evening Post*, 12 January 1796. See also Dunlevy, *Dress in Ireland*, pp. 95–6.

50 Deborah Simonton, 'Apprenticeship: Training and Gender in Eighteenth-Century England' in Maxine Berg (Ed), *Markets and Manufacture in Early Industrial England* (London, 1991), pp. 248–9.

51 *Dublin Falkiner's Journal*, 26–29 January 1771.

52 Collins, 'Women in the Belfast Newsletter, 1738 to 1770', pp. 52–3.

53 *Belfast Newsletter*, 12–16 June 1789.

54 Ibid., 27 April 1762.

55 *Dublin Falkiner's Journal*, 26–29 January 1771.

56 Simonton, 'Apprenticeship: Training and Gender in Eighteenth-Century England', pp. 248–9.

57 Register of Bishop Foy's School in Waterford (Representative Church Body, MS 523).

58 *Belfast Newsletter*, 17 April 1767.

59 Leadbeater, *Cottage Biography*, pp. 44–5.

60 Mary McNeill, *The Life and Times of Mary Ann McCracken, 1770–1866. A Belfast Panorama* (Dublin, 1960), pp. 206, 218.

61 Ibid., p. 112.

62 Ibid., pp. 115, 166.

63 Ibid., p. 218.

64 Ibid., p. 57.

65 Mrs M. J. O'Connell, *The Last Colonel of the Irish Brigade* (Dublin, 1892; reprinted 1977), pp. 33, 46–7; O'Connell Papers, UCD, Dept of Archives, P12/7/127, 129, 130.

66 See William Laffan (Ed), *The Cries of Dublin. Drawn From the Life by Hugh Douglas Hamilton, 1760* (Dublin, 2003).

67 See, for example, payments to butter and milk women in the Dublin accounts of the Kenmare household (PRONI, D/4151/R/2, 18–29 December 1753).

68 Clarkson and Crawford, 'Life After Death: Widows in Carrick-on-Suir, 1799', p. 249.

69 *Memoirs of Mrs Margaret Leeson, Written By Herself and Interspersed with Several Interesting and Amusing Anecdotes, On Some of the Most Striking Characters of Great-Britain and Ireland* (3 vols., 1795–7. Edited by Mary Lyons (Dublin, 1995)).

70 This analysis is based on Rosemary Raughter, 'A Natural Tenderness: Women's Philanthropy in Eighteenth-Century Ireland' (unpublished MA thesis, University College, Dublin, 1992) and the Minutes Books of the Magdalen Asylum in the library of the Representative Church Body, Dublin (MS 551/1-2).

71 Loc. cit., p. 263.

72 Unless otherwise indicated, the information in this section is taken from Mary O'Dowd, 'Women and Paid Work in Ireland, 1500–1800' in Whelan (Ed), *Women and Paid Work in Ireland*, pp. 13–29.

73 Account Book, Brownlow Estate Papers (PRONI, D/1928/A/1/8, pp. 1, 5–6). Miss Lidderdale, employed for a brief period in 1775, and Miss Sinclair, employed in 1778, may have come from England. Miss Julie Gallagher, employed for a few months between 1777 and 1778, may have been Irish or Scottish.

74 Account Book, Brownlow Estate Papers (PRNOI, D/1928/A/2/5, p. 141). See also PRONI, D/1928/A/1/8, pp. 2, 9, 25.

75 *Dublin Evening Post*, 10 February 1791; see also 8 January 1791, 2 April 1791, 21 April 1791, 2 July 1791.

76 See J. Jean Hecht, *The Domestic Servant Class in Eighteenth-Century England* (London, 1956), pp. 61–2 for a similar background for ladies' maids in England.

77 NLI MS 20397, Account of Co. Sligo by Charles O'Hara, c. 1700–1773.

78 For examples see Account Book, Brownlow Estate Records (PRONI, D/1928/A/1/8, D/1928/A/2/5). See also Maria Luddy, 'Martha McTier and William Drennan: a "Domestic" History' in Jean Agnew (Ed), *The Drennan-McTier Letters, Volume 1, 1776–1793* (Dublin, 1998), pp. xxxii–xxxiii.

79 Charles O'Hara the Elder, Wages Book, 1743–1776 (NLI, MS 16705).

80 See NLI, MS 4918, p. 405. Her wage was increased to £15 in 1761.

81 Reynolds, *The Life of Thomas Reynolds, Esq*, i, p. 109.

82 Ibid.

83 Charles O'Hara the Elder, Wages Book, 1743–1776 (NLI, MS 16705, pp. 15–16).

84 Domville Papers (NLI, MS 11844).

85 PRONI, D/1928/A/1/8, p. 12.

86 PRONI, D/1928/A/1/8, p. 31.

87 PRONI, D/1928/A/1/8, pp. 7, 22, 23.

88 *Belfast Newsletter*, 8 April 1777.

89 PRONI, D/1928/A/1/8, p. 30.

90 PRONI, D/1928/A.1/8, p. 32.

91 Keane Oge O'Hara to Eleanor O'Hara, 15 February 1715 (NLI, MS 20278).

92 NLI, MS 11461.

93 PRONI, D/1928/A/1/8, pp. 13, 34, 121.

94 Loc. cit., D/1928/A/2/5, p. 128; D/1928/A/1/8, pp. 5, 82.

95 See, for example, Nurse Sutton who was paid with other servants to travel with children from the Perceval estate in Ireland to England in 1714 (British Library, Egmont Ms 47047, p. 42).

96 National Archives of Ireland, M 2466.

97 D. A. Kent, 'Ubiquitous But Invisible: Female Domestic Servants in Mid-Eighteenth Century London' in *History Workshop Journal*, **28** (Autumn, 1989), p. 111.

98 Mary Leadbeater, *Cottage Dialogues Among the Irish Peasantry* (London, 1811), p. 32.

99 Ibid., pp. 39–53.

100 See, for example, *Retrospections of Dorothea Herbert, 1770–1806* (Dublin, 1929–30, reprinted Dublin, 1988), pp. 14, 17–18, 54, 330.

101 See, for example, NLI, MS 16091, 27 January 1742, 25 December 1745.

102 Mary Donnelly worked on the Brownlow estate as a housemaid for over thirty years at an annual wage of £4 (raised in her last years of service to 4 guineas).

She was retired in 1779 with a pension of 2 guineas per year (PRONI, D/1928/A/1/8, p. 12).

103 NLI, MS 4918, French Papers, p. 407. See also *Belfast Newsletter*, 17–20 September 1776.

104 Marie-Louise Legg (Ed), *The Synge Letters. Bishop Edward Synge to His Daughter Alicia, Roscommon to Dublin 1746–1752* (Dublin, 1996), p. 244. See also pp. 226–8, 233, 240.

105 Mairéad Dunlevy, 'Dublin in the Nineteenth Century: Domestic Evidence' in Brian P. Kennedy and Raymond Gillespie (Eds), *Ireland, Art into History* (Dublin, 1994), p. 206.

106 W. H. Crawford, 'Women in the Domestic Linen industry' in MacCurtain and O'Dowd (Eds), *Women in Early Modern Ireland*, p. 258; Mary E. Daly, *Women and Work in Ireland* (Dundalk, 1997), pp. 12–14; Arthur Young, *A Tour in Ireland With General Observations on the Present State of That Kingdom* . . . (2 parts, London, 1780); 'Illustrations of the Irish Linen Industry in 1783 by William Hincks' in *Ulster Folklife*, **23** (1977), pp. 1–32.

107 Brenda Collins, 'Proto-industrialization and Pre-Famine Emigration' in *Social History*, **7** (1982), p. 130; see also, Young, *A Tour in Ireland*, part I, pp. 161, 182, 193.

108 Collins, 'Proto-industrialization and pre-Famine Emigration' p. 132.

109 L. A. Clarkson, *Proto-Industrialization: the First Phase of Industrialization?* (London, 1985), p. 48.

110 NLI, MS 16091.

111 Young, *A Tour in Ireland*, part I, p. 253.

112 Ibid., part I, p. 302. See also pp. 334, 342.

113 Ibid., p. 361.

114 NLI, MS 16091, 1 February 1742.

115 See, for example, the account book of the Orr family, Co. Down, 1731–1861 (PRONI, T/3301); account book of Patrick Rossiter, Co. Wexford, for the 1780s and 1790s (National Archives of Ireland, Business Records, WEX 15/1).

116 John McEvoy, *Statistical Survey of the County of Tyrone* (Dublin, 1802), p. 155.

117 Account book of the Orr family (PRONI, T/3301).

118 Account Book of Patrick Rossiter, Co. Wexford (National Archives of Ireland, Business Records, WEX 15/1); Account Book of the Orr Family (PRONI, T/3301).

119 David Dickson, *New Foundations: Ireland, 1660–1800* (Dublin, 1987), p. 138.

120 The process is described in Clarkson, 'The Carrick-on-Suir Woollen Industry in the Eighteenth Century', pp. 23–41.

121 Dickson, *New Foundations: Ireland, 1660–1800* (Dublin, 1987), p. 138; Dickson, 'An Economic History of the Cork Region' (unpublished, Ph.D. thesis, Trinity College, Dublin, 1977) pp. 556–9.

122 Young, *A Tour in Ireland*, part II, pp. 18–20, 61–2; Dickson, 'An Economic History of the Cork Region', pp. 564–5.

123 Ibid., p. 355; David Dickson, 'Butter Comes to Market: the Origins of Commercial Dairying in County Cork' in Patrick O'Flanagan and Cornelius G. Buttimer (Eds), *Cork. History and Society. Interdisciplinary Essays on the History of an Irish County* (Dublin, 1993), p. 381; Daly, *Women and Work in Ireland*, pp. 11–12.

124 *A Tour Through Ireland Wherein the Present State of That Kingdom is Considered* (Dublin, 1780), p. 43. See also Hely Dutton, *Statistical Survey of the County of Clare* (Dublin, 1808), pp. 130–1 who noted that wives of tenant farmers sold milk to local towns.

125 O'Connell Papers (UCD Archives, P12/6/A/15, 77, 122, 160).

126 Nuala Cullen, 'Women and the Preparation of Food in Eighteenth-Century Ireland' in MacCurtain and O'Dowd (Eds), *Women in Early Modern Ireland*, p. 267.

127 Leadbeater, *Cottage Dialogues*, pp. 14–18, 31–2.

128 Cullen, 'Women and the Preparation of Food in Eighteenth-Century Ireland', p. 267.

129 NLI, MS 16091. See entries under 15 December 1741, 25 June 1748.

130 Leadbeater, *Cottage Dialogues*, p. 202; Edward Wakefield, *An Account of Ireland, Statistical and Political* (2 vols., London, 1812), vol. ii, p. 739.

131 Cullen, 'Women and the Preparation of Food in Eighteenth-Century Ireland'.

132 Dickson (Ed), *The Gorgeous Mask*, p. viii.

133 Liam Kennedy, 'Marriage and Economic Conditions at the West European Periphery: Ireland, 1600–2000' in Isabelle Devos and Liam Kennedy (Eds), *Marriage and Rural Economy. Western Europe Since 1400* (Brepols, 1999), pp. 85–100.

134 For a discussion on the links between the low status of women in Ireland and their economic contribution to the family economy see Kerby A. Miller with David N. Doyle and Patricia Kelleher, '"For Love and Liberty": Irish Women, Migration and Domesticity in Ireland and America, 1815–1920' in Patrick O'Sullivan (Ed), *Irish Women and Irish Emigration* (London, 1995), pp. 41–65.

PART III

Religion and Education

CHAPTER 5

Women and Religious Change, 1500–1690

Pre-Reformation

And it was this Mac Suibhne who first built the castle of Ráith Maoláin; and it was his wife, namely, Máire, daughter of Eoghan, son of Diarmaid Bacach O Máille, who erected the monastery of Ráith Maoláin. It was Mac Suibhne and this wife who brought to that monastery a community from the south, from Munster . . . This is the manner in which she passed her days: she used to hear Mass once each day, and sometimes more than once; and three days in each week she used to spend on bread and water fare, with lenten fast, and winter fast, and the Golden Fridays. She also caused to be erected a great hall for the Friars Minor in Dūn na nGall. Not only that, but many other churches we shall not here enumerate that woman caused to be built in the provinces of Ulster and Connacht. It was she also who had this book of piety above copied in her own house . . .[1]

Máire O' Malley's patronage of the church in north-west Ireland in the early sixteenth century formed part of a long tradition of women in Gaelic society as benefactresses of ecclesiastical foundations. Throughout the medieval period wives of chiefs were praised for their benevolence towards monasteries and other religious institutions. Female sponsorship of church structures was given a new momentum in the reform movement of the late fifteenth and early sixteenth centuries. Historians and archaeologists have identified the existence of a native Irish ecclesiastical reform at this time through the establishment of new monasteries and the renovation of older ecclesiastical buildings. Scholars have not, however, paid sufficient attention to the fact that this construction programme was heavily dependent on the support of women.[2]

One of the first women connected with the reform movement was Fionnuala O'Brien, wife of Hugh O'Donnell, lord of Tyrconnell, who personally appeared before the meeting of a Provincial Chapter of the Franciscan Observantines in Galway in 1474 and appealed to them to found a monastery in Donegal. According to an account written in the early seventeenth century, Fionnuala said that 'many of her subjects . . . were perishing through lack of pious teachers'. Fionnuala was allegedly so persuasive that the Provincial resigned from the provincialship and accompanied Fionnuala back to Donegal to undertake the new foundation. The building of the church and convent were funded by Fionnuala's 'free use of her own and her husband's fortune'.[3] Fionnuala's sister Margaret, wife of Owen O'Rourke, lord of Breifne, also founded a Franciscan convent at Creevelea in County Leitrim in 1508, while in Galway City in 1506 Margaret Athy was responsible for the building of the Augustinian Church during her husband's absence on a trading journey overseas.[4]

Apart from sponsoring the founding of monasteries, wealthy women supported ecclesiastical foundations through the donation of chalices or other ecclesiastical items to the local church or priest and the building of crosses, usually in memory of a dead husband.[5] In Dublin during the later medieval period, other opportunities for involvement in church affairs were available to women. The confraternities associated with the cathedrals of St Patrick's and Christ Church admitted women. As Dianne Hall has pointed out, nearly half of the admission names listed for the confraternity in St Patrick's were women and many women also feature in the anniversary obits honoured by the clergy in the cathedral.[6]

As the description of Máire O'Malley indicates, her involvement with the foundation at Rathmullan was more than just that of a wealthy patron. She was also observing daily religious exercises. When Máire died in 1523, she was buried in a Carmelite habit in Rathmullan.[7] Fionnuala O'Brien also observed a strict religious life following her husband's death in 1508. She is recorded as having built a house for herself beside Donegal Abbey. 'Here apart from the world she spent peacefully the remainder of her days in almsgiving, prayer, and other good works, assisting with wonderful devotion at Mass and the Divine Office in the Church of the Friars.'[8]

Fionnuala O'Brien and Máire O'Malley were living the life of tertiaries. The Carmelites and Franciscans had developed secular tertiary orders that permitted lay men and women to pursue a structured religious life while remaining in their own homes. Under the Tertiary Rule, members took vows of fasting and abstinence and undertook the recital of daily prayers and attendance at religious ceremonies.[9] On death, members were usually buried in the habit of the Order as both Fionnuala and Máire were.[10]

Separate communities of religious women were relatively rare in late medieval Gaelic Ireland.[11] Prior to the dissolution of the monasteries in the 1530s the vast majority of convents for women were in Anglicised parts of Ireland and the recorded surnames of nuns suggest that most came from Old English or Anglo-Norman gentry families.[12] The monastic revival of the late fifteenth century appears to have been almost exclusively concerned with establishing institutions for men.[13] The option of full-time convent life was not, therefore, available to most women in Gaelic Ireland. The central role of marriage in the dynastic politics of the Gaelic political system may be one reason why this was the case. The daughters of Gaelic lords were considered too useful as marriage partners to permit them to enter a convent. Observing the life of a lay tertiary was, consequently, an attractive alternative for women who wished to follow an ordered religious life in late medieval Gaelic society.

The up to date recent list of female religious houses in sixteenth-century Ireland suggests that almost forty were dissolved in the course of the century. Some, however, may have been no more than a legal entity by 1500, still the nominal owner of property but no longer housing a religious community. Only ten convents can be linked to identifiable nuns.[14] The dissolution records also suggest that the size of the individual communities was small with the majority having no more than six or seven residents who were often connected by marriage or family.[15] Killone Abbey in County Clare appears to have been reserved for members of the O'Brien family. One recent account suggests that the abbey may have been used as a retirement home for 'female relatives who needed to retire from the world when they were found to be embarrassingly with child or had passed their usefulness as political wives'.[16]

The wealthiest convents were within the Pale where one of the most important was that of St Mary of Grace Dieu in Dublin which held extensive property and was described in 1539 as providing a school which 'brought up in virtue, learning, and in the English tongue, and behaviour, – the womenkind of the whole Englishry of this land'.[17] Other convents may also, like Grace Dieu, have had schools or maintained houses for the poor or the sick. In 1567, the convent at Killone in County Clare was described as providing 'relief . . . for the poor, feeding and clothing the needy, naked, hungry and impotent'.[18] Others may have had small hospices or hospitals attached.[19]

We have no information on the teaching of young women in Gaelic society but Máire O'Malley was clearly literate and the book of piety that she had compiled in her own home provides a tantalising glimpse into her spiritual interests. The text is in Irish and occasional notes indicate that Máire's instructions to the scribe included the translation of some texts from Latin. The volume consists of a miscellaneous compilation of brief extracts from the Bible, the writings of Augustine and other ancient writers and brief lives of saints including two female saints, Catherine and Margaret. There are also maxims for good living and notes on the benefits of following a religious life. The book is not unlike the commonplace books compiled by women in Renaissance Europe and it may have been put together for Máire's daily use.[20]

The inclusion of lives of Catherine and Margaret in O'Malley's book of piety is worth noting. They were among the most popular saints in late medieval Europe and were particularly associated with women. Catherine of Alexandra, commemorated for her learning and ability to win converts through reasoned argument, was the patron saint of young unmarried women and female students.[21] The story of her martyrdom when she spurned the Emperor's offer of marriage, choosing Christ as a spouse instead, was 'told in painting cycles, poetry, mystery plays and votive figures all over France as well as in England, Italy and other European countries'.[22] Catherine's popularity in Ireland is testified by the fact that she is the only non-Irish saint to have had a 'bed' dedicated to her at the pilgrimage centre of Lough Derg.[23] An Irish language life of Catherine is also listed among the books belonging to the earl of Kildare in the 1520s and may in fact have been commissioned by his wife or another woman in the Fitzgerald family.[24] Like Catherine, St Margaret of Antioch also refused marriage and miraculously eluded attempts to kill her before being beheaded. Although a virgin, Margaret was designated as the patron saint of pregnant women.[25] Máire O'Malley's acquisition of Irish translations of the lives of Catherine and Margaret suggests, therefore, that she, and, probably, other Irish women, shared many of the same spiritual interests as women in the wider Christian community.

Popular religion

Most women in early sixteenth-century Irish society were neither literate nor wealthy enough to patronise a rural monastery or an urban cathedral. The majority of women, like the majority of men, encountered the church through participation in religious services and ceremonies. Historians have stressed the popular nature of religious practice in early sixteenth century

Ireland. It was a community-based religion in which lay women participated on a virtually equal basis to lay men. Women took part in pilgrimages to holy wells and other places of local spirituality; they participated in celebrations on feast days; they acted as sponsors at baptism; and played a central role in the keening and burial of the dead. Women have also been identified as mediators between traditional beliefs in spirits and more orthodox forms of Christianity. Accusations of witchcraft were rare in medieval and early modern Ireland but 'wise women' are documented administering herbal cures with a mixture of Christian prayers and pagan incantations.[26]

Identification of saints who could act as divine intermediaries was also a central part of Irish Christianity although female saints did not feature strongly in Irish martyrologies and those who did were associated with the early Christian period. The most important was St Brigit, credited with founding a double monastery for men and women in the fifth century.[27] By far the most admired female figure in the Irish church from medieval to modern times was, however, Mary, the mother of God. Marian devotion overshadowed that of other female saints and possibly even prevented cults to other female figures emerging.[28]

Post-Reformation: the Catholic Church

The dissolution of the monasteries that followed the introduction of the Reformation began in Ireland in the late 1530s. The commissioners in charge of the dissolution focused on the monasteries in the Pale. Consequently, many of the female religious communities were among the first to be closed.[29] The fate of the nuns after dissolution is difficult to trace. Most abbesses were offered small pensions and allowed, if they wished, to continue following a religious and celibate life in private. Old English landlords who acquired monastic property may have permitted some communities to remain in residence on their lands.[30] Scattered documents of the late sixteenth and early seventeenth centuries reveal individual nuns living in their family home or under the protection of a wealthy landlord or landlady. In the ecclesiastical visitation of Meath in 1615, for example, Viscount Gormanston was noted as providing lodgings for a priest and for his sister who was a nun. In the Barnewall household at Shankill, another nun, Mary Barnewall, lived with her brother in the family residence where there was also a friar.[31] Lay women continued to take vows and live as tertiaries in their own homes and the distinction between lay and regular members of religious communities must have been, increasingly, difficult to detect. By 1650, the Poor Clares officially instructed its members still in Ireland 'to disperse among their relatives and friends and . . . to live as near as possible to their rule and constitution'.[32] Some may have later travelled to continental convents to be professed as nuns.

The first continental convent catering specifically for Irish women was Bom Successo convent in Lisbon, founded by the Dominicans in 1639. It attracted a number of Irish postulants who had previously been living as tertiaries in Ireland.[33] The majority of Irish women, however, entered convents in France or the Low Countries where there was a more ethnically mixed community. There were, for example, Irish nuns in the English convents at Gravelines and Ypres.[34] The political and economic uncertainties confronting Catholic landed families in the early modern period increased the appeal of life in a convent for girls whose families were no longer in a position to provide dowries for a suitable marriage.[35] Dowries of £60 to £200 were accepted in the Poor Clares in Galway in the late seventeenth century, figures that were considerably below the sum required for a marriage portion among wealthy landed families although still beyond the means of the majority of women.[36] We do not yet have any statistical analysis of the number of Irish women in continental convents but impressionistic evidence suggests that the Irish nun population on the continent, as in Ireland, remained small in size and continued to be dominated by wealthy gentry families.

Throughout the seventeenth century, there were sporadic attempts by Irish nuns living abroad to establish new communities in Ireland. The best known was that of the Poor Clare convent in Dublin in 1629. It was founded by a small group of Irish nuns who had been professed at Gravelines. Finding the political atmosphere in Dublin inhospitable the nuns eventually settled at Bethlehem on Lough Rea in the west of Ireland where they were protected by the patronage of the Dillon family, some members of which had joined the community.[37] The community later moved to Galway but was compelled to disperse in the 1650s when most of the nuns fled to the safety of convents on the continent. Other small communities established in the early seventeenth century had similar experiences.[38]

In continental convents, particularly in France, the strict rules on cloister and contemplative life that had been issued by the Council of Trent for female religious communities were slowly being eroded. New orders like the Ursulines encouraged the development of a more active social and economic role for nuns.[39] In Ireland, however, the scattered female religious communities were from the more traditional orders: the Poor Clares, the

Dominicans and, later in the seventeenth century, the Benedictines. All followed rules of enclosure with the community pursuing a contemplative life having minimal contact with the outside world.[40] The established female communities in Ireland were, therefore, small in number, survived sporadically and were not socially active.

In the absence of female religious, the Catholic lay woman acquired an enhanced status as defender and supporter of the Catholic Church. As in England, the legal non-status of women was exploited by families in which men conformed to the established religion while their wives and children retained an adherence to Catholicism.[41] In 1580, it was reported in Munster that the men attended the church services while the women stayed at home. Among the recusants were wives of men whose husbands served in the Irish establishment.

One of the most prominent supporters of Catholicism in the sixteenth century was Mabel Browne, the wife of Gerald, 11th earl of Kildare (1525–86). The countess, who came from a recusant family in England and had been a lady-in-waiting in the Catholic court of Queen Mary, opened her house to missionary priests in the 1570s and early 1580s. Three of the priests who stayed in the Kildare household were subsequently linked to the revolt of the earl of Baltinglass and were suspected by government officials of fomenting the rebellion in the name of Catholicism.[42]

At the beginning of the reign of James I, there was great optimism within the Irish Catholic community that the new king would grant permission for the public profession of Catholicism. When leading members of the Old English elite were, however, arrested for non-attendance at the established Church, Catholic women in Irish towns are recorded as defending their traditional religious practices.[43] The Catholic seventeenth-century historian Philip O'Sullivan Beare related the story of a funeral which took place in a village near Drogheda. The body was brought to the church surrounded by women, 'the men were not present for fear of the authorities'. In the middle of the celebration of the mass, a Protestant minister entered the church and attempted to arrest the priest. The women, according to O'Sullivan Beare, seized the minister and began to bury him alive in the open grave. He was eventually rescued by the priest, having taken an oath not to prosecute any other priest.[44]

The loyalty of Irish women to Catholicism had far-reaching consequences for the success of the Reformation. The failure to secure the children of the first generation of converts for Protestantism has been recognised by historians as a principal factor in the limited progress of Protestantism in Ireland. Mothers were usually given responsibility for the religious instruction of young children, a task that they undertook themselves or, as in the case of the countess of Kildare, for which they chose a suitable tutor. The priests who led the Counter-Reformation in early seventeenth-century Ireland were products of this maternal instruction. A significant part, therefore, of the failure of the Protestant Reformation in Ireland can be linked to the women who refused to teach their children the new religious practices.[45]

The Society of Jesus in Ireland, as elsewhere, fostered links with wealthy women who could act as patrons and absorb the Jesuits' particular blend of Catholicism.[46] The Jesuits in Ireland may have held traditional views on the passivity of women as being 'weak in judgement and therefore led by authority rather than by reason' but they also praised women who took a more leading role.[47] In the 1580s, the Irish martyrology of the Jesuit missionary John Howlin identified two Irish women, one a widow and the other a single woman, whose lives he presented as examples of 'truly Christian and Catholic' women.[48]

The widow was Margaret Ball who had been married to a prominent Dublin alderman. Howlin described Margaret Ball as a

mother, hostess and receiver of Catholics, and also an instructress of Christian doctrine, for the servants and maids who left her house for other posts or who were given by her to some noble persons who asked for them went out like expert scholars from the finest school and won for Christ not only their fellow servants and maids but also sometimes and indeed very often their masters and mistresses.

Margaret Ball's son, Walter, was a member of the Church of Ireland and, like his father, an alderman of Dublin. His mother tried in vain to convert Walter by bringing to her house Catholic bishops, priests and other learned men to discuss religious matters with him. Margaret Ball, according to Howlin, was arrested several times for her adherence to Catholicism and when her son was made mayor in 1583, she was apprehended again and put in prison where she died in about 1584.[49]

Howlin's brief hagiography of Margaret Ball was elaborated by David Rothe in his martyrology published in 1619.[50] Rothe's main addition to Howlin's story was to emphasise the image of Ball as the ideal Catholic widow. First, as a mother, Margaret Ball performed the crucial role of catechising her 'family' or household. Although the Council of Trent placed a new emphasis on the role of the priest as an instructor of Christian doctrine, there was still a duty on parents and heads of households to ensure that children and servants were educated in the basic tenets of Counter-Reformation Catholicism and, as suggested earlier, this task frequently devolved on the women in the house. Catholic writers applauded women such as Margaret Barnewall who not only trained members of her own household in Catholic doctrine but also provided Catholic servants for other households.[51]

Neither Howlin nor Rothe tell us what books or religious texts were used by Margaret Ball for her catechising classes but in another Jesuit inspired household of the early seventeenth century, that of the Waddings of Waterford, both parents took their catechising role very seriously. The girls as well as the boys were taught to read and given a copy of the Breviary of Pope Pius V. Morning and evening prayers, including the rosary, were said in common. The family and servants also recited 'the Exercises of a Christian Man', the Penitential Psalms, the Office of the Blessed Virgin and the Offium Defunctorum on a regular basis.[52]

Margaret Ball, according to the martyrologists, demonstrated her continued maternal love for Walter despite his rejection of Catholicism. Rothe used the analogy of St Monica whose continual prayer for her son, St Augustine, eventually gave her 'a Catholic son'. Margaret Ball also maintained a vigil for her son. She kept a priest in her house who said mass for Walter on a daily basis. Harbouring a priest was an offence and led to Margaret's frequent arrest. In the eyes of the martyrologists, therefore, it was Margaret Ball's maternal love that led ultimately to her martyrdom.

Apart from Margaret Ball's role as mother and catechiser, Howlin and Rothe also praised her hospitality to priests. As in England, the prosecution of recusants in sixteenth- and seventeenth-century Ireland facilitated the domestication of Catholicism. Priests depended on a network of houses to provide them with lodgings and the finance to carry out their ministry. Margaret Ball and many other women welcomed priests into their homes and prepared rooms in which mass could be said and the sacraments administered to the family and sometimes to others in the locality. The Waddings were reported to have priests staying with them on a regular basis. Anastasia Strong, the mother of Thomas Walsh, the Catholic Bishop of Cashel, was lauded by Catholic sources in the 1620s because 'she kept her house continuously open for clerics, poor students and pilgrims, to whom she gave lodging in her great charity'.[53] A visitation undertaken by a Church of Ireland archbishop of Dublin in 1630 identified over fifty gentlemen and women as 'abettors and harbourers' of priests and friars in the diocese of Dublin. Women in gentry families were thus essential in fostering 'an organised Catholic network, operating parallel to the Church of Ireland parochial system'.[54]

Margaret Ball was one of a number of wealthy women encouraged by the Jesuits in Ireland. In the early seventeenth century, the mission received substantial funding from another widow, Elizabeth Fitzgerald, the dowager countess of Kildare, whose husband died in 1612.[55] When her only son died in 1620 she devoted much of her time to the Jesuit mission. Robert Nugent, the superior of the Jesuits in Ireland from 1627, was her cousin and normally resided in the countess's home. In the 1620s, Elizabeth subsidised the finance for the establishment of a college for the order in Dublin. It consisted of a large building with twenty-six bedrooms and a chapel. The countess claimed to the authorities that the college was her home and the chapel her hall, although Richard Boyle, the earl of Cork and Lord Justice, sardonically pointed out that the room had no chimney and the windows were rather high for a hall.[56] Some years later, the countess gave the Order Kilkea Castle in County Kildare and sufficient funds to finance a Jesuit novitiate in Ireland.[57] The support of Elizabeth Fitzgerald for Catholicism led to her denunciation as a rebel in 1641 but she survived until 1645. In her will she left everything to the Jesuit mission in Ireland. Other wealthy women followed the example of Elizabeth Fitzgerald and bequeathed large sums of money to the Order in their wills.[58]

The hospitable, maternal, pious and generous widow was one ideal of an active Catholic woman presented by the Jesuit Howlin, the other was the single, pious virgin. Howlin's martyrology included the story of Margaret Barnewall who when she was about thirty-three years of age received from a Catholic bishop 'a blessed veil with which it was the custom in Ireland to invest those who had become the spouses of Jesus Christ'. Barnewall subsequently lived among 'holy women, who like herself gave themselves up to prayer and to good works'.[59]

Barnewall, like Margaret Ball, was arrested by the Dublin authorities for practising her faith but she escaped and travelled to France. Significantly, Barnewall chose not to remain on the continent and enter a convent but returned to Ireland where, Howlin concluded, 'her example was the means of bringing many other maidens to consecrate themselves to God'.[60] There is no reference to Margaret Barnewall formally joining a religious order. She may have been among a small group of single Irish women who took vows of chastity and lived a pious life but did not join a traditional community. Scattered evidence suggests the existence of small groups of Catholic women based in Irish towns and cities administering to the poor from the mid-sixteenth century. In the 1560s in Limerick, Helen Stackpole founded a group called *Mena Bocht* (i.e. Poor Women) while in

Drogheda a number of women who had taken vows of chastity were attached to the Franciscan friary. The Dominicans also had single women working as tertiaries in the seventeenth century and performing 'good works'.[61]

In early modern France, the Jesuits were noted for the support that they offered the Ursuline nuns and other congregations of religious women who sought to challenge the limitations imposed by enclosure.[62] In England, members of the Order encouraged Mary Ward whose Institute envisaged a female version of the Jesuits.[63] Against this background, Howlin's choice of Margaret Barnewall in his list of Irish martyrs is worth considering. The Jesuits, like the Franciscans and Dominicans, supported Irish women who took vows of virginity, as Margaret Barnewall had done.[64] The essence of the new communities in France was that women took vows of chastity and sometimes of poverty and obedience but did not take formal religious vows that would have subjected them to the rules of cloister. They were thus free to devote their lives to 'good works' which included establishing schools and taking care of the poor and the sick.[65] This was what the Jesuit-supported *Mena Bocht* were doing in Limerick in the 1560s and Howlin's reference to the 'good works' undertaken by Barnewall and the other women may be an indication that a new type of female religious community was being covertly encouraged in the late sixteenth century. Margaret Barnewall and the *Mena Bocht* were living '"the mixed life" of contemplation and action'.[66]

Another sign of the enhanced role for women in the Irish Catholic Church was the Sodality of the Blessed Virgin established by the Jesuits in the 1590s. By the early seventeenth century there were sodalities in most of the main towns of Ireland. In other countries where the Jesuits had established similar organisations the admission of women was forbidden. In early seventeenth-century Ireland, however, the General of the Irish Jesuits issued an order permitting women in Ireland to enjoy the benefits of the sodality. The members of the sodality were expected to lead a devout life and to perform good works which included giving a good example to family and dependants, instructing the 'ignorant' and taking care of the sick and poor and visiting prisoners.[67] The sodality, therefore, provided a structure through which single, married and widowed women could fulfil an active religious life. It formalised into a group activity the tertiary life that lay women were being encouraged to follow. Through the sodalities, therefore, the Jesuits envisaged a more active lay apostolate for men and women.[68]

The momentum in the Catholic Church in the late sixteenth century and the visible and active role that lay women played in church affairs was dissipated in the course of the seventeenth century. The pope issued a decree dissolving the Institute founded by Mary Ward in 1631, a gesture that signalled the Catholic authority's disapproval of uncloistered female religious orders. The assistance given by leading Franciscans to the new Poor Clare foundation in the west of Ireland in the 1630s identified the approved convent organisation. The Rule for the community, translated by Micheál Ó Cleirigh and Dubhaltach Mac Firbisigh, defined cloister and prohibited contact with outsiders except in particular circumstances.[69] A decade later, when Cardinal Rinuccini arrived in Ireland, he brought with him strongly worded papal instructions to 'attend to the secure cloistering of female religious on the island'.[70] The wars of the 1640s also halted the development of the lay sodalities and in the decades after the wars, women are less visible in the organisation of the Catholic Church. The correspondence of Oliver Plunkett, Archbishop of Armagh 1669–81, suggests that he was dependent on a network of Catholic houses but Plunkett rarely refers to women as activists in church affairs.[71] The sodalities of the earlier period were sporadically revived and women retained their right to membership. In 1696, for example, it was recorded that there were forty-four women and twenty-three men in the Jesuit sodality of the Blessed Virgin Mary in Dublin.[72] By that stage, however, the Jesuits were more circumspect in their activities and were not as energetic as they had been in the early years of their mission in Ireland.

In the tolerant religious atmosphere of the 1680s attempts were made to revive Irish-based female religious communities. In 1688 Irish nuns from the Benedictine convent of Ypres in Belgium founded a convent in Dublin with the support of the countess of Tyconnell. The convent opened a school for girls of Irish gentry families but neither the convent nor the school survived the war of 1689–90.[73]

The social role for the Catholic Church that the Jesuits had tried to develop in the late sixteenth and early seventeenth centuries was, therefore, largely eroded in the second half of the seventeenth century. An impoverished clergy concentrated on its own survival and regular and secular clergy squabbled, often in an unseemly fashion, over the payments due from parishioners for administering the sacraments.[74] There were many complaints that there were too many clergy, particularly within the regular orders. In these circumstances it is perhaps not surprising that there was no great enthusiasm to introduce an additional financial burden for the Church in the form of female religious communities.

Women in the Church of Ireland, 1536–1690

If lay women developed a new role as defenders of Catholicism in late sixteenth- and early seventeenth-century Ireland, what of women in the established Church? In England, the Protestant Reformation has been credited with simultaneously strengthening patriarchy and enhancing the lay woman's role in the family. The role of the father as head of the household was reinforced by allocating to him the responsibility for the religious instruction of his family. At the same time, the influence of the wife and mother in the home was expanded as she was expected to share in the religious teaching of children and servants. The Reformation also encouraged literacy among women as the godly woman read the Scriptures daily and taught her children to read. While Protestant women could not become nuns, they could attain considerable intellectual and emotional satisfaction from their religious reading and devotions. Women attended sermons on a regular basis and often developed close personal contact with individual clergymen as they discussed religious matters and sought the ministers' guidance on their spiritual lives. Life as a clergyman's wife also emerged as a new role for women in the early modern period.[75]

The Protestant community in Ireland was small and the documentation on Protestant women is scanty but there are no indications that women were allotted either an active or visible role in the Irish Church. The woman who married a clergyman had potentially the most opportunities to establish a public role in the Church of Ireland. Nine of the first generation of Reformation bishops married.[76] The Church of Ireland like the Church of England was, however, ambiguous in its attitude to ministers' wives and was consequently slow to given them any official recognition.[77] In sixteenth-century Ireland bishops' wives were subject to abuse and often cruel treatment. George Browne, the first bishop to be appointed by the crown in Ireland, was married to an Irish woman, Elizabeth Miagh, and the couple had three sons. In 1539 legislation in England outlawed clerical marriage and, although the law did not apply in Ireland, Browne was clearly concerned about his domestic position and the legal status of his wife. He reportedly left her and arranged for her to be remarried to one of his servants. In Tudor England, bishops' wives had difficulties having their legal claims to their husbands' estates recognised. Widows had to leave the episcopal home and the church had no responsibility to maintain them. It may have been for this reason that Browne took care to ensure that his wife was legally married. He also made financial arrangements for the support of his children.[78] In the 1550s, when Queen Mary tried to undo the Reformation legislation, clerical wives were once again subject to criticism. Edward Staples, the Bishop of Meath, wrote that he had been thrown out of his house and reduced to poverty because he had married.[79] Bishop John Bale of Ossory also encountered hostility because of his marriage.[80] Spouses of clergymen were criticised by Catholic clergy. In a vitriolic poem written by a Franciscan friar in the 1570s, the families of three Church of Ireland bishops were denounced as illegitimate and their fate determined as eternal damnation:

Your three mothers, your three wives, your three bishops of unclean life, your three illegitimate families – the trios are no equal to the Virgin.
The bishops and their wives shall be reciting vespers heavily,
Lustily and discordantly in the pit of hell, foot to foot, head to head in the hole of sparks.
Jesus shall drive the uxorious clergy, who say no office, from his right hand, with his wife beside him, reciting vespers in hell along with him. . . .[81]

By the seventeenth century, clerical wives were more acceptable but they still had no identifiable role. Some, undoubtedly, quietly assisted their husbands in their episcopal business. The authority exercised by the wife of Thomas Hackett, the Bishop of Down and Connor 1672–94, was, however, unique. Catherine Hackett in conjunction with a widow, Mary Cole, managed all the diocesan affairs while the bishop remained an absentee bishop and lived in London.[82]

An ambiguous attitude to bishops' wives continued to the end of the seventeenth century. William King, appointed chancellor of St Patrick's Cathedral in Dublin in 1679 and archbishop of Dublin in 1703, chose a celibate life but acknowledged missing the companionship that a wife would have brought him. He defined the role of any potential wife in terms of his own domestic comfort. If he had held a country benefice, King asserted, he would have been compelled to marry because he could 'with difficulty comprehend how food and other things requisite for living comfortably, beds, cooking, linen, and other necessaries of domestic life could be cared for in the country without a woman's help'. When King moved to Dublin he knew 'there would be no trouble for me in these matters' and consequently he felt no compulsion to marry.[83] Implicit in King's comment is the belief that the absence of a wife left him unencumbered to pursue his writing and ministry. The biographer of Narcissus Marsh also noted that although Marsh had had many offers of marriage, he rejected all of them in order to serve God.[84] In other words, the celibate bishop scholar remained the ideal spiritual leader until the end of the seventeenth century. It was not until the eighteenth century that clergymen's wives in the Church of Ireland developed a role in their local community as dispensers of charity and organisers of Sunday schools for children.

Irish Church of Ireland writers endorsed the patriarchal view of the family that formed part of the Anglican orthodoxy on women in the sixteenth and seventeenth centuries. In a catechism which James Ussher began, partly for use in his own family, and which appears to have been well known in Ireland in the second half of the seventeenth century, the duties of the husband were clearly laid out and among them was the responsibility to edify his wife 'by instruction and example'.[85] Ezekiel Hopkins, Bishop of Derry 1681–90, agreed, describing the husband as 'the head, the seat and fountain of knowledge and wisdom' of his wife.[86] Both prelates emphasised the weakness of women in the absence of their husbands, an argument which had a particular relevance in the unstable and fluctuating religious world of seventeenth-century Ireland. Conversion of men and women by Catholic priests or by dissenting ministers was not uncommon. Women were considered particularly vulnerable. Ussher's own mother, Margaret Stanihurst, was converted to Catholicism by a group of priests. The fact that the conversion occurred during Ussher's absence in England seems to have particularly distressed him.[87] The account of the Fall in Ussher's catechism may have been composed with women like his mother in mind. Eve's downfall happened, according to Ussher, when she was 'some space removed from her husband'.[88] Satan, recognising her weakness, approached her and persuaded her to disobey God's commandment. Henry Leslie, Bishop of Down and Connor 1635–61, shared Ussher's views on women's susceptibility to heresy although he perceived the main threat to come from Presbyterian ministers who 'advanced their faction, . . . by insinuating into the weaker sex'.[89]

The most secure safeguard against the ensnarement of 'silly' women was well-informed husbands who would protect their wives and households from the dangers represented by Catholicism and non-conformity. Ezekiel Hopkins recommended that a husband 'should be well-grounded and principled with knowledge, that he may help his wife from being led away by the crafty subtlety of those who lie in wait to deceive'.[90] Seventeenth-century biographies of Irish bishops took care to note that their subjects fulfilled their role as religious heads of their households in exemplary fashion. Ussher's family prayed four times a day at each of which the bishop was always present; and on Fridays 'an hour in the chapel was spent going through the principles of religion in the catechism, for the instruction of the family'.[91] Ambrose Bedell, the son of William Bedell, Bishop of Kilmore 1629–42, described his father's 'governing his family upon the Lord's Day':

Being risen himself (most commonly the first in the house), he presently retired to his study, and while he was busied in prayer and meditation, his wife was hastening to get the children ready, a convenient time before the public meeting, that all might be in order against his coming down to prayer in the family. His company being assembled together he would come down among them, but as at all times, so more especially then, with his countenance composed to all possible gravity, piety and solemnity; indeed, the presence of that day, and his deportment together, wrought no small effects both upon children and servants, as to preparation for the service of God, and so truly was he God's vice-gerent in his family.[92]

Similarly Ezekiel Hopkins's household was described as 'a Temple and an Oratory for in it prayers and praises, catechising and reading the scripture were never omitted. He constantly expounded it to his family.'[93]

The head of household leading the family in prayer was, therefore, a common motif in Irish religious tracts of the seventeenth century. It was also a motif enshrined in stone monuments to the dead in Irish churches which incorporated images of a husband, wife and children at prayer.[94] The monuments celebrated the patriarchal godly family. The inclusion of the wife and the children was, nonetheless, also a reminder of the importance of the mother in the family. While women were expected to take instruction from their husbands, they also had a spiritual responsibility in the home as mothers and instructors of the young. Seventeenth-century Irish catechisms followed orthodox Anglican catechisms and included among the common duties of both parents the religious instruction of their children.[95] In many households, women were responsible for the instructing of very young children: teaching them to read and giving them their first lessons in the Scriptures. James Ussher was first taught to read by two blind aunts who knew the Bible by heart while James Bonnell noted that his chiefest benefactress was his mother who 'hath brought me to Heaven', presumably through her instruction of him as a child.[96] Once the child had learnt to read, more formal catechising classes might be given in the church or by the father in a clerical home. Ambrose Bedell recalled that when his mother had taught the children to 'read English and give an account of the heads of the Catechism', his father then 'took them under his own teaching; and two of his sons he thus instructed for some years'.[97] The religious education of the girls in the family might continue to be the responsibility of the mother.

Protestantism encouraged literacy among women but initially there was concern at the dangers of permitting individual interpretation of Scripture. In sixteenth-century England, legislation restricted women's access to the Bible. No similar legislation appeared in Ireland but individual bishops expressed alarm at the encouragement given by Presbyterian ministers to extempore prayer, particularly among women.[98] It is, nonetheless, possible to identify women in the Church of Ireland who read religious literature and probably devoted a considerable amount of private time to religious study. In the Cork home of Mary Boyle, later the countess of Warwick, and her sister, Katherine, later Lady Ranelagh, both their mother and their father encouraged the reading of the Bible and discussion of religious literature.[99] Mary Boyle later remembered attending sermons by James Ussher, Archbishop of Dublin, when she was a child. Similarly, Alice Wandesford, the daughter of Irish Official, Christopher Wandesford, wrote that while a young girl in Dublin, she 'daily read the word of God'.[100] Religious texts dominate the library lists of books belonging to two Irish-based women, Lady Anne Hamilton and Lettice Fitzgerald, Lady Offaly, in the early decades of the seventeenth century, while Phoebe Challoner was left religious books by her father, Luke Challoner, and her name is still to be found on some of the books in her husband, James Ussher's library.[101] Literate women in Ireland also kept commonplace books in to which were copied short extracts from biblical texts, notes on sermons and religious verse.[102]

Membership of the Church of Ireland enabled some literate women, therefore, to develop their own spiritual and intellectual lives. This was not, however, an opportunity available to most women who even within the established Church remained illiterate, content to receive their religious doctrine orally and through guided instruction. It was not until the eighteenth century that literacy began to be considered an essential requirement for full membership of the Church of Ireland.

Presbyterianism

The adverse circumstances in which Presbyterianism existed in Ireland for much of the seventeenth century is important to bear in mind when considering the role of women within it. Presbyterianism was introduced into Ireland through the Scottish settlers in Ulster in the early part of the century. Ministers with Presbyterian sympathies were permitted initially to serve in the Church of Ireland but in the late 1630s, during the lord deputyship of Sir Thomas Wentworth, they were dismissed and replaced by Anglican ministers. In the 1650s and 1660s Presbyterianism again came under attack from supporters of the re-established Church of Ireland but by the 1670s it was more openly tolerated.

The unofficial and, at times, illegal status of Presbyterianism bestowed on women an active role as supporters and benefactresses, responsibilities that had much in common with those undertaken by women in the sixteenth-seventeenth-century Catholic Church. Women in wealthy families offered patronage and hospitality to Presbyterian ministers. Prominent among those who supported ministers in Ulster were the Hamiltons of Clandeboye and the Clotworthys of Massereene. The Clotworthye family were at the centre of a network of aristocratic families in England and Ireland who offered political and financial assistance to Presbyterian ministers in the middle decades of the seventeenth century. Sir Hugh Clotworthy was married to a daughter of Sir Adam Loftus, the Irish lord chancellor, who was a strong advocate of Presbyterianism, as was their son John whose wife, a daughter of another leading Irish official, Sir Roger Jones, was later Lord Ranelagh. The latter's eldest son Arthur married Katherine Boyle, daughter of Richard, 1st earl of Cork, well known for her support for English Puritan ministers in London where she lived in the 1640s. Katherine's sister Mary was also a committed Puritan as is evident from her surviving writings. In addition, the Clotworthy family were linked to a wider English Puritan network through Sir John Pym, whose brother-in-law was married to a sister of Sir John Clotworthy.[103]

Following the war of the 1640s, aristocratic women, particularly in Ulster, continued to offer strong support to Presbyterian ministers. Conventicles were held in the Massereene household and other well-connected women used their political influence to prevent the prosecution of ministers. In the Restoration period when the Church was again under siege, a group of aristocratic women in Ulster offered patronage and financial support to the Church, employing ministers as private chaplains so that they could continue to work in Ireland.[104]

Less wealthy women in 'godly households' also provided places of refuge to ministers forced to flee prosecution from government and ecclesiastical officials.[105] When the Church of Ireland prelates John Bramhall and Henry Leslie excommunicated Presbyterian ministers in the 1630s, the creation of a domestic support network became essential for the survival of the fledgling church. Services were held in private houses and ministers moved quietly from one house to another.[106] As ministers fled to Scotland to avoid arrest, lay members conducted services and discussed Scripture passages among themselves.[107]

The Ulster Presbyterian emphasis on 'family exercise, especially of prayer' gave women access to spiritual activities in the home.[108] In the absence of a minister, lay people prayed and engaged in religious conversation and such informal sessions facilitated women's engagement with the proceedings of the congregation. Ulster Presbyterianism attached particular importance to personal spirituality, private prayer and the reading and discussion of religious texts, and thus gave literate women more direct control over their own spiritual lives and fulfilment than they had either in the Catholic Church or in the Church of Ireland.[109]

The ideal Presbyterian minister preached and catechised in public and also engaged in individual instruction. The autobiography of Robert Blair, who was a Presbyterian minister in County Down in the 1620s and 1630s, presents a picture of a minister who believed that individual instruction was as essential as preaching to a large number of people. Blair engaged in 'private, plain, and familiar instruction of persons, one by one in families, before more public catechising of sundry families together' and these private discussions included men and women.[110] Blair in fact met his second wife, Katherine Montgomery, when she had 'conferred with me privately'.[111] When the Church of Ireland bishop, Henry Leslie outlined his reasons for his dislike of what he called the 'feminine heresie' he noted, in particular, the conversations which women had with Presbyterian ministers:

two things especially make [women] in love with that religion; one is, it is natural unto the daughters of Eve to desire knowledge, and those men puff them up with an opinion of science enabling them to prattle of matters of divinity, which they and their teachers understand much alike: in so much that albeit St Paul hath forbidden women to speak in the church, yet they speak of church-matters more than comes to their share.[112]

There was also a providential and emotional dimension to Presbyterianism that was appealing to women. In the revival movement that spread throughout the north-east in the 1620s and 1630s, prayer meetings, lasting three to five days, attracted hundreds of people who 'swooned, panted, shouted, and wept'.[113] Women were prominent in the revival. It was reported, for example, that women at Larne fell to 'sighing and weeping over their sins' and were afflicted with 'convulsions and trembling'.[114]

Given the necessity of relying on domestic support, it is perhaps not surprising that Presbyterianism, as it developed in seventeenth-century Ulster, also gave more recognition to the minister's wife and her contribution to the ministry of her husband than the Church of Ireland allotted to clergymen's wives. In Blair's autobiography, the ideal minister's wife is portrayed as a spiritual companion, a strong defender of her religious beliefs and a loyal supporter of her husband. Blair wrote warmly about the spiritual companionship of his first wife. The couple frequently prayed together and Blair wrote of his dependence on his wife's spiritual support. His son-in-law later noted that Blair recorded in his private notes that: 'when he was in any soul trouble, or heaviness of mind, she [i.e. his wife] was most comfortable company to him, especially in secret prayer together'.[115] Blair's second wife, Katherine Montgomery, was also praised for her loyalty to her husband in the difficult times of the 1630s when her husband was deprived of his benefice. She and other ministers' wives were willing 'notwithstanding of their desolate and needy condition, to go with their husbands, . . . whither so ever the Lord called them to preach, and so to spread the gospel, though it were by sea and land, even to America'.[116] In addition, there is some scattered evidence to suggest that Presbyterian women were among the first to establish schools in the second half of the seventeenth century and some of these may have been wives or daughters of Presbyterian ministers.[117] The Presbyterian Church, therefore, developed an image of an ideal minister's wife as a spiritual companion, a strong defender of her religious beliefs and a loyal supporter of her husband.

The egalitarian nature of the relationship between the minister and his wife was also perceived by the detractors of Presbyterianism to have infiltrated the homes of lay believers. Another reason listed by Bishop Leslie for condemning the sect was its toleration of women's equality in the home. He argued that the appeal of Presbyterianism for women was partly because of their

desire of liberty and freedom from subjection; for these teachers allow them to be at least quarter-masters with their husbands, in so much that I have not observed that faction to prevail but where husbands have learned to obey their wives, and where will and affection wear the breeches.[118]

Leslie's observations were clearly motivated more by venomous dislike of Presbyterianism than concern to describe accurately the Presbyterian home. His words may, nonetheless, contain some element of truth. A comparison of catechisms used in seventeenth-century Ireland suggests that Irish

Presbyterianism placed more emphasis on the equality of the marriage partners than was the case in Catholicism or the Church of Ireland. In his catechism, dated to 1680, Robert Chambre exonerated Eve from responsibility for the Fall. He acknowledged that the devil had chosen the weaker vessel to seduce but Chambre argued the 'principal cause of the Fall' was Adam's abuse of his own free will. Adam could have chosen not to eat the fruit.[119] Robert Chambre also allotted the mother a special place in the home, pointing out that a number of scriptural texts placed the mother's name before that of the father in the fifth commandment because children 'begin to know her first'. As a wife and 'yoke fellow' of her husband, the wife came nearest in equality to her husband of all those in the home. Chambre also acknowledged the difficulty of women being obliged to be subject to their husbands: 'Of all the duties she owes to her husband this is the most difficult.'[120]

By contrast, James Ussher, in his catechism, places far more emphasis on the weakness of women in the home and in the Fall. It was Eve's 'lustful and wicked eye' that perceived the fruit as 'delectable to eat. Adam did not confer with the Satan or take the fruit. He received it from his wife, and by her was deceived, and she by Satan.'[121] Ezekiel Hopkins's exposition of the ten commandments agreed with Ussher's stress on the weakness of women and strongly supported the subjection of wives to their husbands because 'it was fit and just that she who made all mankind disobedient against God, should herself be made subject and obedient to man . . . there is scarce any other duty which the Scripture doth urge with so much instance and earnestness, with such pressing reasons and inforcing motives, as this of the wives obedience. The duty is frequently express'd, wives submit yourselves.'[122]

The support that women were perceived to give to Presbyterianism resulted in the authorities prosecuting women adherents of the sect in an unprecedented manner. In the late 1630s, when the government of Sir Thomas Wentworth imposed an oath of loyalty on Ulster Scots, members of the established clergy were accused of being particularly concerned to apprehend 'women and maids' who refused to take the oath. In 1641 Sir John Clotworthy presented a petition to the Long Parliament on behalf of the 'Protestant Inhabitants of Ulster'. He noted that

the prelates were the occasion that women and maids should be forced thereunto. Hence commissions issuing to all places for the exacting of it, they were prosecuted with so much rigour, that very many, as if they had been traitors in the highest degree, were searched for, apprehended, examined, reviled, threatened, imprisoned, fettered, by threes and fours, in iron yokes; some carried up to Dublin in chains, and fined in the Star-Chamber in thousands beyond ability, and condemned to perpetual imprisonment. Divers, before delivering of children, were apprehended, threatened, and terrified. Others of them, two or three days after child-birth, so narrowly searched for, that they were fain to fly out of all harbour into woods, mountains, caves, and cornfields . . .[123]

A number of prominent Presbyterian women were arrested. John Clotworthy's wife was summoned before the Irish Court of High Commission to answer for her religious views in 1639, an action that was undoubtedly politically motivated and designed to discourage support for Scottish Presbyterianism among leading members of the New English elite.[124] Subsequently, Sir John Clotworthy initiated the proceedings for the indictment of Strafford in the English House of Commons in the spring of 1642. The attacks on the women in his family undoubtedly contributed to Clotworthy's determined opposition to Strafford. One of the charges levied at Strafford in his trial was his harsh treatment of 'the meaner and poorer sort' which included men and women who had rejected the oath.[125]

Formal legal proceedings against Catholic women were rare in seventeenth-century Ireland. By contrast, women in the Presbyterian community appear to have been deliberately targeted by the authorities in the late 1630s. Presbyterian women, particularly wives of ministers, were also attacked by Catholic mobs on the outbreak of rebellion in October 1641. Some died defending their religious beliefs. It is likely, therefore, that there were more female martyrs among the Presbyterians than there were within the Irish Catholic community in the seventeenth century.

In the Restoration period, the significance of women's role diminished as the state permitted the building of meeting houses and private services were no longer held.[126] The infrastructure of the Presbyterian Church, thus, became more formalised and, as it did so, it became less reliant on the auxiliary services provided by women in earlier decades.[127]

Quakers, Independents and Baptists

Apart from Presbyterianism, congregations of other non-conformist sects appeared in Ireland in the 1640s and 1650s. The Quakers were the largest group but there were also small assemblies of Baptists and other independent congregations. All shared a willingness to allow women to have a more vocal role in the church than they were allocated by the larger Protestant denominations although only the Quakers permitted women to preach. John Rogers's Independent congregation in Dublin in the 1650s is one of the best known, because Rogers published the testimonies of conversion of some of the men and women who spoke in his church. Most were English people who had come to Ireland in the decades before the outbreak of rebellion in 1641 and many had lost family as well as material possessions as a result of the rebellion. The women who gave testimony in the church spoke of the emotional and spiritual comfort that they found in the preaching of Rogers.[128]

Rogers's views on women were radical in that they encouraged women to think of themselves as spiritually equal to men but there were also strict limits to Rogers's perception of women's status in the church. In particular, he did not permit them to hold positions of authority in the church:

Women are forbid to speak by way of teaching, or ruling in the church, but they are not forbid to speak, when it is in obedience, and subjection to the church (for this suits with their sexes) as in this case to give account of their faith, or the like, to answer to any question that the church asks, or the like . . .[129]

Rogers made little impact on Irish society as his congregation was small and it seems to have disappeared when he returned to London, after only a short stay in Dublin.

Of more significance was the Quaker community. Between 1660 and 1740 it has been estimated that there were approximately 6500 members of the Irish Society of Friends. Fundamental to Quaker belief was a rejection of hierarchy within the church. All believers were equal, regardless of sex, and women were permitted to preach and to prophesy. The initiative for women preaching in Ireland came from English women who included Ireland on their missionary journeys but a small number of Irish-born women also preached. Katherine McLoughlin, for example, preached in market places and in private houses throughout the north in the 1670s. She was reported by a fellow Quaker to be of 'great service here, and some were convinced by her and we had very large meetings'.[130] Women preachers were not, however, well received in Irish towns and they were subject to physical and verbal abuse. Within the Irish Quaker community there was an ambiguous attitude towards women preachers and, increasingly in the late seventeenth century, vocal opposition to women preaching outside the home was expressed. Although support for women preachers continued throughout the eighteenth century, most Quaker women confined their public activities to attendance at Women's Meetings which were first started in Ireland in the late 1670s. The existence of separate meetings for women was a recognition of the contribution of women to the movement but, at the same time, it excluded women from some of the affairs discussed in the men's meetings. As Phil Kilroy has documented, the business of the women's meetings was usually centred on what were perceived as women's issues such as the care of children and the welfare of widows and young single women. More important business concerning the organisation of the Society and financial afairs were dealt with by the men.[131]

No special role was allotted to women in the Baptist Church. The memoir of Ann Fowkes, who lived in Kilkenny and Waterford, indicates, however, that women were encouraged to read, listen to sermons and keep spiritual diaries in which they recorded their daily religious feelings and thoughts. Ann Fowkes attended sermons as a child and, with her grandmother's encouragement, was formally accepted into the Baptist community when she was twelve years of age. She records travelling long distances to hear sermons and take notes. The emotional and intellectual commitment of Fowkes to the Baptist Church was the model which was later taken up by evangelical Protestantism and was to prove so appealing to women in the larger Protestant denominations in the eigtheenth century.[132]

Notes

1 Paul Walsh (Ed), *Leabhar Chlainne Suibhne. An Account of the MacSweeney Families in Ireland* (Dublin, 1920), p. 67.

2 Dianne Hall, *Women and the Church in Medieval Ireland, c. 1140–1540* (Dublin, 2003) is the first published study of women's patronage in the medieval Irish Church. On the fifteenth-century religious revival see pp. 60–2, 89–91. See also Mary Ann Lyons 'Lay Female Piety and Church Patronage in Late Medieval Ireland' in Brendan Bradshaw and Dáire Keogh (Eds), *Christianity in Ireland. Revisiting the Story* (Blackrock, Co. Dublin, 2002), pp. 57–75.

3 Cited in Helena Concannon, *The Blessed Eucharist in Irish History* (Dublin, 1932), pp. 187–8; A. Gwynn and R. N. Hadcock (Eds), *Medieval Religious Houses: Ireland* (Dublin, 1970), p. 247. See also Hall, op. cit., p. 61.

4 The Franciscan monastery at Adare, Co. Limerick also benefitted from female patronage. See ibid., p. 198; Gwynn and Hadcock (Eds), *Medieval Religious*

Houses: Ireland, pp. 247, 248, 300; Concannon, *The Blessed Eucharist in Irish History*, pp. 190, 193–5; John O'Heyne, *The Irish Dominicans of the Seventeenth Century* (English transl. by Ambrose Coleman, Dublin, 1902), pp. 227–9.

5 Heather A. King, 'Late Medieval Crosses in County Meath c. 1470–1635' in *Proceedings of the Royal Irish Academy*, **84**, section C (1984), pp. 79–115.

6 Hall, op. cit., pp. 21–41.

7 Walsh (Ed), *Leabhar Chlainne Suibhne. An Account of the MacSweeney Families in Ireland*, pp. 66–9.

8 Concannon, *The Blessed Eucharist in Irish History*, p. 189. Gwynn and Hadcock (Eds), *Medieval Religious Houses: Ireland* (Dublin, 1970), p. 263. For other women living in a similar devout way see ibid., pp. 190–1. See also Hall, op. cit., pp. 239–40, 245–6; Merry E. Wiesner, *Women and Gender in Early Modern Europe* (Cambridge, 1993, 2nd Edition, 2000), p. 183.

9 Gwynn and Hadcock (Eds), *Medieval Religious Houses: Ireland* (Dublin, 1970), p. 263. See also Wiesner, *Women and Gender in Early Modern Europe*, p. 183.

10 See also Hall, *Women and the Church in Medieval Ireland, c. 1140–1540*, pp. 187–90.

11 Ibid., pp. 91–5.

12 Gwynn and Hadcock (Eds), *Medieval Religious Houses: Ireland*, pp. 307–26. See also Brendan Bradshaw, *The Dissolution of the Religious Orders in Ireland Under Henry VIII* (Cambridge, 1974), pp. 36–7.

13 An exception to this is recorded for Galway in 1511: see Gwynn and Hadcock (Eds), *Medieval Religious Houses: Ireland*, pp. 309, 317.

14 Hall, *Women and the Church in Medieval Ireland, c. 1140–1540*, pp. 207–20.

15 Ibid., pp. 200–6.

16 Brian Ó Dálaigh, 'Mistress, Mother and Abbess: Renalda Ní Bhriain (c. 1447–1510)' in *North Munster Antiquarian Journal*, **xxxii** (1990), pp. 50–63; Hall, op. cit., p. 168.

17 Cited in M. V. Ronan, *The Reformation in Ireland 1536–1558* (London, 1926), p. 143.

18 Cited in Ó Dálaigh, 'Mistress, Mother and Abbess: Renalda Ní Bhriain (c. 1447–1510)', p. 60. See also Hall, op. cit., pp. 225–7.

19 Hall, op. cit., pp. 174–6.

20 There is a detailed description of the manuscript in Walsh (Ed), *Leabhar Chlainne Suibhne. An Account of the MacSweeney Families in Ireland.*

21 Jocelyn Wogan-Browne and Glyn S. Burgess (Eds), *Virgin Lives and Holy Deaths. Two Exemplary Biographies for Anglo-Norman Women* (London and Vermont, 1996); Ellen Muller, 'Saintly Virgins. The Veneration of Virgin Saints in Religious Women's Communities' in Lène Dresen-Coenders (Ed),

Saints and She-Devils. Images of Women in the 15th and 16th Centuries (London, 1987), pp. 93–6.

22 Marina Warner, *Joan of Arc. The Image of Female Heroism* (London, 1981), p. 132.

23 Peter Harbison, *Pilgrimage in Ireland. The Monuments and the People* (London, 1991), pp. 60–1, 64.

24 Gearóid Mac Niocaill (Ed), *Crown Surveys of Lands, 1540–41. With the Kildare Rental Begun in 1518* (Dublin, 1992), p. 356. See also T. C. Barnard, 'Introduction: The Dukes of Ormond' in T. C. Barnard and Jane Fenton (Eds), *The Dukes of Ormond, 1610–1745* (Woodbridge, 2000), p. 35, for a portrait of St Catherine in the Butler household in the late seventeenth century. For a female religious community dedicated to St Catherine see Hall, *Women and the Church in Medieval Ireland c. 1140–1540*, pp. 84–5.

25 Warner, *Joan of Arc. The Image of Female Heroism*, pp. 135–6. See online version of *Catholic Encyclopedia* (www.newadvent.org/cathen). See also the catalogue of 'Medieval Wall Painting in the English Parish Church' compiled by Anne Marshall (www.paintedchurch.org).

26 Raymond Gillespie, *Devoted People. Belief and Religion in Early Modern Ireland* (Manchester, 1997), p. 65.

27 Máirín Ní Dhonnchadha (Ed), 'Mary, Eve and the Church, c. 600–1800' in Angela Bourke *et al.* (Eds), *Field Day Anthology of Irish Writing, Vol. IV* (Cork, 2002), pp. 49–57, 62–89.

28 Margaret MacCurtain has noted the absence of female saints in 'the long period of medieval Ireland, when Rome gradually assumed control of who should be "raised to the altars of the church"' (Margaret MacCurtain, 'Women and the Religious Reformation in Early Modern Ireland' in Bourke *et al.* (Eds), *Field Day Anthology of Irish Writing, Vol. IV*, p. 465). See also pp. 244–5 below.

29 Ibid., pp. 465–6; Hall, *Women and the Church in Medieval Ireland, c. 1140–1540*, pp. 201–6.

30 The community of Grace Dieu was alleged to have survived by moving their home to a more remote part of their original estate which had been acquired by the Barnewall family. See Bradshaw, *The Dissolution of the Religious Orders in Ireland*; MacCurtain, op. cit., p. 466; Hall, op. cit., pp. 205–6.

31 John Brady, 'Keeping the Faith at Gormanston, 1569–1629' in The Franciscan Fathers (Eds), *Father Luke Wadding Commemorative Volume* (Dublin, 1957), pp. 409–10.

32 Cited in Avril De Búrca, 'The Poor Clares, Galway, 1642–1996 – the Complete Story' (unpublished, BA dissertation, University of Limerick, 1996), p. 24.

33 Helena Concannon, *The Queen of Ireland. An Historical Account of Ireland's Devotion to the Blessed Virgin* (Dublin, 1938), pp. 136–41; Margaret

MacCurtain, 'Women, Education and Learning in Early Modern Ireland' in Margaret MacCurtain and Mary O'Dowd (Eds), *Women in Early Modern Ireland* (Edinburgh, 1991), pp. 169–70.

34 Cathaldus Giblin, *A History of Irish Catholicism, Volume IV. Irish Exiles in Catholic Europe* (Dublin, 1971), pp. 54–63; Phil Kilroy, 'Women and the Reformation in Seventeenth-Century Ireland' in MacCurtain and O'Dowd (Eds), *Women in Early Modern Ireland*, p. 192; Margaret MacCurtain, 'Women, Education and Learning in Early Modern Ireland' in MacCurtain and O'Dowd (Eds), *Women in Early Modern Ireland*, pp. 169–70.

35 Ibid., pp. 163–4; F. X. Martin, *Friar Nugent. A Study of Francis Lavalin Nugent (1569–1635) Agent of the Counter-Reformation* (Rome and London, 1962), p. 265; Gráinne Henry, *The Irish Military Community in Spanish Flanders, 1586–1621* (Dublin, 1992), p. 78.

36 De Búrca, 'The Poor Clares, Galway, 1642–1996 – the Complete Story', appendix v.

37 Helena Concannon, *The Poor Clares in Ireland (A.D. 1629–A.D. 1929)* (Dublin, 1929), pp. 1–50.

38 Ibid.; Mrs Thomas Concannon, *Irish Nuns in Penal Times* (London, 1931); Kilroy, 'Women and the Reformation in Seventeenth-Century Ireland', pp. 191–2; MacCurtain, 'Women, Education and Learning in Early Modern Ireland', pp. 168–70.

39 Olwen Hufton, *The Prospect Before Her. A History of Women in Western Europe* (London, 1995), pp. 359–96; Elizabeth Rapley, *The Dévotes. Women and Church in Seventeenth-Century France* (Montreal, 1990).

40 Eleanor Knott (Ed), 'An Irish Seventeenth-Century Translation of the Rule of St Clare' in *Eriú*, **15** (1948); MacCurtain, 'Women, Education and Learning in Early Modern Ireland', pp. 168–9; MacCurtain, 'Women and the Religious Reformation in Early Modern Ireland', pp. 460–1.

41 See, for example, Gillespie, *Devoted People*, p. 13; Alan Ford, *The Protestant Reformation in Ireland* (Frankfurt am Main, 1985), pp. 32–3; C. Litton Falkiner (Ed), 'Barnabe Rich's "Remembrances of the State of Ireland, 1612" With Notices of Other Manuscript Reports by the Same Writer, on Ireland Under James the First' in *Proceedings of the Royal Irish Academy*, **xxvi**, Section C (1906), p. 131; Richard Bagwell, *Ireland Under the Tudors* (3 vols., London, 1885–90), vol. iii, pp. 245–6; *Calendar of State Papers: Ireland*, 1596–8, p. 487; Tadhg Ó hAnnracháin, 'Theory in the Absence of Fact: Irish Women and the Catholic Reformation' in Christine Meek and Catherine Lawless (Eds), *Studies on Medieval and Early Modern Women. Pawns or Players?* (Dublin, 2003), pp. 141–54.

42 Vincent P. Carey, *Surviving the Tudors. The 'Wizard' Earl of Kildare and English Rule in Ireland, 1537–1586* (Dublin, 2002), pp. 193–4. See also p. 10 above.

43 Ó hAnnracháin, op. cit., pp. 141–54; Concannon, *The Blessed Eucharist in Irish History*, pp. 211–320.

44 Concannon, *The Blessed Eucharist in Irish History*, pp. 223–4.

45 Colm Lennon, 'Mass in the Manor-House: the Counter-Reformation in Dublin, 1560–1630' in James Kelly and Dáire Keogh (Eds), *History of the Catholic Diocese of Dublin* (Dublin, 2000), pp. 112–43; Ó hAnnracháin, op. cit., pp. 141–54.

46 Hufton, *The Prospect Before Her*, p. 379.

47 Cited from the 1613 annual letter of the Dublin-based Jesuits in Fergus M. O'Donoghue, 'The Jesuit Mission in Ireland 1598–1651' (unpublished, Ph.D. thesis, Catholic University of America, Washington, 1981), p. 74.

48 See translation of excerpt concerning Margaret Ball in MacCurtain, 'Women and the Religious Reformation in Early Modern Ireland', pp. 472–3. For other Jesuit biographies of holy women see Hufton, *The Prospect Before Her*, pp. 377–9. See also Marie B. Rowlands, 'Recusant Women 1560–1640' in Mary Prior (Ed), *Women in English Society 1500–1800* (London, 1985), pp. 162–6.

49 Bourke *et al.* (Eds), *Field Day Anthology of Irish Writing, Vol. IV*, p. 472.

50 David Rothe, *Analecta Sacra, Nova et Mira de Rebus Catholicorvm in Hibernia Pro Fide & Religione Gestis, Diuisa in Tres Partes* (Cologne, 1617); edited by P. F. Moran, *The Analecta of David Rothe, Bishop of Ossory* (Dublin, 1884). The section on Margaret Ball is translated in Bourke *et al.* (Eds), *Field Day Anthology of Irish Writing, Vol. IV*, pp. 473–4.

51 We know from the wills of Margaret Ball's two sons that they had strong religious convictions which suggests that they had been reared in a religious household. See W. Ball Wright, *Ball Family Records* (York, 1908), appendix, pp. x–xx.

52 Concannon, *The Blessed Eucharist in Irish History*, pp. 209–10; Gregory Cleary, *Father Luke Wadding and St. Isidore's College, Rome: Biographical and Historical Notes and Documents* (Rome, 1925), pp. 5–6.

53 Cathaldus Giblin, 'The Processus Datariae and the Appointment of Irish Bishops in the Seventeenth Century' in The Franciscan Fathers (Ed), *Father Luke Wadding Commemorative Volume*, pp. 542–3. See also P. J. Corish, *The Catholic Community in the Seventeenth and Eighteenth Centuries* (Dublin, 1981), p. 27.

54 Lennon, 'Mass in the Manor-House: the Counter-Reformation in Dublin, 1560–1630', pp. 121–3.

55 The information on the countess of Kildare is taken from O'Donoghue, 'The Jesuit Mission in Ireland 1598–1651'. See also Concannon, *The Blessed Eucharist in Irish History*, pp. 313–15.

56 O'Donoghue, 'The Jesuit Mission in Ireland 1598–1651', p. 203.

57 Ibid., pp. 208–9.

58 Ibid., pp. 211, 273; Lennon, 'Mass in the Manor-House: the Counter-Reformation in Dublin, 1560–1630', p. 121.

59 Edmund Hogan, *Distinguished Irishmen of the Sixteenth Century* (London, 1894), p. 34.

60 Ibid., p. 37.

61 Colm Lennon, *The Urban Patriciates of Early Modern Ireland: A Case-Study of Limerick* (NUI O'Donnell Lecture, Dublin, 1999), p. 16; Kilroy, 'Women and the Reformation in Seventeenth-Century Ireland', pp. 189–91; Concannon, *The Queen of Ireland,* pp. 111–14; Brady, 'Keeping the Faith at Gormanston, 1569–1629', p. 409.

62 Rapley, *The Dévotes. Women and Church in Seventeenth-Century France.*

63 Ibid., pp. 28–34.

64 See Kilroy, 'Women and the Reformation', p. 189.

65 Rapley, *The Dévotes. Women and Church in Seventeenth-Century France.*

66 Ibid., p. 46.

67 John McErlean, *The Sodality of the Blessed Virgin Mary in Ireland. A Short History* (Dublin, 1928), pp. 5–16. See also R. S. Devane, 'A Pioneer of Catholic Action (1584–1934). A Forgotten Chapter of History' in *Irish Ecclesiastical Record,* vol. xliv (1934), pp. 581–2; O'Donoghue, 'The Jesuit Mission in Ireland 1598–1651', pp. 147–8; Corish, *The Catholic Community in the Seventeenth and Eighteenth Centuries,* pp. 37–9.

68 The Dominicans and Franciscans also established lay confraternities in Dublin in the 1620s although it is not clear if their membership included women. See Giblin, 'The Processus Datariae and the Appointment of Irish Bishops in the Seventeenth Century', pp. 530–1.

69 Knott (Ed), 'An Irish Seventeenth-Century Translation of the Rule of St. Clare'. On Mary Ward see Hufton, *The Prospect Before Her,* pp. 379–80.

70 Ó hAnnracháin, 'Theory in the Absence of Fact: Irish Women and the Catholic Reformation', p. 149.

71 John Hanly (Ed), *The Letters of Saint Oliver Plunkett 1625–1681* (Dublin, 1979).

72 James Kelly, 'The Impact of the Penal Laws' in James Kelly and Dáire Keogh (Eds), *History of the Catholic Diocese of Dublin,* p. 146.

73 Concannon, *Irish Nuns in Penal Days,* pp. 96–9; Patrick Nolan, *The Irish Dames of Ypres. Being a History of the Royal Irish Abbey of Ypres* (Dublin, 1903).

74 Corish, *The Catholic Community in the Seventeenth and Eighteenth Centuries,* pp. 58–9.

75 For a summary of the impact of the Reformation on English women see Diane Willen, 'Women and Religion in Early Modern England' in Sherrin Marshall (Ed), *Women in Reformation and Counter-Reformation Europe. Private and Public Worlds* (Bloomington, Indiana, 1989), pp. 140–65; and Diane Willen, 'Godly Women in Early Modern England: Puritanism and Gender' in *Journal of Ecclesiastical History*, **43** (4), (1992), pp. 561–80. See also Patricia Crawford, *Women and Religion in England 1500–1720* (London, 1993).

76 MacCurtain, 'Women and the Religious Reformation in Early Modern Ireland', *Vol. IV*, p. 466.

77 Mary Prior, 'Reviled and Crucified Marriages: the Position of Tudor Bishops' Wives' in Prior (Ed), *Women in English Society 1500–1800*, pp. 118–48; Wiesner, *Women and Gender in Early Modern Europe*, p. 226.

78 James Murray, 'Ecclesiastical Justice and the Enforcement of the Reformation: the Case of Archbishop Browne and the Clergy of Dublin' in A. Ford, J. McGuire and K. Milne (Eds), *As By Law Established. The Church of Ireland Since the Reformation* (Dublin, 1995), pp. 49–50.

79 E. P. Shirley (Ed), *Original Letters and Papers . . . of the Church in Ireland Under Edward VI, Mary and Elizabeth* (London, 1851), pp. 87–8. See also Henry A. Jefferies, 'Primate George Dowdall and the Marian Restoration' in *Seanchas Ard Mhacha* (1998), **17**, no. 2, pp. 10–11.

80 MacCurtain, 'Women and the Religious Reformation in Early Modern Ireland', p. 466; J. A. George, '*The Vocacyon of Johan Bale* (1553): a Retrospective Sermon From Ireland' in Alan J. Fletcher and Raymond Gillespie (Eds), *Irish Preaching, 700–1700* (Dublin, 2001), p. 99.

81 Cuthbert Mhág Craith (Ed and trans.), *Dán na mBráthar Mionúr* (2 vols., Dublin, 1967, 1980), vol. II, pp. 61, 66. See also Bourke *et al.* (Eds), *Field Day Anthology of Irish Writing, Vol. IV*, pp. 156–9.

82 See Phil Kilroy (Ed), 'Memoirs and Testimonies: Nonconformist Women in Seventeenth-Century Ireland' in Bourke *et al.* (Eds), *Field Day Anthology of Irish Writing, Vol. IV*, pp. 485–6.

83 William King, *A Great Archbishop of Dublin, Quaedam Vitae Meae Insigniora. Edited by Sir Charles Simeon King* (London, 1908), p. 17.

84 G. T. Stokes, *Some Worthies of the Irish Church* (edited by H. J. Lawlor) (London, 1900), pp. 76–8.

85 James Ussher, *A Body of Divinities, or the Sum and Substance of Christian Religion, Catechistically Propounded and Explained, by Way of Question and Answer* (2nd edition, London, 1657), pp. 260–1. Ussher denied responsibility for publishing the catechism which seems to have been compiled from notes taken at catechising classes. See C. R. Elrington (Ed), *The Whole Works of the Most Rev. James Ussher, D.D.* (Dublin, 1847), **i**, pp. 249–50; Nicholas Bernard, *The Life and Death of the Most Reverend and Learned Father of Our Church*

Dr James Ussher (London, 1656), p. 41. For its use see I. M. Green, '"The Necessary Knowledge of the Principles of Religion": Catechism and Catechizing in Ireland, c. 1560–1800' in Ford, McGuire and Milne (Eds), *As By Law Established. The Church of Ireland Since the Reformation*, pp. 61, 86; William P. Bourke, *History of Clonmel* (2nd Edition, Waterford, 1907, reprinted, Kilkenny, 1983), p. 333.

86 Ezekiel Hopkins, *The Works of the Right Reverend and Learned Ezekiel Hopkins, Late Lord Bishop of London-Derry in Ireland* (London, 1701), p. 165.

87 Bernard, *The Life and Death of the Most Reverend and Learned Father of Our Church Dr James Ussher*, pp. 19–20.

88 Ussher, *A Body of Divinities, or the Sum and Substance of Christian Religion*, p. 129.

89 James Seaton Reid, *History of the Presbyterian Church in Ireland* (2 vols., London, 1853), vol. i, p. 182.

90 Hopkins, *The Works of the Right Reverend and Learned Ezekiel Hopkins*, p. 165. For Hopkins's concern with non-conformity see Richard L. Greaves, '"That's No Good Religion That Disturbs Government": The Church of Ireland and the Nonconformist Challenge' in Ford, McGuire and Milne (Eds), *As By Law Established. The Church of Ireland Since the Reformation*, pp. 127, 129.

91 Bernard, *The Life and Death of the Most Reverend and Learned Father of Our Church Dr James Ussher*, p. 58.

92 Thomas Wharton Jones (Ed), *A True Relation of the Life and Death of . . . William Bedell . . .* (Camden Society, London, 1872), p. 19.

93 Hopkins, *The Works of the Right Reverend and Learned Ezekiel Hopkins*, preface. See also F. R. Bolton, *The Caroline Tradition of the Church of Ireland With Particular Reference to Bishop Jeremy Taylor* (London, 1958), pp. 182–7.

94 R. Loeber, 'Sculptured Memorials to the Dead in Early Seventeenth-Century Ireland: A Survey from *Monumenta Biblanae* and Other Sources' in *Proceedings of the Royal Irish Academy*, vol. 81 C (1982), 267–93.

95 See, for example, Ussher, *A Body of Divinities, or the Sum and Substance of Christian Religion*, p. 261; Hopkins, *The Works of the Right Reverend and Learned Ezekiel Hopkins*, p. 153.

96 Bernard, *The Life and Death of the Most Reverend and Learned Father of Our Church Dr James Ussher*, p. 22; William Hamilton, *The Life and Character of James Bonnell Esq* (Dublin, 1703), p. 255. See also Gillespie, *Devoted People*, p. 12.

97 Wharton Jones (Ed), *A True Relation of the Life and Death of . . . William Bedell . . .* , p. 17.

98 Henry Leslie, *A Discourse of Praying With the Spirit, and With the Understanding whereof Extemporary Premeditate Set Forms of Prayer . . .* (London, 1660), p. 33.

99 Raymond Gillespie, 'Reading the Bible in Seventeenth-Century Ireland' in Bernadette Cunningham and Máire Kennedy (Eds), *The Experience of Reading: Irish Historical Perspectives* (Dublin, 1999), pp. 17, 22, 29.

100 Cited in ibid., p. 25. See also p. 206 below.

101 Ibid., p. 23; Dublin Thosel Records, Dublin City Archive, C1/J/2/4; See also verse attributed to Lady Offaly in *Journal of the Co. Kildare Archaeological Society*, **10** (1922–28), p. 108.

102 See p. 226 below.

103 Jane Ohlmeyer, 'Strafford, the "London Business" and the "New British History"' in J. F. Merritt (Ed), *The Political World of Thomas Wentworth, Earl of Strafford, 1621–1641* (Cambridge, 1996), p. 237; *DNB*; Michael Perceval-Maxwell, *The Outbreak of the Rebellion of 1641* (Dublin, 1994), pp. 56, 117, 143, 309. See also Patrick Little, 'Providence and Posterity: A Letter From Lord Mountnorris to his Daughter, 1642' in *Irish Historical Studies*, **xxii**, no. 128 (2001), pp. 556–66.

104 Richard L. Greaves, *God's Other Children, Protestant Nonconformists and the Emergence of Denominational Churches in Ireland, 1660–1700* (Stanford, 1997), pp. 49, 89–90, 127.

105 W. D. Killen (Ed), *A True Narrative of the Rise and Progress of the Presbyterian Church in Ireland (1623–1670), By the Reverend Patrick Adair* (Belfast, 1866), pp. 16–17, 191, 218–19, 246–7, 281, 319; Reid, *History of the Presbyterian Church in Ireland*, i, 178.

106 Killen (Ed), *A True Narrative of the Rise and Progress of the Presbyterian Church in Ireland (1623–1670)*, pp. 39–40.

107 Reid, *History of the Presbyterian Church in Ireland*, i, 266–7; Thomas M'Crie (Ed), *The Life of Mr Robert Blair* . . . (Edinburgh, 1848), p. 148.

108 Ibid., p. 116; Raymond Gillespie, '"Into Another Intensity": Prayer in Irish Nonconformity, 1650–1700' in Kevin Herlihy (Ed), *The Religion of Irish Dissent, 1650–1800* (Dublin, 1996), pp. 35–9.

109 For Ulster Presbyterian support for private prayer meetings see David Stevenson, 'The Radical Party in the Kirk, 1637–45' in *Journal of Ecclesiastical History*, **xxv**, no. 2 (1974), pp. 135–65.

110 M'Crie (Ed), *The Life of Mr Robert Blair . . .*, p. 116. The autobiography was completed by Blair's son-in-law who was also a minister.

111 Ibid., pp. 104–5.

112 Reid, *History of the Presbyterian Church in Ireland*, I, pp. 182–3. See also Kilroy, 'Women and the Reformation in Seventeenth-Century Ireland', pp. 179–80.

113 Marilyn J. Westerkamp, *Triumph of the Laity. Scots-Irish Piety and the Great Awakening 1625–1760* (Oxford, 1988), pp. 16, 24–5. See also Peter Brooke,

Ulster Presbyterianism. The Historical Perspective 1610–1970 (Dublin, 1987), pp. 17–19.

114 Cited in Gillespie, *Devoted People*, p. 22.

115 M'Crie (Ed), *The Life of Mr Robert Blair . . .*, pp. 117, 129.

116 Ibid., p. 141.

117 King, *A Great Archbishop of Dublin*, pp. 2–4; Phil Kilroy, *Protestant Dissent and Controversy in Ireland 1660–1714* (Cork, 1994), p. 34.

118 Reid, *History of the Presbyterian Church in Ireland*, i, pp. 182–3.

119 Robert Chambre, 'An Explanation of the Shorter Catechism of the Reverend Assembly of Divines' (unpublished manuscript, 1680, Union Theological College, Belfast), pp. 101, 108.

120 Ibid., pp. 357, 359.

121 Ussher, *A Body of Divinities, or the Sum and Substance of Christian Religion*, pp. 131–3.

122 Hopkins, *The Works of the Right Reverend and Learned Ezekiel Hopkins*, p. 167. See also pp. 248–50 below.

123 Reid, *History of the Presbyterian Church in Ireland*, i, pp. 274–5.

124 Perceval-Maxwell, *The Outbreak of the Irish Rebellion of 1641*, p. 56; Reid, *History of the Presbyterian Church in Ireland*, i, pp. 218–20, 280–1; Killen (Ed), *A True Narrative of the Rise and Progress of the Presbyterian Church in Ireland (1623–1670)*, p. 61.

125 John Rushworth (Ed), *Historical Collections of Private Passages of State* (8 vols., London, 1659–1701), vol. 8, pp. 236–40.

126 Greaves, *God's Other Children*, pp. 59, 91, 142.

127 The emergence of Presbyterianism as a denominational church is documented in Greaves, *God's Other Children*.

128 John Rogers, *Ohel or Beth-shemesh. A Tabernacle for the Sun: or Irenicum Evangelicum . . .* (London, 1653). See also Kilroy, 'Memoirs and Testimonies: Nonconformist Women in Seventeenth-Century Ireland', pp. 480–9.

129 Rogers, *Ohel or Beth-shemesh. A Tabernacle for the Sun: or Irenicum Evangelicum . . .*, p. 294.

130 Cited in Phil Kilroy, 'Women and the Reformation in Seventeenth-Century Ireland', pp. 184–5.

131 Ibid., pp. 180–8. Phil Kilroy, 'Quaker Women in Ireland, 1660–1740' in *Irish Journal of Feminist Studies*, 2, no. 2 (1997), pp. 1–30. I am grateful to Dr Kilroy for sending me a copy of her article.

132 *A Memoir of Mistress Ann Fowkes Née Geale Died Aged 82 Years, With Some Recollection of Her Family A.D. 1642–1774. Written By Herself* (Dublin, 1892); Kilroy, 'Memoirs and Testimonies: Nonconformist Women in Seventeenth-Century Ireland'; Kevin Herlihy, '"A Gay and Flattering World": Irish Baptist Piety and Perspective, 1650–1780' in Kevin Herlihy (Ed), *The Religion of Irish Dissent, 1650–1800* (Dublin, 1996), p. 65.

CHAPTER 6

Charity, Catechising and Convents: Women and Religious Institutions, 1690–1800

Reforming, manners, family prayer and evangelicalism

In 1704 the Presbyterian minister Joseph Boyse preached at the funeral of Mrs Anne Reading of Rathfarnham, County Dublin. Boyse, a well-known advocate for Presbyterianism, used the opportunity to urge the necessity for the daily practice of piety, a common theme in his sermons. Predictably, he praised Mrs Reading's charity and Christian love but he also took care to note 'how constant she was in her secret converses with God'. Following her death, he told the congregation that there had been found among Mrs Reading's possessions, 'many papers of her own writing . . . containing meditations and prayers'.[1] Boyse was not alone in his encouragement of women to read, write and engage in conversations about the Scriptures. As we have seen, private reading of the Bible was a fundamental tenet of Presbyterianism and funeral sermons by Presbyterian ministers regularly praised the subject's daily religious exercises.[2] Fourteen years after his sermon at Mrs Reading's funeral, Boyse was scathingly critical of the Roman Catholic Church that discouraged independent reading of Scripture by women:

It is an illusion to persuade oneself, that the knowledge of the mysteries of religion must not be imparted to women, by reading of the sacred books. The abuse of Scripture and heresies are not sprung from the simplicity of women, but from the proud knowledge of men.[3]

Boyse was an advocate of the campaign to reform Irish manners of the 1690s. The campaign promoted family prayer and more moral behaviour, particularly among young men, and was widely supported by clergy in the Church of Ireland. Unlike Presbyterian ministers, however, the Anglican clergy stressed the role of the father or head of household as instructor and religious guide of his family.[4] The Church of Ireland shared some of the concerns of the Catholic Church with the potential dangers of individuals engaging in religious exercises without guidance. It was for this reason that the reform campaign approved the publication of books in Ireland, designed to provide instruction on what prayers to say at particular times and on particular occasions. By the early eighteenth century there was a proliferation of this type of literature, intended to assist families with morning and evening prayers and prayers to be said by specific members of the family. *The Whole Duty of Prayer*, for example, included prayers for a husband, wife, child, widow, orphan, young man or maid, servant and a woman with child.[5] It was in the 1690s too that the first Irish editions of *The Whole Duty of Man* appeared. Directed at the 'meanest reader' it provided sermon-like texts to be read on Sundays by the head of the household or, if he or she could not read, by another member of the family who could.[6]

The Whole Duty of Man listed among the duties of parents the catechising of young people. Despite the patriarchal tone of the religious societies associated with the reforming of manners, the emphasis on family prayer helped to reinforce the role of the mother in instructing her children. When Thomas Pollard published his *The Necessity and Advantages of Family Prayer*, he dedicated it to Lady Capell, the wife of the lord lieutenant, and praised her 'regular and constant observance of family prayer'.[7] Similarly in his *An Exhortation to the Inhabitants of Down and Connor, Concerning the Religious Education of their Children* . . . which appeared in 1695, Samuel Foley, Bishop of Down and Connor 1694–5, assumed throughout that he was addressing two parents and exhorted them by their own lives to give a good example to their children, and to instruct them in the Christian faith as soon as they were capable of understanding.[8] Catechisms that could be used by both parents in the home were also on the lists of books published in Ireland at this time.[9]

Literacy was not considered an essential requirement for full membership of the Church of Ireland but it was increasingly by the early decades of the eighteenth century a recommended one, even for those at the lower end of the social scale. In 1739, Edward Synge, the Archbishop of Tuam, published a short pamphlet for use in the preparation of servant girls for confirmation. The pamphlet was specifically written in words which were 'easy and familiar' so that it could be easily read by literate servants. The accessible language also meant that it could still be learnt by rote by those who could not read. The literate servant was also encouraged to read the Scriptures to her illiterate colleague on a regular basis.[10]

Whether they were reading the recommended prayers of the *Whole Duty of Man* or following the Scriptures on their own, more women within the main Protestant denominations were thinking, reading, writing and talking about religion in early eighteenth-century Ireland than at any previous time. Not surprisingly, therefore, they were attracted to societies that fostered new and often more intense ways of expressing their spirituality. By the mid-1740s, Dublin had an informal network of evangelical groups and membership lists show 'an unmistakable preponderance of women'.[11] Among the leading advocates of evangelical Protestantism were women from aristocratic and landed families, often connected by marriage to descendants of families that had opened their homes to Presbyterian ministers in the seventeenth century.[12]

By the early eighteenth century, however, Presbyterianism had established a formal church network which, as indicated in the last chapter, was less dependent on the auxiliary support services of women. Women involved in the evangelical revival of the eighteenth century were, consequently, drawn to newer sects such as the Moravian society and, particularly, Methodism. As was the case for Presbyterianism in the seventeenth century, early Irish Methodism was dependent on a support structure of sympathetic women who made their homes available for meetings and provided hospitality and lodgings for itinerant preachers. In the class meetings held by Methodists, women could engage in discussion of their daily spiritual lives, share in mutual confession of sins and participate in prayer meetings.[13] Members were also encouraged to keep journals that were circulated among members or read aloud at class meetings. Eighteenth-century Methodism, like the early Quaker movement, also allowed women to preach and to take a leadership role in classes.[14]

The appeal of Methodism for an Irishwoman can be traced through the journal of Angel Anna Slack. Slack was born in 1748, the year after John Wesley's first visit to Ireland, and lived as a child with her godmother and cousin, the countess of Roscommon. She also spent time in her uncle's home near Dublin where she had access to his library and acquired a 'taste for serious authors', partly through the encouragement of her uncle's housekeeper. Slack's family were members of the Church of Ireland and her uncle took his duties as religious head of the household seriously. As his niece noted in her journal, he 'seldom ever neglected the public service of the Church, and every Sabbath called his servants to hear a sermon and prayer in the parlour'.[15]

Slack married her cousin, a landlord, and went to live in his family home near Drumshanbo in County Leitrim when she was about sixteen or seventeen. In Leitrim, Slack encountered Methodism for the first time through the wife of the local church clerk. Subsequently, Slack visited Dublin where she became ill and while recovering overheard two Methodist men praying and singing. She was so overcome by the sound of their prayers that she requested one of them to take her to the Methodist preaching-house that the two men attended. The intensity of the preacher at the meeting triggered a strong emotional response in Slack: 'My heart throbbed and I was obliged to press myself against the seat where I kneeled to prevent my sobs from being taken notice of, but when I found others as much affected as myself, I gave an unconfined scope to my tears.'

When she returned to Leitrim, Slack made contact with local Methodists including a minister, Mr Creighton, with whom she developed a friendship and a long-term correspondence. She also wrote to her Methodist contacts in Dublin for their assistance in getting 'preachers to call at a little farm house near mine, for I feared to ask them at first lest Mr Slack should forbid them'. Later, Slack helped to form a Methodist class in her local area in which, she wrote, she 'was obliged to take the office of leader'.

Slack's journal manifests the emotional appeal of Methodism and its centrality in her daily life. When she returned to Leitrim she eagerly awaited the spiritual experience of being justified and was a little disappointed that although she looked for 'thunderings and lightning' the Lord came to her in a 'still small voice' while she was praying with the wife of a visiting minister. Even then, however, she described the experience in physical terms:

when I arose from my knees I found all my fears were gone, that condemnation vanished and that I could tread as light as if mounted on air – a pleasing inward warmth diffused through my heart, I felt peace indeed.

Slack's husband did not initially join the Methodist movement but, persuaded by his wife, he eventually became a member and the couple raised their children as Methodists. As Hempton and Hill have noted, this was a common pattern in many Methodist families in which the wife or daughter were the first to be converted.[16] Slack's contacts with sympathetic ministers were an important source of her religious belief but her journal suggests that she drew her strongest emotional strength from her friendships with other women, particularly those who participated in the Leitrim network of the Society. She also wrote regularly to female relatives and other women who, like her, were followers of Wesley.[17]

Methodism gave Slack a strong sense of identity and of belonging to a community set apart from the rest of the world. One of the attractions of Methodism for young middle- and upper-class women lay in its promotion of an austere lifestyle that eschewed their more regular, and possibly rather dull, social obligations. Slack revelled in abandoning the normal social round of women in her class. She shunned attendance at the theatre, the playing of cards and the wearing of 'shining ornaments' and rejoiced when some neighbours commented on the oddness of her dress.[18] Meetings of the small Methodist congregation in the north-west were often held in an atmosphere of considerable local hostility and this also must have engendered mixed feelings of excitement and fear at belonging to a community under siege for the sake of its religious beliefs.

There is very little direct comment on contemporary politics in the journal but Methodism inevitably provoked a questioning of the establishment and an awareness of being in conflict with it. Slack was not a political radical but her advocacy of Methodism compelled her to view her wealthy, landed conformist background from a new questioning perspective. She and her family remained within the Church of Ireland but she was critical of what she perceived as the lack of piety demonstrated by Church of Ireland clergy, a view which led her to sympathise with local Catholic agitation against the payment of tithes.

The common people are really very much burdened to support bishops and rectors in luxury, nor do I think it just that they should be oppressed for clergy whom they receive no benefit from, either in public or private; and almost every person in this parish have declared that they will not pay any more tithes, and that they will not oppose the Proctors when they take up pledges for the same, but will let their cattle go to pound peacefully, and when the day of sale comes they will murder any who buy or attempt to buy any of them. They have given notice of their intention by putting up papers on the church and chapel doors.

Slack held traditional views of women advocating that they should be 'decked with modesty and ornamented with a meek and quiet spirit' but through Methodism she had a more public role than many of her social contemporaries. Within her class Slack was the only member justified, a fact that endowed her with a leadership role in the group. She also assumed a controlling position in her family with her husband following her lead in adopting Methodism.

Methodism initially permitted women to preach but, like women preachers among the Society of Friends, not all Methodists approved. Slack makes no reference to women preachers in her diary which suggests that they were not a common phenomenon in Ireland. One of the few known Irish women preachers in the eighteenth century was Alice Cambridge, who was born in Bandon in 1762 and preached as a young woman in towns in the south of Ireland. Cambridge encountered considerable opposition from the crowds who gathered to hear her and she was booed and subjected to physical as well as verbal abuse. In 1802 the Methodist Conference in Ireland resolved 'that it is contrary both to Scripture and to prudence that women should preach or exhort in public'.[19] As Hempton and Hill have suggested, women's preaching within Methodism should be seen 'as exceptional and transitional rather than officially sanctioned and accepted'.[20]

Women and philanthropy

Women were traditionally associated with charitable works, alms-giving and patronage to the poor. Irish annals routinely praised the generosity of the wives of Irish chieftains.[21] In the sixteenth century a new form of institutional charity developed in Ireland as it did in other European countries. The building of almshouses and other charitable institutions was sponsored by private donations and legacies. Women were associated with donations through their husbands but widows also began to make bequests for the poor, especially for poor widows and other destitute women.[22]

A strong focus of early eighteenth-century Irish charity institutions was on the provision of schools to teach the poor useful skills as well as the fundamentals of Protestantism.[23] The charity schools were generally small and often built by the local landlord on estate property. Wives and widows of landlords were prominent among those who fostered this type of reforming activity. Lady Lanesborough, for example, was patroness of a school in Buttevant, County Cork, while her husband maintained schools in Leitrim and Longford as well as promoting a workhouse in Dublin.[24] In Armagh in the 1730s, a widow, Mrs Mary Drelingcourt, left money in her will for the founding of a school.[25] Wealthy women were also important in the funding of voluntary hospitals in Irish towns in the first half of the eighteenth century. Three of the largest hospitals in Dublin: Steevens', Mercer's and the Foundling Hospital, could trace their origins to female sponsorship.[26]

As indicated in Chapter 4, the expansion in the Irish population in the second half of the eighteenth century coincided with an economic recession. Poor men and women crowded into Irish towns and particularly into Dublin, looking for work of any kind. The consequent problems of prostitution, vagrancy and children abandoned by parents who could not afford to keep them led to heightened concern with the fate of poor, single girls. Women philanthropists were particularly encouraged to take a charitable interest in destitute young women.

There was a close association between women's involvement in charity work and their attachment to evangelical Protestantism which 'promoted personal sobriety and social stability', a sentiment that was at the core of much of the philanthropic projects sponsored by Protestant women.[27] One of the most famous Irish women philanthropists was Lady Arbella Denny whose charity work has been noted elsewhere. Denny was a committed Methodist and much of her philanthropic endeavour was predicated on persuading young women to follow a religious regime in the ordering of their lives. Other women connected with Methodism also became involved in charity projects.[28] In 1790, the Female Orphan Society was established in Dublin for the 'support of destitute female children' who were to be kept in the orphanage from the age of five until they were sixteen years of age. Like Denny's Magdalen Society, the orphanage had strong Methodist support. The initial inspiration for the institution came from Margaret Este, an English Methodist based in Dublin who in the late 1780s went on a fact-finding visit to London to identify institutions that could serve as a model for a Dublin orphanage. The Methodist group centred around the Tighe family: Mrs and Mrs Edward Tighe and Mrs Theodosia Blachford were enthusastic patrons of the orphanage and served on its first committee. When Este died in 1791, she was succeeded as 'Chief guardian' by Mrs Elizabeth Latouche, another Methodist sympathiser and a member of the Dublin banking family.[29] Other women, mainly from Protestant aristocratic or Dublin commercial families, also visited the orphanage on a regular basis. The matron was instructed to read from the New Testament to the girls every morning and any girl who could read was given her own book to 'fix her attention'. They were then 'put to plain work, and in the afternoon knitting or spinning'. After supper in the evening their rooms were to be cleaned. It was expected that most of the girls would be employed as servants on leaving the orphanage. Employment was usually found for them in the households of the lady visitors who in return for financial sponsorship could identify a particular girl whom they wished to employ at a later stage in their own household.[30]

The Female Orphan Society was a public institution that raised money through private subscription and public sermons. A small number of women also experimented with establishing model institutions on their family estates. In the late eighteenth century, Lady Kingston created a model village in Mitchelstown, County Cork, in which there was an orphan school, weaving and spinning schools for girls, a Sunday school and a village library 'well-stocked with select books, religious and entertaining' as well as shops which sold goods and clothes for the poor.[31] In Delgany, County Wicklow, Elizabeth Latouche ran a small orphanage and school.[32]

The demographic crisis of the late eighteenth century resulted in a dramatic increase in the number of infants born to women who could not afford to look after them. Many also crowded into Irish towns and cities. This in turn led to a new concern within philanthropic circles with the fate of poor married or single mothers and their offspring, a task that was perceived as particularly appropriate charitable work for women. In the 1790s there was an expansion in the number of foundling and maternity hospitals established with female assistance.[33] Most were, however, too small to make any impact on infant mortality. The overcrowding in the Dublin Foundling Hospital was the subject of a series of damning parliamentary reports that suggested that infants admitted into the hospital had little chance of survival.[34]

Throughout Europe in the early modern period there was a move away from private alms-giving towards more formal and larger projects designed to reform and educate the poor rather than simply alleviate their destitute state.[35] This trend can be documented in eighteenth-century Ireland with the new emphasis on founding charity schools and the careful selection of suitable candidates for admittance to institutions such as the Magdalen Asylum in Dublin or the Female Orphan Society.[36] The absence of an Irish poor law or of any form of regular parish or government sponsored relief for the destitute meant, however, that private alms-giving remained an essential part of charity in Ireland until the 1830s. Household accounts document the extent to which private or one-to-one charity remained a significant part of the total amount spent on charitable donations. In times of serious dearth in rural Ireland, private charity, much of it administered by women, was often the chief means of relief available. Rosemary Raughter estimated that more women were involved in private benevolence in eighteenth-century Ireland than in the better documented institutional charity. Private charity encompassed a broader cross-section of the female population involving, as it did, women from every social and religious background. It was also less prescriptive in scope than institutional charity and probably reached far more people than the small numbers accepted into the charitable institutions.[37]

In the absence of a parish system of relief, wives of local clergymen also developed a social role as providers of food, occasional lodgings and, sometimes, medical care for the destitute. Edward Synge, Bishop of Elphin, wrote of his wife ministering medical care to his parishioners, a responsibility which he took on after her death. Dorothea Herbert described in her memoirs the waifs and strays that her mother looked after in the vicarage in County Tipperary. They included a foundling child left at the door as well as a drunken Frenchwoman who seems to have earned her keep by teaching French to the Herbert girls.[38]

Even in towns where the poor had access to institutional care, individual women administered care in a private capacity. In the Baptist Geale family in Kilkenny in the early eighteenth century, Mrs Geale, whose husband had a shop in the town, 'always kept a cupboard well stor'd with salves, plaisters and cordials to give away and often dress'd their sores herself, which caus'd her to be much lamented when she quitted her own house to go to live at Waterford . . .'.[39] Geale's daughter Ann implied that her mother helped everyone who asked for her assistance regardless of religious belief. Protestant poor, however, figure largely among those who benefitted from institutional care. Consequently, Catholic gentry families generated their own informal and, of necessity, private charitable structure to assist poor relatives and make donations to needy Catholics.[40]

The absence of a poor law thus gave Irish women more opportunities to be involved in charitable work than in other western countries where the trend towards institutionalised forms of philanthropy was more marked in the eighteenth century. In the early nineteenth century, the writer Anna Maria Hall was struck by the involvement of young women in Ireland in charity work:

one can hardly enter a house where the ladies, young and old, are not engaged in some plan for the relief of their fellow creatures. They bestow quantities of food and clothing and are truely zealous of good works. The sums expended in private charities, considering the limited means of the expenders, is astonishing, for they are ever anxious to relieve the wants of others – even beyond their means.[41]

Lay Catholic women, education and convents

The penal legislation of the late seventeenth century weakened the ability of the Catholic Church to function in public. The laws were intermittently enforced but, until about 1730, there was 'active if sporadic persecution' of

Catholic clergy. Nuns were not specifically included in any of the legislation but they were occasionally harassed. In the late seventeenth century, Irish nuns began to return to Ireland and establish small communities, the most notable being that of the Benedictines in Channel Row in Dublin where the order had a boarding school for daughters of Old English families and provided lodgings for some of the Catholic clergy of the diocese.[42]

The model provided by the Channel Row convent was imitated by a series of Dominican and Poor Clare convents that were established in the early decades of the eighteenth century.[43] By the 1720s, the Poor Clares and the Dominicans had communities in Galway and sent recruits to found convents in Dublin, with the Dominicans taking over the Benedictine Convent in Channel Row, and within a short number of years small Dominican communities were also based in Drogheda and Waterford.[44] Like the Benedictine Convent the purpose of the new convents was two-fold. First, most of the convents had boarding schools attached and provided Irish-based education for girls from wealthy Catholic families. Secondly, the convents provided an auxiliary support service for the Catholic clergy. With the establishment of a more stable, resident hierarchy and clergy in the eighteenth century, housekeeping facilities for Catholic clergy became more structured. The Dominican convents in Dublin and Drogheda had lodgings for bishops and other clergy; and the chapel in the Dublin convent was used to consecrate Catholic bishops.[45] Thus the nuns began to take over some of the services which had been provided by lay women in the seventeenth century. In the absence of a convent, bishops continued to rely on female members of their own family, particularly single nieces who were nominated as housekeepers for their uncles.[46] A life dedicated to the care of a bishop or a priest was particularly praised in one of the few texts in the Irish language addressed to women.[47]

The Dublin Dominican convent also provided rooms for lay Catholic women. Some were elderly and seem to have regarded the convent as a retirement home but others, like Lady Fingall who had a suite of rooms in the convent or the countess of Tyrconnell whose own house was located nearby, seem to have used the facilities of the convent as lay tertiaries and thus, in this way, they continued the strong tertiary tradition within the Irish Church.[48]

The convents of the early eighteenth century focused on educating the elite, the daughters of wealthy Catholic families. The education of the poor, however, became an increasing concern of the Catholic Church in Ireland in the 1730s and 1740s. The success of the government-sponsored Charter Schools as well as private charity schools created anxiety among Catholic clergy that children were being converted to Protestantism.[49] The need for a more structured form of catechising was recognised and the possibility of utilising women to teach young girls began to be appreciated. From the 1740s onwards the correspondence of Irish Catholic clergy demonstrates an awareness of the usefulness of women as teachers and catechisers. Some, like the Dominican bishop of Killala, John Brett, looked to nuns to be employed in this task as teachers of girls. Brett wrote in 1747 of 'how useful the religious ladies are . . . by bringing up young maidens to piety and everything else that is becoming, and consequently the great advantage that would arise from multiplying their houses as much as possible'.[50] Priests returning from France and other Catholic countries were, however, also increasingly critical of the regular orders in Ireland for not catering for the poor and such criticism was particularly levied at female religious orders. In 1750 the Jesuit John Murphy reported to the Vatican on the state of Catholic schools in Ireland. He presented a negative picture of Irish nuns who, he suggested, should take more interest in catechising and teaching the poor. Murphy also delivered a number of sermons to the Poor Clares in Dublin in which he reprimanded them for their lack of adherence to a spiritual life, suggesting that many of them had entered the convent because it was a fashionable thing to do rather than out of a sense of religious commitment.[51]

The small number of convents in Ireland meant, in any case, that relying on them to catechise the masses was impractical. Rather than depend on female religious for catechising the poor, the Catholic clergy increasingly looked to the laity.[52] The lay tradition of involvement in sodalities and confraternities of the seventeenth century was revived. One of the first eighteenth-century societies to be instituted was the Sodality of the Name of Jesus established in Dublin in the 1740s. Its membership was open to 'heads of family, or those who have the charge of others with some authority to punish them for their faults. Both the Husband and Wife (tho' they have no one under their command) that they may charitably admonish one another.'[53] The aim of this sodality was to prevent the use of profane language but the educational value of sodalities was also appreciated by Irish bishops. When the Archbishop of Tuam died in 1749 it was noted that he had formed sodalities for 'teaching catechism to young and old' and more and more bishops were following his example.[54] By the 1780s the Irish Catholic Church was heavily dependent on confraternities and sodalities to teach the catechism and women were frequently in the majority in these associations.[55] In 1799, for example, all the members of the Confraternity of the Blessed Sacrament and Christian Doctrine in St Michan's parish in Dublin were women.[56]

One of the strongest advocates of sodalities was Daniel Delany, appointed Bishop of Kildare and Leighlin in 1783. Delany began his catechism classes in the 1770s when he was a parish priest in Tullow, County Carlow. He soon found 'useful assistants of both sexes amongst the education portions of his flock, who gave aid in training choirs . . . and teaching the catechism'.[57] Following his consecration as bishop, Delany established the Confraternity of the Most Holy Sacrament from which he recruited teachers. By 1788 he had developed a more elite group which became part of the Church-wide Confraternity of Christian Doctrine and which included 'maiden female catechists, spiritual readers and other devout teachers of that description'. They 'constantly attend every morning and evening on all Sundays and Holy Days – for the religious and moral instruction of all, without distinction'. The group was particularly charged with the teaching of single women. Apart from catechising in the Church, the members of the Confraternity were also 'in a private domestic manner to inform and direct . . . families and neighbours' and to perform acts of charity.[58] Delany was an enthusiastic supporter of lay women's involvement in the Church and visited homes in his diocese enlisting wives and daughters. He also acknowledged that women were far more likely to join his Confraternity 'with ten times more ardent zeal' than the men.[59]

It was from this mobilisation of Catholic lay women that the most important development in relation to eighteenth-century Catholic women emerged – the founding of new female religious communities which looked to French religious communities for their inspiration rather than to the more traditional orders already established in Ireland. Two women, in particular, are identified with this development, Teresa Mulally and Nano Nagle. Both women began their religious activities as lay women teaching poor children in Dublin. Teresa Mulally was the daughter of a provisions trader. She initially earned her living by means of a millinery business which she opened in her father's parlour. As her business flourished, Mulally became active in lay Catholic circles in St Michan's parish in Dublin. She prepared ointments and medicines for the poor and visited the sick of the parish. In 1766, with the support of a Jesuit priest, she opened a school for poor girls. The curriculum combined catechising with more practical skills of reading, writing and needlework. With the help of two other single women, Mulally was soon teaching more than a hundred girls. In 1771, she started an orphanage and taught the children glove-making as well as dressmaking and housework. The goods produced by the orphans were sold for the upkeep of the house.[60]

Nano Nagle came from a Catholic merchant family from Cork. She was educated in a Catholic school in Paris and gave some thought to entering a French convent but was encouraged by a Jesuit priest to return to Ireland and work among the poor there. In the early 1760s she lived with her mother and sister in Dublin where she taught in a Catholic school and undertook visits to poor households. Nagle subsequently moved to Cork to live with her brother and his wife and started a school for girls. By 1769, Nagle, having benefitted from a substantial legacy from her uncle, was financing seven schools in Cork, two for boys and five for girls. The schools, modelled on the *petits écoles* which she had encountered in France, had, like that of Mulally's in Dublin, a curriculum which consisted of a mixture of catechism, literacy skills (mainly reading) and 'work' such as sewing and housewifery.[61] Nagle also built an almshouse for elderly impoverished women in Cork and had plans before her death to establish an asylum for prostitutes.[62]

Nagle employed female mistresses in her schools but expressed dissatisfaction with the lay teachers because they lacked what she considered sufficient zeal for the task of caring for the poor.[63] Nagle concluded that a religious community would be the most appropriate foundation for the development and continuation of her charitable work. Once again, she looked to France for inspiration. With the advice of the local clergy she provided £2000 to found an Ursuline convent in Cork. The Ursulines, however, wanted to focus on providing an education for the daughters of Cork's Catholic elite and were unwilling to relax their rule of cloister to work among the poor.[64] They did not, therefore, fulfil Nagle's desire for a female religious community dedicated to the education of the poor in Cork. Consequently, Nagle began to lay the foundations for a new type of religious community in the city. She invited a number of young women to live with her and follow a monastic discipline while also engaging in charitable work in teaching as well as visiting the poor and the sick. Nagle wrote to a number of French religious communities to ask for copies of their rules that could be adapted to Irish circumstances. Nagle closely examined the balance between the spiritual life and charity work of each convent.[65] In 1776, Nagle's small community was designated as the Sisters of the Charitable Instruction of the Sacred Heart and in 1791 it was given formal papal recognition. The duties of the new group were identified as three-fold: the instructions of girls in catechism; the instruction of girls in 'arts suitable to their sex' and the visitation of sick women in public infirmaries.[66]

In Dublin, Teresa Mulally also concluded that a formal religious community was the only means to secure a permanent future for her school.

She communicated regularly with Nagle and on hearing of her Institute, Mulally determined to send women to Cork to be trained as members of the new community. When they returned to Dublin they lived in a convent adjacent to the school on the new premises that Mulally had purchased in George's Hill.[67]

Mulally never joined the new order, preferring to remain a lay woman. She remained, nonetheless, closely involved with the community and took an active part in the business affairs of the new convent, securing its financial longevity.[68] It was quickly apparent, however, that Mulally's priorities were different to those of the nuns. Mulally believed that as much as possible the children should be kept in the school and away from what she perceived as the harmful influence of life in the home and on the streets of Dublin. The nuns, for their part, were concerned to incorporate their spiritual programme into their schedule. They, therefore, much to Mulally's annoyance, took an annual monthly break from teaching in the summer and did not teach in the evening.[69]

In Cork, also, after Nagle's death in 1784, there was tension between the community and the local clergy concerning the religious and charitable mission of the new order. While the male clergy were keen supporters of the active role which the Rule of the Insitute identified for its members, the community did not flourish. The absence of enclosure led to a lack of esteem for the Institute. The difficult work of visiting sick and impoverished women did not appeal to many young women. The enclosed orders were perceived as more prestigious and possibly more fashionable. Life in them was certainly more comfortable. In 1801, the Ursuline convent in Cork had a community of forty while there were only six sisters in the Institute. Consequently, the Presentation nuns in Cork adopted a 'form of voluntary enclosure'. They informed the Vatican that they wished to concentrate on teaching within the precincts of the convent and to relinquish their responsibility for visiting the sick.[70]

Both Mulally and Nagle were at the vanguard of a new momentum in Catholic Ireland. The social feminism which Hufton identified as emerging in seventeenth-century France came to Ireland in the eighteenth century.[71] It evolved from the increasing use of the laity in catechising to the establishment of French-style religious communities. Further developments were temporarily halted after the death of Nagle and Mulally but by the mid-nineteenth century, more non-cloistered religious orders had been founded and quickly began to dominate the provision of Catholic social and educational services. Thus, the movement initiated by Mulally and Nagle had a profound long-term impact on Irish society.

Notes

1 Joseph Boyse, *The Works of the Reverend and Learned Mr Joseph Boyse of Dublin* (2 vols., London, 1728), i, 173.

2 See, for example, Robert Craghead, *A Funeral Sermon on the Occasion of the Death of the Right Honourable Catherine, Countess Dowager of Granard: Who Dyed December the 9th, 1714* (Dublin, 1714), pp. 26–7.

3 Boyse, *The Works of the Reverend and Learned Mr Joseph Boyse of Dublin*, i, p. 386.

4 For the movement in general see T. C. Barnard, 'Reforming Irish Manners: the Religious Societies in Dublin During the 1690s' in *The Historical Journal*, **35** (4) (1992), pp. 805–8. See also [William Hamilton], *A Discourse Concerning Zeal, Against Immorality and Prophanences Delivered in Two Sermons in St Michael's Church, Dublin, 29 October, 26 November 1699* (Dublin, 1700) which includes a section addressed to women.

5 *The Whole Duty of Prayer. By the Author of The Whole Duty of Man. Necessary For All Families* (London, 1749). See also John Mears, *A Short Explanation of the End and Design of the Lord's Supper* (Dublin, 1758).

6 *The Whole Duty of Man Laid Down in a Plain and Familiar Way For the Use of All, But Especially the Meanest Reader* (Dublin, 1699). *Private Devotions for Several Occasions, Ordinary and Extraordinary* was also produced by the same printer (John Brocas) in Dublin in 1699.

7 Thomas Pollard, *The Necessity and Advantages of Family Prayer, in Two Sermons, Preached at St Peters Dublin* (Dublin, 1696), dedication.

8 Samuel Foley, *An Exhortation to the Inhabitants of Down and Connor, Concerning the Religious Education of their Children . . .* (Dublin, 1695). See also the publication of the Irish edition of George Saville, Earl of Halifax's *The Lady's New-Year's Gift: Or, Advice to a Daughter* (Dublin edition, 1699) which may also have been linked to the movement for the reform of manners.

9 Ian Green, '"The Necessary Knowledge of the Principles of Religion": Catechisms and Catechizing in Ireland, c. 1560–1800' in A. Ford, J. McGuire and K. Milne (Eds), *As By Law Established. The Church of Ireland Since the Reformation* (Dublin, 1995), pp. 73–81.

10 Edward Synge, *A Discourse of Confirmation in a Dialogue Between the Minister of a Parish, and a Young Servant Maid Named Sarah* (Dublin, 1739).

11 David Hempton and Myrtle Hill, *Evangelical Protestantism in Ulster Society 1740–1890* (London, 1992), p. 131.

12 Ibid., pp. 6–8.

13 Ibid., p. 12.

14 David Hempton and Myrtle Hill, 'Women and Protestant Minorities in Eighteenth-Century Ireland' in Margaret MacCurtain and Mary O'Dowd (Eds),

Women in Early Modern Ireland (Edinburgh, 1991), pp. 196–211; David Hempton, *The Religion of the People. Methodism and Popular Religion c. 1750–1900* (London, 1996), pp. 179–96.

15 Unless otherwise stated, this section is based on an analysis of Angel Anna Slack's journal which is in the County Cavan Public Library. I am grateful to the Women's History Project for giving me access to a copy of the typescript.

16 Hempton and Hill, *Evangelical Protestantism in Ulster Society 1740–1890*, p. 12. See also Rosemary Raughter, '"Mothers in Israel": Women, Family and Community in Early Irish Feminism' in Alan Hayes and Diane Urquhart (Eds), *Irish Women's History* (Dublin, 2004), pp. 29–42.

17 Among Slack's correspondents was the writer Charlotte Brooke.

18 Another young eighteenth-century Methodist woman Theodosia Blachford (née Tighe), was described by her relatives as 'eccentric' because of her adherence to a stringent daily regime. See Wicklow Papers in National Library of Ireland.

19 C. H. Crookshank, *Memorable Women of Irish Methodism in the Last Century* (London, 1882), p. 196.

20 Hempton and Hill, *Evangelical Protestantism in Ulster Society 1740–1890*, p. 134.

21 Bernadette Cunningham, 'Women and Gaelic Literature, 1500–1800' in MacCurtain and O'Dowd (Eds), *Women in Early Modern Ireland*, p. 148.

22 See, for example, *Calendar of Ancient Records of Dublin*, iii, pp. 338–9; National Archives of Ireland, Saved Chancery Pleadings, B/166.

23 David Hayton, 'Did Protestantism Fail in Early Eighteenth-Century Ireland? Charity Schools and the Enterprise of Religious and Social Reformation, c. 1690–1730' in Ford, McGuire and Milne (Eds), *As By Law Established. The Church of Ireland Since the Reformation*, pp. 166–86; Rosemary Raughter, 'A Natural Tenderness: Women's Philanthropy in Eighteenth-Century Ireland' (unpublished MA thesis, University College, Dublin, 1992).

24 Hayton, 'Did Protestantism Fail in Early Eighteenth-Century Ireland?', p. 173.

25 James Stuart, *Historical Memoirs of the City of Armagh* (Newry, 1819), pp. 539–40.

26 Mary Butler, duchess of Ormond provided, the site on which the Foundling Hospital was later built; Richard Steevens' sister, Griselda, fulfilled her brother's bequest to found a hospital in Dublin while Mary Mercer left a bequest to found Mercer's Hospital in the city in the 1730s. Other women sponsored beds in Steevens' hospital in return for which they had the right to recommend sick persons to occupy the bed. See Walter Harris, *The History and Antiquities of the City of Dublin, From the Earliest Accounts* (Dublin, 1766), pp. 443–55.

27 Hempton and Hill, *Evangelical Protestantism in Ulster Society 1740–1890*, p. 131.

28 Rosemary Raughter, 'Eighteenth-Century Catholic and Protestant Women' in Angela Bourke *et al.* (Eds), *Field Day Anthology of Irish Writing, Vol. IV* (Cork,

2002) pp. 493–4; Raughter 'Philanthropic Institutions of Eighteenth-Century Ireland', ibid., Vol. V, pp. 681–4; Representative Church Body, MS 551/1, 2. See also Chapter 4.

29 Raughter, 'Philanthropic Institutions of Eighteenth-Century Ireland', pp. 687–9.

30 Minute book of the Female Orphan Society, Representative Church Body, Dublin, MS 517, pp. 22–4.

31 Horatio Townsend, *Statistical Survey of the County of Cork, with Observations on the Means of Improvement . . .* (Dublin, 1810), pp. 528–32.

32 John Ferrar, *A View of Ancient and Modern Dublin. With Its Improvements to the Year 1796. To Which is Added a Tour to Belvue in the County of Wicklow, the Seat of Peter La Touche* (Dublin, 1796), pp. 87–100. See also William Tighe, *Statistical Observations Relative to the County of Kilkenny Made in the Years 1800 and 1801* (Dublin, 1802), pp. 510–43.

33 See, for example, R. W. M. Strain, *Belfast and its Charitable Society. A Story of Urban Social Development* (London, 1961), pp. 161–4.

34 Mary Hayden, 'Charity Children in Eighteenth Century Dublin' in *Dublin Historical Record*, **5** (1942–3), pp. 92–107. See also p. 56 above.

35 See the essays in Hugh Cunningham and Joanna Innes (Eds), *Charity, Philanthropy and Reform from the 1690s to 1850* (Basinstoke and London, 1998).

36 See pp. 131–2 above.

37 Rosemary Raughter, 'A Natural Tenderness: Women's Philanthropy in Eighteenth-Century Ireland', pp. 97–8; David Dickson, *Arctic Ireland. The Extraordinary Story of the Great Frost and Forgotten Famine of 1740–41* (Belfast, 1998).

38 *Retrospections of Dorothea Herbert, 1770–1806* (Dublin, 1929–30, reprinted Dublin, 1988), pp. 83–4, 133.

39 *A Memoir of Mistress Ann Fowkes Née Geale Died Aged 82 Years, With Some Recollections of her Family A.D. 1642–1774. Written By Herself* (London, 1892), pp. 36–7.

40 See, for example, Patrick Fagan, *Dublin's Turbulent Priest. Cornelius Nary 1658–1738* (Dublin, 1991), pp. 67–78.

41 Michael Scott (Ed), *Hall's Ireland. Mr & Mrs Hall's Tour of 1840* (2 vols., London and Sydney, 1984), p. 290.

42 Helena Concannon, *Irish Nuns in Penal Times* (London, 1931), pp. 95–9.

43 P. J. Corish, *The Catholic Community in the Seventeenth and Eighteenth Centuries* (Dublin, 1981), pp. 73–81.

44 Concannon, *Irish Nuns in Penal Times*, pp. 41–5, 65–71, 74–8; Helena Concannon, *The Poor Clares in Ireland (A.D. 1629–A.D. 1929)* (Dublin, 1929); Fagan, *Dublin's Turbulent Priest. Cornelius Nary 1658–1738*, pp. 67–78. The Poor

Clares had initially taken over the premises from the Benedictines at the request of the Catholic archbishop Cornelius Nary but after a short time they were replaced by the Dominicans, probably because the archbishop preferred the educational services which they provided. See ibid., pp. 72–4.

45 Ibid., pp. 74–5.

46 See William Carrigan (Ed), 'Catholic Episcopal Wills in the Public Record Office, Dublin, 1683–1812' in *Archivium Hibernicum*, vol. i (1912), pp. 148–200; vol. ii (1913), pp. 220–41; **iii** (1914), pp. 160–202; **v** (1915), pp. 66–95.

47 Bourke *et al.* (Eds), *Field Day Anthology of Irish Writing, Vol. IV*, p. 161.

48 Fagan, *Dublin's Turbulent Priest. Cornelius Nary 1658–1738*, pp. 74–5.

49 On the Charter Schools see Kenneth Milne, *The Irish Charter Schools, 1730–1830* (Dublin, 1997); on charity schools, see Hayton, 'Did Protestantism Fail in Early Eighteenth-Century Ireland?, pp. 166–86.

50 See Hugh Fenning, 'Some Problems of the Irish Mission, 1733–1774' in *Collectanea Hibernica* **8** (1965), p. 77.

51 Corish, *The Catholic Community in the Seventeenth and Eighteenth Centuries*, pp. 80–1; Hugh Fenning, *The Undoing of the Friars of Ireland* (Louvain, 1972), pp. 165–6, 196–9; Concannon, *The Poor Clares in Ireland (A.D. 1629–A.D. 1929)*, p. 98. John Fottrell, Provincial of the Irish Dominicans also criticised female convents during his visitations in 1738/9. See Hugh Fenning (Ed), *The Fottrell Papers* (Belfast, 1980), pp. 113–20. Máirín Ní Dhonnchadha has suggested that a new version of the Irish text, 'Páirliament Na mBan', which included the story of Máire Lawless, a nun living in the community, may have been prepared as a 'devotional text for Catholic ladies, including would-be nuns' (Bourke *et al.* (Eds), *Field Day Anthology of Irish Writing, Vol. IV*, pp. 159–61).

52 Corish, *The Catholic Community in the Seventeenth and Eighteenth Centuries*, p. 217.

53 Hugh Fenning, 'Letters From a Jesuit in Dublin on the Confraternity of the Holy Name, 1747–1748' in *Archivium Hibernicum*, **xix** (1970), p. 141.

54 Hugh Fenning, 'The Parish Clergy of Tuam 1717–1809' in *Collectanea Hibernica*, **39** and **40** (1997–98), p. 166.

55 For the diocese of Dublin see Dáire Keogh, ' "The Pattern of the Flock": John Thomas Troy, 1786–1823' in James Kelly and Dáire Keogh (Eds), *History of the Catholic Diocese of Dublin* (Dublin, 2000), pp. 229–30. See also Kevin Whelan, 'The Regional Impact of Irish Catholicism 1700–1850' in W. J. Smyth (Ed), *Common Ground. Essays on the Historical Geography of Ireland Presented to T. Jones Hughes* (Cork, 1998), pp. 260–1; Corish, *The Catholic Community in the Seventeenth and Eighteenth Centuries*, pp. 85–100.

56 M. V. Ronan, *An Apostle of Catholic Dublin Father Henry Young* (Dublin, 1944), p. 123.

57 M. Brenan, 'The Confraternity of Christian Doctrine in Ireland' in *Irish Ecclesiastical Record*, **43** (1934), p. 571. See also Sister Mary O'Riordan, 'Bishop Daniel Delany (1747–1814)' in Pádraig G. Lane and William Nolan (Eds), *Laois. History and Society Interdisciplinary Essays on the History of an Irish County* (Dublin, 1999), pp. 459–86.

58 M. Brenan, 'The Confraternity of Christian Doctrine in Ireland' in *Irish Ecclesiastical Record*, **44** (1934), pp. 11–12.

59 O'Riordan, 'Bishop Daniel Delany (1747–1814)', pp. 467, 471.

60 Roland Burke Savage, *A Valiant Dublin Woman. The Story of George's Hill (1766–1940)* (Dublin, 1940), pp. 49–66.

61 Ibid., pp. 67–74. See also T. J. Walsh, *Nano Nagle and the Presentation Sisters* (Dublin, 1959), pp. 43, 372.

62 Ibid., pp. 377, 394.

63 Burke Savage, *A Valiant Dublin Woman. The Story of George's Hill (1766–1940)*, p. 87.

64 Ibid., pp. 78–80.

65 Ibid., pp. 97–100. See also Mary Peckham Magray, *The Transforming Power of the Nuns. Women, Religion, and Cultural Change in Ireland, 1750–1900* (New York, 1998), pp. 16–17.

66 Walsh, *Nano Nagle and the Presentation Sisters*, pp. 101–2, 136.

67 Burke Savage, *A Valiant Dublin Woman. The Story of George's Hill (1766–1940)*, pp. 110–41.

68 See ibid. for the details of the business negotiations undertaken by Mulally to secure the finances of the George's Hill establishment.

69 Burke Savage, *A Valiant Dublin Woman. The Story of George's Hill (1766–1940)*, pp. 142–5.

70 Walsh, *Nano Nagle and the Presentation Sisters*, pp. 173–4.

71 Olwen Hufton, *The Prospect Before Her. A History of Women in Western Europe*, Volume One, 1500–1800 (London, 1995), pp. 367–96. See also pp. 158–64 above.

CHAPTER 7

Reading, Writing and Intellectual Interests

Literacy and education in the sixteenth and seventeenth centuries

In 1632 when Alice Wandesford was six years old she travelled to Dublin with her mother and her two younger brothers. The family were going to join Alice's father, Christopher Wandesford, who had been appointed Master of the Rolls in the administration of the new Irish lord deputy, Sir Thomas Wentworth. By the time she arrived in Ireland, Alice could read the Psalms, but while in Dublin she was tutored more formally along with the lord deputy's two daughters in Dublin Castle: 'learning those qualities with them which my father ordered, namelie, – the French language, to write and speake the same; singing; danceing; plaieing on the lute and theorboe'. Wandesford was also taught 'such other accomplishments of working silkes, gummework, sweetmeats, and other sutable huswifery, as by my mother's virtuous provision and caire, she brought me up in what was fitt for her qualitie and my father's childe'.[1] The priorities of Thornton's education are clear. First, she learnt to read religious texts and then she was taught social and domestic skills that would equip her to be an attractive and competent marriage partner.

Scattered evidence suggests that other girls in wealthy Protestant families had a similar training. In the Boyle family in the early seventeenth century, religion was also central to the girls' education. Extracts from Scripture, sermons and theological tracts were read by, and sometimes to, the Boyle children. The Boyles also, however, read plays, novels and poetry.[2] Richard Boyle gave the children presents of books, not all of which were religious texts. In 1637, for example, he gave his youngest daughter, Mary, a copy of the countess of Pembroke's edition of her brother Philip's *Arcadia* as a New Year's gift.[3] In the Savage family in County Down in the 1640s, the girls were taught singing and the playing of musical instruments but also had a 'school mistris to other purposes'.[4] Among the books in Lady Hamilton's possession on her death in Dublin in 1638 were religious books but also an English translation of Virgil, a French dictionary and a French religious book.[5] Another tantalising glimpse into the sort of education that some girls in wealthy New English families received is the survival of a school book belonging to Anne Loftus. The small copybook listed geographical locations in Latin and suggests that a classical education was provided for some young women in seventeenth-century Ireland.[6]

There were also educated, literate women in Gaelic society and there too reading was mainly used for religious purposes, as the account of Máire O'Malley suggests.[7] Although women were excluded from the formal training of the bardic poets, the chance survival of the poetry of Caitlín Dubh indicates that, like the Latin education of Anne Loftus, a small number of Gaelic women were taught the rudiments of composing classical Irish poetry.[8] Women were also prominent among the patrons of literature in Gaelic society. As noted in Chapter 1, Chieftains' wives traditionally offered patronage to poets and ecclesiastical scribes and were frequently thanked for their generosity in bardic poetry.[9]

The printing press and the advance of English as the language of politics, commerce and Protestantism revolutionised reading habits in the English language but made little initial impact on the reading or composition of Irish texts that continued to be circulated in manuscript form. While the majority of the population spoke Irish, far fewer could read or write in their native language. Consequently, acquisition of literacy skills increasingly meant proficiency in the English language. As indicated elsewhere, an ability to speak and read (if not, write) English was perceived as an attractive skill for a potential wife by sixteenth-century Irish lords. In the pre-Reformation Pale, Old English convents like Grace Dieu in County Dublin boasted proudly that the girls in their care were brought up 'in virtue, learning, and in the English tongue'.[10] Among the Old English community in Galway, girls were also educated in English. At the end of the sixteenth century, the Elizabethan writer, Sir John Harington, paid two visits to the western town where he encountered young women who had, to his surprise, read his translation of the *Orlando Furioso*.[11]

Well-educated women were, therefore, not unusual in sixteenth- and seventeenth-century Ireland. In Tudor and Stuart England, a small group of elite women achieved renown as authors of literary texts and a surprising number of them had links with Ireland through male relatives who served in the Dublin administration. Mary Sidney, Eleanor Davies and Elizabeth Carey all spent time in the country although there is little evidence of their Irish experiences in their writings.[12] Alice Thornton and Mary Boyle were, however, among the daughters of English officials who were inspired by religious conviction to write about their Irish childhood while the commonplace book of Lady Anne Southwell indicates the intellectual interests of an English woman in the Munster colony in the 1630s.[13] Predictably, much of Southwell's writing is concerned with religious topics but she also read widely in classical and English literature. She copied extracts from and wrote commentaries on well-known texts including Augustine's *City of God* and Edward Topsell's *The Historie of Foure-Footed Beastes* (1607) and its companion volume *The Historie of Serpents* (1608).[14] Southwell's letter to Lady Cecily MacWilliam in 1626 was a defence of poetry in which, according to one commentator, she demonstrated her 'knowledge of Renaissance critical theory, particularly that of Phillip Sidney's *Apologie for Poetrie* (1595)'.[15] Cecily MacWilliam also connected Southwell to a wider network of literary contacts in Ireland and England. MacWilliam was a former maid of honour to Queen Elizabeth and the wife of Sir Thomas Ridgeway who served as treasurer in Ireland, 1606–16.[16] In 1612, Barnabe Rich dedicated his polemical pamphlet on the differences between Roman Catholicism and Anglicanism to MacWilliam, asserting that although the contents were 'not to be aspired by every ordinary capacity' he knew that they were within the reach of MacWilliam's 'exquisite judgement'.[17]

Throughout the seventeenth century, wealthy Protestant women continued to be taught formally by private tutors and informally by their parents, particularly their mothers. Reading was considered both a religious necessity and a fulfilling leisure activity. As Anne Southwell's writings and correspondence with MacWilliam indicate, literature and reading were valued as intellectually satisfying. Reading could also provide solace for English women living in rural Ireland, isolated from family and friends. In the 1650s, Lady Anne Conway, for example, described the time she enjoyed in 'the privacy of my own closett' as her only source of happiness in her life in Ireland.[18] Some time later, in 1681, when Lady Frances Keightley, the wife of the Irish attorney general, Sir John Keightley, wrote a letter of advice to her daughter, Katherine, who had established a home with her Irish husband, Lucius O'Brien of Dromoland Castle, she praised the benefits of reading widely. Lady Keightley advised her daughter to read religious texts but also recommended history, classical literature and philosophy.[19]

Literacy and numeracy skills were essential for women who had responsibility for managing a landed estate or supervising payments to domestic staff. The collection and exchange of cooking recipes, medical prescriptions and household tips that were written into commonplace books was also a popular pastime among women in landowning families. Lady Frances Keightley started her collection of recipes and prescriptions about 1660 and passed it on to her daughter, Katherine, who added to the collection, often noting in the margin the names of the women who had given her new recipes or cures, many of them members of Irish peerage families. The volume was preserved in the family archives and was clearly perceived as a valuable heirloom that was passed down through several generations of women in the O'Brien family.[20]

By the seventeenth century, girls in Catholic families might be sent to a continental convent to be educated. The number of lay 'scholars' resident in convents where Irish pupils were enrolled was, however, usually small. So, unless a young Irish Catholic woman opted to take religious vows her chances of acquiring a formal education were limited.[21] The research of Ciarán Ó Scea reveals that the overwhelming majority of women who arrived in Spain from Ireland in the sixteenth and seventeenth centuries were illiterate.[22] By the end of the seventeenth century, this situation may have begun to change as many of the Irish women associated with the French Stuart court could sign their name, a reflection perhaps of the small boarding schools linked to the convents established in Dublin and elsewhere during the reign of James II.[23]

Even when a family could afford to send a girl to the continent she may have spent only a short period of time there and not received a very literate education. Catholic Counter-Reformation culture did not encourage women to record their daily spiritual thoughts and practices in the way that Protestantism did. The emphasis in convent schools was on religion and, above all, on learning the catechism by rote. Reading, writing and arithmetic were of secondary importance. In French convents, literacy in Latin was taught first. Subsequently, pupils were taught to read and write in French, with varying degrees of success. Commentators in seventeenth-century France mocked the inability of convent-educated women to write correctly, many having difficulty forming the correct shapes of letters on a page. Literacy in English was not on the curriculum of most French convents.[24] The Catholic Church authorities also shared a more general belief that women did not need to learn to write and, at times, actively discouraged women from writing. Mr Ó Scea suggests that the acquisition of literacy skills by Irish women who travelled to Spain was stimulated not by the Church or convent but by the necessity of dealing with Spanish bureaucracy.[25] The silent historical record of Irish convent-educated women in the sixteenth and seventeenth centuries may, therefore, reflect not just the non-survival of their writing but also the inability of the majority of them to write.

We know practically nothing about the schooling or education of girls from less well-off Gaelic or English families. School books were imported into the towns of the Ulster plantation in the early seventeenth century but there is no record on whether or not these books were used to educate girls. A popular import in Munster was Francis Seager's, *The School of Virtue and Booke of Good Nourture for Children and Youth to Learne Theyr Dutie* (London, 1557).[26] Written in verse, it included daily prayers for children as well as guidance on good behaviour, dress, serving food and table manners. Although aimed mainly at young boys, *The School of Virtue* could have been used in a family to teach all children how to read, pray and behave appropriately. The existence of women teachers in Ulster schools indicates that at least some women were being educated in the new plantation.[27] This suggestion is corroborated by an analysis of depositions made by Protestant women in the 1640s which provides evidence that almost a third of them could sign their names. The religious imperative of Protestantism was clearly making an impact on literacy within the new settler communtiy.[28]

Most men and women in sixteenth- and seventeenth-century Ireland, however, could not read or write; and most people had little daily need to develop literacy skills. The religious faith of the majority did not depend on literacy nor were there notable economic advantages to be gained through its acquisition. The Catholic Church promoted catechetical knowledge through verse that could be recited rather than read or written down.[29] As noted elsewhere, it was not until the eighteenth century that literacy began to be identified as a desirable skill for religious and economic reasons, particularly for women.

Education in the eighteenth century

In the first half of the eighteenth century, as Toby Barnard has documented, there was a marked increase in literacy among the mainly Protestant 'middling sort' of Irish towns, particularly in Dublin.[30] Although Barnard's analysis does not include women, cumulative impressionistic evidence suggests that urban middle-class women were a significant group within the new literate population. Education through private tuition or attendance at a small fee-paying school became a common experience for girls from middle-class urban families. The number of newspaper advertisements for girls' schools increased significantly in the last quarter of the century and by 1800 all of the major cities and most medium-sized provincial towns such as Mullingar, Athlone and Castlebar had small boarding schools that catered for girls from well-off rural and urban families, all anxious to have their daughters educated as 'young ladies'. Girls from Protestant gentry families in the midlands as well as in the hinterland of Dublin, attended Samuel Whyte's famous school in the capital.[31] Similarly, boys and girls were on the roll call of David Manson's school in Belfast.[32] Irish girls were also sent to schools in England from whence, according to one critical commentator, the 'englisied ladies' returned to Ireland speaking English in a Lancashire dialect and incomprehensible French.[33]

In rural areas, small schools for poor children also appeared in the course of the eighteenth century. Some, as noted in the last chapter, were charitable endeavours while others were opened by men and women keen to make a respectable living through teaching. In a survey of schools in the diocese of Killala in 1808, 25 per cent of the pupils were girls. The schools with the most female pupils were located in the small towns of the region as well as in Limerick City.[34]

Most of the schools that advertised in newspapers catered for girls from the age of ten or eleven. These establishments were, therefore, intended to develop the basic literacy skills that many middle-class children would have acquired at home. The school curriculum usually included classes in writing, French and English as well as social skills such as music, dancing and drawing and was, therefore, not that different from that experienced by Alice Thornton and her fellow students in the 1630s. By the eighteenth century, a knowledge of history and geography was also, however, perceived as a useful conversational skill for young women. The annual fees in the urban boarding schools ranged from twelve to twenty-five guineas as well as an initial entrance fee. Such rates placed the girls' schools beyond the reach of all but the reasonably well off, although in some of the larger towns, evening classes were advertised for girls who were occupied during the day. In the 1790s in Cork, an evening school provided classes in book-keeping in addition to the usual curriculum.[35] Some of the schools in the linen towns in the north also offered practical skills. In 1773, Mrs Fossett advertised her boarding school in Moy, County Tyrone. The curriculum included the English language, needlework, knitting and making up lace, as well as lessons in 'making different kinds of pastry, pickling, preserving, jellies, blomage, the oeconomy of a table, and clear startching, etc.' Mrs Fossett undertook to 'form the minds and manners of her pupils so as to render them happy in themselves and useful to society'.[36] In the diocese of Killala in 1808, the rural day schools provided a cheap and basic curriculum in reading (1s. 1d.

a quarter); reading and writing (2s. 2d. a quarter) and reading, writing and arithmetic (3s. 3d. a quarter). Girls were also taught sewing.[37]

The proliferation of schools for girls did not necessarily mean that the pupils who attended them had a very structured education. Some went to school on a weekly basis; and, while others were enrolled for more frequent classes, they may have received lessons in a number of different establishments. In 1770, for example, William Eccles opened his writing classes to young ladies from twelve to one o'clock at his house in Belfast. Eccles arranged the hours of his classes so that pupils could also attend classes in other subjects and premises.[38] In the middle decades of the eighteenth century, the five daughters in the Dublin Bayley family enrolled for writing lessons with Mathew Haskins while music and dancing classes were provided by separate teachers.[39] As the Dublin school teacher, Samuel Whyte, caustically remarked, the employment of a succession of instructors could be more fashionable than educational. Whyte wrote of how 'the French master, the music master, the drawing master, the dancing master, the writing master, etc.' were 'poured' in upon young women. Consequently, Whyte maintained, the girls comprehended little of what they were taught.[40]

In the absence of a school, the local parish clerk might provide lessons for Protestant children. Caroline Hamilton, looking back in the nineteenth century at the education received by her mother's generation, noted that 'an old nurse generally taught to read and the parish clerk, to write'.[41] The level of education provided depended on the quality of the teacher as well as of the pupil. The poet Constantia Grierson who, according to Laetitia Pilkington, was 'mistress of Hebrew, Greek and French; and understood mathematics as well as most men' was educated by the local minister.[42] Dorothea Herbert was taught 'writing, reading and grammar' by the parish clerk employed by her father, a Church of Ireland rector; and French, dancing and music by a succession of men and women who stayed in the rectory for brief periods of time, some of them homeless foreigners who were provided with lodgings by Minister Herbert and his wife in return for teaching their children.[43] It may have been an indication of changing attitudes to the education of girls that Dorothea Herbert's younger sisters were sent to a school in Carrick on a daily basis in the 1780s.[44] Clearly, however, the education of the boys in the family was taken more seriously and their enrolment in the boarding school at Cashel was considered by their sister as a major landmark in the history of the family.[45]

Although Catholic clergy did not get involved in the education of young women in the same way as Church of Ireland ministers and their clerks, it is clear that the Catholic Church was increasingly concerned in the eighteenth century to provide formal educational facilities for girls in Ireland. When convents began to be re-established in the country, a priority was, as we have seen, the opening of small boarding schools for girls from wealthy Catholic families.[46] The curriculum taught in these convent schools is unknown but it is likely that it was similar to continental convents where, as in the seventeenth century, emphasis was placed on religious catechising and the acquisition of social skills. By the 1770s, however, the latter would have included literacy. Among the first generation of pupils to attend the Ursuline Convent founded by Nano Nagle in Cork in the 1770s, was Margaret Carey, who was literate in French and English. It is very likely that Carey acquired her proficiency in French, if not also English, in the Cork school.[47] The provision of convent schools in Ireland marked, therefore, an important stage in the development of education of Catholic girls, initiating the process by which they routinely acquired an education beyond the literacy skills taught at home or in the small rural schools.

Despite the expansion in Irish-based convent education, the tradition of sending girls to spend some time in convents on the continent continued among wealthy families, partly because of the social esteem attached to this type of education. Continental convents served as finishing schools for young Catholic women. Eleanor Butler's time abroad as a young woman was reported to have given her a 'certain degree of refinement and literature, and a distaste for Irish priests and popery'.[48] Rose and Julia Reynolds, the aunts of Catholic Committee member Thomas Reynolds, attended an Ursuline convent in Liège, while their brothers went to a Jesuit College in the city. When Rose left the convent in 1784 she was 'placed for a year and a half at the Royal Abbaye de Forît, near Brussels, as a proper place to give her the polish and manners of good society. None but persons of noble families could be admitted as members in that community . . .'[49]

The expansion in the number of schools for girls in Ireland is evidence of the increased public interest in women's education in the last quarter of the eighteenth century. Throughout Europe, Enlightenment ideas provoked a debate on the necessity and purpose of women's education.[50] Evidence of this discussion filtering into public discourse in Ireland can be detected throughout the eighteenth century and particularly from the 1770s. The popular periodical *Walker's Hibernian Magazine*, which championed radical ideas, encouraged the debate in Ireland and regularly printed articles on women's education. Many were extracts from texts first published in England or America while a smaller number were of Irish origin.

The discussion initially focused on the merits and value of educating girls. While there was general agreement that women should be literate in order to read religious texts, there was less agreement on what other subjects they should study or whether they should write, particularly for publication. The image of the 'literary lady' was conjured up by those who argued that women should not pursue serious study. Too much learning could make a young woman vain, arrogant and neglectful of her domestic duties.[51] The Dublin school teacher, Samuel Whyte, made an enlightened response to such views:

> *O lord! A* learned *lady! So impertinent! So conceited! So full of herself! Nobody else can put in a word! She is dreadful! Intolerable! – And what great sirs, are your* learned *gentlemen? Infinitely worse, ferocious! Overbearing! Assuming! Ostentatious! Self opinionated! And every way insufferably disagreeable! A similar character in both sexes; a pedant is a pedant be it male or female . . .*[52]

Whyte and others contrasted the situation in Ireland with that prevailing on the continent, and particularly in France, where educated women were esteemed for their knowledgeable conversation. Consequently, they argued that a more structured and academic education for girls benefitted society as a whole. It made young women better companions as wives. As the author of 'The Female Advocate' wrote in 1779: 'The more they [i.e. women] extend their ideas, the more subjects of intercourse they will find with us, and the more interesting will that intercourse become.'[53] Others stressed the need to educate women for their roles as mothers and managers of household budgets.[54]

Samuel Whyte deserves credit as one of the earliest Irish advocates of education for girls. His views, on female education, first appeared in an appendix to *The Shamrock, or Hibernian Cresses* (Dublin, 1772), a collection of poems and short plays that had been performed in Whyte's school and was published by subscription of his pupils and their parents. Some of the poems in the volume had been written in response to lines penned by Whyte's female pupils. The composition of poetry was clearly used by Whyte as a pedagogical tool for boys as well as girls. Subsequently, Whyte published the appendix on education as a separate pamphlet. The long title made clear his support for girls' education: *Modern Education. . . . With Particular Proposals for a Reformation. In the Course of Which the Female Right to Literature is Asserted. . . . Clearly Demonstrating that the Weakness and Depravity Imputed to the Fair Sex, is Wholly Owing to Our Utter Neglect of Their Minds; and That the Proper Cultivation of Them is the First and Grand Principle of All Human Excellence, As Well As of All Our Social and Domestic Felicity* (Dublin, 1775). Whyte berated parents and guardians who neglected the education of children and, particularly that of young women. If women were brought up in ignorance then it was unfair to accuse them in later life of lack of understanding. While Whyte did not challenge the view that the female mind might be 'less happily endowed by nature' than that of men, he suggested that this was all the more reason why care should be taken with their education. Women might not require education for the public world of affairs but this did not mean that they should be 'precluded from the privilege of being rational creatures'. Like Mary Wollstonecraft twenty years later, Whyte condemned society's preference to train women in trivial and vain pastimes, arguing instead that women should have their 'reason faculties' cultivated from an early age. He praised women who had taken the time to acquire for themselves an education as they were manifest proof of the 'inclination and capacity' of women for intellectual activity.

Whyte believed, above all, in the social utility of educating young women. He proposed a curriculum that concentrated on making young women knowledgeable and gracious social companions. It included the traditional subjects of English literature, geography and history as well as writing and speaking English. Whyte shared the commonly held view that there was no necessity for women to learn Latin or Greek but, like others, he suggested that they could follow some of the sentiments expressed in classical literature through English writers like Dryden, Pope, Milton and Shakespeare. Included in the *Shamrock, or Hibernian Cresses* were annotated translations of classical texts which appear to have been completed by Whyte for teaching purposes

Apart from reprinting extracts from Whyte's article, *Walker's Hibernian Magazine* also published some of the most advanced views on women's education appearing in American and English periodicals. In January 1791, it reproduced the address of John Swanwick, one of the Board of Visitors to the Young Ladies' Academy of Philadelphia, an establishment that pioneered women's education in the new American republic. Swanwick also stressed the utilitarian value of educating young middle-class women as they had a vital role in forming the young citizens of the new state.[55] In the following year, in 1792, *Walker's Hibernian Magazine* published a long extract from Mary Wollstonecraft's new pamphlet, *A Vindication of the Rights of Women,* in which she argued that far from making women vain, education helped to develop women's modesty and purity of mind.[56] When Wollstonecraft died in 1797, the magazine underlined its support for her views by printing an engraving of the dead author on its front page and reproducing a review of William Godwin's recollection of their life together, a controversial text that defended Wollstonecraft's personal life and her views on marriage.[57]

While it is impossible to assess the wider social impact of the debate on women's education in the pages of periodicals like *Walker's Hibernian Magazine*, it is clear that parents expressed more concern about the best methods of educating their children in the eighteenth century than is evident in earlier periods. In the 1750s, the dowager countess of Leinster was reluctant to foster her son's children because she claimed that he and his wife fussed too much over their upbringing. She may have had a point. Emily Fitzgerald embraced many of the latest fashions on children's education. She briefly contemplated employing the French writer and philosopher Rousseau as a tutor for her children. When he refused the offer, the Fitzgeralds employed the Scot William Ogilvie, who proved a popular teacher with the children and encouraged both the boys and the girls in the family to read widely.[58] Caroline Hamilton recalled in her family memoir that her mother was also influenced by Rousseau and 'adopted some of his ideas' when educating her sons. When Mrs Tighe began to consider how she ought to educate her two daughters, she enquired of her brother-in-law in England whether a learned education was suitable for women, a question that suggests that she was aware of the discussion on 'literary ladies'. Her brother-in-law 'gave her many instances of learned ladies in the highest rank, who were better wives and mothers than those who had received a frivolous education'. Accordingly, Caroline recorded that her mother, 'caring little what expense she incurred for our improvement', employed an Irish governess, a drawing master, a music master and a writing master who also taught arithmetic and 'the use of the globes'.[59] Unusually, Caroline and her sister were also given lessons in Latin grammar although Caroline admitted that she was not a very attentive student.[60]

Parents and commentators were also preoccupied with the best methods of teaching children. Should it be done by a parent or was it better to employ a governess and did an English school education bestow a social advantage on Irish boys and girls? The unreliability of governesses who stayed in employment for short periods of time, and like Mary Wollstonecraft in the Kingsborough household in County Cork, disliked and resented their position, was recognised.[61] The Methodist activitist Theodosia Blachford believed that 'women could not be so usefully employed as in teaching their children' and refused to employ a governess for her children.[62] The Edgeworth family experimented with different pedagogical methods for the instruction of children in the home, and Richard and Maria Edgeworth jointly compiled texts on how to educate children.[63]

The careful parent, like Mrs Blachford and Mr Edgeworth, was actively involved in the children's education, even when a governess was employed.

Alicia Synge, for example, had a live-in French companion as well as a male tutor but Synge's father, Edward, was also deeply concerned with his daughter's education. He corrected her grammar and sentence structure in her letters, advised her on which books to read and requested her views on some of the books that she had read.[64] In a similar fashion, Emily Fitzgerald's children sent their mother regular reports of their studies, outlining their reading and displaying their writing skills in their letters.[65]

In the absence of a careful and attentive parent, middle- and upper-class girls who continued their education beyond basic literacy were, to a large extent, self-taught. The wealthy woman had always developed her own intellectual interests through private reading and this trend was accelerated in the eighteenth century as books circulated more widely in society and the creation of libraries in estate houses gave women easier access to them. In the mid-nineteenth century Caroline Hamilton looked back critically on the education that her mother's generation had received. After they had acquired basic literacy skills:

if a young lady professed any taste for literature, she was permitted to read what she pleased in her father's library which generally consisted of old romances, books of divinity, and tedious histories.[66]

Other women also recalled reading at random in the family library. As noted already, Anna Slack read unsupervised in her uncle's library, while Melissa Chenevix Trench remembered reading 'Shakespeare, Ovid's Metamorpheses, Sterne, the Arabian Nights, an abundance of plays and several works of imagination' in her grandfather's study.[67] Theodosia Blachford turned self-education into a principle rather than a necessity, believing that when children were 'very young they must be forced to learn, but a time arrives, when if they have been taught certain dry rudiments . . . and habits of application . . . they will cheerfully continue their education themselves, it will then afford them great pleasure to read and think alone, without the troublesome interference of a governess, who would imagine them idle when only reading'.[68] Blachford did, however, employ music and drawing masters for her daughter, who later vindicated her mother's educational views by achieving renown as a poet.[69]

The growth of evangelical Protestantism that Blachford supported was also a strong motivation for self-education. As noted in Chapter 6, the Presbyterians, Methodists and Quakers encouraged women to keep spiritual diaries. Methodist woman Dorothea Johnson taught herself to write, presumably in order to keep a record of her religious thoughts, while the Methodist preacher Alice Cambridge recorded that she was taken from school 'when very young' but endeavoured subsequently to educate herself through reading.[70]

More secular intellectual pursuits could also be pursued independently. Attending public lectures on philosophy and science and pursuing the fashionable study of botany could enable a young woman to broaden her mind and occupy her time. Public lectures were regularly advertised in the Dublin newspapers inviting 'ladies' as well as 'gentlemen' to attend.[71] Sarah Lennox wrote excitedly to her sister Emily of her newly discovered passion for botanical studies:

> *. . . would you believe it, I am actually studying and deeply engaged in a science – Botany? And a most delightful one it is. Dear little Lady Edward*[72] *first put me upon it last summer at Carton in our walks. . . . I am always diverted with* dissecting *the spring flowers now coming up, and finding out by books the* classes, orders, *etc. they belong to.*[73]

Other women in landed families developed their skills in drawing, architecture and house design or pursued their own private study.[74]

Books that offered guidance on self-education were, not surprisingly, among the best-selling publications on Irish booksellers' lists. One of the most popular texts in Ireland in the last quarter of the eighteenth century was Hester Chapone's *Letters on the Improvement of the Mind. Addressed to a Lady*, which was first published in London in 1773 and which was reprinted five times in Dublin between 1773 and 1786.[75] The book was in the form of a series of letters addressed to a fifteen-year-old niece. Chapone provided advice on reading the Bible, as well as guidance on other types of literature. Chapone's curriculum included the subjects taught in schools: English literature, French, history and writing as well as information on household management and domestic economy. Chapone, like other educators, commended the study of nature but agreed with the prevailing view that Latin and Greek were 'generally incompatible with our natures'. She did, however, like Samuel Whyte, recommend reading classical texts in English translation.

The public debate on women's education was concerned with girls in middle- and upper-class families. There was general agreement that basic literacy and a limited knowledge of arithmetic were all that was needed for girls from lower-class families. As indicated in Chapter 6, reform through education was the core philosophy of charitable institutions founded in the eighteenth century. This, undoubtedly, helped boost literacy figures at the lowest social level but the overall impact of charity schools on literacy rates was limited. Most charity schools were small, usually catering for no more than fifty or sixty pupils. Many were also of short duration, lasting as long as the patron retained interest or until he or she was distracted by another social fashion. The school curriculum for female education in most charity schools placed the emphasis on the learning of useful skills and religious instruction. The latter usually entailed reading the Scriptures and other religious literature but did not always involve learning to write. When the charter schools were established in the 1730s, they too devoted most of the school day to instructing the girls in housewifery with only two hours a day spent on reading and writing which was primarily intended for religious instruction.[76]

Nano Nagle's description of the curriculum followed by boys and girls in her Cork schools illustrates the sort of literacy deemed necessary for poor Catholic girls. The boys 'learn to read, and when they have the Douay Catechism by heart, they learn to write and cypher. . . . the girls learn to read; and when they have the Catechism by heart, they learn to work' i.e. to sew or spin.[77] In Teresa Mulally's Dublin school in the 1760s, more emphasis was placed on the girls' ability to spell; arithmetic tables were also recited but the curriculum centered, like that of Nagle's, on learning by rote, 'work' skills and reading.[78]

Emphasis on reading rather than writing was, however, increasingly out of date in the last quarter of the eighteenth century when both skills began to be considered useful for all social classes. In the charter schools from the 1770s, as Kenneth Milne has noted, more care was taken that all the children could write as well as read. As the rule adopted by the Society responsible for the schools noted in 1774: '. . . reading and writing and cyphering (in some degree) are useful in the lowest stations of life and . . . the better the children in the schools are educated the less likely they will be to relapse into popery'.[79]

Among poor women the reasons for learning to read and write may have been based on more pragmatic considerations. By the eighteenth century, a literate woman was more employable than an illiterate one. Servants with basic literacy and numeracy skills were more useful than those who lacked them as they could undertake a wider variety of jobs including account keeping and reading to children. Impoverished, middle-class women used their literacy skills to find employment as teachers and governesses as well as supervisors in charitable institutions or as lady's companions.

Information on levels of literacy in Irish society at any time during the early modern period is meagre, fraught with difficulties of interpretation and too specific for general conclusions. Throughout the period, literacy rates among women remained considerably lower than among men but it is also clear that far more women could read and write at the end of the eighteenth century than at the beginning of it. And, perhaps more importantly, more people, including women, wanted to learn to read and write in the English language. There was still a strong oral culture in the Irish language but the growth of a print culture meant that society increasingly expected men and women to be literate in English. By 1800, therefore, there was a general recognition of literacy as a desirable acquisition, even if it remained an aspiration rather than a reality for many poor women.

Books and reading

The growth in literacy was partly a by-product of the new consumer market in books. The Irish book trade developed initially in Dublin in the late seventeenth century but by the second half of the eighteenth century books were being sold in most provincial towns. General merchants included books in their lists of goods for sale while travelling chapmen increased access to cheaper forms of literature, mainly novels. Newspapers, national and provincial, also proliferated. Women as well as men were enthusiastic consumers in the new book trade as they read, purchased and borrowed books. Circulating libraries enabled women with a relatively modest income to borrow the latest publications. In Dublin in the 1780s and 1790s, the annual subscription was 16s. 3d. a year.[80] This sum was beyond the means of most working-class people but could have been easily paid by those of the 'middling' ranks in society. Poorer women and men had access to books in less expensive ways. Reading clubs existed in the linen areas of the north where chapbooks, pamphlets and 'novels for the women' were circulated.[81] Incidental information suggests newspapers were increasingly read at all levels of society.[82]

Women were not only reading books for private pleasure and for educational and religious purposes, but social occasions were often centered around reading and the discussion of literature. The Thursday literary salons of Mary and Patrick Delany and their friend Jonathan Swift in Dublin were described by Laetitia Pilkington.[83] Poetry was read and critiqued and literature was discussed. At the end of the eighteenth century, Lady Moira was noted as inviting to her house in Dublin 'all who had any pretensions to literary or professional celebrity' while Lady Moira's daughter, Selina, hosted literary evenings at her home, Castle Forbes in County Longford, at which, Maria Edgeworth recalled, 'Lady Moira's taste for literature, general knowledge, and great conversational talents, drew around her cultivated and distinguished persons'.[84] The Edgeworth household in Edgeworthstown close to Castle Forbes was also a centre for literary salons.[85]

Many of the Irish literary hosts like the Edgeworths, Swift and Delanys had links with the larger and more fashionable London salons. Among the leading female hosts in the capital in the mid-eighteenth century was Elizabeth Vesey whose library in her home at Lucan included English and French literature, translations of classical literature and other works on geography, science, philosophy and politics. The purchase and collection of books was important to Mrs Vesey and her books were distinguished from those collected by her husband and other members of her family through the insertion of her personal book plate and autograph.[86] A number of the books were gifts from authors who attended Mrs Vesey's 'bluestocking' salon in London, including Elizabeth Carter, George Lyttleton, Elizabeth Montagu, Hannah More and Richard Glover.[87] Mary Delany and Anne Donnellan were also acquainted with the women in the bluestocking group and shared many of the same reading interests as them.[88]

More modest literary affairs were the evening reading parties that Dorothea Herbert described as taking place in her family home in County Tipperary and which usually included the local school mistress, a Church of Ireland minister, the daughters of an apothecary from the local town, and a Mrs Cooke 'who was a great amateur and transcriber of poetry'.[89] On other evenings a visiting minister read to the family and lent Dorothea books.[90] Later, when it was learnt that Dorothea wrote poetry, copies of her poems were brought to Cashel where they were read at the morning levees of officers from the local garrison and 'the literati of the place'.[91] In smaller family groups reading a book out loud as women worked at needlework, drawing or painting was common practice.[92]

If women were reading more in the eighteenth century, what were they reading? Edward Synge, Mary Delany, Anne Donnellan, Elizabeth Vesey and her friends and Martha McTier all shared a belief that reading should be morally uplifting as well as pleasurable. As Synge wrote to Alicia, 'I allow and approve of reading for amusement, and entertainment, as well as for instruction . . . your general reading might be books of instruction, in virtue, Politenesss, or something that may improve your mind, or behaviour.'[93] Synge recommended that his young daughter read books which would not only educate her but also develop writing style. These included the letters of Madame de Sévigné, the writings of Jonathan Swift (for grammar), the works of Dryden for literary merit and Clarendon's *History* as well as religious books and sermons. Synge also praised the historical memoir, *Princess of Clèves* by Marie-Madeleine de la Fayette,

French courtier and a friend of de Sévigné's. Alicia, for her part, sent her father Charlotte Lennox's first novel, *The Life Of Harriet Stuart, Written By Herself* (2 vols., London, 1751) and *Constantia: Or, A True Picture of Human Life, Represented in Fifteen Conversations, After the Manner of Boccace* (Dublin, 1751). The latter consisted of fifteen stories told by young men and women as they attended an evening literary assembly. It was slightly more lightweight than the volumes recommended by her father but was still, nevertheless, in the category of serious reading.[94]

The reading list of Mary Delany and her companion Letitia Bushe was also serious and intellectually demanding. The main focus was on history and literature. Bushe read Thomas Carte's *Life of Ormond* aloud as they worked in the evenings while Delany read Clarendon's *History* with her husband.[95] Delany's friend Anne Donnellan read the publications of English women writers such as Elizabeth Montagu, Carte's *Life of Ormond*, classical literature in translation and Shakespeare. She was also acquainted with Edward Young, author of the hugely popular *Night Thoughts*, a volume that was on the reading list of many Protestant women in Ireland.[96]

The bluestocking circles of Delany and Donnellan maintained what they considered to be a respectful distance from contemporary politics. By contrast, Martha McTier's reading was dominated by political ideas and controversies. She read with enthusiasm the publications of most of the radical writers of her time including Thomas Paine, Mary Wollstonecraft and William Godwin. McTier also read the *Star* newspaper to which her brother, William, and other friends in the United Irishmen contributed. McTier and William exchanged ideas about books and reviews of their reading on a daily basis. When McTier established a small school for poor girls in the 1790s she began to read more of the literature on women's education by female writers such as Mary Wollstonecraft, Elizabeth Hamilton (whom she also knew personally), Mrs Barbauld and Mrs Radcliffe, as well as works by Irish women writers such as Mary Barber, Maria Edgeworth, and Sydney Owenson.[97]

The countess of Moira and her daughter, Lady Granard, also exchanged correspondence on their reading and both women read avidly, mainly in contemporary politics and history. Lady Granard ordered books from the continent through Denys Scully, the Catholic lawyer and campaigner who visited her mother's house in Dublin and was also a regular visitor at Castle Forbes.[98] Lady Moira was an enthusiastic historian of her family and read history and work on genealogy. She supported the publication of *Anthologia Hibernica* which appeared in the mid-1790s and for which she wrote and may also have encouraged others to do so. The countess was also one of the leading literary patrons in late eighteenth-century Dublin and very few Irish publications of serious literary merit were printed which did not include her name in the list of subscribers.

The intellectual interests of women like Delany, Donnellan, McTier and the countess of Moira are reflected in their particular reading lists. In less academically inclined circles, the mixture of books is more eclectic. The reading list of Mrs Katherine Bayley in Dublin in the mid-eighteenth century was probably a fairly typical selection of the books read by middle-class Protestant women. They included popular religious texts (including Edward Young's *Night Thoughts*), conduct books addressed to women and novels and books that were probably used for the education of children. Virtually all of the books had first appeared in English editions and were printed in Irish editions either in the year of publication or shortly thereafter. Among the latter were Homer's *Iliad* and the letters of Madame de Sévigné as well as three books specifically addressed to young women: James Fordyce, *Sermons to Young Women*, first published in Dublin in 1766; Wethenhall Wilke, *A Letter of Genteel and Moral Advice to a Young Lady*, first published in Dublin in 1740 and reprinted in 1741; and *The Ladies' Monitor: Or, Instruction for the Fair Sex*, written initially for schoolgirls in France and translated into English and printed in London and Dublin in 1758. Mrs Bayley subscribed to a lending library managed by the Dublin printer, George Faulkner, from which she seems to have borrowed most of the novels that she read. Among the books of fiction read in the Bayley household were Samuel Richardson's *Clarissa* as well as *Henrietta*, another novel by Charlotte Lennox; and *The History of Charlotte Villars* by Isaac Mukins, printed in Dublin in 1756. Mrs Bayley and her family were also regular attendees at the theatre in Dublin and read plays.[99]

Novels were undoubtedly among the most successful items in a bookseller's list. Many commentors condemned the proliferation of cheap novels and romances. In 1729 James Arbuckle wrote dismissively of the lack of books in the home of an Irish country Protestant gentleman but his account, paradoxically, reveals that the women in the household in fact read a great deal. Most gentlemen, he wrote, have

. . . never once a book or have any such furniture in their houses. I must indeed except a Bible, a Prayer-Book, and a Weekly Preparation, which are the property of the lady of the house, who is generally the better scholar, as well as the better Christian of the two. Her woman may also happen to have a Robinsoe Crusoe, Gulliver's Travels and Aristotle's masterpiece, both for her own edification and the instruction of the Young Ladies as soon as they are

grown up; not to mention Tommy Pots, Jack the Giant-Killer, the cobler of Canterbury, and several other notable pieces of literature carried about in the baskets of itinerant pedlars, for the improvement of his majesty's liege people.[100]

Martha McTier also gave a condescending description of the reading of novels out loud in her Belfast household:

. . . once begun, let it be even the very vilest of trash, Miss Young will have it finished, or it is matter of serious complaint. The last one was called Margaret of Stafford with Madame De Stael's name to it, which, with anecdotes of the revolution tempted me to bring out. Alas! Five volumes. It beggars all description . . . One might wander over such nonsense to themselves, but to read them out and throughout is a task not to be endured . . .[101]

Despite the misgivings of Arbuckle and McTier, novels were popular with women readers. Dorothea Herbert wrote of reading romances and novels with her friends and the romantic tone of her own memoirs was, undoubtedly, influenced by such reading.[102] Even Edward Synge permitted his daughter to read some novels although he warned her to be judicious in her choice: 'Too much dwelling on these, is apt to give the mind, a very fantastical, if not a wrong turn.'[103] The novels of Samuel Richardson were as popular in Ireland as they were in England and were among the few works of fiction approved by Synge as well as by the moralising bluestocking group because they carried a strong, uplifting message for the virtuous young woman.

It is also clear that Irish publishers targeted potential women readers from the mid-eighteenth century. An increasing number of books appeared that were specifically written for women.[104] Some novels were clearly in this category but books for schoolgirls were another aspect of the market as were self-help books such as that by Hester Chapone or books on cooking and household management that were regularly advertised in Irish newspapers.[105] English compilations of readings for young women such as Eliza Haywood's *The Female Spectator* and her *Epistle for Ladies* were printed in Dublin in 1746 and 1747 respectively.[106] Another magazine aimed at young women, mainly for use in the classroom, was the French language *Magazin à La Mode* which appeared for twelve issues from 1777–1778 and included lessons on geography, news of theatrical and musical events as well as foreign news. An engraved musical score accompanied each volume.[107]

Commercially-minded editors of periodicals also recognised the potential of a female readership. From the beginning the *Hibernian Magazine* catered for a female readership with articles often specifically addressed to women.[108] These included items which would not be out of place in a modern women's magazine: fashion reports, serialised novels, inserts of embroidery patterns which could be pulled out and traced on to cloth; and prints of fashionable men and women with occasional titbits about their lives. In addition, the magazine encouraged women to send in poetry for the poetry column.

Writing

Many women could read and write in early modern Ireland but only a few had their work published. In the sixteenth and first half of the seventeenth centuries, the most important literary texts were not printed but circulated in manuscript form within a social network. As J. W. Saunders noted:

. . . there was a sharp distinction between the courtier or gentleman poet for whom print publications would have been a social disgrace, and more humbly born aspirants for patronage who turned to the press as a means of self-advertisement.[109]

The social stigma attached to publications by men had disappeared by the end of the seventeenth century but it remained a strong deterrent against women writing for publication for most of the early modern period. Even in the 1780s, Martha McTier appeared to blush at the suggestion of her brother that he publish a work (on which she had advised him) in her name.[110]

To avoid social notoriety, the writings of women were often circulated within a select group of friends and acquaintances rather than being exposed to the wider world through commercial publication. The compilation of the writings of Lady Anne Southwell by her husband after her death in 1636 was, for example, intended for circulation among their friends.[111] Two of Southwell's poems also appear in a presentation copy for King Charles.[112] As Victoria Burke suggested, 'Southwell, and probably her husband, had a select but powerful readership in mind for her work'.[113] Similarly, in the 1660s Katherine Philips built her reputation as one of the most admired poets of the century 'largely through manuscript transmission, initially within a circle of intimates in Ireland and later on a wider scale'.[114] Among those who received copies of Philips's poetry was a group of Irish women associated with court circles in Dublin, including the duchess of Ormond and several members of the extended Boyle family.[115] As Elaine Hobby noted of Philips, 'the "public" she was interested in reaching was the coterie of court and leading poets, not the wider world'.[116] Philips made use of the printing press to have a limited edition of her translation of the play *Pompey* printed which she circulated to her friends.[117] In the same fashion, in the eighteenth century, Mary Tighe's husband persuaded her to have fifty copies of her poem *Psyche* printed which he distributed among her friends as well as sending copies to public figures, which had the effect of enhancing her reputation as a talented poet.[118] Presentation of literary work at house salons could also encourage women to publish their work in small print runs. Lady Elizabeth Tuite attended the literary gatherings at Castle Forbes where she probably read some of the poetry that was later published in 1796.[119] Scribes and authors of Gaelic poetry also circulated their work among elite groups of patrons and poets. The poems were distributed in manuscript form and recited and sung at house gatherings. Women attended these sessions and, as the research of Máirín Nic Eoin has uncovered, a small number of women also composed and recited poetry of a professional standard, most of which no longer survives.[120]

Radical Protestant groups like the Quakers, the Baptists and, later, the Methodists encouraged women to keep spiritual diaries which were sometimes read aloud or circulated within the religious group. Keeping a daily journal demanded a self-discipline that many found hard to maintain and most diaries survive for only a part of a woman's life, usually her youth or at a time when she was particularly devout, the exception being the diary kept by Mary Leadbeater for over forty years. Regular recording of events in a diary could also lead to other forms of writing. Leadbeater drew on her diaries for her published writings while Mary Boyle wrote a memoir of her life based on her diaries, as did the Irish Baptist Ann Fowkes.[121]

By the end of the eighteenth century, the keeping of commonplace books was a standard part of a young middle- or upper-class woman's education and a number survive among family papers. Most, like diaries, were kept for a short period of a young girl's life although a small number of women kept commonplace books later in life. Commonplace books were used, as in the seventeenth century, by young women as scrap books in which they recorded their thoughts on religion, copied extracts from Scripture and poetry and, sometimes, composed their own verse and prose.[122]

The most common form of writing by women was, however, the letter and in Ireland, as elsewhere, letter writing became an increasingly popular occupation for women in the early modern period. In the sixteenth century, surviving letters by women were formal undertakings, written in formulaic language, often pleading for clemency for an errant husband or for relief for the woman and her children. Most women who signed such letters employed a clerk or secretary to write them. In the seventeenth century women like the 1st duchess of Ormond wrote more private letters, usually in their own hand, but they were still largely impersonal and businesslike in tone and usually concerned with estate management and the family accounts. By the eighteenth century, letters by women had became more personal and concerned with social and family affairs. The composition of letters formed part of the education of young girls and it was undoubtedly one of the priorities in the writing classes which many attended. Letter writing was considered a skill to be learnt, practised and polished. Letters were written to be read out loud on social occasions and the style of writing was given a great deal of thought. The letters of Madame de Sévigné were cited as models to be emulated by young girls and, as we have seen, appeared in the reading lists of many wealthy women. The ideal letter was a mixture of family news and literary comments on books being read. Many women spent hours writing letters on a daily basis, as the vast correspondence produced by the Lennox sisters, the countess of Moira and her daughter, Lady Selina Granard, and other women testifies. The time spent writing letters also helps to explain the popularity of books by Hester Chapone and Samuel Richardson that were written in letter form.

Some women clearly used letter writing as an outlet for their literary pretensions and as an alternative to publishing. Like manuscript texts, the letters were written for circulation within the family and a wider social circle. The correpondence of Mary Delany was written as a journal of her time in Ireland for her sister and, later, for her niece. The letters of Anne Donnelan, Elizabeth Vesey and their bluestocking acquaintances were written to impress the reader and the listener with their author's literary knowledge.[123] And, as already noted, later in the century, Martha McTier utilised her lengthy correspondence with her brother to express her political and intellectual views on contemporary politics and on the books which she had read. Martha's brother, William Drennan, was aware of the literary value of their letters and expressed the hope that they might in time form the basis for a publication.[124] The countess of Moira kept up a wide-ranging correspondence with politicians, writers, genealogists and antiquarians and commented on the intellectual pleasure that she derived from reading and writing, praising the 'independence' that she believed it developed.[125]

In the early decades of the eighteenth century, poetry writing was not considered as morally ambiguous as writing novels and it was the first genre through which more women moved into the world of print. Male literary figures such as Jonathan Swift and Patrick Delany offered patronage to women poets and wrote letters on their behalf to potential subscribers and printers. The assistance given by Swift to Mary Barber, Constantia Grierson and, initially, Laetitia Pilkington is well known.[126] Pilkington also used Swift's name to make contact with literary figures in London, including Samuel Richardson, while Henrietta Battier acknowledged her debt to Samuel Johnson who encouraged her to publish her satirical poetry.[127] The social acceptance of women publishing their poetry was also announced in periodicals like the *Hibernian Magazine* and the *Cork Journal* which welcomed the submission of poetry for publication by women.

From the second half of the eighteenth century, a small number of Irish women advanced the publishing field for women a little further as they began to publish novels and plays. The majority, however, made use of an English rather than an Irish publisher to produce their first work; and the most successful Irish women writers lived in England for a substantial part of their lives. In Ireland, it seems that there was still a lingering social stigma attached to women writers. The fact that most of the Irish women writers resorted to publication for financial reasons served only to confirm the image of the woman writer as someone who, like the woman actor, not only worked for a living but led a private life that was often perceived as morally suspect. Irish publishers were also reluctant to subsidise publications by relatively unknown and untried Irish women writers. Charlotte McCarthy tried to publish her work in Ireland but failed. As she explained in the preface to *Justice and Reason* which was published in London in 1767:

> *. . . the Printers of that Country are so extremely avaricious, and have so very little judgement; that no man there would print it, unless I laid down the whole charge for printing, paper, and every other requisite, beforehand; which was not in my power to do.*[128]

Other women who published work in Ireland did so at their own expense or with the help of wealthy patrons and subscribers.[129]

Slowly, therefore, in the late eighteenth century, the social ambiguity of women writers was eroded. In England, Anne Donnellan's and Elizabeth Vesey's friend Elizabeth Montagu overcame her personal reservations and agreed to the publication of her work. And she was joined by other women. The popularity of the moral and religious publications of English women writers such as Elizabeth Hamilton, Mrs Barbauld, Hannah More, Hester Chapone and Catherine Talbot helped to create a new image of the woman writer as one who not only led an impeccably moral life but whose writings aimed to teach virtue to the young and poor.[130] In Ireland in the 1790s, a small number of Irish women writers took on a similar role. Charlotte

Brooke, Mary Leadbeater and Maria Edgeworth all wrote texts for children and Edgeworth went on, as we have seen, to write, with her father, a number of books on the education of children.[131] Leadbeater's publications also had a strong didactic purpose. The Irish women writers of the 1790s projected a new image of the 'literary lady' which replaced that of the unattractive and domestically uncouth woman of the earlier part of the century. The woman writer was now a respected figure in society but her sphere of writing was also carefully defined. She was not only concerned with the education of children but wrote texts that were morally uplifting. Few women stepped outside the space in the literary world established by Brooke, Edgeworth and Leadbeater.

Notes

1. Alice Thornton, *The Autobiography of Mrs. Alice Thornton of East Newton, Co. York* (London, 1875), p. 8. For Alice's reading of the Psalms when she was five see pp. 6–7.
2. Raymond Gillespie, 'Reading the Bible in Seventeenth-Century Ireland' in Bernadette Cunningham and Máire Kennedy (Eds), *The Experience of Reading: Irish Historical Perspectives* (Dublin, 1999), p. 29.
3. Margaret MacCurtain, 'Women, Education and Learning in Early Modern Ireland' in Margaret MacCurtain and Mary O'Dowd (Eds), *Women in Early Modern Ireland* (Edinburgh, 1991), p. 171; Charlotte Fell Smith, *Mary Rich, Countess of Warwick (1625–1678): Her Family and Friends* (London, 1901), pp. 47, 170–1.
4. George Hill (Ed), *The Montgomery Manuscripts, 1603–1706. Compiled from Family Papers by William Montgomery of Rosemount, Esq* (Belfast, 1879), p. 409.
5. Pearse Street Library, Dublin, Dublin City Records, C1/J/2/24. See also list of books lent by Sir James Ussher which included two women (Bodleian Library, Rawlinson MS D 1290). I am grateful to Professor Alan Ford for this reference.
6. Barrett Leonard Muniments, D/DL F106, Essex Record Office. See description in Brian C. Donovan and David Edwards, *British Sources for Irish History 1485–1641* (Dublin, 1997), p. 56.
7. See p. 153 above. See also Peter O'Dwyer, *Mary: A History of Devotion in Ireland* (Dublin, 1988), p. 106; *Aithdioghliom Dana. A Miscellany of Irish Bardic Poetry*, Ed. Lambert McKenna (2 vols., Dublin, 1939–40), i, pp. 40–4.
8. Máirín Ní Dhonnchadha (Ed), 'Courts and Coteries II: c. 1500–1800' in Angela Bourke *et al.* (Eds), *Field Day Anthology of Irish Writing, Vol. IV* (Cork, 2002) pp. 399–402, 452. See also Jane Stevenson and Peter Davidson (Eds), *Early Modern Poets (1520–1700). An Anthology* (Oxford, 2001) pp. xliii–xlvi, 164–7, 174–8, 436–9.

9 Paul Walsh, *Irish Men of Learning* (Dublin, 1947), pp. 179–205; Máirín Nic Eoin, *B'Ait Leo Bean. Gnéithe den Idé-eolaíocht Inscne i dTraidisiún Liteartha na Gaeilge* (Dublin, 1998), pp. 150–69. Bernadette Cunningham, 'Women and Gaelic Literature, 1500–1800' in MacCurtain and O'Dowd (Eds), *Women in Early Modern Ireland*, pp. 147–59; Máirín Ní Dhonnchadha, 'Courts and Coteries I, 900–1600' in Bourke *et al.* (Eds), *Field Day Anthology of Irish Writing, Vol. IV*, pp. 300–1; O'Dwyer, *Mary: A History of Devotion in Ireland*, p. 106. *Aithdioghliom Dana*, Ed McKenna (ITS, xxxvii, xl), i, pp. 40–4. See also p. 24 above.

10 Cited in M. V. Ronan, *The Reformation in Ireland 1536–1558* (London, 1926), p. 143. See also pp. 25–8, 155 above.

11 John Harington (1561–1612). His *A Short View of the State of Ireland* was printed in *Nugae Antiquae; Being a Miscellaneous Collection of Printed Papers in Prose* (London, 1779). Margaret MacCurtain, 'Women, Education and Learning in Early Modern Ireland' in MacCurtain and O'Dowd (Eds), *Women in Early Modern Ireland*, pp. 160–1. Women were also portrayed holding books in paintings and on funeral monuments. See, for example, the picture of Lady Offaly reprinted in *Journal of Co. Kildare Archaeological Society and Surrounding Districts*, **10** (1922–8), p. 108.

12 Esther S. Cope, *Handmaid of the Holy Spirit. Dame Eleanor Davies, Never Soe Mad a Ladie* (Michigan, 1992), pp. 8–25.

13 Thornton, *The Autobiography of Mrs. Alice Thornton of East Newton, Co. York; Memoirs of Lady Warwick . . .* (London, 1847); Jean Klene, C.S.C. (Ed), *The Southwell-Sibthorpe Commonplace Book Folger MS. V.b.198* (Tempe, Arizona, 1997).

14 Victoria Burke, 'Women and Early Seventeenth-Century Manuscript Culture: Four Miscellanies' in *The Seventeenth Century*, **xii**, no. 2 (1997), p. 142.

15 Klene, C.S.C. (Ed), *The Southwell-Sibthorpe Commonplace Book Folger MS. V.b.198*, pp. xviii, 4–5. The text of the letter was also edited in Jean C. Cavanaugh, 'Lady Southwell's Defense of Poetry' in *English Literary and Renaissance*, Vol. 14 (1984). Not paginated. See also Jean Klene, '"Monument of an Endless Affection": Folger Ms V.b.198 and Lady Anne Southwell' in Peter Beal and Margaret J. M. Ezell (Eds) *English Manuscript Studies* (London, 2000), pp. 165–86.

16 Klene, C.S.C. (Ed), *The Southwell-Sibthorpe Commonplace Book Folger MS. V.b.198*; Victoria Burke, 'Women and Early Seventeenth-Century Manuscript Culture: Four Miscellanies' in *The Seventeenth Century*, **XII** (2) (1997), pp. 135–50.

17 *A Catholick Conference Betweene Syr Tadg Mac. Mareall a Popish Priest of Waterford, and Patricke Plaine, a Young Student of Trinity Colledge by Dublin in Ireland* (London, 1612).

18 Marjorie Hope Nicholson (Ed), *The Conway Letters. The Correspondence of Anne, Viscountess Conway, Henry Moore and Their Friends* (London, 1930), p. 191.

19 Lady Frances Keightley to Mrs O'Brien of Dromoland, 1681 (NLI, O'Brien Papers, MS 1843, typescript copy in TCD, MS 5098/1).

20 NLI, O'Brien Papers, Ms 14786. See also NLI, Inchiquin Papers, MS 14887; NLI MS 19332.

21 See, for example, Ann M. C. Forster, 'The Chronicles of the English Poor Clares of Rouen – I' in *Recusant History*, **18** (1986–7), pp. 59–102.

22 I am grateful to Dr Marian Lyons and Mr Ciarán Ó Scea for discussing this topic with me. See also Ciarán Ó'Scea, 'The Devotional World of the Irish Catholic Exile in Early-Modern Galicia, 1598–1666' in Thomas O'Connor (Ed), *The Irish in Europe, 1580–1815* (Dublin, 2001), p. 40.

23 Based on the research of Dr Marian Lyons.

24 Wendy Gibson, *Women in Seventeenth-Century France* (Basingstoke, 1989), pp. 26–37; Elizabeth Rapley, *The Devotés; Women and the Church in Seventeenth-Century France* (Montreal, 1990), pp. 161–2.

25 Mr Ó Scea is currently completing a doctoral thesis on the Irish Community in Spain in the seventeenth century.

26 Raymond Gillespie, 'The Book Trade in Southern Ireland, 1590–1640' in Gerard Long (Ed), *Books Beyond the Pale. Aspects of the Provincial Book Trade in Ireland Before 1850* (Dublin, 1994), pp. 3–6.

27 See p. 172 above.

28 Based on a sample of depositions for Counties Kilkenny, Dublin and Carlow (Trinity College, Dublin, MSS 810, 812). See also the group petition signed by twenty-four women, only one of whom signed with a mark (TCD, MS 840, fo. 27).

29 Mary O'Reilly, 'Seventeenth-Century Irish Catechisms – European or Not?' in *Archivium Hibernicum*, **i** (1996), pp. 102–12; Nicholas Canny, *Making Ireland British, 1580–1650* (Oxford, 2001), p. 423.

30 Toby Barnard, 'Reading in Eighteenth-Century Ireland: Public and Private Pleasures' in Cunningham and Kennedy (Eds), *The Experience of Reading: Irish Historical Perspectives*, pp. 60–77; 'Learning, the Learned and Literacy in Ireland, c. 1660–1760' in Toby Barnard, Dáibhí Ó Cróinín and Katharine Simms (Eds), *'A Miracle of Learning'; Studies in Manuscripts and Irish Learning* (Aldershot, 1998), pp. 209–35.

31 Samuel Whyte, *The Shamrock: or Hibernian Cresses* (Dublin, 1772).

32 Paul J. Kane, 'The Life and Works of David Manson. A Belfast School-Teacher, 1726–1792' (unpublished, M.Ed. thesis, Queen's University, Belfast 1984). See also Hamilton Moore, *Young Gentlemen and Ladies Monitor, Being a Collection of Select Pieces From Our Best Modern Writers: Particularly Calculated to Form the Mind and Manners of the Youth of Both Sexes, and Adapted to the Uses of Schools and Academies* (Belfast, 1788).

33 *Walker's Hibernian Magazine*, September 1782, pp. 453–4.

34 Return of Endowed Schools in Killala, 1808, BL, Add MS 31882, fos. 314–71.

35 *Cork Gazette*, 25 May 1793.

36 *Belfast Newsletter*, 16 March 1773.

37 BL, Add MS 3182, fos. 314–71.

38 *Belfast Newsletter*, 6 March 1770; J. Kane, 'The Life and Works of David Manson. A Belfast School-Teacher, 1726–1792', pp. 34–5.

39 H. F. Berry, 'Notes From the Diary of a Dublin Lady in the Reign of George II' in *Journal of the Royal Society of Antiquaries of Ireland*, **28** (1898), p. 143.

40 Samuel Whyte, 'On Female Education' reprinted in *Walker's Hibernian Magazine*, May 1772, p. 370.

41 Caroline Hamilton, 'Anecdotes of Our Family, Written For My Children' (National Library of Ireland, MS 4810), p. 1.

42 A. C. Elias, Jr (Ed), *Memoirs of Laetitia Pilkington* (Athens and London, 2 vols., 1997), vol. i, p. 178.

43 *Retrospections of Dorothea Herbert 1770–1806* (Dublin, 1929–30, reprinted, Dublin, 1988), pp. 18, 41, 83–4, 147.

44 Ibid., p. 82.

45 Ibid., pp. 39–42, 55.

46 See pp. 164, 196 above.

47 Kerby Miller *et al.* (Eds), *Irish Immigrants in the Land of Canaan. Letters and Memoirs From Colonial and Revolutionary America, 1675–1815* (New York, 2003), pp. 349–62; letters by Margaret Carey Murphy Burke to Mathew Carey, 1 August 1830, 22 August 1841 (Mathew Carey Letterbooks, Lea and Febriger Collection, the Historical Society of Pennsylvania, Philadelphia). I am very grateful to Professor Kerby Miller for sending me copies of his transcripts of these letters. Susan O'Brien has suggested that the education in the Bar Convent, York, was through the medium of French throughout the eighteenth century. See her 'Women of the "English Catholic Community": Nuns and Pupils at the Bar Convent, York, 1680–1790' in Judith Loades (Ed), *Monastic Studies. The Continuity of Tradition* (Bangor, Gwynned, 1990), p. 272.

48 National Library of Ireland, MS 4811.

49 Thomas Reynolds, *The Life of Thomas Reynolds, Esq* (2 vols., London, 1839), vol. i, pp. 72–3.

50 For the wider debate see Karen Offen, *European Feminisms 1700–1950. A Political History* (Stanford, 2000), pp. 37–41; Jane Rendall, *The Origins of Modern Feminism: Women in Britain, France and the United States, 1780–1860* (London, 1985), pp. 7–32.

51 See, for example, 'A Copy of a Letter, on a Proper Education for Young Ladies; Addressed to a Gentleman, Who Was About to Undertake the Tuition of a Female Pupil' in *Walker's Hibernian Magazine*, October 1774, pp. 595–6.

52 'On Female Education' in *Walker's Hibernian Magazine*, May 1772, p. 268.

53 *Walker's Hibernian Magazine*, August 1779, p. 467.

54 'Reflections on the Importance of Forming the Female Character by Education' in *Hibernian Magazine*, January 1798.

55 'Thoughts on Education . . .' reprinted in *Hibernian Magazine*, January 1791, pp. 52–9. On the Young Ladies' Academy in Philadelphia see Linda K. Kerber, *Women of the Republic. Intellect and Ideology in Revolutionary America* (Chapel Hill, North Carolina, 1980), pp. 210–13; *Towards an Intellectual History of Women* (Chapel Hill and London, 1997), pp. 29–34.

56 'On Modesty' in *Walker's Hibernian Magazine*, March 1792, pp. 244–8.

57 *Walker's Hibernian Magazine*, April 1798.

58 Stella Tillyard, *Aristocrats* (London, 1994), pp. 238–51.

59 Reminiscences of Caroline Hamilton (National Library of Ireland, MS 4811).

60 Hamilton, 'Anecdotes of Our Family, Written For My Children', p. 11.

61 Janet Todd, *Mary Wollstonecraft. A Revolutionary Life* (London, 2000), pp. 82–120. See also letter to editor entitled 'Character of Governesses Examined' in *Walker's Hibernian Magazine*, October 1780, pp. 539–40.

62 Hamilton, 'Anecdotes of Our Family, Written For My Children', p. 9. For the influence of Rousseau's ideas on the education of girls see Martine Sonnet, 'A Daughter to Educate' in Natalie Zemon Davis and Arlette Farge (Eds), *A History of Women in the West, III. Renaissance and Enlightenment Paradoxes* (Cambridge, Massachusetts and London, 1993), pp. 108–9.

63 Marilyn Butler, 'Irish Culture and Scottish Enlightenment: Maria Edgeworth: Histories of the Future' in Stefan Collini, Richard Whatmore and Brian Young (Eds), *Economic Policy and Society. British Intellectual History 1750–1950* (Cambridge, 2000), pp. 158–80.

64 Marie-Lou Legg (Ed), *The Letters of Bishop Edward Synge to his Daughter Alicia. Roscommon to Dublin, 1746–1752* (Dublin, 1996).

65 NLI, MS 13022.

66 Hamilton, 'Anecdotes of Our Family, Written For My Children', pp. 1–2.

67 Cited in Frances A. Gerard, *Some Fair Hibernians* (London, 1897), p. 114.

68 Hamilton, 'Anecdotes of Our Family, Written For My Children' (National Library of Ireland, MS 4810), pp. 13–14.

69 Mary Tighe (1772–1810), author of *Psyche, With Other Poems* (London, 1811).

70 C. H. Crookshank, *Memorable Women of Irish Methodism in the Last Century* (London, 1882), pp. 56, 192.

71 Patricia Phillips, *The Scientific Lady. A Social History of Women's Scientific Interests, 1520–1918* (London, 1990), pp. 94, 120, 130. See also the advertisement in the *Freeman's Journal*, 13 April 1780, for lectures by Mr Dinwiddie on geography and astronomy, open to ladies and gentlemen; Mary Delany attended a series of philosophical lectures with her husband in Dublin in 1755 (Angelique Day (Ed), *Letters from Georgian Ireland. The Correspondence of Mary Delany 1731–68* (Belfast, 1991), p. 279). Delany also took an interest in botany from which she developed her famous paper collages.

72 Pamela Fitzgerald (née Sims) married to Emily Fitzgerald's son, Lord Edward.

73 Countess of Bellamont to Emily Fitzgerald, 10 March 1794 (NLI, MS 13022, Folder 26, p. 387).

74 Frank Mitchel, 'The Evolution of Townley Hall' in *Bulletin of the Irish Georgian Society*, vol. 30 (1987), pp. 5–43; Christopher Moore, 'Lady Louisa Conolly: Mistress of Castletown 1759–1821' in Jane Fenlon, Nicola Figgis and Catherine Marshall (Eds), *New Perspectives: Studies in Art History in Honour of Anne Crookshank* (Dublin, 1987), pp. 123–41. David J. Griffin, 'Castletown, Co. Kildare: the Contribution of James, First Duke of Leinster' in *Irish Architectural and Decorative Studies*, Vol. 1 (1998), pp. 120–45.

75 Chapone's text was among those recommended by Lady Anne O'Brien to her children, see TCD, MS 5096; Lucy Fitzgerald wrote to her mother that she was reading the Bible in 'Mrs Chapoon's way' (NLI MS, folder 23, p. 372). See also Janet Todd, *The Signs of Angellica. Women, Writing and Fiction, 1660–1800* (London, 1989), pp. 108–20.

76 Kenneth Milne, *The Irish Charter Schools 1730–1830* (Dublin, 1997), p. 18.

77 Roland Burke Savage, *A Valiant Dublin Woman. The Story of George's Hill (1766–1940)* (Dublin, 1940), p. 73.

78 Ibid., pp. 61–2.

79 Milne, *The Irish Charter Schools 1730–1830*, p. 118.

80 Máire Kennedy, 'Women and Reading in Eighteenth-Century Irish Historical Ireland' in Cunningham and Kennedy (Eds), *The Experience of Reading: Irish Historical Perspectives*, p. 82. See also Berry, 'Notes From the Diary of a Dublin Lady in the Reign of George II', p. 143.

81 C. J. Woods (Ed), *Journals and memoirs of Thomas Russell 1791–5* (Belfast, 1991), p. 84.

82 Ibid.; see also p. 150 above.

83 Elias, Jr (Ed), *Memoirs of Laetitia Pilkington* vol. i, p. 283, vol. ii, p. 387. See also T. C. Barnard, '"Grand Metropolis" or "The Anus of the World"? The Cultural Life of Eighteenth-Century Dublin' in Peter Clark and Raymond

Gillespie (Eds), *Two Capitals. London and Dublin 1500–1840* (Oxford, 2001), pp. 185–6.

84 Cited in Rolf Loeber and Magda Stouthamer-Loeber, 18th–19th Century Irish Fiction Newsletter (October 1998), no. 10. I am grateful to Dr Loeber for sending me copies of the newsletter; J. T. Gilbert, *A History of the City of Dublin* (3 vols., Dublin, 1854), vol. i, p. 395.

85 Loeber and Stouthamer-Loeber, 18th–19th Century Irish Fiction Newsletter, no. 10.

86 *The Library of Mrs. Elizabeth Vesey 1715–1791* (William H. Robinson, Newcastle-on-Tyne, 1926); Phillips, *The Scientific Lady. A Social History of Women's Scientific Interests, 1520–1918*, pp. 94–8.

87 For the bluestocking circle see Sylvia Harcstark Myers, *The Bluestocking Circle. Women, Friendship, and the Life of the Mind in Eighteenth-Century England* (Oxford, 1990), esp. pp. 251–3, 265–7; Deborah Heller, 'Bluestocking Salons and the Public Sphere' in *Eighteenth-Century Life*, **22** (1998), pp. 59–82. I am grateful to Lisa Townshend, a graduate student in Queen's University Belfast, for drawing my attention to this article.

88 Patrick Kelly, 'Anne Donnellan: Irish Proto-Bluestocking' in *Hermathena*, **152** (Summer, 1992), pp. 39–68.

89 *Retrospections of Dorothea Herbert 1770–1806*, p. 83.

90 Ibid., p. 131.

91 Ibid., p. 324.

92 See, for example, Sophia Fitzgerald's Journal, February 1785 (National Library of Ireland, MS 35012 (1)); Angelique Day (Ed), *Letters from Georgian Ireland. The Correspondence of Mary Delany 1731–68* (Belfast, 1991), pp. 166, 279–86.

93 Legg (Ed), *The Letters of Bishop Edward Synge to his Daughter Alicia. Roscommon to Dublin, 1746–1752*, pp. 209–10.

94 Ibid., pp. 145, 203, 209–10, 292, 306, 307, 332, 335. On Charlotte Lennox see Todd, *The Sign of Angellica. Women, Writing and Fiction, 1660–1800*, pp. 151–60.

95 S. J. Connolly, 'A Woman's Life in Mid-Eighteenth-Century Ireland: the Case of Letitia Bushe' in *The Historical Journal*, **43** (2) (2000), p. 436; Day (Ed), *Letters from Georgian Ireland. The Correspondence of Mary Delany 1731–6*, pp. 166, 279–86.

96 Patrick Kelly, 'Anne Donnellan: Irish Proto-Bluestocking', pp. 49–51. See also Bourke *et al.* (Eds), *Field Day Anthology of Irish Writing, Vol. V*, pp. 633–4.

97 Jean Agnew (Ed), *The Drennan-McTier Letters, 1776–1819* (3 vols., Dublin, 1998–99).

98 Brian MacDermot (Ed), *The Catholic Question in Ireland and England 1798–1822 The Papers of Denys Scully* (Dublin, 1988), pp. 2–56.

99 Berry, 'Notes From the Diary of a Dublin Lady in the Reign of George II', pp. 143–4. The CD-Rom version of *Short Title Catalogue* has been used to check Irish editions.

100 Mary Pollard, *Dublin's Trade in Books, 1550–1800* (Oxford, 1989), pp. 220–1.

101 Agnew (Ed), *The Drennan-McTier Letters, 1776–1819*, vol. iii, p. 212.

102 *Retrospections of Dorothea Herbert 1770–1806.*

103 Legg (Ed), *The Letters of Bishop Edward Synge to his Daughter Alicia. Roscommon to Dublin, 1746–1752*, pp. 209–10.

104 Kennedy, 'Women and Reading in Eighteenth-Century Ireland', pp. 78–98.

105 In the 1790s when Anne O'Brien compiled a book of advice for her children she recommended Hester Chapone's *Letters on the Improvement of the Mind. Addressed to a Young Lady* and the writings of Catherine Talbot Pollard.

106 Kennedy, 'Women and Reading in Eighteenth-Century Ireland', pp. 78–98.

107 Máire Kennedy, 'The Distribution of a Locally-Produced French Periodical in Provincial Ireland: *The Magazin à La Mode*, 1777–1778' in *Eighteenth-Century Ireland*, **7** (1992), pp. 83–98.

108 Kennedy, 'Women and Reading in Eighteenth-Century Ireland', pp. 81–2.

109 Cited in Harold Love, *Scribal Publication in Seventeenth-Century England* (Oxford, 1993), p. 50.

110 Agnew (Ed), *The Drennan-McTier Letters, 1776–1819*, vol. i, p. 189.

111 Klene, C.S.C. (Ed), *The Southwell-Sibthorpe Commonplace Book Folger MS. V.b.198*; Burke, 'Women and Early Seventeenth-Century Manuscript Culture: Four Miscellanies' in *The Seventeenth Century*, **XII** (1997), pp. 141–2.

112 Ibid., p. 12; British Library, Lansdowne MS 740.

113 Burke, 'Women and Early Seventeenth-Century Manuscript Culture: Four Miscellanies', p. 142.

114 Love, *Scribal Publication in Seventeenth-Century England*, p. 56.

115 Patrick Thomas (Ed), *The Collected Works of Katherine Philips. The Matchless Orinda* (Stump Cross, Essex, 1992), vol. ii, pp. 47–9, 60–1.

116 Elaine Hobby, *Virtue of Necessity: English Women's Writing 1649–88* (London, 1988), p. 129.

117 Thomas (Ed), *The Collected Works of Katherine Philips. The Matchless Orinda*, vol. ii, p. 79.

118 Hamilton, 'Anecdotes of Our Family, Written For My Children', pp. 36–7.

119 Loeber and Stouthamer-Loeber, 18th–19th Century Irish Fiction Newsletter, no. 10.

120 Nic Eoin, *B'Ait Leo Bean*, pp. 229–88; Eiléan Ní Chuilleanáin, 'Women as Writers: *Dánta Grá* to Maria Edgeworth' in Eiléan Ní Chuilleanáin (Ed), *Irish*

Women: Image and Achievement (Dublin, 1985), pp. 111–26. Ní Dhonnchadha, 'Courts and Coteries II: C. 1500–1800', pp. 358–66.

121 *Memoir of Lady Warwick: Also Her Diary From A.D. 1666 to 1672. Now First Published to Which are Added Extracts from Her Other Writings* (London, 1847); Thomas Crofton Croker (Ed), *Some Specialiaties in the Life of M. Warwick* (London, 1848); *A Memoir of Mistress Ann Fowkes Née Geale Died Aged 82 Years, With Some Recollection of Her Family A.D. 1642–1774. Written By Herself* (Dublin, 1892); Bourke *et al.* (Eds), *Field Day Anthology of Irish Writing, Vol. IV*, pp. 483–5, 486–9; *Vol. V*, pp. 499–500. Professor Kevin O'Neil is preparing a major study based on the Leadbeater diaries.

122 See, for example, NLI MS 2176, the commonplace book of Harriet King, 1796.

123 See Bourke *et al.* (Eds), *Field Day Anthology of Irish Writing, Vol. V*, pp. 633–7. For Anne Donnellan's correspondence, see Kelly, 'Anne Donnellan: Irish Proto-Bluestocking', pp. 39–68. Letters by Elizabeth Vesey are among the papers of Elizabeth Montagu in the Huntington Library, San Marino, California.

124 Agnew (Ed), *The Drennan-McTier Letters, 1776–1819.*

125 MacDermot (Ed), *The Catholic Question in Ireland and England 1798–1822*, pp. 30–1. Transcripts of the countess of Moira's correspondence are among the Granard Papers in PRONI.

126 On eighteenth-century women writers see Siobhán Kilfeather, 'The Profession of Letters, 1700–1810' in Bourke *et al.* (Eds), *Field Day Anthology of Irish Writing, Vol. V*, pp. 772–832.

127 See Elias, Jr (Ed), *Memoirs of Laetitia Pilkington* for Swift's relationship with Pilkington. For Grierson and Barber see ibid., pp. 375–6, 391–3. See also Andrew Carpenter, *Verse in English From the Eighteenth Century* (Cork, 1998), pp. 194–6, 201–6.

128 Bourke *et al.* (Eds), *Field Day Anthology of Irish Writing, Vol. IV*, p. 795.

129 See, for example, ibid., p. 818.

130 Todd, *The Signs of Angellica. Women, Writing and Fiction, 1660–1800*, pp. 101–287.

131 Brooke published in 1791 *School for Christians* which consisted of a series of dialogues for the use of children. Leadbeater's first publication was also a book for children: *Extracts and Original Anecdotes for the Improvement of Youth* (1794) and her subsequent publications were full of moralising lessons for the middle and upper classes of Ireland.

PART IV

Ideas

CHAPTER 8

Ideas and Laws About Women

'Corraghliochas na mBan' (Female Policy Detected)

In the late eighteenth century a young Irish scholar from Carrigtohill in County Cork, Dáibhi de Barra, embarked on his first scholarly work. De Barra set himself the task of translating into Irish Edward Ward's *Female Policy Detected. Or the Arts of a Designing Woman Laid Open*. Ward's text first appeared in print in London in 1695 and was reprinted in Dublin editions in 1749 and 1780, one of which may have been the source of De Barra's translation.[1] Ward wrote for a popular audience and *Female Policy Detected* was intended as an amusing contribution to the contemporary debate on women, the famous *Querelle Des Femmes*.[2] Addressed to young apprentices in London, the volume was strongly misogynistic in tone. The format, as well as the message, of Ward's book may have appealed to the young De Barra. Divided into three parts, the first section consisted of a series of maxims of advice to young men on the dangers and snares of women. The brief paragraph format was not unlike the lists of epigrams or 'dánfhocail' to be found in Irish manuscript texts with which de Barra may have been familiar and which often included similar sentiments about women to those expressed by Ward.[3] The scholarly gloss in the second part of Ward's volume may also have engaged de Barra's intellectual interest. Citing a wide range of examples from classical and Christian literature, Ward amply demonstrated that distrustful, jealous and inconstant women had existed throughout time. In the third and final section, Ward debated the merits of marriage for men, advising young men to proceed with caution in their choice of a suitable wife.

Dáibhí de Barra's 'Corraghliochas na mBan' was more, however, than just an exercise in translation. While he adhered carefully to the original in section 1, de Barra was more discriminating in his translation of the second part of Ward's volume, omitting portions of it and substituting his own local examples of perfidious Irish women. Drawing on Irish literature, he recited the stories of mythical women such as Aoife whose jealousy led her to turn her stepchildren into swans or Queen Maedbh whose bad advice resulted in the death of her husband Ferdia and many of his followers; and, perhaps more surprisingly, Queen Elizabeth who, also consumed by jealousy, according to de Barra, ordered the execution of her favourite courtier and suitor, the earl of Essex.[4] Moreover, De Barra eschewed translating most of the third section of Ward's text, preferring instead to add a new section on the laziness of wives and a story about Hamlet's relationship with Gertrude and Ophelia, both of which were consistent with the overall theme of the volume on the folly and perfidy of women and the threat they represented for men.[5]

De Barra clearly, therefore, empathised with the misogynistic message of Ward's text and 'Corraghliochas na mBan' testifies to the shared store of ideas about women held by English and Irish writers in the early modern period. The fact that Ward drew on the work of the French author Jacob Oliver for much of the second part of his book illustrates also the pervasiveness of these views throughout western Europe.[6]

The final chapter in this volume essays a brief survey of the ideas and laws concerning women that prevailed in early modern Ireland. Conducting an audit of ideas about women is always an exercise fraught with tension between theory and reality. In the Irish context, the problem is compounded by paucity of evidence and over-dependence on the surviving writings of a small literate, male elite whose influence on a largely illiterate society is impossible to quantify. The misogyny reflected in literary texts like that by de Barra was also often circumscribed in practice by compromising courts, assertive and independent-minded women and humane men. Despite these misgivings, ideas about women as articulated in literary, religious and legal texts are worth considering for a number of reasons. First, religious and legal codes were rooted in theoretical constructs of womanhood. Secondly, literary works such as 'Corraghliochas na mBan' incorporated more popular views on women as reflected in the 'dánfhocail' and may, therefore, provide a tantalising glimpse of 'ordinary people's' ideas and perceptions of women.[7] Charting contemporary views on women also enables us to raise important questions about the relationship between theory and empirical change in women's lives. Is it possible to identify any significant shifts in attitudes to women during the early modern period?

Or, do misogynistic views retain their vigour despite significant transitions in women's economic, religious and legal status? If religious and legal infrastructures incorporate particular constructions of womanhood how, if at all, did the revolutionary changes in both spheres change views on and ideas about Irish women? Did the colonial status of Ireland have any implications for views on women? And what impact did the emerging debate on virtuous women and the reform of manners have on Irish women?

Christian ideology

A blinkered search for change would, however, be an inappropriate way to approach early modern ideas about women. Christian ideology prevailed in Ireland in 1500 just as it did in 1800; and Christian doctrine on women remained largely the same throughout the three-hundred-year period. In early medieval Ireland the Church competed with indigenous traditions of female divinities and earth goddesses whose power included the selection of mortal kings. By 1500, however, the omnipotent female goddess of earlier times had metamorphosed into a symbolic representation of Ireland (Éire) as a passive and vulnerable young woman dependent on the military prowess of the human male sovereign for her protection and survival. The ideal woman in late medieval bardic poetry was chaste, silent, pious and renowned for her charity and hospitality. In other words, by the early sixteenth century the Gaelic bard's view of women derived more from Christian ideology than it did from pre-Christian tradition.[8]

Most of the key texts of medieval Christianity were circulated in Ireland in Latin and, frequently, in Irish translations. For Irish clerics, as for Christian scribes throughout the western world, the starting point for an explanation of women's status in society was to be found in the Garden of Eden. Eve's transgression and her responsibility for the subordinate position of women was unquestioned. In the words attributed to Eve by an eleventh-century Irish poet:

I plucked the apple from the spray
Because of greed I could not rule;
Even until their final day
Women will still play the fool.[9]

Ecclesiastical scribes, often unsuccessfully pursuing the ideal of a celibate life, condemned Eve the temptress and constantly warned one another to be wary of the snares of women. The lives of male saints were told in terms of overcoming the 'lusts of lascivious maidens'. Virginity was the attribute most lauded in female saints, an emphasis which was perhaps aimed as much at clerics and their concubines as it was at constructing a role model for other women to follow. A popular Irish tale of the fifteenth century, for example, portrayed the priest's concubine as the personification of the devil.[10]

The 'queen of the virgins' was Mary the mother of God who, in Ireland as elsewhere, was portrayed as the antithesis of Eve.[11] As an eighth century Irish poem explained:

Through a woman and wood mankind had perished –
Through the power of a woman mankind returned to safety (salvation).[12]

Devotion to Mary was popular in Ireland from early Christian times but in the late medieval period literary images of Mary underwent a subtle transformation. In early Irish literature, Mary was depicted as a woman with access to power. Her family relations with God were described in Gaelic kinship terms. As the mother and spouse of Christ, she was in an extraordinary position to intercede with God on man's behalf. By the end of the medieval period, however, this active image was being replaced by a more passive one. The reforming Observantine Franciscans, in particular, lauded Mary's virginity and her unquestioning obedience. The Franciscan poet Pilib Bocht Ó hUiginn wrote warmly of Mary's humility and subordinate relationship with her son:

. . . her teacher was God's Son; so precious a gift was He, you would say she had Him for nothing . . . She was not only humble but called herself His maid. Hearing the glorious message she was not proud of heart, honour had no peril for the Virgin; she was as a couch for pleasure or pain.[13]

Ó hUiginn, who addressed some of his poetry specifically to women, acknowledged the superior role of Mary among women but he also suggested that her virtues as an obedient daughter, mother and nurse could be emulated by other women. Catholic reformers continued to celebrate Mary's chastity and the miracle of the virgin birth throughout the early modern period.[14]

The most well-known Irish female saint was Brigit whose life was told in several recensions in the medieval period. Brigit was often given the epitaph of a 'second Mary', an appellation that associated her with Mary's virginity and chastity. The earliest lives of Brigit portrayed her as a powerful figure equal in status and authority to her male colleagues, including St Patrick. By the late Middle Ages, however, like the images of Mary and the female goddess, that of Brigit was also transformed into a modest, holy virgin:

She never looked into a man's face. She never spoke without blushing. She was abstinent, innocent, liberal, patient, rejoicing to God's commandments, steadfast, humble, forgiving, charitable. She was a Consecrated Casket for the keeping of Christ's Body.[15]

There was, therefore, nothing unusual about the Irish Church's view on women in the early sixteenth century. It conformed to Christian orthodoxy. Like other clerics, Irish ecclesiastical scribes relied on the Bible and the accumulated writings of the Church Fathers to elucidate the role of women. As elsewhere, Paul's famous letter to the Corinthians, urging women to 'keep silent in church', was quoted in early Irish manuscripts that continued to be in wide circulation throughout the medieval period.[16] In the fifteenth century, Franciscan friars reiterated this message and integrated it into their depiction of the ideal woman as passive and unquestioningly submissive. Pilib Bocht Ó hUiginn almost strayed into blasphemy when he reminded even the Virgin Mary of her female status and unsuitability as a teacher. Echoing the words of St Paul he urged the mother of God to

Get thy dear Son to teach us, though thou too canst do it; yet, even when folk's frenzy is least, 'tis no woman's work to bring them to reason.[17]

As indicated in Chapter 5, one of the most popular non-Irish female saints in late medieval Ireland was St Catherine of Alexandria. Ó hUiginn, and probably other medieval Irish writers, was uncomfortable with the popular image of St Catherine as an intelligent woman who could debate complex theological issues with learned men. The story of Catherine's life and death seemed to challenge St Paul's message. In his poem dedicated to Catherine, Ó hUiginn felt compelled to provide Catherine with a male protector, Michael the Archangel, and mirroring the words of St Paul he noted that

In Michael I trust while yet in danger on Defence Day:
For Catherine by herself to defend me is no task for a woman ever so glorious.[18]

Like Mary and Brigit, Catherine's active image of the early medieval period was transformed into a more passive role by the later Middle Ages.

Science and medicine

In fifteenth-century Europe, the Renaissance revived interest in classical literature and led to new commentaries on the writings of Greek doctors and philosophers on the human body. Aoibheann Nic Dhonnchadha has demonstrated the surprising extent to which this literature was circulated in Ireland, usually in Irish translations, from the late medieval period through to the seventeenth century.[19] The scientific discussion on female physiology, prevalent in these texts, fitted neatly into the Christian view of women. The most frequently cited work in the Irish texts was that by the Greek physician Galen of Pergammon, who believed that a woman's body was physically an imperfect form of a man's. Men and women had similar reproductive organs but those in a woman were internal while in the more complete body of a man they were external. Men's bodies were warmer than women's and were, therefore, stronger and more fully formed. The male body was also pre-eminent in the act of reproduction because men could 'convert surplus nutriment into semen that has power to generate'. The woman's body, being colder, produced menstrual blood instead of semen, which was 'devoid of generative power'. Even the uterus was perceived as a gendered space as Galen and his followers believed that the male body was formed in the warmer right side of the womb while the female embryo was developed in the cooler left side. For this reason, it was argued that the female embryo developed more slowly than that of the male although it was thought that once born the female body aged more quickly than the male. The commentary on this phenomenon demonstrates the mixture of scientific deductivism and subjective analysis to be found in these scientific texts. As an anonymous text, translated into Irish in the mid-fifteenth century, noted:

It is asked here why it is that a son grows better in his mother's womb than a daughter, and that a daughter grows better after her birth.
We reply to that according to Averroes, who says these words: Herba mala cicius cresit quam bona, *i.e. a bad plant grows sooner than a good plant; and Averroes applies this analogy to the female: because of her badness she grows sooner than the male.*[20]

Protestant Reformation and Catholic reform

Neither the Protestant nor the Catholic reformation fundamentally transformed the late medieval ideological legacy concerning women. Within the Catholic Church, celibate male clergy continued to portray women as a source of temptation and potential entrapment. Moreover, as Máirín Nic Eoin has noted, two leading Counter-Reformation clerics Geoffrey Keating and Aodh Mac Aingil not only feminised sin in general but also associated women with particular sins, especially those of lust and greed.[21] The chastity and virginity of the Virgin Mary remained the ideal. The zeal with which Irish clergymen promoted the cause of the Immaculate Conception in the seventeenth century is also indicative of their conservative attitude towards women. Under clerical influence, the Confederate Assembly at Kilkenny nominated Mary as the Patroness of the Kingdom of Ireland and, in 1650, it confirmed that the Feast of the Immaculate Conception should be observed in Ireland although it was not an official feast day in the church calendar until 1708.[22] Irish clergymen also amended the official Tridentine catechism to include prayers and devotion to Mary.[23]

The traditional attitude of the Irish Catholic Church towards women can also be discerned in 'Páirliament na mBan', a popular text that was first compiled in the 1670s but survives in over forty manuscript versions dating to the eighteenth and nineteenth centuries.[24] Its author, Domhnall Ó Colmáin, a Catholic priest, borrowed the format of 'Páirliament na mBan' i.e. a parliament of women, from one of the *Colloquia* of Erasmus entitled 'The Council of Women'. The initial section of Ó Colmáin's manuscript is essentially a translation into Irish of Erasmus's text.[25] Thereafter, 'Páirliament na mBan' consists of a series of brief speeches presented by the women parliamentarians on aspects of Catholic doctrine including prayer, different types of sin, the Virgin Mary and the cardinal virtues. For these, too, it is likely that Ó Colmáin drew on other printed sources, circulating within the Irish clerical community.[26] 'Páirliament na mBan' had a didactic purpose and, judging from its popularity, was probably used by parochial clergy in the eighteenth century as a guide for the compilation of sermons. Some of the sermons are directed at its female audience but the majority were not. The use of women's voices served more to reinforce the religious instruction than to convey a particular moral message to women.[27]

In the spirit of the *Querelle Des Femmes* Erasmus had begun his 'Council of Women' with a debate on the role of women in society and in this part of his text Ó Cólmain followed the original closely. Some of the women's speeches appear to promote a radical view of women's education and a role for them in public affairs.[28] In other writings Erasmus promoted the education of women and in the 'Council of Women' he used the amusing idea of a parliament of women to raise serious questions about sexual and political inequality. This more subtle intention of the original text was overlooked by Ó Cólmain who undermined the impact of the women's debate by assigning the speakers mocking surnames such as 'Fionnghuala Ní Stanganéifeacht', i.e. 'Useless Fionnghuala', or 'Caitríona Ní Chorsarasair', i.e. 'Caitríona Trampled-Underfoot'.[29] In the main part of the manuscript,

'Páirliament na mBan' conveys a traditional image of women whose sexual allure and flattering talk was often the source of men's sinfulness. A number of sermons commend the Virgin Mary and women are urged to imitate her passive qualities of quietness, meekness, charity, humility, purity and chastity.[30] As Máirín Ní Dhonnchadha notes, 'Ó Colmáin's work was significantly more conservative and more reductive of women than that of Erasmus'.[31]

There is, therefore, sufficient evidence to document the continuity of a misogynistic tradition within the Irish Catholic Church. It is, however, a more problematic exercise to discern any change in the Church's views on women in the course of the early modern period. As Chapters 5 and 6 have demonstrated, the Catholic Church in Ireland was heavily dependent on the auxiliary services of women. The extent to which this activity shifted perceptions of women in the Church is, however, difficult to gauge. For the most part, the work undertaken by women was incorporated into prevailing views on gender. The welcoming householder, the wealthy widow, the lay tertiary and the chaste teaching sisters were praised for their exercise of the ideal female virtues: charity, chastity and humility. In the sixteenth and early seventeenth centuries, the Jesuits praised wealthy benefactresses of the Catholic Church in Ireland while at the same time noting women's propensity for heresy and laying down careful limits to the services that they offered priests.[32] Successive synods of Irish Catholic bishops in the seventeenth and eighteenth centuries also relentlessly warned priests of the dangers of friendships with women.[33]

Nonetheless, a case can be made for a subtle, almost imperceptible, shift in attitudes to women within the Irish Catholic Church from the mid-eighteenth century. As described in Chapter 6, the emerging public profile of the Church opened up a more active role for women. The encouragement given by Irish Catholic clergy to non-cloistered female communities, such as those fostered by Nano Nagle and Teresa Mulally, suggests that by that time priests were beginning to focus more on what were perceived as women's positive qualities rather than dwell on their negative and more threatening ones. As Bishop Daniel Delany recognised, women were usually more zealous in their support for his religious reforms than men.[34]

Clergy in the Protestant denominations shared many of the same ideas about women as their Catholic counterparts. Inevitably, however, it is possible to discern more variation of opinion among Protestant clergymen than is evident within the Catholic clerical community. The original tale of Adam and Eve maintained its centrality in the perception of women in all the early modern Christian denominations but some clerics interpreted Eve's role in a less harsh light than others. As discussed in Chapter 5, the late seventeenth-century Presbyterian catechiser Robert Chambre refused to blame Eve, arguing that Adam should not have heeded her advice, although he agreed that women had from their first creation been subject to men and that Eve's actions had intensified that subjection.[35] Ezekiel Hopkins, Church of Ireland Bishop of Raphoe 1671–81 and Bishop of Derry 1681–90, took a much harsher view:

Because by the occasion of the Woman Sin entered into the world; So . . . Adam was not deceived, but the Woman being deceived, was in the Transgression. *And therefore it is but fit and just, that She who made all Mankind disobedient against God, should herself be made subject and obedient unto Man.*[36]

Such severe assertions of women's subordination were, however, increasingly rare. By the mid-eighteenth century, most Protestant clergy wrote of the differences between men and women as a creation of God and nature rather than as a consequence of Eve's transgressions. As the Church of Ireland cleric Philip Skelton noted, men's physical strength explained their superior position:

It is true that, in nature and reason, the right of governing ought to go with the superior understanding, whether placed in the husband or wife. But, then in regard to each particular couple, who shall decide its place? . . . the God of peace and order, who alone can judge in such a matter, . . . hath, . . . commanded the [wife] obey the [husband] in all things lawful and honest. I will not say this rule is founded on a greater degree, generally speaking of natural capacity in men than in women, for I know, although much may be said for it, yet a good deal may be said against it. But one thing is certain, that men in general have more strength of body than women.[37]

The Irish Presbyterian philosopher Francis Hutcheson concurred and, like Skelton, he questioned the universality of the belief that men were always endowed with greater intellectual ability than women. Even if this was the case, Skelton and Hutcheson shared the view, that was to become increasingly common in the eighteenth century, that women were endowed with 'other amiable dispostions' that men often lacked.[38]

Printed discourses on the commandment: Honour Thy Father and Thy Mother, usually included a commentary on the respective duties of wives and husbands. Within the Catholic Church, throughout the early modern period, Irish catechisms followed the traditional analogy of Christ's relationship with the Church to explain the relationship between a husband and wife.[39]

This analogy was also used by Protestant clergymen but there were variations in the interpretations of its meaning. While some argued that it justified the inferior role of women in marriage, others maintained that it meant that marital relationships should be based on mutual love and support. Like many of his clerical colleagues, Jeremy Taylor, Bishop of Down and Connor 1660–7, asserted that a husband's power over his wife should be 'paternal and friendly, not magesterial and despotic'. Taylor, however, went further than many other writers and diffused a harsh interpretation of a wife's subordinate role by suggesting that it was a matter of semantics:

. . . there is scarce any matter of duty but it concerns them both alike, and is only distinguished by names, and hath its variety by circumstances and little accidents: and in what in one is called 'love', in the other is called 'reverence', and what in the wife is 'obedience', the same in the man is 'duty': he provides, and she dispenses; he gives commandments, and she rules by them; he rules her by authority, and she rules him by love; she ought by all means to please him, and he must by no means displease her.[40]

The Presbyterian Hutcheson followed this line of thought to its logical conclusion by describing marriage as 'a state of equal partnership or friendship'.[41]

Taylor, Hutcheson and Skelton may have been among the more open-minded of the cohort of Presbyterian and Protestant writers who considered the role and status of women during this period but their views reflect a more general concern to stress the mutuality of the marital relationship and, as in the Catholic Church, to focus on women's positive qualities rather than to dwell on their negative ones.

Colonial discourse and gender

Despite their differences, all ecclesiastical denominations in Ireland drew on a shared intellectual inheritance, an inheritance that was familiar to church authorities throughout western Europe. The colonial context of early modern Ireland, however, distinguished it from other European countries and placed gender at the centre of public policy in a way that was not common elsewhere. Regulation of the home and family formed an essential part of Tudor reform in Ireland. Consequently, the nature of Irish womanhood was given serious consideration by Elizabethan writers on Ireland who constructed a particular view of the Irish woman as the antithesis of the ideal Christian woman. She was deemed to have all the worst characteristics traditionally associated with women and none of the redeeming ones. In Elizabethan literature, the Irish woman was portrayed as lustful, licentious, deceitful and lacking in personal and domestic hygiene. Consequently, she was unsuitable as a spouse for a civilised Englishman or as a mother to his offspring.[42] The Irishwoman represented not only a threat to male colonial settlers but to the whole civilising influence of English society in Ireland. The failure of the first government-sponsored plantation scheme in Laois and Offaly in the 1560s was partly attributed to sexual liaisons between the soldier-settlers and local women. Subsequent plantation schemes endeavoured to limit the contact between English men and local women. The plans for the two largest projects in Munster and Ulster envisaged a segregated colonial society. In Ulster, the original intention was to clear the indigenous population totally from certain areas and settle them entirely with British settlers and thus avoid contamination through contact with local women.[43] The concern of the planners with relations between English men and Irish women is also evident in the final colonial project undertaken in Ireland in the 1650s. In the atmosphere of the religious zeal of the Commonwealth, however, official attitudes to Irish women appear to have changed. Although liaisons with Irish sexual partners were still viewed with distaste it was accepted that conversion to Protestantism might assist the reconstruction of Irish womanhood. Irish women converts were, however, often suspected of conforming 'for some corrupt or carnal ends' rather than for religious reasons. Accordingly, intermarriage between serving soldiers and local women was forbidden unless the woman could pass an oral examination 'by a board of military saints' to prove that her conversion was genuine. The artful and deceitful image of Irish women continued to flourish despite the growth in the belief of the redeeming power of Protestantism.[44]

The traditional dual image of the benign and malign powers of women was, therefore, given a particular formulation in Irish colonial theory. While Irish women were portrayed as guileful and licentious creatures capable of destroying the colonial ideal, English women were hailed as a positive force on whom the future of the colony depended. The Protestant, English mother had a function in colonial Ireland as a transmitter of English manners and morals to her children, a task that was inherited by the philanthropically-minded landlord's wife of the eighteenth century. In the late sixteenth century, Gaelic lords who sought wives from outside Gaelic society also implicitly endorsed the negative construction of Irish women and the idealisation of the English Protestant mother of Irish colonial discourse. As Hugh O'Neill explained to the London administration, he married Mabel Bagenal to 'bring civility into my house'.[45]

The low status of women in Gaelic society was also offered as a moral justification for Tudor and Stuart colonial projects in Ireland. The prohibition on women heiresses, the lack of economic security for widows and the ease with which Irish men divorced their wives were frequently cited as examples of barbaric customs in Gaelic society. Colonisation was, therefore, presented as beneficial to Irish women. It would not only reconstruct Irish womanhood but it would also offer women more economic and legal security as wives, widows and heiresses.[46] Such views can still be found in commentaries on Ireland in the eighteenth century although by then they were directed more at the rural poor than at the Irish population as a whole.

The feminisation of the iconography of Ireland was another gendered theme of Irish colonial discourse. As noted already, the metaphor of Ireland as a woman first appeared in early Irish literature and was revived in the *aisling* poetry of the eighteenth century in which Ireland is depicted as a beautiful woman expecting deliverance through a foreign (usually a Stuart or, later, French) prince.[47] The feminisation of Ireland was also a common literary trope of colonial discourse. Elizabethan and Commonwealth writers used the analogy of Ireland as a virgin, awaiting fertilisation or penetration by English colonists. In the eighteenth century, Protestant political rhetoric also borrowed the imagery of a feminised Ireland to portray Anglo-Irish relations in familiar terms as sisters or as a paternal father and a loving daughter.[48] Although the depiction of Ireland varied in its form and intent, the representation of women in this type of literature remained constant and served to reinforce rather than challenge prevailing views of women. Whether she was awaiting deliverance by a continental prince or being cared for by a concerned English father, Ireland was constructed as a passive and defenceless creature, incapable of independent action.

Marriage, patriarchy and the law

Another consequence of the colonial status of Ireland was, of course, the legal revolution which occured in the sixteenth and seventeenth centuries. The transition from Irish to English law was the most profound change implemented by the Tudor and Stuart regimes in Ireland. As described elsewhere, there were significant differences in practice between Gaelic and English law in relation to women, particularly in the areas of property, inheritance and divorce. The two codes shared, however, a common recognition of women's dependent status. Katharine Simms noted of women in Gaelic society that they 'lived in a state of perpetual tutelage under father, brother, husband or son from the cradle to the grave'.[49] Similarly, under English common law fathers left the custody of unmarried daughters to their male heirs and married women were legally represented by their husbands. Both legal systems demanded that women present themselves as passive supporters of a patriarchal society.

Women who appeared to challenge the hapless image identified for them by the legal systems were treated harshly. They were shunned by local custom and severely punished by the judiciary. The powerful images of strong, independent women in Gaelic society are a later folk tradition. The military deeds of Gráinne O'Malley's are ignored in contemporary Gaelic literature.[50] The annalist and the bardic poet preferred to construct an image of the generous and charitable chieftain's wife rather than praise the woman who engaged in military conflict. Similarly, in English literature the activities of O'Malley were mocked rather than admired. In local custom the violent woman was socially ostracised. In the 1630s when a woman in the Liberties in Dublin beat her husband, her neighbours were so outraged at the role reversal that they revived a medieval custom of placing a horse in front of the man's house to indicate his shaming in public. As one participant in the ritual explained, the woman's behaviour 'tended to the discredit of the rest of the inhabitants and unfit to be practised within the liberties of so sacred a place'.[51] Similarly, in eighteenth-century courts women murderers were more likely to receive the death penalty than men because they were perceived to have offended against the agreed norms of behaviour for their sex.[52]

The shift from Gaelic to English law was the most significant legal change of the period but other legal developments also had implications for attitudes to women. Reform of the laws on marriage was central to the political debate in early modern Ireland; and the state's attempt to outlaw marriage services not conducted by a Church of Ireland minister led to an increasingly bitter debate about what constituted a valid marriage. The discussion also raised important questions about the nature of patriarchy in Irish society.[53] While Protestant patriarchy was bolstered by the state and the established Church through its legislation on marriage and property, the patriarchal control of Catholic men was officially undermined. In particular, the penal legislation approved by the Irish parliament in the late seventeenth century embodied an unprecedented attack on the legal rights of Catholic men. Catholic husbands of Protestant heiresses or landowners were denied their common law rights to their wives' property. Under the new legal restrictions, a Protestant heiress who married a Catholic man was deemed no longer to exist in law and, consequently, her property passed to the next

Protestant heir. The children of Catholic male landowners were also encouraged to disobey their fathers and convert to Protestantism. The rewards for a son who did so were particularly attractive as he could inherit the entire estate of his father. If the sons remained Catholic, the property was divided between them, thus undermining Catholic male ownership in subsequent generations. Protestant wives of Catholic husbands were also permitted to leave their husbands without securing a divorce. If a woman chose this option, the Chancery Court had the power to seize maintenance for her from the husband's estate. A daughter who converted to Protestantism could also make a legal claim for maintenance from her Catholic father.[54] As one contemporary noted, 'the ties of nature . . . are torn to pieces. . . . the Papist must . . . watch day and night against the legal assaults of his wife, his children and his kindred'.[55]

The efforts to maintain Protestant landed security also reinforced the Protestant father's dominance in the family in other ways. Throughout the seventeenth century there was a concern to prevent the marriage of young heiresses without the consent of their parents. The law in this area became progressively more severe as the control of the father over the marriages of his daughters was strengthened by successive legislation. In 1634, legislation was enacted that prohibited the marriage of heiresses under sixteen years of age without the consent of father and mother. By an act of 1708, the age limit was raised to eighteen and in 1735 new legislation was approved by the Irish parliament that prohibited heiresses under twenty-one years of age marrying without their father's consent. There was no reference in the Act to the consent of the mother being necessary.[56]

The Irish legislation was unique. There was no English equivalent. The first attempt to introduce reform of the marriage laws in England was the 1753 Hardwicke Act. Like the 1735 Irish Act, it was designed to prevent clandestine marriages. The English legislation was, however, primarily directed at unregistered clergymen who performed marriage ceremonies, inexpensively, in informal settings. In Ireland, on the other hand, the concern of the legislators in 1735 and in the earlier marriage laws was mainly with 'clandestine' marriages between Protestant women heiresses and Catholic men. The contrasting responses to the Irish and English legislation reflected the different circumstances in each country. In England, the Hardwicke Act provoked a public debate with opponents of the bill arguing, among other things, that it curbed the ability of a young woman to choose her own marriage partner. The supporters of the bill, on the other hand, favoured the power that it bestowed on parents to prevent their daughters marrying unwisely.[57] There is little evidence that the legislation of 1735 provoked a similar debate in Ireland where the new law was perceived above all as bolstering the landed security of the Protestant elite and, as a consequence, the patriarchal control of Protestant men over the inheritance of their property.

The strengthening of Catholic patriarchy?

The official Catholic response to the state reinforcement of Protestant patriarchy was an endeavour to strengthen Catholic patriarchy. Catholic bishops, for example, urged priests to support the patriarchal status of Catholic men married to Protestant women by baptising their children as members of the Catholic community. As Dublin Archbishop Cornelius Nary angrily asked when a priest hesitated:

How could . . . the said priest refuse to do his duty, when he was desired by the fathers, whom I hope you will allow to be the heads of their families, though the mothers should expressly forbid it . . .[58]

Other reports also suggest that Catholic priests had little tolerance for Protestant wives of Catholic men and urged their husbands to assert their authority.[59]

The cult of the Holy Family was never as strong in Irish Christian tradition as that of the Virgin Mary but a rare sermon on the subject by the mid-eighteenth-century Catholic warden of Galway provides some intriguing insights into Catholic clerical views on the man's authority in the home. The warden was particularly exercised by the role and status of St Joseph in the Holy Family. Joseph, as the husband of Mary and the father of Jesus, was, according to the warden, the dominant figure in the household. Mary, therefore, owed him obedience and respect, an awkward position, the warden acknowledged, for the spouse of God. The warden was convinced, however, that Mary, the ideal woman, was endowed with all the essential female virtues and would, therefore, have recognised Joseph's superior role in the family despite her close association with God. The warden also pondered on Joseph's relationship with Jesus. As the male head of household, Joseph should have demanded obedience from his step-son, a difficult expectation if your son is God. The warden resolved the dilemma, as he had done with Mary's position, by asserting that Joseph would have been spiritually inspired to have recognised the special connection that he enjoyed with Jesus. The warden's conclusions concerning relations within the Holy Family are of less significance than the fact that the issue concerned him. Even in the exceptional family of Mary and Joseph, it was essential that patriarchal principles be at least recognised and respected, if not followed precisely as in other families.[60]

John Bossy has suggested that the withdrawal of Catholic men from political life in early modern England strengthened the role of the father in the household and resulted in a 'patriarchal revival among the Catholic gentry'.[61] The Bossy thesis may also have a relevance for Ireland. In the eighteenth century, Catholic gentry families formed tightly bonded networks that seemed to have left few openings for women to exercise financial, spiritual or intellectual independence. In one of the largest collections of Catholic family correspondence, that of the O'Connells of Derrynane, County Kerry, women are noticeable by their silence. In the second half of the eighteenth century, the family was governed by the dominant male figure of Maurice O'Connell who presided over a large extended family stretching from Ireland to France. In the pages of the family correspondence, Maurice O'Connell emerges as a strong, patriarch who took a close interest in the activities of his nephews and brothers. It is striking, however, how little is written by or about the women in the family. The most extensive correspondence relates to two 'difficult' women, Maurice O'Connell's widowed sister-in-law Mary Falvey and her daughter Abigail. O'Connell was outraged that the former departed from the O'Connell family home shortly after she was widowed. O'Connell's distress was focused not on concern for the widow's welfare but on the social shame her sudden return to her parents' house might inflict on the O'Connell family. Later, when Abigail wanted to leave a violently abusive husband, O'Connell told her bluntly that she should bear her situation 'with that patience that becomes a good Christian and the calmness of a gentle woman'.[62] In the nineteenth century folk memory of the O'Connells, Maurice O'Connell's mother, Máire Dhubh, emerges as a strong matriarchal figure whom members of the family feared as much as loved. But even she was subjected to the patriarchal rule of her son following her husband's death.[63]

Further down the social scale patriarchal control was strong within rural families. The message behind many of the epigrams and proverbs of Irish popular culture was that men should exercise a strong control over their wives. As one seventeenth-century maxim put it: 'da leige tu dhi saltradh ar do chois anocht sailteoraid si ar do chionn amaireach [for if you let her stamp on your foot to-night, she will stamp on your head tomorrow'].[64] While such expressions might be considered the common currency of popular literature in most rural societies, visitors to Ireland commented on what they perceived as the exceptionally low status of women in Irish marriages. Edward Wakefield famously noted:

An Irishman assumes over the partner of his bed an authority which is seldom claimed or submitted to in England. . . . Females in Ireland are treated more like beasts of burden than rational beings. . . .[65]

One of the reasons offered for the strong authority of Irish men in the home by the late eighteenth century was the prevalence of arranged marriages, particularly within the farming or substantial tenant class. Young men and women accepted that their fathers could 'claim a substantial voice both in the timing of these marriages and in the choice of a partner'. Economic considerations were central to the negotiations and, as Sean Connolly has noted, the interests of the family took precedence over that of the individual.[66]

It could be argued, therefore, that a powerful mixture of the political powerlessness of Catholic gentry, the conservative tradition of Catholicism and the economic priorities of rural families served to reinforce the leadership role of the male head of the family in Irish Catholic families in the eighteenth century. Political, religious and economic circumstances, thus, combined to prolong stereotypical views of women in many Irish households.

Behavioural and conduct books and the virtuous woman

In sixteenth- and seventeenth-century England, the message to women in the Church and the law courts was reinforced in print through a proliferation of advice books for women. The printing press was slower to develop in Ireland. Consequently, there was not the same growth in this type of literature, although some English publications undoubtedly found their way into Irish homes in the sixteenth and seventeenth centuries. In the Catholic community, clergymen drew on a large store of texts produced since the Council of Trent. Some were communicated orally through verse and sermons and others through the circulation of manuscript texts such as 'Páirlement na mBan' which, as noted already, survives in an impressive number of manuscript versions, one of which was addressed to young women.[67] The most popular Catholic author of printed texts was Francis de Sales whose *Introduction to the Devout Life* (1619) promoted the virtues of married life and encouraged women to remain widows rather than remarry.[68] In the eighteenth century Richard Challoner's *Considerations Upon Christian Truths and Christian Duties* presented a similar message and was also read in the Irish Catholic community.[69] In the absence of printed texts women, and occasionally, men also composed their own letters of advice to young female relatives.[70]

There was, however, no Irish-authored conduct book for girls or women printed before 1800. From the late seventeenth century, the Irish book market relied heavily on texts that had first been printed in England and then reprinted in Irish editions. Irish reprints were aimed, of course, at an English-speaking as well as, probably, a largely Protestant middle- and upper-class readership although, as de Barra's translation of *Female Policy Detected* clearly demonstrated, English printed books had a wide circulation in eighteenth-century Ireland.[71] One of the earliest advice books for girls to be printed in an Irish edition was George Saville, earl of Halifax's *The Lady's New-Year's Gift: Or, Advice to a Daughter* (Dublin edition, 1699). Halifax praised women's special virtues but at the same time clearly limited their sphere of influence to house and family. Like others, he suggested that the 'inequality in the sexes' was based on the laws of nature that bestowed the 'larger share of Reason' on men, but he acknowledged that women had a greater share of other characteristics such as gentleness 'to soften, and to entertain' men; and, as mothers, women had considerable influence over young children.[72]

In England from the 1770s there was a major expansion in the production of behaviour and conduct books, a development that also made an impact on the Irish book market as most were also reprinted in at least one Irish edition. John Gregory's *Father's Legacy to his Daughter* and Hester Chapone's letters to her niece were among the most popular texts in Ireland and appeared in several reprints from the early 1770s through to the 1790s.[73] They, like Halifax, placed the emphasis on the special qualities of women, particularly their modesty and domestic skills.

As noted in the last chapter, Hester Chapone also recommended an educational programme for her niece and the popularity of Chapone's text in Ireland, as in England, reflected the growing awareness of the virtues of the educated woman. The debate on women's education initiated a wider discussion on women's role in society and support for a less passive attitude on the part of women than that advocated by Halifax and others. From its first issue in 1771, *Walker's Hibernian Magazine* regularly featured articles on the history of women and descriptions of customs and laws relating to women found in other countries and civilisations, often extracted from recently printed books. Implicit in many of these items was a recognition that the status of women in contemporary English society (and, therefore, to the readers of *Walker's Hibernian Magazine* in Irish society) was too restrictive and that there were other ways in which the respective roles of men and women in society could be regulated.[74] As noted in Chapter 7, the editor of *Walker's Hibernian Magazine* was an admirer of Mary Wollstonecraft and reprinted extracts from *A Vindication of the Rights of Women* in 1792, the year in which it was first published. Wollstonecraft's text was printed in a number of Irish editions and read with approval by Martha McTier and Mary Ann McCracken, both from politically-minded Presbyterian families in Belfast. The latter was one of the few women to write about the contemporary debate on the status of women that the writings of Wollstonecraft and others had provoked. Yet, it is also worth noting that neither McTier nor McCracken translated their radical beliefs into public activity. Both preferred to remain in the background while their brothers engaged with political affairs. When both women took on a more public role it was through philanthropic work rather than politics and they, thus, implicitly lived their lives according to the model of the virtuous woman of the conduct books.[75]

The radical nature of the woman promoted in magazines like *Walker's Hibernian Magazine* should not, therefore, be exaggerated. The ideal new woman was literate and politically aware but not actively involved in public discourse. She may have provided support for the Volunteers or the United Irishmen but neither she nor the editors of *Walker's Hibernian Magazine* believed that women should become political activists. The new woman was sufficiently well educated to take part in social conversations but she had no intellectual ambitions. She engaged in charitable work outside the home but she did not neglect her domestic responsibilities. Mary Wollstonecraft's views on women's education were admired but her personal life weakened the acceptability of her message. As Martha McTier commented to her brother on Wollstonecraft's life: 'Virtue and prudence must ever be absolutely necessary to independence.'[76]

The debate on the role of women in society and the conservative backlash against Wollstonecraft was part of a wider shift in social attitudes and behaviour that historians have detected in late eighteenth-century England. The emergence of the culture of sensibility with its emphasis on benevolence, moral sense and tenderness had profound consequences for the status and perception of women in society. English conduct literature increasingly promoted the ideal woman as the virtuous woman who had a strong sense of morality and fellow feeling. She eschewed the superficiality of 'polite' society in favour of more genuine sentiments of charity, morality and generosity.[77] Janet Todd has noted that women writers such as Hester Chapone won public approval through promoting sensibility in their publications while Judith Lewis has suggested that by the end of the century aristocratic women were increasingly withdrawing from engagement with political life and transferring their energies to evangelical religion.[78] The new public awareness of women's intellectual abilities was tempered, therefore, by society's increasing restrictions on women's public and social behaviour.

In Ireland, too, historians have identified changes in manners and behaviour in the course of the eighteenth century although the extent to which these mirrored the social transition of English society is not clear. Toby Barnard has suggested that the emergence of a 'polite society' within the Irish Protestant community was slow and uneven. Other scholars have also argued that Irish landed society lagged behind that of its English counterpart in terms of manners and behaviour. The latter had abandoned in the late seventeenth century the raucous and drunken behaviour still attributed to the former in the mid-eighteenth century.[79] The abduction of young women is often cited as evidence of the acceptance of violent conduct in Irish rural society.[80] Historians agree, however, that toleration of such behaviour declined in the last decades of the eighteenth century. Neal Garnham, in particular, has noted the increased prosecution of crimes of rape, a development that he attributes to a decreasing acceptance of violence against women.[81] Similarly, James Kelly has pointed to the dwindling tolerance of duelling in the 1780s and identified as one of the principal reasons for this trend the 'growing disposition among elements of the Protestant middle-classes . . . for root-and-branch moral and religious regeneration'. The intensification of the evangelical revival created a new awareness of the need for public and private morality, a development that would also lead to a new appreciation of the virtuous woman.[82]

Other indicators of changing attitudes to behaviour and morals can be tentatively detected. Sean Connolly incorporated his analysis of the life of Letitia Bushe into the English debate on changing fashions, suggesting that Bushe's 'lack of verbal inhibition' in her private correspondence of the 1740s would not have been socially acceptable at the end of the century.[83] Similarly, in the middle decades of the eighteenth century, the sons of Emily Fitzgerald, 1st duchess of Leinster, wrote to their mother about their mistresses, illegitimate children and occasional sexual adventures in ways that were, perhaps, less common by the end of the century.[84]

It is difficult, however, to trace the extent to which this 'moral and religious regeneration' filtered downwards into the Irish countryside or impacted on the majority Catholic population. The reforming ethos of the Irish Catholic Church in the 1790s did, undoubtedly, serve to bolster the image of the virtuous woman. The appearance of new female Catholic religious communities throughout the country provided local models of virtuous women as well as a training ground for more. Furthermore, as the penal legislation against the Catholic Church in Ireland was relaxed, the hierarchy began to concentrate on moral reform. An effort was made to tighten up the enforcement of marriage regulations and to eradicate informal ceremonies presided over by 'couple beggars' or unregistered priests. In addition, the Catholic hierarchy gave new attention to the problems presented by prostitution, particularly in Dublin where Archbishop Troy sanctioned the opening of two Magdalen Asylums and a number of orphanages, the first of many such institutions to be founded by the Catholic Church in the following century.[85]

The effect of the reform in morals and manners remained, however, very uneven, if not superficial by 1800. Popular publications such as *Walker's Hibernian Magazine* may have promoted the virtuous woman but they also retained a fascination with the fallen woman. The magazine regularly printed stories about young women led astray by older and wealthier men and seemed to present a rather ambiguous moral message concerning prostitution and illicit sex. Some of its more titillating stories on fallen women were clearly published with an eye to the crowded magazine market while others seemed to offer a critique of the fashionable promotion of 'virtue'. In 1795, the magazine printed extracts from the memoirs of the well-known Dublin prostitute Margaret Leeson that wryly mocked the hypocrisy of those that condemned the moral depravity of the prostitute with the question: 'is chastity the only virtue?' Leeson was critical of women who denounced sexual misdemeanours while at the same time failing to demonstrate many Christian virtues in their own lives. Leeson publicly made fun of Lady Arbella Denny, Ireland's most famous virtuous woman, by appearing at a charity masquerade in the Rotunda in Dublin, dressed as the goddess of Chastity accompanied by women from her brothel as her Magdalens. She also attempted to register her establishment as a boarding school for young women! Although it was possible to interpret Leeson's *Memoirs* as a warning against the pitfalls of prostitution as a way of life, her readers were more likely to have been interested in the salacious details that she provided about the politicians and churchmen who visited her brothel. Nor do Leeson's revelations appear to have been a source of public scandal or to have damaged the reputation of her well-known clients whose names she made little attempt to disguise.[86]

Another literary indicator of the limited impact of the moral reform might also be cited. In the 1780s, a mathematics teacher from County Clare composed one of the most sexually explicit poems in the Irish literary canon. In 'Cúirt an Mheón-Oíche' Brian Merriman utilised the format of an assembly of women to write a comic satire on the plight of unmarried women and reluctant male suitors. There is little evidence of the virtuous woman in the voices of Merriman's young women who describe with considerable frankness their sexual frustration and desire. It might indeed not be too fanciful to suggest that, like Leeson, the poet composed his work partly in response to the expanding body of printed literature on the merits of the chaste and modest young woman.[87] The texts of Leeson and Merriman serve also as a reminder that the cruder and more reductive image of women to be found in 'Corraghliochas na mBan' continued to be popular in Ireland at the end of the eighteenth century. The moral reform that was to characterise Irish Catholicism in the nineteenth and twentieth centuries was only in its initial stages.

Conclusion

The introduction to this chapter queried whether ideas and attitudes to women in Ireland changed in the course of the early modern period; and, if they did, what were the forces that drove the process of change. The answer to these questions is not intellectually tidy nor can it be more than tentative, given the current limited state of research into the history of ideas in Ireland. Christianity remained at the core of the construction of womanhood throughout the period but in the last quarter of the eighteenth century Enlightenment thinking began to infiltrate the debate on women's education and influenced some writers to consider the possibility of the intellectual equality of men and women. The most significant development was, however, a shift in emphasis rather than the introduction of a new paradigm. In the long term, nonetheless, the increased awareness of women's special attributes laid the basis for the later nineteenth century debate on the moral superiority of women. In addition, there were more local developments that impacted on perceptions of women. The colonial status of Ireland in the sixteenth century demonised indigenous Irish women while idealising the Protestant English woman. In the seventeenth century, the official policy of the state attempted to undermine Catholic patriarchy in landed families, a development that in turn may have led to a strengthening of the role of the father as head of the household in the Irish Catholic community as a whole.

Notes

1 Breandán O Conchúir (Ed), *Corraghliochas na mBan Le Dáibhí de Barra* (Dublin, 1991) is a printed edition of De Barra's manuscript text. See introduction for

editions of *Female Policy Detected*, pxii. See also Máirín Nic Eoin, *B'Ait Leo Bean. Gnéithe de Idé-eolaíocht Inscne I d'Traidisiún Llitleartha na Gaeilge* (Dublin, 1998), pp. 139–40.

2 O Conchúir, op. cit., p. xii; Howard William Troyer, *Ned Ward of Grubstreet. A Study of Sub-Literary London in the Eighteenth Century* (Harvard, 1946), pp. 11–12.

3 Carl Marstrander (ed. and translator), 'Bídh Crínna' in *Eriú*, **v** (1911), pp. 136–7; T. F. O'Rahilly (Ed), *Dánfhocail. Irish Epigrams in Verse* (Dublin, 1921), pp. 15–19; O'Rahilly (Ed), *Búrdún Bheaga. Pithy Irish Quatrains* (Dublin, 1925). See also Nic Eoin, *B'Ait Leo Bean*, pp. 128, 176–82.

4 De Barra also told stories of other women, less noble in status but equally perfidious in their treatment of their husbands. See O Conchúir (Ed), *Corraghliochas na mBan*, pp. xiii–iv, 42, 60–4, 72–3.

5 Ibid., xiii–iv.

6 See Troyer, *Ned Ward of Grubstreet*, p. 12.

7 Nic Eoin, *B'Ait Leo Bean*, pp. 176–82.

8 Máire Herbert (Ed), 'Society and Myth, c. 700–1300' in Angela Bourke *et al.* (Eds), *Field Day Anthology of Irish Writing, Vol. IV* (Cork, 2002), pp. 250–72; Máirín Nic Eoin, 'Sovereignty and Politics, c. 1300–1900', ibid., pp. 273–92; Nic Eoin, *B'Ait Leo Bean*, pp. 150–69.

9 Ibid., p. 125.

10 Ibid., p. 150. See also pp. 148–9.

11 Peter O'Dwyer, *Mary. A History of Devotion in Ireland* (Dublin, 1988), p. 78.

12 Ibid., pp. 14, 45.

13 Ibid., pp. 100–99. See especially, p. 116.

14 See pp. 246–7 above.

15 Bourke *et al.* (Eds), *Field Day Anthology of Irish Writing, Vol. IV*, p. 73.

16 See ibid., pp. 99–102. I am grateful to Professor Máirín Ní Dhonnchadha and Dr Máire Herbert for advice on this point.

17 O'Dwyer, *Mary: A History of Devotion in Ireland*, p. 117.

18 Lambert McKenna (Ed), *Philip Bocht Ó hUiginn* (Dublin, 1931), p. 178. See also p. 156 above.

19 Aoibheann Nic Dhonnchadha, 'Irish Medical Writing, 1400–1600' in Bourke *et al.* (Eds), *Field Day Anthology of Irish Writing, Vol. IV*, pp. 341–57. See also Olwen Hufton, *The Prospect Before Her. A History of Women in Western Europe, Volume One, 1500–1800* (London, 1995), pp. 39–44.

20 Bourke *et al.* (Eds), *Field Day Anthology of Irish Writing Vol. IV*, p. 347.

21 Nic Eoin, *B'Ait Leo Bean*, pp. 126–31.

22 Helena Concannon, *The Queen of Ireland An Historical Account of Ireland's Devotion to the Blessed Virgin* (Dublin, 1938), pp. 1–11.

23 Mary O'Reilly, 'Seventeenth-Century Irish Catechisms – European or Not?' in *Archivium Hibernicum*, vol. 50 (1996), pp. 102–12. For Marian devotion in the eighteenth century see Patrick J. Corish, *The Catholic Community in the Seventeenth and Eighteenth Centuries* (Dublin, 1981), pp. 108–9.

24 The text was edited by Brian Ó Cuiv in 1977 for the Dublin Institute for Advanced Learning. See Ó Cuiv's introduction for a list of the manuscript copies of the text.

25 Máirín Ní Dhonnchadha (Ed), 'Mary, Eve and the Church, c. 600–1800' in Bourke *et al.* (Eds), *Field Day Anthology of Irish Writing, Vol. IV*, pp. 159–61.

26 Nic Eoin, *B'Ait Leo Bean*, pp. 132–3

27 Ibid., p. 137.

28 Ibid., pp. 132–9; *Párliament na mBan*, pp. 9–23.

29 Ní Dhonnchadha (Ed), 'Mary, Eve and the Church, c. 600–800', p. 160.

30 Nic Eoin, *B'Ait Leo Bean*, pp. 137–8; Brian Ó Cuiv (Ed), *Páirliament na mBan* (Dublin, 1977), pp. 63–4.

31 Ní Dhonnchadha, op. cit., p. 160.

32 According to Henry Fitzsimon, for example, no woman should make responses at Mass or serve the priest at the altar even in circumstances where the service was being held in the woman's house and she and her family may have been the only people attending the service. See Henry Fitzsimon, *The Justification and Exposition of the Divine Service of the Masse, and of All Rites and Ceremonies Thereto Belonging* (1611), p. 194; *Words of Comfort to Prosecuted Catholic* (1608, edited by Edmund Hogan, Dublin, 1881), p. 85.

33 Alison Forrestal, *Catholic Synods in Ireland, 1600–1690* (Dublin, 1998), pp. 128, 182–3; James Gerard McGarry, 'The Statutes of Tuam From the Council of Trent to the Nineteenth Century' (unpublished, MA thesis, St Patrick's College, Maynooth, 1932).

34 See p. 198, above.

35 Robert Chambre, 'An Explanation of the Shorter Catechism of the Reverend Assembly of Divines' (unpublished manuscript, 1680, Union Theological College, Belfast), p. 359. See pp. 172–3 above.

36 Ezekiel Hopkins, *The Works of the Right Reverend and Learned Ezekiel Hopkins* (4 parts, London, 1701), part ii, pp. 166–7.

37 Robert Lynam (Ed), *The Complete Works of Philip Skelton* (3 vols., 1824), vol. 3, pp. 304–5.

38 Francis Hutcheson, *A System of Moral Philosophy* (2 vols., London, 1755), vol. ii, p. 163. This work was published posthumously and dedicated to Edward Synge, Archbishop of Tuam (1716–41) and father of Alicia Synge. See pp. 217, 221–2 above.

39 Brian Ó Cuiv (Ed), 'Flaithrí Ó Maolchonaire's Catechism of Christian Doctrine' in *Celtica*, **1**, part 2 (1950), p. 178. See also Andrew Donlevy, *An Teagasg Críosduidhe. Do Réir Cearda agus Freagartha. The Catechism or Christian Doctrine By Way of Question and Answer* (Paris, 1742), pp. 348–9; Michael Tynan, *Catholic Instruction in Ireland, 1720–1950* (Dublin, 1985), p. 29; Hopkins, *The Works of the Right Reverend and Learned Ezekiel Hopkins*, part ii, pp. 166–70. In one of the few known sermons by a Catholic cleric on marriage, a priest in the mid-eighteenth century urged a newly married woman that she should have for her husband 'that friendship, that complacence, that respect and submission which the Church had always had for Christ her spouse'. See Galway Diocesan Archives, Box 7/D13/F1.

40 Jeremy Taylor, 'The Marriage Ring' in Thomas K. Carroll, *Wisdom and Wasteland. Jeremy Taylor in his Prose and Preaching Today* (Dublin, 2001), p. 140. See also William King, *A Great Archbishop of Dublin, Quaedam Vitae Meae Insigniora. Edited by Sir Charles Simeon King* (London, 1908), p. 157.

41 Hutcheson, *A System of Moral Philosophy*, vol. ii, p. 163.

42 See, for example, the extracts from Fynes Moryson's *Itinerary*, published in C. L. Falkiner, *Illustrations in Irish History and Topography* (London, 1904), pp. 225–32, 310–25; Máirín Ní Dhonnchadha, 'Courts and Coteries II, c. 1500–1800' in Bourke *et al.* (Ed), *Field Day Anthology of Irish Writing, Vol. IV*, p. 366. See also Kathleen Brown, *Good Wives, Nasty Wenches, and Anxious Patriarchs: Gender, Race, and Power in Colonial Virginia* (Chapel Hill, 1996).

43 Mary O'Dowd, 'Women and the Colonial Experience in Ireland, c. 1550–1650' in Terry Brotherstone, Deborah Simonton and Oonagh Walsh (Eds), *Gendering Scottish History. An International Approach* (Glasgow, 1999), pp. 156–71.

44 J. P. Prendergast, *The Cromwellian Settlement of Ireland* (3rd edition, Dublin, 1922), pp. 231–4. For the continuation of such views in perceptions of Irish prostitutes in eighteenth-century Britain see Siobhán Kilfeather, 'Sexual Discourses, 1685–1801' in Bourke *et al.* (Eds), *Field Day Anthology of Irish Writing, Vol. IV*, p. 782.

45 C. P. Meehan, *The Fate and Fortunes of Hugh O'Neill, Earl of Tyrone, and Rory O'Donel, Earl of Tyrconnel; Their Flight From Ireland, and Death in Exile* (Dublin, 1870), p. 448.

46 Mary O'Dowd, 'Women and the Colonial Experience in Ireland, c. 1550–1650'.

47 Nic Eoin, 'Sovereignty and Politics, c. 1300–1900'; *B'Ait Leo Bean*, pp. 183–228.

48 S. J. Connolly, 'Precedent and Principle: the Patriots and their Critics' in S. J. Connolly (Ed), *Political Ideas in Eighteenth-Century Ireland* (Dublin, 2000), p. 141; See also *An Utilist to the Agregrate Body of the Irish Nation; Proposing the Parliamentary Reform by a New Method of Electing by Ballot in the Venal Boroughs* (Dublin, 1784) which suggested that it would be more appropriate to use the analogy of brothers rather than sisters for the Anglo-Irish relationship because 'as females, we may be suspected to be more the slaves of our habits; but as men are supposed superior to them.'

49 Katharine Simms, 'The Legal Position of Irishwomen in the Later Middle Ages' in *The Irish Jurist*, **x**, n.s. (1975), p. 111. See also Donnchadh Ó Corráin, 'Early Medieval Law, c. 700–1200' in Bourke *et al.* (Eds), *Field Day Anthology of Irish Writing, Vol. IV*, pp. 6–44.

50 Anne Chambers, *Granuaile. The Life and Times of Grace O'Malley c. 1530–1603* (Dublin, new edition, 1988). On the construction of the ideal woman in Irish literature see Nic Eoin, *B'Ait Leo Bean*, pp. 165–9, 206–7.

51 National Archives of Ireland, M2448, pp. 362–77.

52 Neal Garnham, *The Courts, Crime and the Criminal Law in Ireland, 1692–1760* (Dublin, 1996), pp. 236–7.

53 See, for example, [John McBride,] *A Vindication of Marriage As Solemnised by Presbyterians in the North of Ireland* (no place of publication given, 1702); Moses West, *A Treatise Concerning Marriage Wherein the Unlawfulness of Mixt Marriage, is Laid Open From the Scriptures of Truth* (Dublin, 1735); document entitled 'What Method Must the Judge of the Ecclesiastical Court Take in Prosecuting Irregular Marriages by Popish Priests and Presbyterian Ministers?' (Marsh's Library, MS Z.2.1.7(33)). There was considerable confusion within the Irish Catholic hierarchy as to the canonical status of a 'mixed' marriage with some dioceses opting to issue dispensations while others followed the strict Tridentine rules prohibiting such marriages. It was not until 1785 that marriages between Catholics and Protestants were formally approved by Pope Pius VI. See Patrick Corish, 'Catholic Marriage Under the Penal Code' in Art Cosgrove (Ed), *Marriage in Ireland* (Dublin, 1985), pp. 67–77; 'Calendar of the Papers of Butler Archbishops of Cashel and Emily, 1712–1791' (typescript copy in National Library of Ireland, Special List, 170B), pp. 102, 140–9; Forrestal, *Catholic Synods in Ireland, 1600–1690*, pp. 105, 142, 171–2.

54 Based on Mary O'Dowd, 'Women and the Law in Early Modern Ireland' in Christine Meek (Ed), *Women in Renaissance and Early Modern Europe* (Dublin, 2000), pp. 95–108.

55 'A Short Sketch of the Political History of Ireland' (NLI, Joly MS 29), pp. 21–2.

56 Deborah Wilson's recently completed doctoral thesis includes an analysis of Irish marriage laws in the seventeenth and eighteenth centuries. See Deborah Wilson, 'Women, Marriage and Property in Ireland, 1750–1850' (unpublished, Ph.D. thesis, Queen's University, Belfast, 2003).

57 David Lemmings, 'Marriage and the Law in the Eighteenth Century: Hardwicke's Marriage Act of 1753' in *The Historical Journal* **39** (1996), pp. 339–60.

58 Patrick Fagan, *Dublin's Turbulent Priest. Cornelius Nary 1658–1738* (Dublin, 1991), p. 171.

59 William King, *The State of the Protestants of Ireland Under the Late King James's Government* (Cork, 1768), p. 278. See also O'Dowd, 'Women and the Law in Early Modern Ireland', pp. 104–8.

60 Galway Diocesan Archives, Box 9.

61 John Bossy, *The English Catholic Community, 1570–1850* (London, 1975), p. 159.

62 O'Connell Papers (UCD Archives, P/12/2A/34. See also P/12/7/10, 11, 17, 18, 53.); Mrs M. J. O'Connell, *The Last Colonel of the Irish Brigade* (Dublin, 1892; reprinted 1977), pp. 1–47, 110, 114–15, 159, 168–9, 172.

63 Ibid., pp. 168–9.

64 Marstrander (Ed and translator), 'Bídh Crínna', pp. 136–7.

65 Edward Wakefield, *An Account of Ireland, Statistical and Political* (2 vols., London, 1812), **ii**, p. 801; S. J. Connolly, 'Marriage in Pre-Famine Ireland' in Art Cosgrove (Ed), *Marriage in Ireland* (Dublin, 1985), p. 84; Toby Barnard, *Irish Protestants. Ascents and Descents* (Dublin, 2004), p. 81.

66 Connolly, op. cit., p. 84.

67 See Bourke *et al.* (Eds), *Field Day Anthology of Irish Writing, Vol. IV*, pp. 159–61; McKenna (Ed), *Philip Bocht Ó hUiginn* (Dublin, 1931); Hugh Fenning, 'Dublin Imprints of Catholic Interest: 1701–1739' in *Collectanea Hibernica*, nos. 39–40 (1997–8), pp. 106–54.

68 De Sales was also read by Protestant readers. See *An Introduction to a Devout Life . . . Fitted for the Use of Protestants.* (Dublin, 1673). Additional editions were printed in Ireland in the eighteenth century.

69 Corish, *The Catholic Community*, pp. 86–9, 109–10; Bourke *et al.* (Eds), *Field Day Anthology of Irish Writing, Vol. IV*, pp. 497–8.

70 Lady Frances Keightley to Lucy O'Brien, 1681 (NLI MS 1843 (typescript copy in TCD, MS 5098/1)); Katharine Conolly's Advice to Molly Burton, 1720 (transcript in Barnard, *Irish Protestants. Ascents and Descents, 1641–1770*, pp. 287–9.); 'Book of Anne, Lady O'Brien (TCD, MS 5096); Patrick Little, 'Providence and Posterity: A Letter From Lord Mountnorris to his Daughter, 1642' in *Irish Historical Studies*, **xxxii**, no. 128 (2001), pp. 556–66.

71 See Marjorie Morgan, *Manners, Morals and Class in England, 1774–1858* (London, 1994), p. 15 on the cost of popular conduct books in London.

72 *The Lady's New-Year's Gift: Or, Advice to a Daughter* (Dublin edition, printed in 1699).

73 For Irish editions see the bibliography. Lord Chesterfield's *Letters To His Son* was also very popular but this may have been because of his Irish political connections rather than his rather dismissive views of women.

74 See for example, 'The Female Advocate' in August 1779; the comments on Thomas Gisbourne, *Duties of the Female Sex* in May 1797; article entitled 'Moral and Intellectual Excellence of the Fair Sex' in June 1786.

75 John Gray, 'Mary Anne McCracken: Belfast Revolutionary and Pioneer of Feminism' in Dáire Keogh and Nicholas Furlong (Eds), *The Women of 1798* (Dublin, 1998), pp. 47–63. Mary McNeill, *The Life and Times of Mary Ann McCracken, 1770–1866. A Belfast Panorama* (Dublin, 1960); Jean Agnew (Ed), *The Drennan-McTier Letters, 1776–1819* (3 vols., Dublin, 1998–99); Bourke *et al.* (Eds), *Field Day Anthology of Irish Writing, Vol. V*, pp. 53–9.

76 Ibid., p. 59.

77 Philip Carter, *Men and the Emergence of Polite Society in Britain, 1660–1800* (London, 2001); Muriel Jaeger, *Before Victoria* (London, 1956); Morgan, *Manners, Morals and Class in England, 1774–1858.*

78 Janet Todd, *The Signs of Angelica. Women, Writing and Fiction, 1660–1800* (London, 1989); Judith S. Lewis, *Sacred to Female Patriotism, Gender, Class and Politics in Late Georgian Britain* (New York and London, 2003).

79 Toby Barnard, *A New Anatomy of Ireland. The Irish Protestants, 1649–1770* (New Haven, 2003), pp. 71–4l; S. J. Connolly, *Religion, Law and Power. The Making of a Protestant Elite* (Oxford, 1992), pp. 65–73.

80 L. M. Cullen, *The Emergence of Modern Ireland, 1600–1900* (London, 1981), pp. 244–9; James Kelly, 'The Abduction of Women of Fortune in Eighteenth-Century Ireland' in *Eighteenth-Century Ireland*, **ix** (1994), pp. 7–43.

81 Neal Garnham, 'How Violent Was Eighteenth-Century Ireland?' in *Irish Historical Studies*, **xxx** (1997), p. 385; James Kelly, '"Most Inhuman and Barbarous Piece of Villainy": An Exploration of the Crime of Rape in Eighteenth-Century Ireland' in *Eighteenth-Century Ireland*, **x** (1995), pp. 78–107.

82 James Kelly, *'That Damn'd Thing Called Honour'. Duelling in Ireland, 1570–1860* (Cork, 1995), p. 199, 66–223. See also Cullen, *The Emergence of Modern Ireland, 1690–1900*, p. 247.

83 S. J. Connolly, 'A Woman's Life in Mid-Eighteenth Century Ireland: the Case of Letitia Bushe' in *The Historical Journal*, **43**, 2 (2000), pp. 438–9.

84 Most of the letters have been edited in a typescript by Brian Fitzgerald. See NLI, MS 13022.

85 John, Brady, 'Dr Troy's Pastoral on Clandestine Marriages, 1789' in *Reportium Novum*, **1**, no. 2 (1956), pp. 481–5; James Kelly, 'The Impact of the Penal Laws' in James Kelly and Dáire Keogh (Eds), *History of the Catholic Diocese of Dublin* (Dublin, 2000), pp. 172–3. See also David Ryan, '"That Most Serious Duty": Catholic Preaching in Ireland, 1760–1840' (unpublished MA thesis, National University of Ireland, Galway, 1998), pp. 102–4, 130.

86 *Memoirs of Mrs Margaret Leeson, Written By Herself and Interspersed with Several Interesting and Amusing Anecdotes, On Some of the Most Striking Characters of Great-Britain and Ireland* (3 vols., 1795–7; edited by Mary Lyons (Dublin, 1995).

87 See headnote by Patrick Crotty in Bourke *et al.* (Eds), *Field Day Anthology of Irish Writing, Vol. IV*, pp. 242–4.

Conclusion

There are two questions at the centre of this book: What were women doing in early modern Ireland? What changed in women's lives during the period? Individual chapters have explored these questions in the context of the history of Ireland over three centuries. Inevitably, at times, the answers have been broadly sketched, the approach impressionistic and, on occasion, perhaps, too narrow. The aim was to establish a basic framework for the history of women in Ireland, 1500–1800. Some of the individual parts of the framework may be familiar to early modern historians but the intention has been to link the parts into a structure that might provoke further discussion and research.

One of the most striking features of the framework is the importance of the eighteenth century as a time of significant change in women's lives. The prosperous economy of the middle decades of the century widened economic opportunities for women at all levels of society. For the first time, single women could make, if they chose, an independent living. In the eighteenth century, also, ecclesiastical institutions and the state formally recognised women's philanthropic endeavour. Politically, women were more visibly active in the last quarter of the eighteenth century than they had been at any time previously. An essential medium for change in women's lives was the acquisition of literacy. Initially confined to wealthy women, by the 1790s reading (and usually, by that stage, also writing) was considered a desirable skill for all women. Literacy broadened the work opportunities for women and facilitated the development of spiritual and intellectual independence. It also gave women access to political discourse and debate through the reading of newspapers and political pamphlets. Within the wider context of the Enlightenment, the education of women instigated a debate on women's role and status in society. Slowly, the Irish intellectual elite began to consider the possibility of women's intellectual equality with men.

Changes in women's lives in the eighteenth century were part of a more long-term and sustained process of evolution. The debate on women's education eventually led to women's admission into the universities and professional occupations. It was also the opening salvo in the campaign for women's suffrage that culminated in the commitment to women's political equality by nationalist and unionist leaders in the early decades of the twentieth century. The involvement of Catholic women in education and the founding of new female religious orders by Nano Nagle and Teresa Mulally marked the beginning of Catholic domination of education and social services that was to have profound consequences for the shaping of nineteenth- and twentieth-century Ireland. Politically, the abolition of the Irish parliament undermined the influence of elite women but the involvement of women in the crowds that supported the Volunteers and the United Irishmen was continued in the mobilisation of the masses by Daniel O'Connell and, later, by the Irish Land League and Charles Stewart Parnell. The second half of the eighteenth century was, therefore, crucial in the history of women in Ireland.

The theme of a progressive eighteenth century that opened up a myriad of opportunities for women can, of course, be overstated. As Chapter 8 has indicated, empirical change did not develop in tandem with changes in society's attitude to or perception of women. Throughout the period women remained legally unequal and barred from holding political office. Until the last decades of the eighteenth century, it is very difficult to discern any shift in social attitudes to women and even then change was not only muted but compounded by a new emphasis on the virtuous woman that strengthened rather than weakened restrictions on women's behaviour. Economically, there may have been more opportunities for paid work but they were usually in the form of part-time, low-paid and labour-intensive jobs. Single and widowed women were economically free to function in the commercial world of urban tradesmen and merchants but few chose to do so. Most opted for the social security of marriage and economic and legal representation by their husbands or other male relatives. The churches endorsed women's philanthropic work but Christian teaching on women remained largely unchanged from 1500 to 1800.

Nor were all the changes of the eighteenth century permanent. The prosperity of the middle decades of the century had disappeared by 1800 and with it went much of the paid work available to women in rural Ireland. Women's economic contribution to the household was undermined which may also have led to a loss of status and power in the home. The looming demographic crisis of the late eighteenth century impacted most severely on poor women who gave birth to children they could not support and who increasingly found themselves destitute and without any means of subsistence.

Any consideration of historical change must also be formulated within the context of real women's lives and circumstances. Change was filtered through various combinations of ethnic, religious and economic experiences and backgrounds. The rich woman, the poor woman, the urban woman, the rural woman, the Gaelic woman, the Anglo-Irish woman, the Catholic woman and the Protestant woman all experienced change in different ways. An underlying theme in the volume has been to assess the relative status of women in Gaelic and Anglo-Irish societies and in Catholic and Protestant families. In terms of modern perceptions of economic and intellectual independence, the argument favours Anglo-Irish women and Protestant women. Anglicisation improved the legal standing of women, led to more women property owners and gave greater financial security to widows. It also fostered urbanisation which opened up new economic opportunities for women. Protestantism encouraged female literacy while Presbyterianism and other dissenting groups facilitated women's spiritual and intellectual development. An attempt to argue the case for Gaelic or Catholic society falters on lack of evidence. The silence of the documents may, however, be revealing in itself. Gaelic women in the sixteenth century and Catholic women in the seventeenth and eighteenth centuries were neither as literate nor as visible in public as their Anglo-Irish or Protestant counterparts. Gaelic women had limited access to economic resources. They could not inherit property and separated and widowed women were in a dependent and often precarious financial position. In the seventeenth and eighteenth centuries, the Catholic Church was slow to encourage literacy and, although women were utilised as catechisers, the Church remained wary of women reading and writing on their own and carefully supervised uncloistered female religious orders.

It is, perhaps, unfair to judge Gaelic society against modern criteria for women's independence and find it wanting. Patriarchy is a complex phenomenon that manifests itself in a multitude of forms in different societies. Both Gaelic and English laws and structures were fundamentally patriarchal. Barbara Harris has suggested that within the patriarchal structure of early Tudor England, aristocratic women found space to negotiate 'considerable power, resources and prestige'.[1] The regional power vested in the Tudor aristocracy compelled men to rely on their wives as partners in the enterprise of enhancing their families' social, economic and political status. Young women were educated to take responsibility for the management of large aristocratic households, foster political networks and manage the extensive estates of the family. Aristocratic mothers had responsibility for childcare that included the arrangement of economically and politically suitable marriages. In English common law women were subordinate to men but in reality women heiresses, widows and remarried women enjoyed considerable economic control. Many of these characteristics can also be documented for aristocratic women in Anglo-Irish society in the early Tudor period as the lives of the women in the Fitzgerald family demonstrate.

By contrast, the political structure in Gaelic Ireland was not dependent on women's active participation. Power was regionally based, as in early Tudor England, but it was imposed predominantly through male military control. Wives of Gaelic chiefs presided over feasts and other forms of hospitality for their husband followers but the tower house had a more limited socio-political function than the English magnate's large multi-roomed manor house. Estate management was also far less complex in the pastoral economy of Gaelic Ireland than it was on the more carefully documented estates of the English aristocrat. A vivid indication of the need for a strong military leader in Gaelic society was manifest in O'Donnell's territory as late as 1607. The tenants of the recently created earl of Tyrconnell rejected his wife as a landlady because, it was claimed, she could not defend them.[2] Men in Gaelic society were not, therefore, obliged to entrust their wives with a leadership role in their absence as they were in England. While the custom for entailing land to male heirs declined rapidly in sixteenth-century England, Gaelic lords insisted on a male line of descent in their agreements with English administrators. Nor did they remember their wives in their negotiations with the crown. As Gráinne O'Malley pointed out to Queen Elizabeth, the Composition Book of Connacht contained no provision for wives or widows.[3] Gaelic and Anglo-Irish societies were, therefore, both patriarchal in stucture, but the organisation of Anglo-Irish society, like that in early Tudor England, gave women more space to be involved in the political, social and financial affairs of their families.

Patriarchy is endorsed by the organisation of society but it also manifests itself in familiar structures. Patriarchal figureheads can be found in every ethnic group in early modern Ireland. Gerald Fitzgerald, 8th earl of Kildare, Hugh O'Neill, 1st earl of Tyrone, Richard Boyle, 1st earl of Cork and later, in the eighteenth century, Maurice O'Connell are among the most well known.[4] All were recognised as governors of extended family networks. Men as well as women acknowledged their ruling position. Hugh O'Neill's sons-in-law were as obedient to his wishes as his own sons and daughters. Similarly, the male relatives of Gerald Fitzgerald or Richard Boyle disobeyed the patriarch's orders at their financial, or in the case of Fitzgerald, military, peril. Fitzgerald, O'Neill and Boyle all gave careful consideration to the selection of marriage partners for themselves and their children. A comparison of the fate of the women in all three families appears to endorse more general conclusions that the lives of women in Gaelic society were most restricted and determined by the head of family. The women in the O'Neill family rarely appear in the historical record and usually only in connection with their father or husband. Women in both the Fitzgerald and Boyle families had more freedom of manoeuvre despite the patriarchal nature of their family structure. The ease with which marriages could be ended and the lack of financial security for wives and widows hindered the ability of Gaelic women to gain access to economic, political or social power.

Religious divisions had largely replaced those of ethnicity by the eighteenth century. It is impossible to be conclusive as to the relative control of Catholic and Protestant male heads of household. The study of private and intimate relations can rarely be undertaken by historians. It is clear, however, that increasing use of legal equity and the literacy demands of Protestantism gave women more flexibility and facilitated more of a sense of personal authority and control than was available to women in Catholic families.

Finally, what does a study of women in early modern Ireland contribute to our understanding of the history of the period? It does not dramatically change our interpretation of events but it does add considerably to our understanding of the complexity and subtlety of that interpretation. Sixteenth-century dynastic politics was impossible without the co-operation of aristocratic women while the emergence of the heiress was of central importance in the transfer of property in late seventeenth-century Ireland. In the eighteenth century, the smooth management of parliamentary politics by Dublin Castle depended on the social interaction of women and the century's economic boom was heavily reliant on the labour of women. The growing confidence of the Catholic Church in the period was built on the ever-expanding army of women who serviced Catholic schools and institutions. Moreover, women participated in all the significant mobilisations of popular agitation from the 1641 rebellion through to that of 1798.

A recognition of the presence of women in these events should not be considered simply as a politically correct balancing of the historical record. Rather, an analysis of women's involvement subtly changes our understanding of the event itself. Until recently, historians failed to notice the women in the gallery in Francis Wheatley's famous portrait of the Irish House of Commons in 1779, despite the fact that one of them is dramatically dressed in a red Volunteer uniform. Yet, understanding why the women were in the gallery adds considerably to a nuanced understanding of the parliamentary debate and the popular agitation it provoked. Seeing the women, therefore, widens our perception of the whole picture.[5]

Notes

1 Barbara J. Harris, *English Aristocratic Women, 1450–1550: Marriage and Family, Property and Careers* (Oxford, 2002), pp. 9–11.

2 C. P. Meehan, *The Fate and Fortunes of Hugh O'Neill, Earl of Tyrone, and Rory O'Donel, Earl of Tyrconnel; Their Flight From Ireland, and Death in Exile* (Dublin, 1870), p. 246.

3 Angela Bourke *et al.* (Eds), *Field Day Anthology of Irish Writing, Vol. V* (Cork, 2002), p. 21.

4 For a discussion of Richard Boyle as a patriarchal figure within his family see Nicholas Canny, *The Upstart Earl: A Study of the Social and Mental World of Richard Boyle, First Earl of Cork, 1566–1643* (Cambridge, 1982), pp. 77–123. See also Patrick Little, 'Providence and Posterity: A Letter From Lord Mountnorris to his Daughter, 1642' in *Irish Historical Studies*, **xxxii**, no. 128 (2001), pp. 556–66.

5 See Mary O'Dowd, 'The Women in the Gallery. Women and Politics in 18th Century Ireland' in Sabine Wichert (Ed), *From the United Irishmen to the Act of Union* (Dublin, 2004), pp. 35–47.

Bibliography

Birr Castle

Parsons Papers (microfilm in NLI)

Bodleian Library, Oxford

Add C 39 A Brief Declaration of the Order and Forme of Government in Sir John Perrot's House During the Time He Was Lord Deputy of Ireland

Eng hist. d. 155 Patrick Thomson's Narrative of his Life and Adventures c. 1750

British Library

Add MS 31881–2 Papers of the Consistory Court of Killaloe, 1671–1824

Add MS 11722 Carrick-On-Suir Census

Lansdowne MS 740

Egmont Manuscripts

Centre for Kentish Studies

De L'Isle and Dudley Papers

County Cavan Public Library

Angel Anna Slack's Journal (typescript copy provided by Women's History Project)

Dublin City Archives

Dublin Thosel Court Records

Essex Record Office

Barrett Leonard Muniments

Galway Diocesan Archives
Records of Warden of Galway

Huntington Library, San Marino, California
Correspondence of Elizabeth Vesey in Montagu Papers (microfilm)

Linenhall Library, Belfast
Records of the Belfast Charitable Society

National Archives of Ireland
Chancery Pleadings
M2446 Elphin Census
M2448 Star Chamber Court Book
Undated Chancery Pleadings
Vernon-Bardon Papers
Diary of Mary Martin (Small Collections, 999/775/1)
Business Records, Ros 13/1, Account Book
Business Records, Wex 15/1, Account Book of Patrick Rossiter, Co. Wexford
Record Commission Records (RC 5/1, 4, 5, 8, 19, 20, 21, 24, 25, 30)
Calendar of Prisoners, Petitions and Cases, 1778–1826
Carew Shapland Papers

Marsh's Library, Dublin
MS Z.2.1.7(33) 'What Method Must the Judge of the Ecclesiastical Court Take in Prosecuting Irregular Marriages by Popish Priests and Presbyterian Ministers?'

National Library of Ireland
Blake Papers
De Vesci Papers (on microfilm)
Domville Papers (MS 11844)
Drogheda Manuscripts (MS 9682, 3)
Edgeworth Beaufort Papers (MS 13176)
Fingall Papers (MS 8041)
Flower Papers (MS 11461)
French Papers (MS 4918)
Heron Papers (MS 13049)
Inchiquin Papers
Joly MS 29, 'A Short Sketch of the Political History of Ireland'
Kemmis Papers (MS 15159)

Lennox/Fizgerald/Campbell Papers (MS 35005, 35012)
O'Brien Papers
O'Hara Papers
Ormond Papers
Parsons Papers (on microfilm)
Powerscourt Estate Papers (MS 4876)
Rich Papers (MS 8014/9)
Wicklow Papers (MS 4810, 4811)
MS 14101 Diary of Member of Lucas Family, 1739–1741
MS 1467–70 Lists of Attendance at Lord Lieutenant Dinners, 1761–70
MS 1471 Memorandum Book for the Earl of Buckingham; Printed *Gazette*, 1777–8
MS 16091 Diary of Nicholas Peacock
MS 19332 Book of Recipes
MS 19729 Book of Recipes and Household Hints Compiled by Jane Burton
MS 2176 Commonplace Book of Harriet King
MS 2178 Accounts of Jane Creighton, Lady Erne
MS 23254 Poems by Olivia Elder
MS 3575
MS 4152 Commonplace Book by Female Member of St George family, 1786–1830
MS 4481 Household Accounts of Mrs Meliosa Adlercorn
MS 5695 Cork Farm Book
MS 7861
MS 8064, Fragment of Earl of Halifax's Journal
'Calendar of the Papers of Butler Archbishops of Cashel and Emily, 1712–1791' (typescript copy in National Library of Ireland, Special List, 170B)

Public Record Office, Kew
State Papers Ireland (SP61, 63)

Public Record Office, Northern Ireland
D/1140
D/1518/2/3, 4 Adam Papers, Account Books
D/1556 Maxwell Papers
D/1721 Account Book
D/1759/1A/1, Presbyterian Session Book, Antrim 1654–1658
D/1928 Brownlow Estate Papers
D/4123/9/1/1 Farm Account Book of Lawless Family

D/4151 Kenmare Papers
D/530 Papers relating to the Shipboy family
D/671/A8/1A
D/717/1–2 Blair Papers
T/581 Will Transcripts
T/640 Papers related to the McClelland Family
T/681 Will Transcripts
T/1461 Transcript of documents concerning the founding of a convent by the Order Poor Clares in Newry
T/2854/1, 2 Story Papers
T/3301 Account book of the Orr family, Co. Down
T/3765 Granard Papers, Transcripts and Calendar
Letter-book contained bound in-letters to Florinda Gardiner (Calendar, Registers of Irish Archives, Miscellaneous Collections)

Registry of Deeds, Dublin
Transcript Books

Representative Church Body
MS 517/1 Minute Book of the Female Orphan Society, 1790–1814
MS 523 Register of Bishop Foy's School in Waterford
MS 551/1–2 Minute Books of the Magdalen Asylum

Trinity College Dublin
Conolly Papers
MSS 812–39, 1641 Depositions
MS 5098/1 Typescript Copy of NLI MS 1843
MS 5096 Book of Lady Anne O'Brien c. 1780
MS 4460 Jane Bingham's Book of Devotions

Union Theological College, Belfast
Robert Chambre, 'An Explanation of the Shorter Catechism of the Reverend Assembly of Divines' (unpublished manuscript, 1680)

University College, Dublin, Archives Department
O'Connell Papers

Wiltshire Record Office
John Clavel's Commonplace Book

Printed Manuscript Sources

'Autobiography of Pole Cosby, of Stradbally, Queen's County, 1705–1737(?)' in *Co. Kildare Archaeological Society and Surrounding Districts*, **5** (1906–8).

'Illustrations of the Irish Linen Industry in 1783 By William Hincks' in *Ulster Folklife*, **23** (1977).

'Report on the State of Popery in Ireland, 1731' in *Archivium Hibernicum*, **i, iv** (1912, 1915).

'The Diary of Anne Cooke' in *Journal of Co. Kildare Archaeological Society and Surrounding Districts*, **8** (1915–17).

A Memoir of Mistress Ann Fowkes Née Geale Died Aged 82 Years, With Some Recollection of Her Family A.D. 1642–1774. Written By Herself (Dublin, 1892).

Agnew, Jean (Ed), *The Drennan-McTier Letters, 1776–1819* (3 vols., Dublin, 1998–99).

Anonymous, 'Old Waterford Wills' in *Journal of the Waterford and South-East of Ireland Archaeological Society*, **ix–xiii** (1906–1910).

Appleby, John C. (Ed), *Calendar of Material Relating to Ireland from the High Court of Admiralty Examinations* (Dublin, 1992).

Bartlett, Thomas (Ed), *Macartney in Ireland 1768–72. A Calendar of the Chief Secretaryship Papers of Sir George Macartney* (Belfast, 1978).

Bell, G. H. (Ed), *The Hanwood Papers of the Ladies of Llangollen and Caroline Hamilton* (London, 1930).

Blake, Martin (Ed), *Blake Family Records, 1300 to 1700: A Chronological Catalogue With Copious Notes and Genealogies* (2 vols., London, 1902, 1905).

Bolster, Evelyn (Ed), 'The Moylan Correspondence in Bishop's House, Killarney: Part 1' in *Collectanea Hibernica*, **14** (1971).

Bourke, Angela *et al.* (Eds), *Field Day Anthology of Irish Writing, Vols. IV–V* (Cork, 2002).

Brady, Ciarán (Ed), *A Viceroy's Vindication? Sir Henry Sidney's Memoir of Service in Ireland, 1556–1578* (Dublin, 2002).

Brady, John (Ed), 'Catholic Schools in Dublin in 1787–8' in *Reportium Novum*, **i**, no. 1 (1955).

(Ed), 'Dr Troy's Pastoral on Clandestine Marriages, 1789' in *Reportium Novum*, **i**, no. 2 (1956).

Brimley Johnson, R. (Ed), *Bluestocking Letters* (London, 1926).

Callanan, M. (Ed), 'The De Burgos or Burkes of Ileagh' in *North Munster Antiquarian Journal*, **ii** (1940–41).

Calendar of Carew Manuscripts. Preserved in the Archiepiscopal Library at Lambeth, 1515–1624 (6 vols., London, 1867–73).

Calendar of State Papers: Ireland, 1571–1575, Mary O'Dowd (Ed) (London, 2000).

Calendar of State Papers Relating to Ireland, 1509–1670 (24 vols., London, 1860–1912).

Calendar of the Manuscripts of the Marquess of Ormonde, Preserved at Kilkenny Castle (11 vols., London, 1895–1920).

Carpenter, Andrew (Ed), *Verse in English From the Eighteenth Century* (Cork, 1998).

(Ed), *Verse in English From Tudor and Stuart Ireland* (Cork, 2003).

Carrigan, William (Ed), 'Catholic Episcopal Wills in the Public Record Office, Dublin, 1683–1812' in *Archivium Hibernicum*, **i–v** (1912–15).

Caulfield, Richard (Ed), 'Wills and Inventories, Cork, temp. Elizabeth' in *The Gentleman's Magazine* (May 1861–September 1862).

(Ed), *The Council Book of the Corporation of Kinsale From 1652 to 1800* (Guildford, 1879).

Cavanaugh, Jean C. (Ed), 'Lady Southwell's Defense of Poetry' in *English Literary and Renaissance*, **14** (1984).

Clare, Wallace, 'A Brief Directory of the City of Cork, 1769–1770' in *The Irish Genealogist*, **i** (1937–42).

Clark, Mrs Godfrey (Ed), *Gleanings From an Old Portfolio* (3 vols., Edinburgh, 1895).

Corish, P. J. (Ed), 'Bishop Wadding's Notebook' in *Archivium Hibernicum*, **xxix** (1970).

Crofton Croker, Thomas (Ed), *Some Specialities in the Life of M. Warwick* (London, 1848).

Curran, M. J. (Ed), 'Instructions, Admonitions, etc. of Archbishop Carpenter, 1770–1786' in *Reportium Novum*, **2**, no. 1 (1957–8).

Curtis, Edmund (Ed), *Calendar of Ormond Deeds, Volumes III–VI, 1413–1603* (Dublin, 1935–43).

Danaher, Kevin and Simms, J. G. (Eds), *The Danish Forces in Ireland, 1690–1691* (Dublin, 1961).

Day, Angelique (Ed), *Letters from Georgian Ireland. The Correspondence of Mary Delany 1731–68* (Belfast, 1991).

Elrington, C. R. (Ed), *The Whole Works of the Most Rev. James Ussher, D.D.* (Dublin, 1847).

Falkiner, C. Litton (Ed), 'Barnabe Rich's "Remembrances of the State of Ireland, 1612" With Notices of Other Manuscript Reports by the Same Writer, on Ireland Under James the First' in *Proceedings of the Royal Irish Academy*, **xxvi**, Section C (1906).

Fenning, Hugh (Ed), 'Some Problems of the Irish Mission, 1733–1774' in *Collectanea Hibernica*, **8** (1965).

(Ed) 'John Kent's Report on the State of the Irish Mission, 1742' in *Archivium Hibernicum*, **xxviii** (1966).

(Ed), 'Letters From a Jesuit in Dublin on the Confraternity of the Holy Name, 1747–1748' in *Archivium Hibernicum*, **xxix** (1970).

(Ed), 'Dublin Imprints of Catholic Interest: 1701–1739' in *Collectanea Hibernica*, **39–40** (1997–8).

(Ed), 'The Parish Clergy of Tuam 1717–1809' in *Collectanea Hibernica*, **39–40** (1997–8).

Fewer, Thomas G. and Nicholls, Kenneth W. (Eds), 'The Will of Robert Forstall of Kilferagh, 1645' in *Decies*, **48** (1993).

Fitzgerald, Brian (Ed), *Correspondence of Emily Duchess of Leinster, 1731–1814* (3 vols., Dublin, 1949–57).

Forster, Ann M. C. (Ed), 'The Chronicles of the English Poor Clares of Rouen – I' in *Recusant History*, **18** (1986–7).

Gilbert, J. T. (Ed), *Facsimiles of the National Manuscripts of Ireland* (4 vols., Dublin, 1874–84).

(Ed), *A Jacobite Narrative of the War in Ireland, 1688–1691* (Dublin, 1892; reprinted, 1971).

Gilbert, J. T. and Mulholland, Rosa (Eds), *Calendar of Ancient Records of Dublin in the Possession of the Municipal Corporation* (18 vols., 1889–1922).

Griffith, Margaret C. (Ed), *Calendar of Inquisitions Formerly in the Office of the Chief Remembrancer of the Exchequer Prepared From the Mss of the Irish Record Commission* (Dublin, 1991).

Grosart, A. B. (Ed), *Lismore Papers* (2 series, 10 vols., London, 1886–8).

Hanly, John (Ed), *Letters of Saint Oliver Plunkett 1625–1681* (Dublin, 1979).

Harington, John, *A Short View of the State of Ireland in Nugae Antiquae; Being a Miscellaneous Collection of Printed Papers in Prose* (London, 1779).

Hickson, Mary Ann (Ed), *Ireland in the Seventeenth Century, or the Irish Massacres of 1641–2 . . .* (2 vols., London, 1884).

Hill, George (Ed), *The Montgomery Manuscripts, 1603–1706. Compiled From Family Papers by William Montgomery of Rosemount, Esq* (Belfast, 1879).

Historical Manuscripts Commission, *Report on the Manuscripts of the Earl of Egmont*, vol. i (London, 1905).

Hogan, Edmund, *Distinguished Irishmen of the Sixteenth Century* (London, 1894).

Holt, Joseph, *Memoirs of Joseph Holt. General of the Irish Rebels in 1798* (London, 1838).

Hore, Herbert J. and Graves, James (Eds), *The Social State of The Southern And Eastern Counties of Ireland in the Sixteenth Century, Being the Presentments of the Gentlemen, Commonalty, and Citizens of Carlow, Cork, Kilkenny, Tipperary, Waterford, and Wexford, Made in the Reigns of Henry VIII and Elizabeth* (Dublin, 1870).

Hughes, Charles (Ed), *Shakespeare's Europe. Unpublished Chapters of Fynes Moryson's Itinerary* (London, 1903).

Ilchester, Countess of and Stavordale, Lord (Eds), *The Life and Letters of Lady Sarah Lennox 1745–1826* (2 vols., London, 1901).

Joy, Henry (Ed), *Historical Collections Relative to the Town of Belfast* (Belfast, 1817).

Kelly, Gary *et al.* (Eds), *Bluestocking Feminism. Writings of the Bluestocking Circle, 1738–1785*, volume 3 (London, 1990).

Kelly, James (Ed), *Gallows Speeches From Eighteenth-Century Ireland* (Dublin, 2001).

Killen, W. D. (Ed), *A True Narrative of the Rise and Progress of the Presbyterian Church in Ireland (1623–1670), By the Reverend Patrick Adair* (Belfast, 1866).

King, Heather A., 'Late Medieval Crosses in County Meath, c. 1470–1635' in *Proceedings of the Royal Irish Academy*, **84**, Section C (1984).

Klene, Jean, C.S.C. (Ed), *The Southwell-Sibthorpe Commonplace Book Folger MS. V.b.198* (Tempe, Arizona, 1997).

Knott, Eleanor (Ed), 'An Irish Seventeenth-Century Translation of the Rule of St Clare' in *Eriú*, **15** (1948).

Laffan, William (Ed), *The Cries of Dublin. Drawn From the Life by Hugh Douglas Hamilton, 1760* (Dublin, 2003).

Latimer, William T. (Ed), 'The Old Session-Book of Templepatrick Presbyterian Church, Co. Antrim' in *Royal Society of Antiquaries of Ireland Journal*, **xxxi** (1901).

Legg, Marie-Lou (Ed), *The Letters of Bishop Edward Synge to his Daughter Alicia. Roscommon to Dublin, 1746–1752* (Dublin, 1996).

Little, Patrick, 'Providence and Posterity: A Letter From Lord Mountnorris to his Daughter, 1642' in *Irish Historical Studies*, **xxxii**, no. 128 (2001).

Llanover, Lady (Ed), *The Autobiography and Correspondence of Mary Granville, Mrs Delany With Interesting Reminiscences of King George the Third and Queen Charlotte* (3 vols., 1st series, London, 1862).

Luddy, Maria (Ed), *The Diary of Mary Mathew* (Thurles, 1991).

Lysaght, Edward (Ed), *The Kenmare Manuscripts* (Dublin, 1942).

M'Crie, Thomas (Ed), *The Life of Mr Robert Blair, Minister of St Andrews . . .* (Edinburgh, 1848).

MacDermot, Brian (Ed), *The Catholic Question in Ireland and England 1798–1822. The Papers of Denys Scully* (Dublin, 1988).

Mac Niocaill, Gearóid (Ed), *Crown Surveys of Lands, 1540–41. With the Kildare Rental Begun in 1518* (Dublin, 1992).

McKenna, Lambert (Ed), *Philip Bocht Ó hUiginn* (Dublin, 1931).

(Ed), *Aithdioghliom Dana. A Miscellany of Irish Bardic Poetry* (2 vols., Dublin, 1939–40).

Maley, Willy (Ed), 'The Supplication of the Blood of the English Most Lamentably Murdered in Ireland Cryeng Out of the Yearth for Revenge (1598)' in *Analecta Hibernica*, **36** (1995).

Marstrander, Carl (Ed and translator), 'Bídh Crínna' in *Eriú*, **v** (1911).

Memoir of Lady Warwick: Also Her Diary From A.D. 1666 to 1672. Now First Published to Which are Added Extracts from Her Other Writings (London, 1847).

Mhág Craith, Cuthbert (Ed and translator), *Dán na mBráthar Mionúr* (2 vols., Dublin, 1967, 1980).

Miller Kerby *et al.* (Eds), *Irish Immigrants in the Land of Canaan. Letters and Memoirs From Colonial and Revolutionary America, 1675–1815* (New York, 2003).

Montgomery, William, *The Montgomery Manuscripts* (Belfast, 1869).

Moran, P. F., *The Analecta of David Rothe, Bishop of Ossory* (Dublin, 1884).

Murray, R. H. (Ed), *The Journal of John Stevens* (Oxford, 1912).

Nicholls, K. W. (Ed), 'Some Documents on Irish Law and Custom in the Sixteenth Century' in *Analecta Hibernica*, **6** (1970).

(Ed), 'The Lynch Bloss Papers' in *Analecta Hibernica*, **29** (1980).

Nicholson, Marjorie Hope (Ed), *The Conway Letters. The Correspondence of Anne, Viscountess Conway, Henry Moore and Their Friends* (London, 1930).

O Conchúir, Breandán (Ed), *Corraghliochas na mBan Le Dáibhí de Barra* (Dublin, 1991).

Ó Cuiv, Brian (Ed), 'Flaithrí Ó Maolchonaire's Catechism of Christian Doctrine' in *Celtica*, **1**, part 2 (1950).

(Ed), *Páirliament na mBan* (Dublin, 1977).

Ó Donnchú, Donncha (Ed), *Fíliocht Mháire Bhuidhe Ní Laoghaire* (Dublin, 1931).

O'Donovan, John (Ed), *The Genealogies, Tribes and Customs of the Hy Fiachrach in Ireland* (Dublin, 1844).

(Ed), *Annála Rioghachta Eireann: Annals of the Kingdom of Ireland by the Four Masters From the Earliest Period in the Year 1616. Edited and Translated by John O'Donovan* (7 vols., Dublin, 1851; reprinted, New York, 1966).

O'Heyne, John, *The Irish Dominicans of the Seventeenth Century* (English transl. by Ambrose Coleman, Dublin, 1902).

Ó Murchú, Liam P. (Ed), *Cúirt an Mheon-Oíche* (Dublin, 1982).

O'Rahilly, T. F. (Ed), *Danfhocail. Irish Epigrams in Verse* (Dublin, 1921).

(Ed), *Búrdún Bheaga. Pithy Irish Quatrains* (Dublin, 1925).

O'Shaughnessy, Peter (Ed), *Rebellion in Wicklow. General Joseph Holt's Personal Account of 1798* (Dublin, 1998).

Offaly, Lady, Verse attributed to, in *Journal of the Co. Kildare Archaeological Society and Surrounding Districts*, **10** (1922–28).

Ohlmeyer, Jane and Ó Ciardha, Éamonn (Eds), *The Irish Statute Staple Books, 1596–1687* (Dublin, 1998).

Piers, Henry, *A Choreographical Description of the County of West-Meath* (Meath Archaeological and Historical Society, 1981).

Public Record Office of Northern Ireland, *Irish Elections, 1750–1832* (PRONI, *Education Facsimiles*) (Belfast, 1972).

Retrospections of Dorothea Herbert 1770–1806 (Dublin, 1929–30, reprinted, Dublin, 1988).

Sayles, G. O., 'Contemporary Sketches of the Members of the Irish Parliament in 1782' in *Proceedings of the Royal Irish Academy*, vol. 56, section C (1953–4).

Shirley, E. P. (Ed), *Original Letters and Papers . . . of the Church in Ireland Under Edward VI, Mary and Elizabeth* (London, 1851).

Simmington, Robert C. (Ed), *The Transplantation To Connacht, 1654–58* (Dublin, 1970).

State Papers During the Reign of Henry the Eighth (11 vols., London, 1830–52), vols. ii–iv.

Stevenson, Jane and Davidson, Peter (Eds), *Early Modern Women Poets (1520–1700). An Anthology* (Oxford, 2001).

The State Letters of Henry Earl of Clarendon . . . During the Reign of King James the Second (2 vols., Oxford and Dublin, 1765).

The Whole Works of the Most. Rev. James Ussher, D.D., . . . (16 vols., 1847), vol. 1.

Thomas, Patrick (Ed), *The Collected Works of Katherine Philips. The Matchless Orinda*, vol. ii (Stump Cross, Essex, 1992).

Thornton, Alice, *The Autobiography of Mrs. Alice Thornton of East Newton, Co. York* (London, 1875).

Trevelyan, Walter Calverley and Trevelyan, Charles Edwards (Eds), *Trevelyan Papers, Part III* (London, 1872).

Walsh, Paul (Ed), 'The Flight of the Earls' in *Archivium Hibernicum*, **ii–iv** (1913–15).

(Ed), *Leabhar Chlainne Suibhne. An Account of the MacSweeney Families in Ireland* (Dublin, 1920).

(Ed), *The Will and Family of Hugh O'Neill, Earl of Tyrone* (Dublin, 1930).

Warwick Bond, R. (Ed), *The Marlay Papers, 1778–1820* (London, 1937).

Wharton Jones, Thomas (Ed), *A True Relation of the Life and Death of . . . William Bedell . . .* (London, 1872).

Wogan-Browne, Jocelyn and Burgess, Glyn S. (Eds), *Virgin Lives and Holy Deaths. Two Exemplary Biographies for Anglo-Norman Women* (London and Vermont, 1996).

Woods, C. J. (Ed), *Journals and Memoirs of Thomas Russell, 1791–5* (Dublin and Belfast, 1991).

Young, R. M. (Ed), *The Town Book of the Corporation of Belfast, 1613–1816* (Belfast, 1892).

Young, Robert M. (Ed), *Historical Notices of Old Belfast and Its Vicinity* (Belfast, 1896).

Contemporary Newspapers and Journals

Anthologica Hibernica
Belfast Newsletter
Cork Gazette
Dublin Evening Post
Dublin Faulkner's Journal
Freeman's Journal
Hibernian Journal
Magee's Weekly Packet
Northern Star
The Universal Advertiser
Volunteer Evening Post
Walker's Hibernian Magazine

Contemporary Printed Material (1500–1800)

A Catholick Conference Betweene Syr Tadg Mac. Mareall a Popish Priest of Waterford, and Patricke Plaine, a Young Student of Trinity Colledge by Dublin in Ireland (London, 1612).

A Lover of His Country, *Considerations on the Present State of the Silk Manufacture in Ireland* (Dublin, 1765).

A Lady, *To the Ladies of Dublin, A Poem. To Which is Added, Ierne's Answer to Albion. By a Lady* (Dublin, 1745).

An Heroic Epistle from Kitty Cut-A-Dash to Oroonoko (Dublin, 1778).

An Utilist to the Agregrate Body of the Irish Nation; Proposing the Parliamentary Reform by a New Method of Electing by Ballot in Venal Boroughs (Dublin, 1784).

Anonymous, *A Description How All States and Degrees of Men, Women and Children Spend Sunday in Dublin; From the Hours of Six in the Morning Untill Nine at Night* (Dublin, no date).

Anonymous, *A Scheme to Prevent the Running of Irish Wools to France and Irish Woollen Goods to Foreign Countries . . .* (Dublin, 1745).

Anonymous, *A Tour Through Ireland Wherein the Present State of That Kingdom is Considered* (Dublin, 1780).

Anonymous, *An Essay on the Necessity of Protecting Duties* (Dublin, 1783).

Anonymous, *Private Devotions for Several Occasions, Ordinary and Extraordinary* (Dublin, 1699).

Anonymous, *The Prelude to a Levee; Calculated for the Meridian of the Castle of Dublin* (Dublin, 1757).

Anonymous, *The Whole Duty of Man Laid Down in a Plain and Familiar Way For the Use of All, But Especially the Meanest Reader* (Dublin, 1699).

Anonymous, *The Whole Duty of Prayer. By the Author of* The Whole Duty of Man. *Necessary For All Families* (London, 1749).

Anonymous, *Thoughts On the Misery of a Numerous Class of Females Particularly Addressed to Their Own Sex, Whom God Has Entrusted With Affluence; For Which They Must Shortly Give Account* (Dublin, 1793).

B[our]ke, T[homas], *A Catechism. Moral and Controversial . . .* (Lisbon, 1752).

Barclay, Robert, *A Catechism and Confession of Faith* (8th Edition, Dublin, 1741).

Berkeley, George, *The Querist Containing Several Queries Proposed to the Consideration of the Public.* Edited by J. M. Hone (Dublin and Cork, 1935).

Bernard, Nicholas, *Life and Death of the Most Reverend and Learned Father of Our Church Dr James Ussher* (London, 1656).

Birkett, Mary, *A Poem on the African Slave Trade, Addressed To Her Own Sex* (Dublin, 1792).

Boyse, Joseph, *The Works of the Reverend and Learned Mr Joseph Boyse of Dublin* (2 vols., London, 1728).

Broadsides (Early Modern Printed Books, TCD, OLS X-1-924).

Brooke, Charlotte, *The School for Christians, in Dialogues, For the Use of Children* (Dublin, 1791).

By a Friend of the Nation, *An Address to the Representatives of the People, Upon Subjects of Moment, To the Well-Being and Happiness of the Kingdom of Ireland* (Dublin, 1771).

Chapone, Hester, *Letters on the Improvement of the Mind. Addressed to a Young Lady* (London, 1773; reprinted in Dublin, 1773, 1774, 1775, 1777, 1786).

Chesterfield, Philip Dormer Stanhope, *Letters to his Son. The Accomplished Gentleman: or, Principles of Politeness, and of Knowing the World . . .* (Dublin edition, 1772, 1774, 1775, 1776, 1782, 1783, 1790).

Craghead, Robert, *A Funeral Sermon on the Occasion of the Death of the Right Honourable Catherine, Countess Dowager of Granard: Who Dyed December the 9th, 1714* (Dublin, 1714).

De Lambert, Marchioness, *Advice of a Mother to Her Daughter* (Dublin, 1790).

De Sales, Francis, *An Introduction to a Devout Life . . . Fitted For the Use of Protestants* (Dublin edition with preface by Henry Dodwell, 1673).

Derricke, John, *The Image of Irelande* (London, 1581; reprinted, Belfast, 1985).

Dobbs, Arthur, *An Essay on the Trade and Improvement of Ireland* (Dublin, 1729).

Donlevy, Andrew, *An Teagasg Críosduidhe. Do Réir Cearda agus Freagartha. The Catechism or Christian Doctrine By Way of Question and Answer* (Paris, 1742).

Female Mentor or Select Conversation (Dublin edition, 1793).

Ferrar, John, *A View of Ancient and Modern Dublin. With Its Improvements to the Year 1796. To Which is Added a Tour to Belvue in the County of Wicklow, the Seat of Peter La Touche* (Dublin, 1796).

The Limerick Directory . . . (Limerick, 1799).

Fitzsimons, Henry, *The Justification and Exposition of the Divine Service of the Masse, and of All Rites and Ceremonies Thereto Belonging . . .* (1611).

Words of Comfort to Prosecuted Catholics (1608, edited by Edmund Hogan, Dublin, 1881).

Flynn, William, *An Abstract of the Doway Catechism. For the Use of Children, and Ignorant People* (Cork, 1774).

Foley, Samuel, *An Exhortation to the Inhabitants of Down and Connor, Concerning the Religious Education of their Children . . .* (Dublin, 1695).

Fordyce, James, *The Character and Conduct of the Female Sex, and the Advantages to be Derived by Young Men from the Society of Virtuous Women . . .* (Belfast edition, 1776; Dublin edition, 1776; Newry edition, 1776).

Gregory, John, *A Father's Legacy To His Daughters* (Dublin edition, 1774, 1788, 1790; Newry edition, 1775).

Griffith, Richard, Junior, *Thoughts on Protecting Duties* (Dublin, 1784).

Halifax, Earl of, *The Lady's New-Year's Gift: Or, Advice to a Daughter* (Dublin and Drogheda edition, printed in 1699; new Dublin edition, 1724).

Hall, Thomas, *A Plain and Easy Explication of the Assemblies Shorter Catechism . . .* (Edinburgh, 1697).

Hamilton, Andrew, *A True Relation of the Actions of the Inniskilling-Men From Their First Taking Up Arms in December 1688 for the Defence of the Protestant Religion, and Their Lives and Liberty* (London, 1690).

Hamilton, William, *A Discourse Concerning Zeal, Against Immorality and Prophanences Delivered in Two Sermons in St Michael's Church, Dublin, 29 October, 26 November 1699* (Dublin, 1700).

The Life and Character of James Bonnell Esq (Dublin, 1703).

Harris, Walter, *The History and Antiquities of the City of Dublin, From the Earliest Accounts* (Dublin, 1766).

Haywood, Eliza, *Female Spectator* (4 vols., Dublin edition, 1746).

Holinshed, Ralph, *Chronicles of England, Scotlande, and Irelande* (London, 1577; edited by Liam Miller and Eileen Power, Dublin, 1979).

Hopkins, Ezekiel, *The Works of the Right Reverend and Learned Ezekiel Hopkins, Late Lord Bishop of London-Derry in Ireland* (London, 1701).

Hutcheson, Francis, *A System of Moral Philosophy* (2 vols., London, 1755).

[Jennings, Soame], *Thoughts on a Parliamentary Reform* (3rd edition, Dublin, 1784).

Journals of the House of Commons of the Kingdom of Ireland (23 vols., Dublin, 1763–86).

Kenrick, William *The Whole Duty of a Woman By A Lady* (Dublin edition, 1753).

Keogh, John, *Thoughts on Equal Representation, With Hints for Improving the Manufactures and Employment of the Poor of Ireland* (Dublin, 1784).

King, William, *The State of the Protestants of Ireland Under the Late King James's Government* (Cork, 1768).

Leadbeater, Mary, *Extracts and Original Anecdotes for the Improvement of Youth* (1794).

Leslie, Henry, *A Discourse of Praying With the Spirit, and With the Understanding Whereof Extemporary Premeditate Set Forms of Prayer . . .* (London, 1660).

A Treatise of the Authority of the Church (Dublin, 1637).

Lodge, John, *The Peerage of Ireland* (London, 1789).

Lucas, Richard, *The Cork Directory for . . . 1787, Including the Adjacent Outports of Youghal, Kinsale, Cove, Passage and the Manufacturing Towns of Inishannon and Bandon* (Cork, 1787).

Madden, R. R., *The Literary Life and Correspondence of the Countess of Blessington* (London, 1855).

Malantius, *Letters Addressed to Mrs Peter La Touche by Malantius. Containing a State of the Orphan-Houses of England, Zeland and Ireland* (Dublin, 1793).

Mears, John, *A Short Explanation of the End and Design of the Lord's Supper* (Dublin, 1758).

Memoirs of Laetitia Pilkington (vols. i–ii, Dublin, 1748; vol. iii, London, 1754; new edition by A. C. Elias Jr, 2 vols., Athens, Georgia and London, 1997).

Memoirs of Mrs Margaret Leeson, Written By Herself and Interspersed with Several Interesting and Amusing Anecdotes, On Some of the Most Striking Characters of Great-Britain and Ireland, 3 vols., Dublin 1795–7; edited by Mary Lyons (Dublin, 1995).

Memoirs of the Right Honourable the Marquis of Clanricarde, Lord Deputy General of Ireland (Dublin, 1744).

Moore, Edward, *Fables for the Female Sex* (Dublin, 1790).

Moore, Hamilton, *Young Gentlemen and Ladies Monitor, Being a Collection of Select Pieces From Our Best Modern Writers: Particularly Calculated to*

Form the Mind and Manners of the Youth of Both Sexes, and Adapted to the Uses of Schools and Academies (Belfast, 1788).

Nevill, John, *Seasonable Remarks on the Linen-Trade of Ireland With Some Observations on the Present State of that Country* (Dublin, 1783).

Pennington, Lady, *An Unfortunate Mother's Advice to Her Absent Daughters* (Dublin edition, 1790).

Pollard, Thomas, *The Necessity and Advantages of Family Prayer, in Two Sermons, Preached at St Peters, Dublin* (Dublin, 1696).

Rogers, John, *Ohel or Beth-shemesh. A Tabernacle for the Sun: or Irenicum Evangelicum . . .* (London, 1653).

Rushworth, John (Ed), *The Trial of Thomas, Earl of Strafford* (London, 1680).

Rushworth, John (Ed), *Historical Collections of Private Passages of State* (8 vols., London, 1659–1701), vol. 8.

Swift, Jonathan, *A Proposal That All Ladies and Women of Ireland Should Appear Constantly in Irish Manufactures* (Dublin, 1722).

Directions to Servants (Dublin, 1752, reprinted, London, 2003).

Synge, Edward, *A Gentleman's Religion: In Three Parts* (Dublin, 1730).

A Discourse of Confirmation in a Dialogue Between the Minister of a Parish, and a Young Servant Maid Named Sarah (Dublin, 1739).

Teate, Joseph, *A Sermon Preached at the Cathedral Church of St Canice Kilkenny, Feb. 27 1669* (Dublin, 1670).

The Assembly's Shorter Catechism Explained (Belfast edition, 1764).

The Church-Catechism Explained and Proved by Apt Texts of Scripture (Belfast, 1769).

The Hardships of the English Laws in Relation to Wives. With an Examination of the Original Curse of Subjection Passed Upon the Woman. In an Humble Address to the Legislature (London, 1735; Dublin edition, 1735).

The Statutes at Large. Passed in the Parliaments Held in Ireland (Dublin, 1786–1804).

The Young Lady's Pocket Library, or Parental Monitor (Dublin edition, 1790).

Twiss, Richard, *A Tour in Ireland in 1775* (London, 1776).

Ussher, James, *A Body of Divinities, or the Sum and Substance of Christian Religion, Catechistically Propounded and Explained, by Way of Question and Answer . . .* (2nd edition, London, 1657).

Ward, Edward, *Female Policy Detected. Or the Arts of a Designing Woman Laid Open.* (1st edition, London, 1695; 1761 edition used).

Ware, James, *The Antiquities and History of Ireland* (English version, Dublin, 1705).

Watson, John, Watson, Samuel, and Watson, Stewart John, *The Gentleman and Citizens Almanack* (Dublin, 1752–1800).

West, Moses, *A Treatise Concerning Marriage Wherein the Unlawfulness of Mixt Marriage, Laid Open From the Scriptures of Truth* (Dublin, 1735).

Whyte, Samuel, *The Shamrock: or Hibernian Cresses* (Dublin, 1772).

Wollstonecraft, Mary, *A Vindication of the Rights of Woman: With Strictures on Political and Moral Subjects* (Dublin edition, 1793).

W. W., *A Letter to a Lady in Praise of Female Learning* (Dublin, 1739).

Young, Arthur, *A Tour in Ireland With General Observations on the Present State of That Kingdom Made in the Years 1776, 1777 and 1778* (2 parts, London, 1780).

Young, Edward, *The Works of the Author of the Night-Thoughts* (4 vols., Dublin, 1764).

Secondary Sources

A Report Upon Certain Charitable Establishments in the City of Dublin which Receive Aid From Parliament (Dublin, 1809).

Appleby, J. C., 'Women and Piracy in Ireland: From Gráinne O'Malley to Anne Bonney' in Margaret MacCurtain and Mary O'Dowd (Eds), *Women in Early Modern Ireland* (Edinburgh, 1991).

Arnold, L. J., *The Restoration Land Settlement in County Dublin, 1660–1688* (Dublin, 1993).

Bagenal, Philip H., *Vicissitudes of an Anglo-Irish Family 1530–1800. A Story of Romance and Tragedy* (London, 1925).

Bagwell, Richard, *Ireland Under the Tudors* (3 vols., London, 1885–90).

Ireland Under the Stuarts and During the Interregnum (3 vols., London, 1909–16).

Ball Wright, W., *Ball Family Records* (York, 1908).

Barash, Carol, *English Women's Poetry, 1649–1714. Politics, Community, and Linguistic Authority* (Oxford, 1996).

Barker, Hannah and Chalus, Elaine (Eds), *Gender in Eighteenth-Century England* (London, 1997).

Barnard, Toby, 'Reforming Irish Manners: the Religious Societies in Dublin During the 1690s' in *The Historical Journal*, **35** (4) (1992).

'Learning, the Learned and Literacy in Ireland, c. 1660–1760' in Toby Barnard, Dáibhí Ó Cróinín and Katharine Simms (Eds), *'A Miracle of Learning'; Studies in Manuscripts and Irish Learning* (Aldershot, 1998).

The Abduction of a Limerick Heiress. Social and Political Relations in Mid-Eighteenth Century Ireland (Dublin, 1998).

'The World of Goods and County Offaly in the Early Eighteenth Century' in William Nolan and Timothy P. O'Neill (Eds), *Offaly History and Society. Interdisciplinary Essays on the History of an Irish County* (Dublin, 1998).

'Reading in Eighteenth-Century Ireland: Public and Private Pleasures' in Bernadette Cunningham and Máire Kennedy (Eds), *The Experience of Reading: Irish Historical Perspectives* (Dublin, 1999).

'The Viceregal Court in Later Seventeenth-Century Ireland' in Eveline Cruickshanks (Ed), *The Stuart Courts* (Stroud, Gloucestershire, 2000).

'"Grand Metropolis" or "The Anus of the World"? The Cultural Life of Eighteenth-Century Dublin' in Peter Clark and Raymond Gillespie (Eds), *Two Capitals. London and Dublin 1500–1840* (Oxford, 2001).

A New Anatomy of Ireland. The Irish Protestants, 1649–1770 (New Haven and London, 2003).

Irish Protestants. Ascents and Descents, 1641–1770 (Dublin, 2004).

Barnard, Toby and Fenlon, Jane (Eds), *The Dukes of Ormond, 1610–1745* (Woodbridge, 2000).

Baron, Caroline M., 'London 1300–1540' in D. M. Palliser (Ed), *The Cambridge Urban History of Britain, Vol. I, 600–1540* (Cambridge, 2000).

Barrington, Jonah, *Historic Memoirs of Ireland; Comprising Secret Records of the National Convention, the Rebellion and the Union; With the*

Delineations of the Principal Characters Connected with Those Transactions (2 vols., Dublin, 1835).

The Rise and Fall of the Irish Nation (London 1833, reprinted Dublin, 1843).

Bartlett, Thomas, *The Fall and Rise of the Irish Nation. The Catholic Question, 1690–1830* (Dublin, 1992).

'Bearing Witness: Female Evidences in Courts Martial Convened to Suppress the 1798 Rebellion' in Dáire Keogh and Nicholas Furlong (Eds), *The Women of 1798* (Dublin, 1998).

Bean, J. M. W., *The Decline of English Feudalism 1215–1540* (Manchester, 1968).

Berry, H. F., 'Notes From the Diary of a Dublin Lady in the Reign of George II' in *Journal of the Royal Society of Antiquaries of Ireland*, **28** (1898).

Berry, Henry F., *A History of the Royal Dublin Society* (London, 1915).

Bilbao Acedos, Amala, *The Irish Community in the Basque Country c. 1700–1800* (Dublin, 2003).

Bishop, Erin I., *The World of Mary O'Connell, 1778–1816* (Dublin, 1999).

Blades, Brooke S., '"In the Manner of England": Tenant Housing in the Londonderry Plantation' in *Ulster Folklife*, **27** (1981).

Bolton, F. R., *The Caroline Tradition of the Church of Ireland With Particular Reference to Bishop Jeremy Taylor* (London, 1958).

Bonfield, Lloyd, *Marriage Settlements, 1601–1670. The Adoption of the Strict Settlement* (Cambridge, 1983).

Bossy, John, *The English Catholic Community, 1570–1850* (London, 1975).

Bourke, Angela 'More in Anger Than in Sorrow: Irish Women's Lament Poetry' in Joan Newlon Radner (Ed), *Feminist Messages. Coding in Women's Folk Culture* (Urbana and Chicago, 1993).

Bourke, William P., *History of Clonmel* (2nd edition, Waterford, 1907, reprinted, Kilkenny, 1983).

Boylan, Lena, 'The Connollys of Castletown. A Family History' in Quarterly *Bulletin of the Irish Georgian Society*, **xi** (1968).

Bradshaw, Brendan, *The Dissolution of the Religious Orders in Ireland Under Henry VIII* (Cambridge, 1974).

Bradshaw, Thomas, *Belfast General and Commercial Directory for 1819* (Belfast, 1819).

Brady, Ciarán, 'Political Women and Reform in Tudor Ireland' in Margaret MacCurtain and Mary O'Dowd (Eds), *Women in Early Modern Ireland* (Edinburgh, 1991).

The Chief Governors. The Rise and Fall of Reform Government in Tudor Ireland, 1536–1588 (Cambridge, 1994).

'The Captains' Games: Army and Society in Elizabethan Ireland' in Thomas Bartlett and Keith Jeffery (Eds), *A Military History of Ireland* (Cambridge, 1996).

Shane O'Neill (Dublin, 1996).

Brady, John, 'Keeping the Faith at Gormanston, 1569–1629' in The Franciscan Fathers (Eds), *Father Luke Wadding Commemorative Volume* (Dublin, 1957).

Brenan, M., 'The Confraternity of Christian Doctrine in Ireland' in *Irish Ecclesiastical Record*, 43–44 (1934).

Brooke, Peter, *Ulster Presbyterianism. The Historical Perspective 1610–1970* (Dublin, 1987).

Brophy, Imelda, 'Women in the Workforce' in David Dickson (Ed), *The Gorgeous Mask* (Dublin, 1987).

Brown, Kathleen, *Good Wives, Nasty Wenches, and Anxious Patriarchs: Gender, Race, and Power in Colonial Virginia* (Chapel Hill, 1996).

Brown, Michael, *Francis Hutcheson in Dublin, 1719–30: The Crucible of His Thought* (Dublin, 2002).

Bryan, Donough, *Gerald Fitzgerald. The Great Earl of Fitzgerald (1456–1513)* (Dublin, 1933).

Burke Savage, Roland, *A Valiant Dublin Woman. The Story of George's Hill (1766–1940)* (Dublin, 1940).

Burke, Victoria, 'Women and Early Seventeenth-Century Manuscript Culture: Four Miscellanies' in *The Seventeenth Century*, **xii** (2) (1997).

Butler, Beatrice Bayley, 'Lady Arbella Denny, 1707–1792' in *Dublin Historical Record*, **9** (1) (1946–7).

Butler, Marilyn, *Maria Edgeworth. A Literary Biography* (London, 1972).

'Irish Culture and Scottish Enlightenment: Maria Edgeworth: Histories of the Future' in Stefan Collini, Richard Whatmore and Brian Young (Eds), *Economic Policy and Society. British Intellectual History 1750–1950* (Cambridge, 2000).

Butler, W. F. T., *Gleanings From Irish History* (London, 1925).

Campbell, Gerald, *Edward and Pamela Fitzgerald* (London, 1904).

Campbell Ross, Ian, *Public Virtue, Public Love. The Early Years of the Dublin Lying-In Hospital. The Rotunda* (Dublin, 1986).

Canny, Nicholas, 'The 1641 Depositions as a Source for the Writing of Social and Economic History: County Cork as a Case Study' in Patrick O'Flanagan and Cornelius Buttimer (Eds), *Cork: History and Society* (Dublin, 1993).

The Upstart Earl: A Study of the Social and Mental World of Richard Boyle, First Earl of Cork, 1566–1643 (Cambridge, 1982).

Making Ireland British 1580–1650 (Oxford, 2001).

Carey, Vincent P., *Surviving the Tudors. The 'Wizard' Earl of Kildare and English Rule in Ireland, 1537–1586* (Dublin, 2002).

Carroll, Thomas K., *Wisdom and Wasteland. Jeremy Taylor in his Prose and Preaching Today* (Dublin, 2001).

Carter, Philip, *Men and the Emergence of Polite Society in Britain, 1660–1800* (London, 2001).

Casway, Jerrold, 'Rosa O Dogherty: a Gaelic Woman' in *Seanchas Ard Mhacha*, **10**, no. 1 (1980–1).

'Irish Women Overseas, 1500–1800' in Margaret MacCurtain and Mary O'Dowd (Eds), *Women in Early Modern Ireland* (Edinburgh, 1991).

'The Decline and Fate of Dónal Ballagh O'Cahan and His Family' in Micheál Ó Siochrú (Ed), *Kingdoms in Crisis. Ireland in the 1640s* (Dublin, 2001).

Chalus, Elaine, 'Elite Women, Social Politics and the Political World of Late Eighteenth-Century England' in *The Historical Journal*, **43** (3) (2000).

Chambers, Anne, *Eleanor Countess of Desmond, c. 1545–1638* (Dublin, 1986).

Granuaile. The Life and Times of Grace O'Malley c. 1530–1603 (Dublin, new edition, 1988).

Clarke, Aidan, 'The Genesis of the Ulster Rising of 1641' in Peter Roebuck (Ed), *Plantation to Partition* (Belfast, 1981).

Clarkson, L. A., *Proto-Industrialization: the First Phase of Industrialization?* (London, 1985).

'The Carrick-on-Suir Woollen Industry in the Eighteenth Century' in *Irish Economic and Social History*, **xvi** (1989).

'Love, Labour and Life: Women in Carrick-On-Suir in the Late Eighteenth Century' in *Irish Economic and Social History*, **xx** (1993).

Clarkson, L. A. and Crawford, E. M., 'Life After Death: Widows in Carrick-on-Suir, 1799' in Margaret MacCurtain and Mary O'Dowd (Eds), *Women in Early Modern Ireland* (Edinburgh, 1991).

Cleary, Gregory, *Father Luke Wadding and St. Isidore's College, Rome: Biographical and Historical Notes and Documents* (Rome, 1925).

Cohen, Marilyn, *Linen, Family and Continuity in Tullyish, County Down, 1690–1914* (Dublin, 1997).

Collins, Brenda, 'Proto-industrialization and Pre-Famine Emigration' in *Social History*, **7** (1982).

Concannon, Helena, *Women of 'Ninety-Eight* (Dublin, 1920).

The Poor Clares in Ireland (A.D. 1629–A.D. 1929) (Dublin, 1929).

Daughters of Banba (Dublin, 1930).

Irish Nuns in Penal Times (London, 1931).

The Blessed Eucharist in Irish History (Dublin, 1932).

The Queen of Ireland. An Historical Account of Ireland's Devotion to the Blessed Virgin (Dublin, 1938).

Condren, Mary, *The Serpent and the Goddess. Women, Religion and Power in Celtic Ireland* (New York, 1989).

Connolly, S. J., 'Illegitimacy and Pre-Nuptial Pregnancy in Ireland Before 1864: The Evidence of Some Catholic Parish Registers' in *Irish Economic and Social History Journal*, **vi** (1979).

Priests and People in Pre-Famine Ireland 1780–1845 (Dublin, 1982).

'Marriage in Pre-Famine Ireland' in Art Cosgrove (Ed), *Marriage in Ireland* (Dublin, 1985).

Religion, Law and Power: The Making of Protestant Ireland, 1660–1760 (Oxford, 1992).

'A Woman's Life in Mid-Eighteenth-Century Ireland: the Case of Letitia Bushe' in *The Historical Journal*, **43** (2) (2000).

'Precedent and Principle: the Patriots and their Critics' in S. J. Connolly (Ed), *Political Ideas in Eighteenth-Century Ireland* (Dublin, 2000).

Coote, Charles, *Statistical Survey of the County of Cavan, With Observations on the Means of Improvement* (Dublin, 1802).

Cope, Esther S., *Handmaid of the Holy Spirit. Dame Eleanor Davies, Never Soe Mad a Ladie* (Michigan, 1992).

Corish, P. J., *The Catholic Community in the Seventeenth and Eighteenth Centuries* (Dublin, 1981).

Cox, Catherine, 'Women and Paid Work in Rural Ireland, c. 1500–1800' in Bernadette Whelan (Ed), *Women and Paid Work in Ireland, 1500–1930* (Dublin, 2000).

Crawford, Patricia, *Women and Religion in England 1500–1720* (London, 1993).

Crawford, W. H., 'Women in the Domestic Linen Industry' in Margaret MacCurtain and Mary O'Dowd (Eds), *Women in Early Modern Ireland* (Edinburgh, 1991).

Crookshank, C. H., *Memorable Women of Irish Methodism in the Last Century* (London, 1882).

Cullen, L. M., *Life in Ireland* (London, 1968).

The Emergence of Modern Ireland, 1600–1900 (London, 1981).

The Irish Brandy Houses of Eighteenth-Century France (Dublin, 2000).

Cullen, Nuala, 'Women and the Preparation of Food in Eighteenth-Century Ireland' in Margaret MacCurtain and Mary O'Dowd (Eds), *Women in Early Modern Ireland* (Edinburgh, 1991).

Cunningham, Bernadette, 'Women and Gaelic Literature, 1500–1800' in Margaret MacCurtain and Mary O'Dowd (Eds), *Women in Early Modern Ireland* (Edinburgh, 1991).

'"Zeal For God and For Souls": Counter-Reformation Preaching in Early Seventeenth-Century Ireland' in Alan J. Fletcher and Raymond Gillespie (Eds), *Irish Preaching, 700–1700* (Dublin, 2001).

Cunningham, Bernadette and Kennedy, Máire (Eds), *The Experience of Reading: Irish Historical Perspectives* (Dublin, 1999).

Cunningham, Hugh and Innes, Joanna (Eds), *Charity, Philanthropy and Reform from the 1690s to 1850* (Basingstoke and London, 1998).

Daly, Mary E., *Women and Work in Ireland* (Dundalk, 1997).

Davis, Natalie Zemon and Farge, Arlette (Eds), *A History of Women in the West. III. Renaissance and Enlightenment Paradoxes* (Cambridge, Massachusetts and London, 1993).

Devane, R. S., 'A Pioneer of Catholic Action (1584–1934). A Forgotten Chapter of History' in *Irish Ecclesiastical Record*, **xliv** (1934).

Devine, T. M. (Ed), *Farm Servants and Labour in Lowland Scotland* (Edinburgh, 1984).

Dickson, David, *New Foundations: Ireland, 1660–1800* (Dublin, 1987; new edition, 2000).

(Ed), *The Gorgeous Mask. Dublin, 1700–1850* (Dublin, 1987).

'Capital and County: 1600–1800' in Art Cosgrove (Ed), *Dublin Through the Ages* (Dublin, 1988).

'No Scythians Here: Women and Marriage in Seventeenth Century Ireland' in Margaret MacCurtain and Mary O'Dowd (Eds), *Women in Early Modern Ireland* (Edinburgh, 1991).

'Butter Comes to Market: the Origins of Commercial Dairying in County Cork' in Patrick O'Flanagan and Cornelius G. Buttimer (Eds), *Cork. History and Society. Interdisciplinary Essays on the History of an Irish County* (Dublin, 1993).

Arctic Ireland. The Extraordinary Story of the Great Frost and Forgotten Famine of 1740–41 (Dublin, 1997).

Dictionary of National Biography.

Dolan, J. T. 'Drogheda Trade and Customs, 1683' in *Country Louth Archaeological Journal*, **iii** (1912–15).

Donovan, Brian C. and Edwards, David, *British Sources for Irish History 1485–1641* (Dublin, 1997).

Dubourdieu, John, *Statistical Survey of Co. Down* (Dublin, 1802).

Statistical Survey of Co. Antrim (Dublin, 1812).

Dunlevy, Mairéad, *Dress in Ireland. A History* (Dublin, 1989).

'Changes in Living Standards in the Seventeenth Century' in M. Ryan (Ed), *Irish Archaeology Illustrated* (Dublin, 1991).

'Dublin in the Nineteenth Century: Domestic Evidence' in Brian P. Kennedy and Raymond Gillespie (Eds), *Ireland, Art into History* (Dublin, 1994).

Dutton, Hely, *Statistical Survey of the County of Clare* (Dublin, 1808).

Edwards, David, 'The Mac Giollapadraigs (Fitzpatricks) of Upper Ossory, 1532–1641' in Padraig G. Lane and William Nolan (Eds), *Laois, History and Society. Interdisciplinary Essays on the History of an Irish County* (Dublin, 1999).

The Ormond Lordship in County Kilkenny, 1515–1642, The Rise and Fall of Butler Feudal Power (Dublin, 2003).

Eger, Elizabeth, Grant, Charlotte, Ó Gallchoir, Clíona and Warburton, Penny (Eds), *Women, Writing and the Public Sphere, 1700–1830* (Cambridge, 2001).

Erickson, Amy Louise, *Women and Property in Early Modern England* (London, 1993).

'Property and Widowhood in England, 1660–1840' in Dandra Cavallo and Lyndan Warner (Eds), *Widowhood in Medieval and Early Modern Europe* (London, 1999).

Ewan, Elizabeth and Meikle, Maureen M. (Eds), *Women in Scotland, c. 1100–c. 1750* (Phantassie, East Linton, 1999).

Fagan, Patrick, *The Second City. Portrait of Dublin, 1700–1760* (Dublin, 1986).

Dublin's Turbulent Priest. Cornelius Nary 1658–1738 (Dublin, 1991).

Fell Smith, Charlotte, *Mary Rich, Countess of Warwick (1625–1678): Her Family and Friends* (London, 1901).

Fenlon, Jane, '"Her Grace's Closet": Paintings in the Duchess of Ormond's Closet at Kilkenny Castle' in *Bulletin of the Irish Georgian Society* (1994).

'The Duchess of Ormonde's House at Dunmore, County Kilkenny' in John Kirwan (Ed), *Kilkenny. Studies in Honour of Margaret M. Phelan* (Kilkenny, 1997).

Fenning, Hugh, 'Laurence Richardson, O.P., Bishop of Kilmore, 1747–53' in *The Irish Ecclesiastical Record*, 5th series, **cix** (1968).

The Undoing of the Friars of Ireland (Louvain, 1972).

Ferguson, Moira, *Subject to Slavery. British Women Writers and Colonial Slavery, 1670–1834* (London, 1992).

Ffolliott, Rosemary, 'Houses in Ireland in the 17th Century' in *The Irish Sword*, **xvii** (1989).

Fitzgerald, Brian, *Emily Duchess of Leinster, 1731–1814. A Study of Her Life and Times* (London, 1949).

Lady Louisa Conolly, 1743–1821 (London, 1950).

Fitzsimons, Fiona, 'Fosterage and Gossiprid in Late Medieval Ireland: Some New Evidence' in Patrick J. Duffy, David Edwards and Elizabeth FitzPatrick (Eds), *Gaelic Ireland c. 1250–c. 1650: land, Lordship and Settlement* (Dublin, 2001).

Fletcher, A. J., *Drama, Performance and Polity in Pre-Cromwellian Ireland* (Cambridge, 2000).

Fletcher, Alan J. and Gillespie, Raymond (Eds), *Irish Preaching, 700–1700* (Dublin, 2001).

Ford, Alan, *The Protestant Reformation in Ireland* (Frankfurt am Main, 1985).

Forrestal, Alison, *Catholic Synods in Ireland, 1600–1690* (Dublin, 1998).

Foster, Sarah, 'Going Shopping in 18th Century Dublin' in *Things*, **4** (Summer, 1996).

Froide, Amy M., 'Old Maids: the Lifecycle of Single Women in Early Modern England' in Judith M. Bennett and Amy M. Froide (Eds), *Single Women in the European Past 1250–1800* (Philadelphia, 1999).

Gardiner, Juliet (Ed), *What is History Today?* (Atlantic Highlands, New Jersey, 1988).

Garnham, Neal, *The Courts, Crime and the Criminal Law in Ireland, 1692–1760* (Dublin, 1996).

'How Violent Was Eighteenth-Century Ireland?' in *Irish Historical Studies*, **xxx** (1997).

George, J. A., 'The Vocacyon of Johan Bale (1553): A Retrospective Sermon From Ireland' in Alan J. Fletcher and Raymond Gillespie (Eds), *Irish Preaching, 700–1700* (Dublin, 2001).

Gerard, Frances A., *Some Fair Hibernians* (London, 1897).

Gerard, Jessica A., 'Invisible Servants: the County House and the Local Community' in *Bulletin of the Institute of Historical Research*, **lvii** (1984).

Gibbs, Vicary (Ed), *The Complete Peerage of England, Scotland, Ireland, Great Britain and the United Kingdom* (13 vols., London, 1910–1940).

Giblin, Cathaldus, 'Processus Datariae and the Appointment of Irish Bishops in the Seventeenth Century' in The Franciscan Fathers (Eds), *Father Luke Wadding Commemorative Volume* (Dublin, 1957).

A History of Irish Catholicism, Volume IV. Irish Exiles in Catholic Europe (Dublin, 1971).

Gibson, Wendy, *Women in Seventeenth-Century France* (Basingstoke, 1989).

Gilbert, J. T., *A History of the City of Dublin* (3 vols., Dublin, 1854).

Gill, Conrad, *The Rise of the Irish Linen Industry* (Oxford, 1925).

Gillespie, Raymond, 'The Book Trade in Southern Ireland, 1590–1640' in Gerard Long (Ed), *Books Beyond the Pale. Aspects of the Provincial Book Trade in Ireland Before 1850* (Dublin, 1994).

'"Into Another Intensity": Prayer in Irish Nonconformity, 1650–1700' in Kevin Herlihy (Ed), *The Religion of Irish Dissent, 1650–1800* (Dublin, 1996).

Devoted People. Belief and Religion in Early Modern Ireland (Manchester, 1997).

'Reading the Bible in Seventeenth-Century Ireland' in Bernadette Cunningham and Máire Kennedy (Eds), *The Experience of Reading: Irish Historical Perspectives* (Dublin, 1999).

Grattan, Henry, *Memoirs of the Life and Times of the Right Honourable Henry Grattan* (5 vols., new edition, London, 1849).

Greaves, Richard L. (Ed), *Triumph Over Silence. Women in Protestant History* (Connecticut, 1985).

'"That's No Good Religion That Disturbs Government": The Church of Ireland and the Nonconformist Challenge' in A. Ford, J. McGuire and K. Milne (Eds), *As By Law Established. The Church of Ireland Since the Reformation* (Dublin, 1995).

God's Other Children, Protestant Nonconformists and the Emergence of Denominational Churches in Ireland, 1660–1700 (Stanford, 1997).

Green, Ian, '"The Necessary Knowledge of the Principles of Religion": Catechisms and Catechizing in Ireland, c. 1560–1800' in A. Ford, J. McGuire and K. Milne (Eds), *As By Law Established. The Church of Ireland Since the Reformation* (Dublin, 1995).

The Christian's ABC. Catechisms and Catechizing in England c. 1530–1740 (Oxford, 1996).

Griffin, David J., 'Castletown, Co. Kildare: the Contribution of James, First Duke of Leinster' in *Irish Architectural and Decorative Studies,* **1** (1998).

Gwynn, Aubrey and Hadcock, R. N. (Eds), *Medieval Religious Houses Ireland* (Dublin, 1970).

Gwynn, Stephen, *Henry Grattan and His Times* (Dublin, 1939).

Hall, Dianne, *Women and the Church in Medieval Ireland, c. 1140–1540* (Dublin, 2003).

Harbison, Peter, *Pilgrimage in Ireland. The Monuments and the People* (London, 1991).

Harcstark Myers, Sylvia, *The Bluestocking Circle. Women, Friendship, and the Life of the Mind in Eighteenth-Century England* (Oxford, 1990).

Hardy, Francis, *Memoirs of the Political and Private Life of James Caulfield, Earl of Charlemont* (London, 1810).

Harris, Amy Louise, 'The Funerary Monuments of Richard Boyle, Earl of Cork' in *Church Monuments,* **xiii** (1998).

Harris, Barbara J., 'Women and Politics in Early Tudor England' in *The Historical Journal,* **33** (2) (1990).

'The View From My Lady's Chamber: New Perspectives on the Early Tudor Monarchy' in *Huntington Library Quarterly,* **60** (3) (1999).

English Aristocratic Women, 1450–1550: Marriage and Family, Property and Careers (Oxford, 2002).

Hayden, Mary, 'Charity Children in Eighteenth Century Dublin' in *Dublin Historical Record,* **5** (1942–3).

Hayes-McCoy, G. A., *Scots Mercenary Forces in Ireland (1656–1603)* (Dublin and London, 1937).

Hayton, David, 'Did Protestantism Fail in Early Eighteenth-Century Ireland? Charity Schools and the Enterprise of Religious and Social Reformation, c. 1690–1730' in A. Ford, J. McGuire and K. Milne (Eds), *As By Law Established. The Church of Ireland Since the Reformation* (Dublin, 1995).

Hecht, J. Jean, *The Domestic Servant Class in Eighteenth-Century England* (London, 1956).

Heller, Deborah, 'Bluestocking Salons and the Public Sphere' in *Eighteenth-Century Life,* **22** (1998).

Hempton, David, *The Religion of the People. Methodism and Popular Religion c. 1750–1900* (London, 1996).

Hempton, David and Hill, Myrtle, 'Women and Protestant Minorities in Eighteenth-Century Ireland' in Margaret MacCurtain and Mary O'Dowd (Eds), *Women in Early Modern Ireland* (Edinburgh, 1991).

Evangelical Protestantism in Ulster Society 1740–1890 (London, 1992).

Henry, Brian, *Dublin Hanged* (Dublin, 1994).

Henry, Gráinne, *The Irish Military Community in Spanish Flanders 1586–1621* (Dublin, 1992).

Herlihy, Kevin, '"A Gay and Flattering World": Irish Baptist Piety and Perspective, 1650–1780' in Kevin Herlihy (Ed), *The Religion of Irish Dissent, 1650–1800* (Dublin, 1996).

Hibbard, Caroline, 'The Role of a Queen Consort: the Household and Court of Henrietta Maria, 1625–1642' in R. Asch and A. Birke (Eds), *Princes, Patronage and the Nobility: the Court at the Beginning of the Modern Age, c. 1450–1650* (London, 1991).

Hill, Bridget, *Women, Work and Sexual Politics in Eighteenth Century England* (Oxford, 1989).

Hill, Jacqueline (Ed), *Luxury and Austerity* (Dublin, 1999).

Hoby, Elaine, *Virtue of Necessity: English Women's Writing 1649–88* (London, 1988).

Hogan, Edmund, *Distinguished Irishmen of the Sixteenth Century* (London, 1894).

Hufton, Olwen, *The Prospect Before Her. A History of Women in Western Europe. Volume One 1500–1800* (London, 1995).

Hunt, Margaret, *The Middling Sort. Commerce, Gender and the Family in England, 1680–1780* (Berkeley and London, 1996).

Jackson, Donald, *Intermarriage in Ireland, 1550–1650* (Montreal and Minneapolis, 1970).

Jacob, Margaret, 'The Mental Landscape of the Public Sphere' in *Eighteenth-Century Studies*, **28** (1994).

Jaeger, Muriel, *Before Victoria* (London, 1956).

Jefferies, Henry A., 'Primate George Dowdall and the Marian Restoration' in *Seanchas Ard Mhacha*, **17** (2) (1998).

Johnston, Edith Mary, *Great Britain and Ireland, 1760–1800. A Study in Political Administration* (Edinburgh, 1963).

Ireland in the Eighteenth Century (Dublin, 1974).

Johnston-Liik, Edith Mary, *History of the Irish Parliament, 1692–1800; Commons, Constituencies and Statutes* (6 vols., Belfast, 2002).

Jones, Vivien (Ed), *Women and Literature in Britain, 1700–1800* (Cambridge, 2000).

Joseph Byrne, 'A Rhapsody on the Carved Oak Chimney-piece of the Assumption of the Blessed Virgin in the Oak Room at Malahide' in *Archivium Hibernicum*, **52** (1998).

Jupp, Peter and Magennis, Eoin (Eds), *Crowds in Ireland, c. 1720–1920* (London and New York, 2000).

Kelly, James, 'Infanticide in Eighteenth-Century Ireland' in *Irish Economic and Social History*, **xix** (1992).

'The Abduction of Women of Fortune in Eighteenth-Century Ireland' in *Eighteenth-Century Ireland*, **ix** (1994).

'"Most Inhuman and Barbarous Piece of Villainy": An Exploration of the Crime of Rape in Eighteenth-Century Ireland' in *Eighteenth-Century Ireland*, **10** (1995).

'That Damn' Thing Called Honour'. Duelling in Ireland, 1570–1860 (Cork, 1995).

Henry Flood. Patriots and Politics in Eighteenth-Century Ireland (Dublin, 1998).

'Reporting the Irish Parliament: the *Parliamentary Register*' in *Eighteenth-Century Ireland*, **15** (2000).

'The Impact of the Penal Laws' in James Kelly and Dáire Keogh (Eds), *History of the Catholic Diocese of Dublin* (Dublin, 2000).

Kelly, James and Keogh, Dáire (Eds), *History of the Catholic Diocese of Dublin* (Dublin, 2000).

Kelly, Patrick, 'Anne Donnellan: Irish Proto-Bluestocking' in *Hermathena*, **152** (Summer, 1992).

'The Politics of Political Economy in Mid-Eighteenth Century Ireland' in Sean Connolly (Ed), *Political Ideas in Eighteenth Century Ireland* (Dublin, 2000).

Kennedy, Liam, 'Marriage and Economic Conditions at the West European Periphery: Ireland, 1600–2000' in Isabelle Devos and Liam

Kennedy (Eds), *Marriage and Rural Economy. Western Europe Since 1400* (Ghent, 1999).

Kennedy, Máire, 'The Distribution of a Locally-Produced French Periodical in Provincial Ireland: *The Magazin à La Mode*, 1777–1778' in *Eighteenth-Century Ireland*, **7** (1992).

'Women and Reading in Eighteenth-Century Ireland' in Bernadette Cunningham and Máire Kennedy (Eds), *The Experience of Reading: Irish Historical Perspectives* (Dublin, 1999).

Kent, D. A., 'Ubiquitous But Invisible: Female Domestic Servants in Mid-Eighteenth Century London' in *History Workshop Journal*, **28** (Autumn, 1989).

Keogh, Dáire, '"The Pattern of the Flock": John Thomas Troy, 1786–1823' in James Kelly and Dáire Keogh (Eds), *History of the Catholic Diocese of Dublin* (Dublin, 2000).

Keogh, Dáire and Furlong, Nicholas (Eds), *The Women of 1798* (Dublin, 1998).

Kerber, Linda, *Women of the Republic. Intellect and Ideology in Revolutionary America* (Chapel Hill, North Carolina, 1980).

Towards an Intellectual History of Women (Chapel Hill and London, 1997).

Kildare, Marquis of, *The Earls of Kildare and Their Ancestors: from 1057 to 1773* (Dublin, 1858).

Kilroy, Phil, 'Women and the Reformation in Seventeenth-Century Ireland' in Margaret MacCurtain and Mary O'Dowd (Eds), *Women in Early Modern Ireland* (Edinburgh, 1991).

Protestant Dissent and Controversy in Ireland 1660–1714 (Cork, 1994).

'Quaker Women in Ireland, 1660–1740' in *Irish Journal of Feminist Studies*, **2**, no. 2 (1997).

King, Heather A., 'Late Medieval Crosses in County Meath c. 1470–1635' in *Proceedings of the Royal Irish Academy*, **84**, section C (1984).

King, William, *A Great Archbishop of Dublin, Quaedam Vitae Meae Insigniora. Edited by Sir Charles Simeon King* (London, 1908).

Kingston, John, 'The Carmelite Nuns in Dublin, 1644–1829' in *Reportium Novum*, **3**, no. 2 (1964).

Klene, Jean, C.S.C., '"Monument of an Endless Affection": Folger Ms V.b.198 and Lady Anne Southwell' in Peter Beal and Margaret J. M. Ezell (Eds), *English Manuscript Studies* (London, 2000).

Kussmaul, Ann, *Servants in Husbandry in Early Modern England* (Cambridge, 1981).

Lacy, Brian, 'Two Seventeenth-Century Houses at Linenhall Street, Londonderry' in *Ulster Folklife*, **27** (1981).

Laurence, Anne, 'The Cradle to the Grave: English Observation of Irish Social Customs in the Seventeenth Century' in *The Seventeenth Century*, **iii** (1988).

Women in England, 1500–1760 (London, 1994).

Lawless, Emily, *Maria Edgeworth* (London, 1904).

Leadbeater, Mary, *Cottage Dialogues Among the Irish Peasantry* (London, 1811).

Cottage Biography. Being a Collection of the Lives of the Irish Peasantry (London, 1822; new edition, Athy, Co. Kildare, 1987).

Leask, H. G., *Irish Castles and Castellated Houses* (Dublin, 1977).

Leerssen, Joep, *Mere Irish and Fíor Ghael* (Cork, 1996).

Lemire, Beverly, 'Developing Counsumerism and the Ready-Made Clothing Trade in Britain, 1750–1800' in *Textile History*, **15** (1984).

Lemmings, David, 'Marriage and the Law in the Eighteenth Century: Hardwicke's Marriage Act of 1753' in *The Historical Journal* **39** (1996).

Lenihan, Maurice, *Limerick: Its History and Antiquities* (1866, reprinted, Cork, 1967).

Lennon, Colm, *Richard Stanihurst. The Dubliner 1547–1618* (Dublin, 1981).

The Lords of Dublin in the Age of Reformation (Dublin, 1989).

Sixteenth-Century Ireland: the Incomplete Conquest (Dublin, 1994).

The Urban Patriciates of Early Modern Ireland: A Case-Study of Limerick (NUI O'Donnell Lecture, Dublin, 1999).

'Mass in the Manor-House: the Counter-Reformation in Dublin, 1560–1630' in James Kelly and Dáire Keogh (Eds), *History of the Catholic Diocese of Dublin* (Dublin, 2000).

Lewis, Judith S., *Sacred to Female Patriotism. Gender, Class and Politics in Late Georgian Britain* (New York and London, 2003).

Little, P. J., 'The Geraldine Ambitions of the First Earl of Cork' in *Irish Historical Studies*, **xxxiii** (2002), pp. 151–68.

Loeber, R., 'Sculptured Memorials to the Dead in Early Seventeenth-Century Ireland: A Survey from *Monumenta Biblanae* and Other Sources' in *Proceedings of the Royal Irish Academy*, **81** C (1982).

Loeber, Rolf and Stouthamer-Loeber, Magda, 18th–19th Century Irish Fiction Newsletter (October 1998), no. 10.

Long, Gerard (Ed), *Books Beyond the Pale. Aspects of the Provincial Book Trade in Ireland Before 1850* (Dublin, 1994).

Love, Harold, *Scribal Publication in Seventeenth-Century England* (Oxford, 1993).

Luddy, Maria, 'Martha McTier and William Drennan: A "Domestic" history' in Jean Agnew (Ed), *The Drennan-McTier Letters, Volume 1, 1776–1793* (Dublin, 1998).

Luddy, Maria, MacCurtain, Margaret, and O'Dowd, Mary, 'An Agenda for Women's History in Ireland, 1500–1900' in *Irish Historical Studies*, **xxviii** (1992).

Lyons, Mary Ann, 'Lay Female Piety and Church Patronage in Late Medieval Ireland' in Brendan Bradshaw and Dáire Keogh (Eds), *Christianity in Ireland. Revisiting the Story* (Blackrock, Co. Dublin, 2002).

McCarthy, B. G., 'The Riddle of Rose O'Toole' in Séamus Pender (Ed), *Féilscríbhinn Torna . . . Essays and Studies Presented to Professor Tadhg ua Donnachadha (Torna)* (Cork, 1947).

McCavitt, John, *The Flight of the Earls* (Dublin, 2002).

McClintock, H. F., *Handbook of the Traditional Old Irish Dress* (Dundalk, 1958).

McClintock Dix, E. R., *Catalogue of Early Dublin-Printed Books, 1601–1700* (Dublin, 1898).

MacCurtain, Margaret, 'Women, Education and Learning in Early Modern Ireland' in Margaret MacCurtain and Mary O'Dowd (Eds), *Women in Early Modern Ireland* (Edinburgh, 1991).

MacCurtain, Margaret and O'Dowd, Mary (Eds), *Women in Early Modern Ireland* (Edinburgh, 1991).

McDonnell-Bodkin, M., *Grattan's Parliament, Before and After* (London, 1912).

McDowell, R. B., 'Historical Revisions: the United Irish Plans of Parliamentary Reform, 1793' in *Irish Historical Studies*, **iii** (1942–3).

Ireland in the Age of Imperialism and Revolution 1760–1801 (Oxford, 1979).

McErlean, John, *The Sodality of the Blessed Virgin Mary in Ireland. A Short History* (Dublin, 1928).

McEvoy, John, *Statistical Survey of the County of Tyrone* (Dublin, 1802).

MacKechnie, John, 'Treaty Between Argyle and O'Donnell' in *Scottish Gaelic Studies*, **vii** (1953).

MacLysaght, Edward, *Irish Life in the Seventeenth Century* (1st edition, Cork, 1939; reprinted, New York, 1969).

McNally, Patrick, *Parties, Patriots and Undertakers: Parliamentary Politics in Early Hanoverian Ireland* (Dublin, 1987).

McNeill, Mary, *The Life and Times of Mary Ann McCracken, 1770–1866. A Belfast Panorama* (Dublin, 1960).

MacNevin, Thomas, *The History of the Volunteers of 1782* (5th edition, Dublin, 1846).

McParland, Edward, *Public Architecture in Ireland 1680–1760* (New Haven and London, 2001).

MacSkimin, Samuel, *The History and Antiquities of the County of the Town of Carrickfergus From the Earliest Records Till 1839* (new edition, Belfast, 1909).

MacSuibhne, Breandán, 'Whiskey, Potatoes and Paddies: Volunteering and the Construction of the Irish Nation in Northwest Ulster, 1778–1782' in Peter Jupp and Eoin Magennis (Eds), *Crowds in Ireland, c. 1720–1920* (London and New York, 2000).

Madden, R. R., *The United Irishmen, Their Lives and Times* (3rd series, 2nd Edition, London, 1860).

Malcomson, Anthony, *The Pursuit Of An Heiress: Aristocratic Marriage in Ireland, 1750–1820* (Belfast, 1982).

'A Woman Scorned?: Theodosia, Countess of Clanwilliam (1743–1817)' in *Familia*, **15** (1999).

Martin, F. X., *Friar Nugent. A Study of Francis Lavalin Nugent (1569–1635) Agent of the Counter-Reformation* (Rome and London, 1962).

Meehan, C. P., *The Fate and Fortunes of Hugh O'Neill, Earl of Tyrone, and Rory O'Donel, Earl of Tyrconnel; Their Flight From Ireland, and Death in Exile* (Dublin, 1870).

Meek, Christine (Ed), *Women in Renaissance and Early Modern Europe* (Dublin, 2000).

Meek, Christine and Lawless, Catherine (Eds), *Studies on Medieval and Early Modern Women. Pawns or Players?* (Dublin, 2003).

Meek, Christine and Simms, Katharine (Eds), *'The Fragility of Her Sex'. Medieval Irish Women in their European Context* (Dublin, 1996).

Meigs, Samantha A., *The Reformations in Ireland* (Dublin, 1997),

Memoirs of the Late Mrs Elizabeth Hamilton With a Selection From Her Correspondence and Other Unpublished Writings By Miss Benger (2 vols., London, 1818).

Mendelson, Sara, *The Mental World of Stuart Women: Three Studies* (Brighton, 1987).

Mendelson, Sara and Crawford, Patricia, *Women in Early Modern England, 1550–1720* (Oxford, 1998).

Merritt, J. F., 'Power and Communication: Thomas Wentworth and Government at a Distance During the Personal Rule, 1629–1633' in J. F. Merritt (Ed), *The Political World of Thomas Wentworth, Earl of Strafford, 1621–1641* (Cambridge, 1996).

Miller, Kerby A. with Doyle, David N. and Kelleher, Patricia, '"For Love and Liberty": Irish Women, Migration and Domesticity in Ireland and America, 1815–1920' in Patrick O'Sullivan (Ed), *Irish Women and Irish Emigration* (London, 1995).

Milne, Kenneth, *The Irish Charter Schools, 1730–1830* (Dublin, 1997).

Mitchel, Frank, 'The Evolution of Townley Hall' in *Bulletin of the Irish Georgian Society*, **30** (1987).

Monahan, Amy, 'An Eighteenth Century Family Linen Business: The Faulkners of Wellbrook, Cookstown, Co. Tyrone' in *Ulster Folklife*, **9** (1963).

Moody, T. W., *The Londonderry Plantation, 1609–41: The City of London and the Plantation in Ulster* (Belfast, 1939).

Moore, Christopher, 'Lady Louisa Conolly: Mistress of Castletown 1759–1821' in Jane Fenlon, Nicola Figgis and Catherine Marshall (Eds), *New Perspectives: Studies in Art History in Honour of Anne Crookshank* (Dublin, 1987).

Morgan, Hiram, *Tyrone's Rebellion. The Outbreak of the Nine Years War in Tudor Ireland* (Woodbridge, Suffolk, 1993).

Morgan, Marjorie, *Manners, Morals and Class in England, 1774–1858* (London, 1994).

Mullen, T. H. *Coleraine in Georgian Times* (Belfast, 1877).

Muller, Ellen, 'Saintly Virgins. The Veneration of Virgin Saints in Religious Women's Communities' in Lène Dresen-Coenders (Ed), *Saints and She-Devils. Images of Women in the 15th and 16th Centuries* (London, 1987).

Munter, Robert, *A Dictionary of the Print Trade in Ireland 1550–1775* (New York, 1988).

Murphy, Denis, *Our Martyrs: A Record of Those Who Suffered for the Catholic Faith Under the Penal Laws in Ireland* (Dublin, 1896).

Murray, Alice E., *A History of the Commercial and Financial Relations Between England and Ireland from the Period of the Restoration* (London, 1903).

Murray, James, 'Ecclesiastical Justice and the Enforcement of the Reformation: the Case of Archbishop Browne and the Clergy of Dublin' in A. Ford, J. McGuire and K. Milne (Eds), *As By Law Established. The Church of Ireland Since the Reformation* (Dublin, 1995).

Nicholls, Kenneth, *Gaelic and Gaelicised Ireland in the Middle Ages* (Dublin, 1972).

'Irishwomen and Property in the Sixteenth Century' in Margaret MacCurtain and Mary O'Dowd (Eds), *Women in Early Modern Ireland* (Edinburgh, 1991).

Ní Chuilleanáin, Eiléan, 'Women as Writers: *Dánta Grá* to Maria Edgeworth' in Eiléan Ní Chuilleanáin (Ed), *Irish Women: Image and Achievement* (Dublin, 1985).

Nic Eoin, Máirín, *B'Ait Leo Bean. Gnéithe den Idé-eolaíocht Inscne i dTraidisiún Liteartha na Gaeilge* (Dublin, 1998).

Nolan, Patrick, *The Irish Dames of Ypres. Being a History of the Royal Irish Abbey of Ypres* (Dublin, 1903).

O'Brien, George, *The Economic History of Ireland in the Eighteenth Century* (Dublin, 1918).

O'Brien, Susan, 'Women of the "English Catholic Community": Nuns and Pupils at the Bar Convent, York, 1680–1790' in Judith Loades (Ed), *Monastic Studies. The Continuity of Tradition* (Bangor, Gwynned, 1990).

O'Connell, Maurice, *Irish Politics and Social Conflict in the Age of the American Revolution* (Philadelphia, 1965).

O'Connell, Mrs M. J., *The Last Colonel of the Irish Brigade* (Dublin, 1892; reprinted 1977).

Ó Crualaoich, Gearóid, 'The Vision of Liberation in Cúirt an Mheán Oíche' in Pádraig de Brún, Seán Ó Coileáin and Pádraig Ó Riain (Eds), *Folia Gadelica* (Cork, 1983).

Ó Dálaigh, Brian, 'Mistress, Mother and Abbess: Renalda Ní Bhriain (c. 1447–1510)' in *North Munster Antiquarian Journal*, **xxxii** (1990).

O'Donnell, Ruan, 'Bridget "Croppy Biddy" Dolan: Wicklow's Anti-Heroine of 1798' in Dáire Keogh and Nicholas Furlong (Ed), *The Women of 1798* (Dublin, 1998).

O'Dowd, Mary, *Power, Politics and Land in Early Modern Sligo, 1568–1668* (Belfast, 1991).

'Women and War in Ireland in the 1640s' in Margaret MacCurtain and Mary O'Dowd (Eds), *Women in Early Modern Ireland* (Edinburgh, 1991).

'From Morgan to MacCurtain, Irish Women Historians from the 1790s to the 1990s' in Maryann Gialanella Valiulis and Mary O'Dowd (Eds), *Women and Irish History* (Dublin, 1997).

'Women and the Colonial Experience in Ireland, c. 1550–1650' in Terry Brotherstone, Deborah Simonton, and Oonagh Walsh (Eds), *Gendering Scottish History. An International Approach* (Glasgow, 1999).

'Women and the Irish Chancery Court in the Late Sixteenth and Early Seventeenth Centuries' in *Irish Historical Studies*, **xxxi** (November 1999).

'Women and Paid Work in Ireland, 1500–1800' in Bernadette Whelan (Ed), *Women and Paid Work in Ireland* (Dublin, 2000).

'Women and the Law in Early Modern Ireland' in Christine Meek (Ed), *Women in Renaissance and Early Modern Europe* (Dublin, 2000).

'The Women in the Gallery. Women and Politics in 18th Century Ireland' in Sabine Wichert (Ed), *From the United Irishmen to the Act of Union* (Dublin, 2004).

O'Dwyer, Peter, *Mary. A History of Devotion in Ireland* (Dublin, 1988).

O'Hanlon, John, *Lives of the Irish Saints* (Dublin and London, no date).

Ó hAnnracháin, Tadhg, 'Theory in the Absence of Fact: Irish Women and the Catholic Reformation' in Christine Meek and Catherine Lawless (Eds), *Studies on Medieval and Early Modern Women. Pawns or Players?* (Dublin, 2003).

O'Mahony, Charles, *The Viceroys of Ireland. The Story of the Long Line of Noblemen and Their Wives Who Have Ruled Ireland and Irish Society for Over Seven Hundred Years* (London, 1912).

O'Neill, Kevin, 'Mary Shackleton Leadbeater: Peaceful Rebel' in Dáire Keogh and Nicholas Furlong (Eds), *The Women of 1798* (Dublin, 1998).

O'Neill, Timothy, *Merchants and Mariners in Medieval Ireland* (Dublin, 1987).

O'Reilly, Mary, 'Seventeenth-Century Irish Catechisms – European or Not?' in *Archivium Hibernicum*, **50** (1996).

O'Riordan, Sister Mary, 'Bishop Daniel Delany (1747–1814)' in Pádraig G. Lane and William Nolan (Eds), *Laois History and Society. Interdisciplinary Essays on the History of an Irish County* (Dublin, 1999).

O'Scea, Ciarán, 'The Devotional World of the Irish Catholic Exile in Early-Modern Galicia, 1598–1666' in Thomas O'Connor (Ed), *The Irish in Europe, 1580–1815* (Dublin, 2001).

O'Sullivan, Harold, 'Women in County Louth in the Seventeenth Century' in *County Louth Archaeological and Historical Journal*, **xxiii** (1995).

O'Sullivan, M. D., 'The Use of Leisure in Old Galway' in *Journal of the Galway Archaeological and Historical Society*, **xviii** (1939).

'The Wives of Ulick 1st Earl of Clanricarde' in *Journal of the Galway Archaeological and Historical Society*, **xxi** (1945).

O'Toole, Fintan, *A Traitor's Kiss. The Life of Richard Brinsley Sheridan* (London, 1997).

Offen, Karen, *European Feminisms 1700–1950. A Political History* (Stanford, 2000).

Ohlmeyer, Jane, 'Strafford, the "London Business" and the "New British History"' in J. F. Merritt (Ed), *The Political World of Thomas Wentworth, Earl of Strafford, 1621–1641* (Cambridge, 1996).

Palmer, William, 'Gender, Violence and Rebellion in Tudor and Early Stuart Ireland' in *Sixteenth-Century Journal*, **xxiii** (1992).

Peckham Magray, Mary, *The Transforming Power of the Nuns. Women, Religion, and Cultural Change in Ireland, 1750–1900* (New York, 1998).

Perceval-Maxwell, Michael, *The Scottish Migration to Ulster in the Reign of James I* (London, 1973).

The Outbreak of the Irish Rebellion of 1641 (Dublin, 1994).

Phillips, Patricia, *The Scientific Lady. A Social History of Women's Scientific Interests, 1520–1918* (London, 1990).

Plowden, Francis, *An Historical Review of the State of Ireland, From the Invasion of That Country under Henry II, to its Union with Great Britain* (2 vols., London, 1803).

Pollard, Mary, *Dublin's Trade in Books, 1550–1800* (Oxford, 1989).

A Dictionary of Members of the Dublin Book Trade, 1550–1800 (London, 2000).

Prendergast, J. P., *The Cromwellian Settlement of Ireland* (3rd edition, Dublin, 1922).

Prior, Mary, 'Reviled and Crucified Marriages: the Position of Tudor Bishops' Wives' in Mary Prior (Ed), *Women in English Society 1500–1800* (London, 1985).

'Women and the Urban Economy: Oxford, 1500–1800' in M. Prior (Ed), *Women in English Society, 1500–1800* (London, 1985).

Quinlan, Maurice J., *Victorian Prelude. A History of English Manners, 1700–1830* (Washington, 1941; reprinted, 1965).

Rapley, Elizabeth, *The Dévotes. Women and Church in Seventeenth-Century France* (Montreal, 1990).

Raughter, Rosemary 'A Natural Tenderness: the Ideal and the Reality of Eighteenth-Century Female Philanthropy' in Maryann Gialanella Valiulis and Mary O'Dowd (Eds), *Women and Irish Society* (Dublin, 1997).

'"Mothers in Israel": Women, Family and Community in Early Irish Feminism' in Alan Hayes and Diane Urquhart (Eds), *Irish Women's History* (Dublin, 2004).

Reid, James Seaton, *History of the Presbyterian Church in Ireland* (2 vols., London, 1853).

Relke, Diana M. 'In Search of Mrs. Pilkington' in Ann Messenger (Ed), *Gender at Work. Four Women Writers of the Eighteenth Century* (Detroit, Michigan, 1990).

Rendall, Jane, *The Origins of Modern Feminism: Women in Britain, France and the United States, 1780–1860* (London, 1985).

'Women and the Public Sphere' in *Gender and History*, **11** (3) (November 1999), p. 479.

Reynolds, Thomas, *The Life of Thomas Reynolds, Esq* (2 vols., London, 1839).

Richardson, Ethel M., *Long Forgotten Days (Leading to Waterloo)* (London, 1928).

Robins, Joseph, *Champagne and Silver Buckles. The Viceregal Court at Dublin Castle 1700–1922* (Dublin 2001).

Robinson, Philip, 'Vernacular Housing in Ulster in the Seventeenth Century' in *Ulster Folklife*, **25** (1979).

The Ulster Plantation. British Settlement in an Irish Landscape, 1600–1670 (London, 1984).

Robinson, Portia, *The Women of Botany Bay* (Melbourne, 1988).

Rogal, Samuel J., *John Wesley in Ireland, 1747–1789* (2 parts, Lampeter, 1993).

Rogers, Katharine M., *Feminism in Eighteenth-Century England* (Brighton, 1982).

Ronan, M. V., *The Reformation in Ireland 1536–1558* (London, 1926).

An Apostle of Catholic Dublin. Father Henry Young (Dublin, 1944).

Rowlands, Marie B., 'Recusant Women 1560–1640' in Mary Prior, *Women in English Society 1500–1800* (London, 1985).

Schwoerer, Lois G. (Ed), *The Revolution of 1688–1689. Changing Perspectives* (Cambridge, 1992).

Scott, Michael (Ed), *Hall's Ireland. Mr & Mrs Hall's Tour of 1840* (2 vols., London and Sydney, 1984).

Seymour, St John D., *Irish Witchcraft and Demonology* (New York, 1992).

Sharpe, Pamela, *Adapting to Capitalism. Working Women in the English Economy, 1700–1850* (London, 1996).

Sheldon, Esther K., *Thomas Sheridan of Smock-Alley* (Princeton, 1967).

Sidney, Philip, *The Sidneys of Penshurst* (London, no date).

Simms, Katharine, 'The Legal Position of Irishwomen in the Later Middle Ages' in *The Irish Jurist*, **x**, n.s. (1975).

'Guesting and Feasting in Gaelic Ireland' in *Journal of the Royal Society of Antiquaries of Ireland*, **108** (1978).

From Kings to Warlords. The Changing Political Structure of Gaelic Ireland into the Later Middle Ages (Woodbridge, Suffolk, 1987).

Simonton, Deborah, 'Apprenticeship: Training and Gender in Eighteenth-Century England' in Maxine Berg (Ed), *Markets and Manufacture in Early Industrial England* (London, 1991).

Smith Clark, William, *The Early Irish Stage. The Beginnings to 1720* (Westport, Connecticut, 1973).

Somerville-Large, Peter, *The Irish Country House: A Social History* (London, 1995).

Sonnet, Martine, 'A Daughter to Educate' in Natalie Zemon Davis and Arlette Farge (Eds), *A History of Women in the West, III. Renaissance and Enlightenment Paradoxes* (Cambridge, Massachusetts and London, 1993).

Souers, Philip Webster, *The Matchless Orinda* (Cambridge, Massachusetts, 1931).

Spring, Eileen, *Law, Land, and Family. Aristocratic Inheritance In England, 1300–1800* (Chapel Hill and London, 1993).

Stevenson, David, 'The Radical Party in the Kirk, 1637–45' in *Journal of Ecclesiastical History*, xxv, no. 2 (1974).

Stokes, G. T., *Some Worthies of the Irish Church* (edited by H. J. Lawlor) (London, 1900).

Strain, R. W. M., *Belfast and its Charitable Society. A Story of Urban Social Development* (London, 1961).

Stuart, James, *Historical Memoirs of the City of Armagh* (Newry, 1819).

Styles, John, 'Clothing the North: the Supply of Non-élite Clothing in the Eighteenth-Century North of England' in *Textile History*, **25** (2) (1994).

Sutherland, Kathryn, 'Writings on Education and Conduct: Arguments For Female Improvement' in Vivien Jones (Ed), *Women and Literature in Britain, 1700–1800* (Cambridge, 2000).

Teeling, Charles Hamilton, *Personal Narrative of the 'Irish Rebellion' of 1798* (London, 1828).

The Library of Mrs. Elizabeth Vesey 1715–1791 (William H. Robinson, Newcastle-on-Tyne, 1926).

Thomas, P. D. G., *The House of Commons in the Eighteenth Century* (Oxford, 1971).

Tighe, Mary, *Psyche, With Other Poems* (London, 1811).

Tighe, William, *Statistical Observations Relative to the County of Kilkenny Made in the Years 1800 and 1801* (Dublin, 1802).

Tilly, A. Louise and Scott, Joan, *Women, Work and Family* (London, 1989).

Tillyard, Stella, *Aristocrats* (London, 1994).

Titley, Alan, 'An Breithiúnas ar Cúirt an Mheán-Oíche' in *Studia Hibernica*, 25 (1990).

Todd, Janet, *The Signs of Angellica. Women, Writing and Fiction, 1660–1800* (London, 1989).

Mary Wollstonecraft. A Revolutionary Life (London, 2000).

Rebel Daughters (London, 2003).

Townsend, Horatio, *Statistical Survey of the County of Cork, with Observations on the Means of Improvement . . .* (Dublin, 1810).

Treadwell, Victor, *Buckingham and Ireland 1616–1628. A Study in Anglo-Irish Politics* (Dublin, 1998).

Troyer, Howard William, *Ned Ward of Grubstreet. A Study of Sub-Literary London in the Eighteenth Century* (Harvard, 1946).

Tynan, Michael, *Catholic Instruction in Ireland, 1720–1950. The O'Reilly/Donlevy Catechetical Tradition* (Dublin, 1985).

Vickery, Amanda, *The Gentleman's Daughter. Women's Lives in Georgian England* (New Haven and London, 1998).

Wakefield, Edward, *An Account of Ireland, Statistical and Political* (2 vols., London, 1812).

Wall, Maureen, 'The Catholic Merchants, Manufacturers and Traders of Dublin, 1778–1782' in *Reportium Novum*, **2**, no. 2 (1959–60).

Wall, Thomas, *The Sign of Doctor Hays* (Dublin, 1958).

Walsh, Micheline, 'Some Notes Towards a History of the Womenfolk of the Wild Geese' in *The Irish Sword*, **v** (1961).

'Some Further Notes Towards a History of the Womenfolk of the Wild Geese' in *The Irish Sword*, **vi** (1962).

Walsh, Paul, *Irish Men of Learning* (Dublin, 1947).

Walsh, T. J., *Nano Nagle and the Presentation Sisters* (Dublin, 1959).

Warner, Marina, *Joan of Arc. The Image of Female Heroism* (London, 1981).

Webb, J. J., *Industrial Dublin Since 1698 and the Silk Industry in Dublin – Two Essays* (Dublin, 1913).

Webster, Mary, *Francis Wheatley* (London, 1970).

Weiner, Margery, *Matters of Felony. A Reconstruction* (London, 1967).

West, William, *A Directory and Picture of Cork and Its Environs* (Cork, 1810).

Westerkamp, Marilyn J., *Triumph of the Laity. Scots-Irish Piety and the Great Awakening 1625–1760* (Oxford, 1988).

Wharton Jones, Thomas, *True Relation of the Life and Death of the Right Reverend Father in God, William Bedell . . .* (London, 1872).

Whelan, Bernadette, 'Women and the "War of the Three Kings" 1689–91' in Ronit Lenin (Ed), *In From the Shadows: The UL Women's Studies Collection*, vol. ii (Limerick, 1996).

(Ed), *Women and Paid Work in Ireland, 1500–1930* (Dublin, 2000).

Whelan, Kevin, 'The Regional Impact of Irish Catholicism 1700–1850' in W. J. Smith (Ed), *Common Ground. Essays on the Historical Geography of Ireland Presented to T. Jones Hughes* (Cork, 1998).

Wiesner, Merry E., *Women and Gender in Early Modern Europe* (Cambridge, 1993, 2nd Edition, 2000).

Willen, Diane, 'Women and Religion in Early Modern England' in Sherrin Marshall (Ed), *Women in Reformation and Counter-Reformation Europe. Private and Public Worlds* (Bloomington, Indiana, 1989).

'Godly Women in Early Modern England: Puritanism and Gender' in *Journal of Ecclesiastical History*, **43** (4) (1992).

Wright, P., 'A Change in Direction: The Ramifications of a Female Household, 1558–1603' in D. Starkey (Ed), *The English Court from the Wars of the Roses to the Civil War* (London, 1987).

Young, Francis Berkeley, *Mary Sidney, Countess of Pembroke* (London, 1912).

CDs and Online Databases

Catholic Encyclopedia www.newadvent.org/cathen

Directory for Sources for Irish Women's History CD, Irish Manuscripts Commission 1998 (Dublin, 1998); online: www.nationalarchives.ie

Early English Books Online (by subscription (www.chadwyck.com)). Available for consultation in the National Library of Ireland. Eighteenth-Century Collections Online (by subscription (www.gale.com)). Available for consultation at the National Library of Ireland.

English Short Title Catalogue, 1473–1800 CD, British Library (London, 2003).

Index to *Belfast Newsletter.* Edited by John C. Green, www.ucs.louisiana.edu/~jcg3525/Main.html

Marshall, Anne, 'Medieval Wall Painting in the English Parish Church' www.paintedchurch.org

Unpublished Theses

Black, Anthony Robert, 'An Edition of the Cavendish Irish Parliamentary Diary: 1776–1778' (unpublished Ph.D. thesis, University of Notre Dame, 1969).

Browne, Róisín, 'Ulster Presbyterianism in the 18th Century' (M. Phil. thesis, Queen's University, Belfast, 1997).

Callen, Robert V., 'The Structure of Anglo-Irish Politics During the American Revolution: Cavendish's, Diary of the Irish Parliament, October 12, 1779 To September 2, 1780; Edition of the Partial Text and a Critical Essay' (unpublished Ph.D. thesis, University of Notre Dame, 1973).

Collins, Michaela, 'Women in the Belfast Newsletter 1738 to 1770' (unpublished MA dissertation, Queen's University, Belfast, 1994).

De Búrca, Avril, 'The Poor Clares, Galway, 1642–1996 – the Complete Story' (unpublished BA dissertation, University of Limerick, 1996).

Dickson, David, 'An Economic History of the Cork Region' (unpublished, Ph.D. thesis, Trinity College, Dublin, 1977).

Ferguson, Kenneth Patrick, 'The Army in Ireland. From the Restoration to the Act of Union' (unpublished PD thesis, Trinity College, Dublin, 1980).

Fitzgerald, Patrick, 'Poverty and Vagrancy in Ireland, 1500–1770' (unpublished, Ph.D. thesis, Queen's University, Belfast, 1995).

Foster, Sarah, 'Going Shopping in Georgian Dublin: Luxury Goods and the Negotiation of National Identity' (unpublished, MA thesis, Victoria and Albert Museum/Royal College of Art, 1995).

Kane, Paul J., 'The Life and Works of David Manson. A Belfast School-Teacher, 1726–1792' (unpublished M.Ed. thesis, Queen's University, Belfast, 1984).

Little, P. J. S., 'Family and Faction, the Irish Nobility and the English Court, 1632–42' (unpublished M. Litt thesis, University of Dublin, 1992).

Lyons, Thomas, 'Sean O'Neill – A Biography' (unpublished, MA thesis, University College, Cork, 1948).

McGarry, James Gerard, 'The Statutes of Tuam From the Council of Trent to the Nineteenth Century' (unpublished, DD thesis, St Patrick's College, Maynooth, 1932).

Moore, Donal, 'English Action, Irish Reaction: the MacMurrough Kavanaghs, 1530–1630' (unpublished, MA thesis, St Patrick's College, Maynooth, 1985).

O'Donoghue, Fergus M., 'The Jesuit Mission in Ireland 1598–1651' (unpublished Ph.D. thesis, Catholic University of America, Washington, 1981).

O'Reilly, Mary, 'Catechists in Exile. An Examination of Seventeenth Century Catechisms Written on the Continent for Use on the Irish Mission' (unpublished, MA thesis, National University of Ireland, Maynooth, 1994).

Raughter, Rosemary, 'A Natural Tenderness: Women's Philanthropy in Eighteenth-Century Ireland' (unpublished MA thesis, University College, Dublin, 1992).

Ryan, David, '"That Most Serious Duty": Catholic Preaching in Ireland, 1760–1840' (Unpublished MA thesis, National University of Galway, 1998).

White, D. G., 'Tudor Plantations in Ireland Before 1571' (2 vols., unpublished Ph.D. thesis, University of Dublin, 1968).

Wilson, Deborah, 'Women, Marriage and Property in Ireland, 1750–1850' (unpublished Ph.D. thesis, Queen's University, Belfast, 2003).

Index